UQ HOLDER!

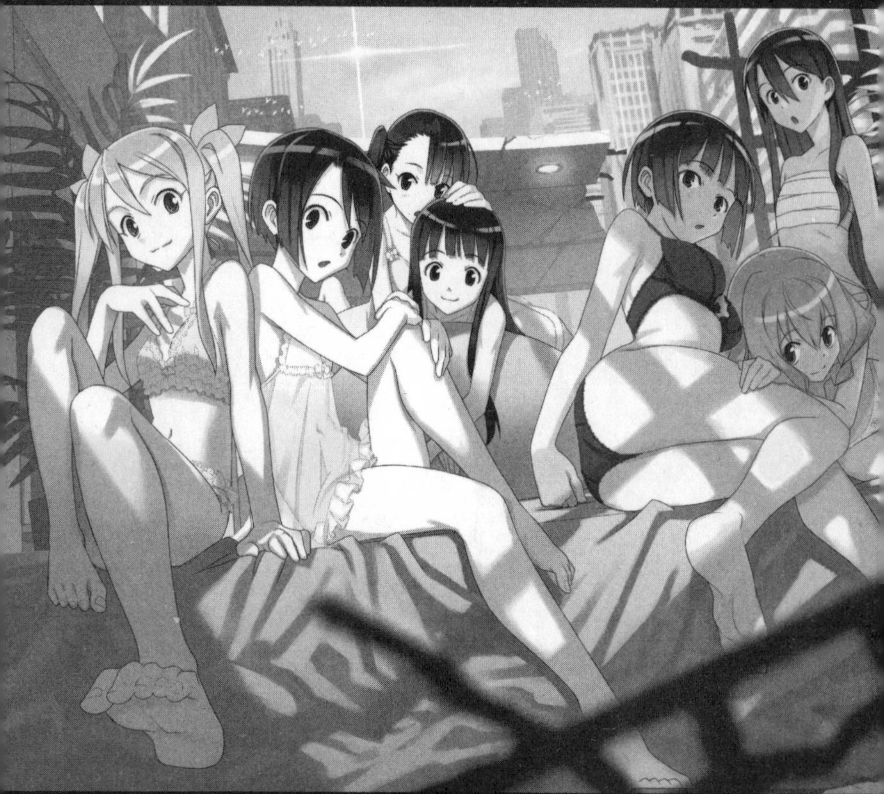

KEN AKAMATSU

vol.24

CHARACTERS

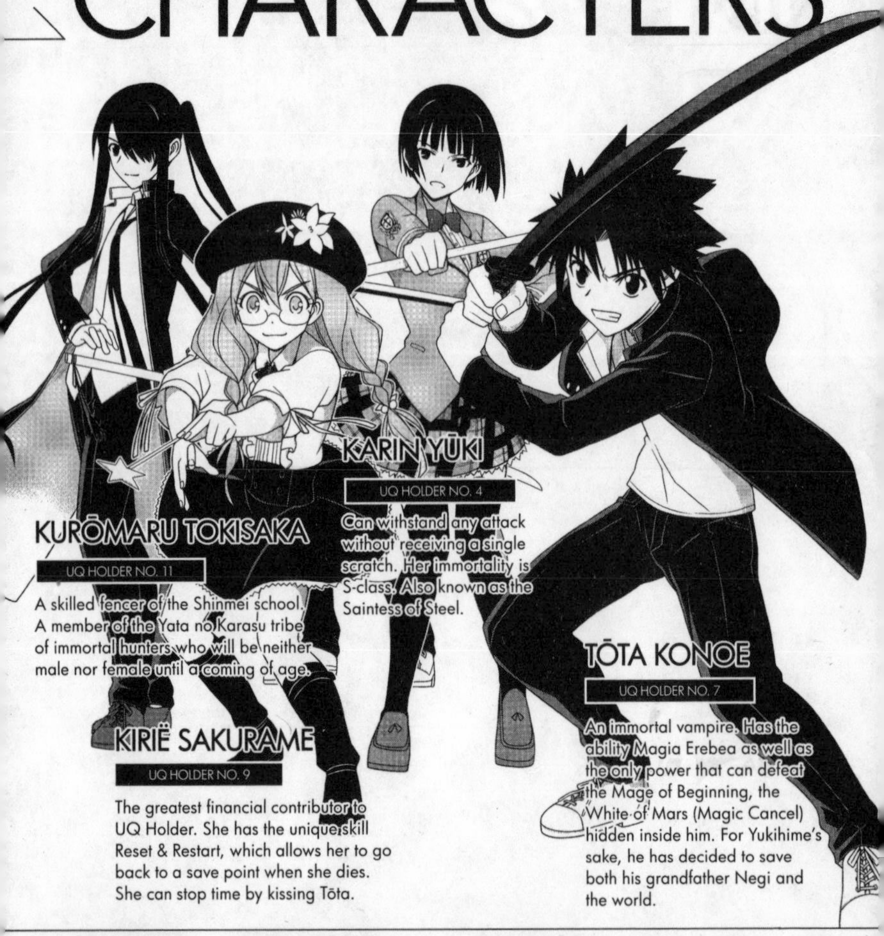

KURŌMARU TOKISAKA

UQ HOLDER NO. 11

A skilled fencer of the Shinmei school. A member of the Yata no Karasu tribe of immortal hunters who will be neither male nor female until a coming of age.

KARIN YŪKI

UQ HOLDER NO. 4

Can withstand any attack without receiving a single scratch. Her immortality is S-class. Also known as the Saintess of Steel.

TŌTA KONOE

UQ HOLDER NO. 7

An immortal vampire. Has the ability Magia Erebea as well as the only power that can defeat the Mage of Beginning, the White of Mars (Magic Cancel) hidden inside him. For Yukihime's sake, he has decided to save both his grandfather Negi and the world.

KIRIË SAKURAME

UQ HOLDER NO. 9

The greatest financial contributor to UQ Holder. She has the unique skill Reset & Restart, which allows her to go back to a save point when she dies. She can stop time by kissing Tōta.

UQ HOLDER IMMORTAL NUMBERS

JINBEI SHISHIDO

UQ HOLDER NO. 2

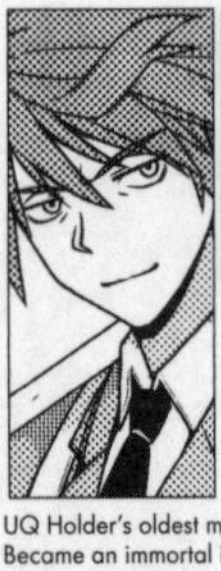

UQ Holder's oldest member. Became an immortal in the Middle Ages, when he ate mermaid flesh in the Muromachi Period. Has the "Switcheroo" skill that switches the locations of physical objects.

SEPT SHICHIJŪRŌ NANAO

UQ HOLDER NO. 3

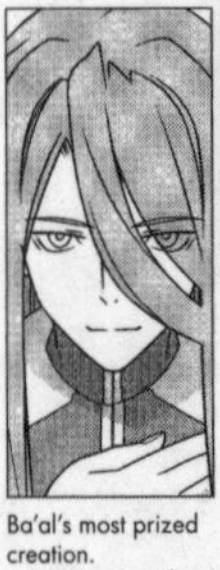

Ba'al's most prized creation.
A high-level artificial light spirit.

JŪZŌ SHISHIMI

UQ HOLDER NO. 5

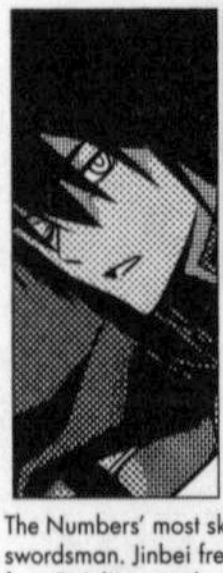

The Numbers' most skilled swordsman. Jinbei freed him from Ba'al's control.

UQ HOLDER!

Ken Akamatsu Presents

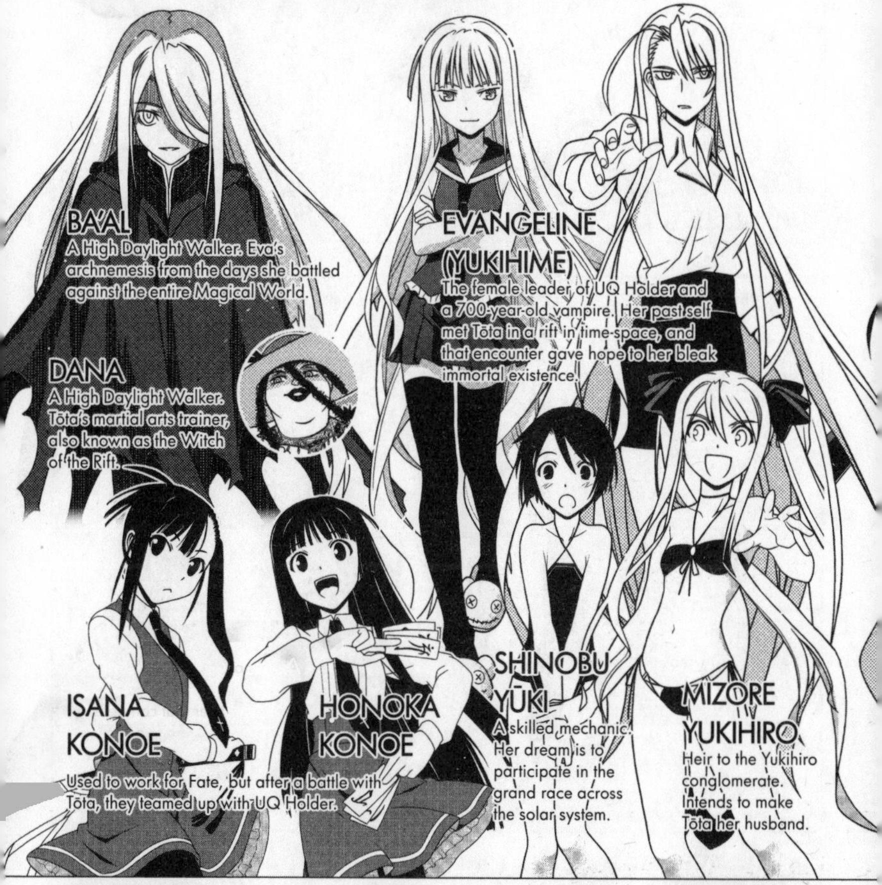
BA'AL
A High Daylight Walker. Eva's archnemesis from the days she battled against the entire Magical World.
EVANGELINE (YUKIHIME)
The female leader of UQ Holder and a 700-year-old vampire. Her past self met Tōta in a rift in time-space, and that encounter gave hope to her bleak immortal existence.
DANA
A High Daylight Walker. Tōta's martial arts trainer, also known as the Witch of the Rift.
ISANA KONOE
HONOKA KONOE
Used to work for Fate, but after a battle with Tōta, they teamed up with UQ Holder.
SHINOBU YŪKI
A skilled mechanic. Her dream is to participate in the grand race across the solar system.
MIZORE YUKIHIRO
Heir to the Yukihiro conglomerate. Intends to make Tōta her husband.

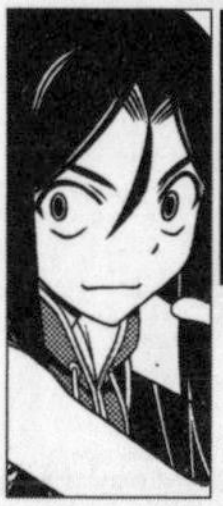

SANTA SASAKI
UQ HOLDER NO. 12

A revenant brought back to life through necromancy. He has multiple abilities, including flight, intangibility, possession, telekinesis, etc.

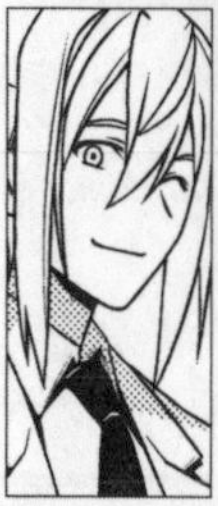

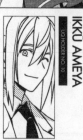

IKKŪ AMEYA
UQ HOLDER NO. 10

After falling into a coma at age 13 and lying in a hospital bed for 72 years, he became a full-body cyborg at age 85. He's very good with his hands. ♡

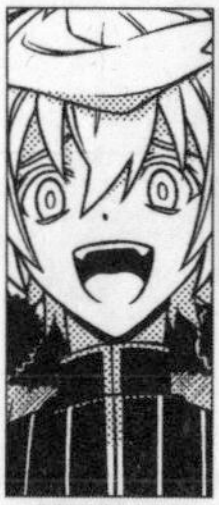

NIKITIS LAPIS
UQ HOLDER NO. 8

A High Daylight Walker. He helped Tōta find his true strength, but his motives remain unclear.

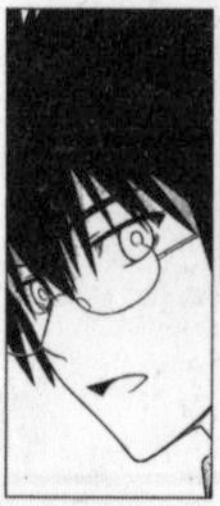

GENGORŌ MAKABE
UQ HOLDER NO. 6

Manages the business side of UQ Holder's hideout and inn. He has a skill known as "multiple lives," so when he dies, another Gengorō appears.

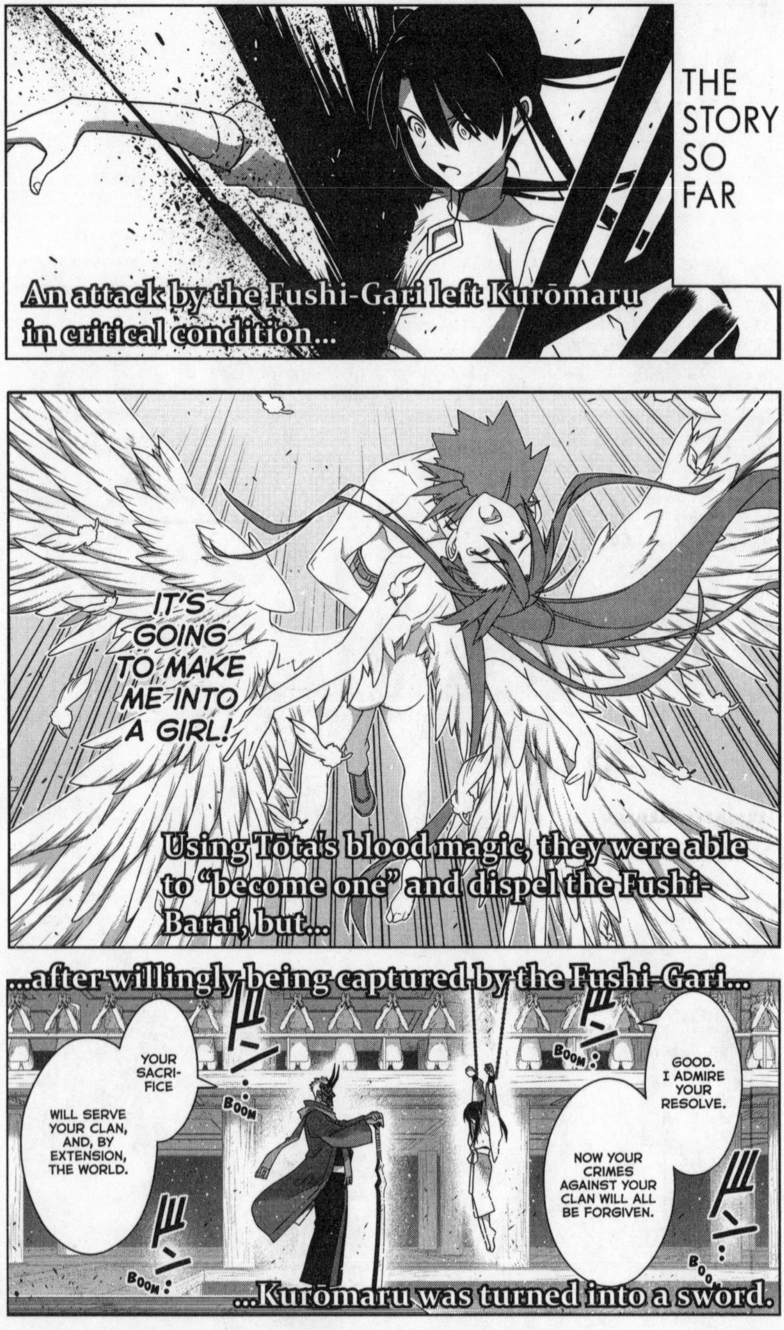

THE STORY SO FAR
An attack by the Fushi-Gari left Kurōmaru in critical condition...
IT'S GOING TO MAKE ME INTO A GIRL!
Using Tōta's blood magic, they were able to "become one" and dispel the Fushi-Barai, but...
...after willingly being captured by the Fushi-Gari...
BOOM
GOOD. I ADMIRE YOUR RESOLVE.
NOW YOUR CRIMES AGAINST YOUR CLAN WILL ALL BE FORGIVEN.
BOOM
YOUR SACRIFICE
WILL SERVE YOUR CLAN, AND, BY EXTENSION, THE WORLD.
BOOM
BOOM
...Kurōmaru was turned into a sword.

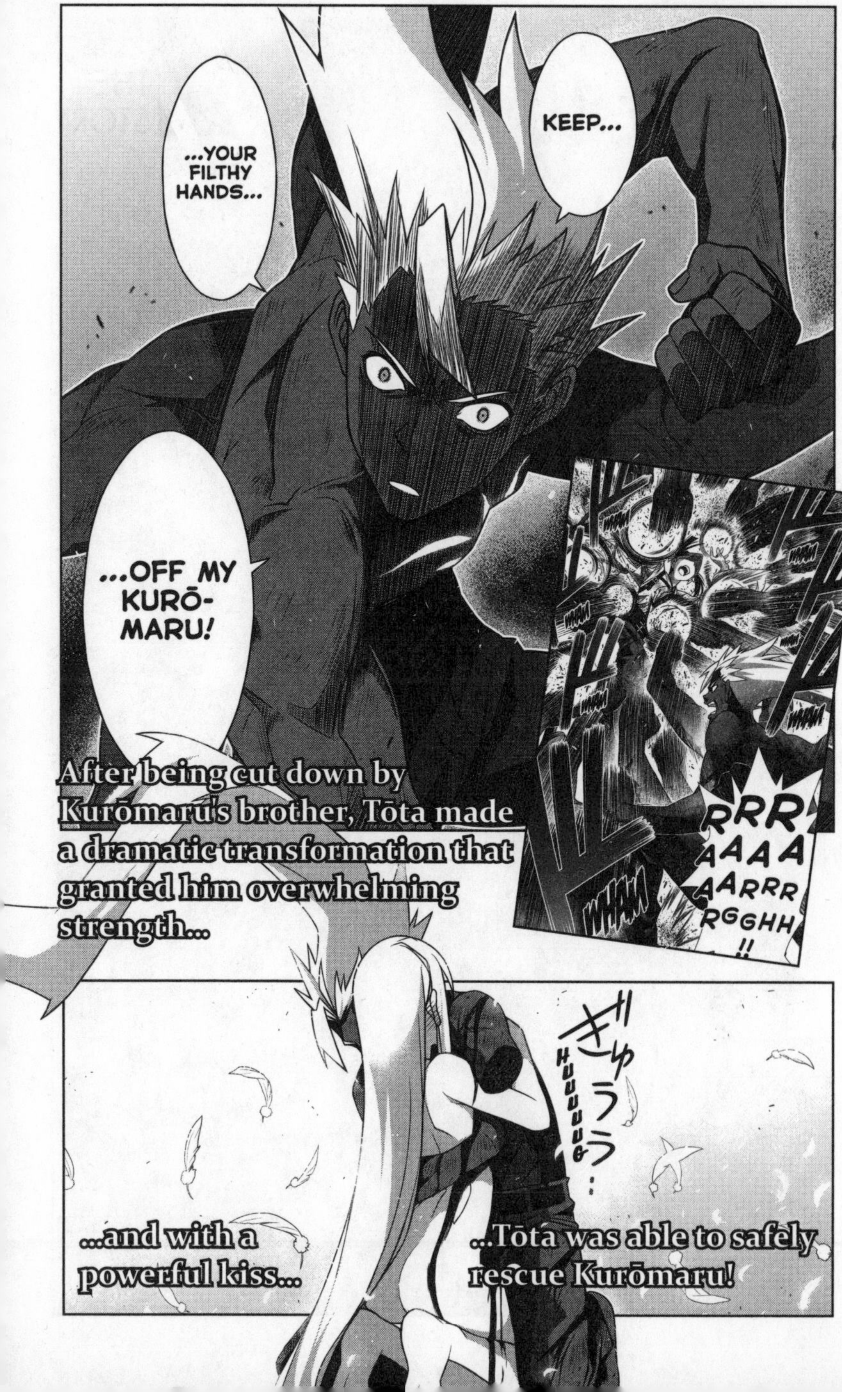
KEEP...
...YOUR FILTHY HANDS...
...OFF MY KURŌMARU!
WHAM
RRRAAAAARRRRGGHH!!
After being cut down by Kurōmaru's brother, Tōta made a dramatic transformation that granted him overwhelming strength...
ぎゅううう
HUUUUUUG
...and with a powerful kiss...
...Tōta was able to safely rescue Kurōmaru!

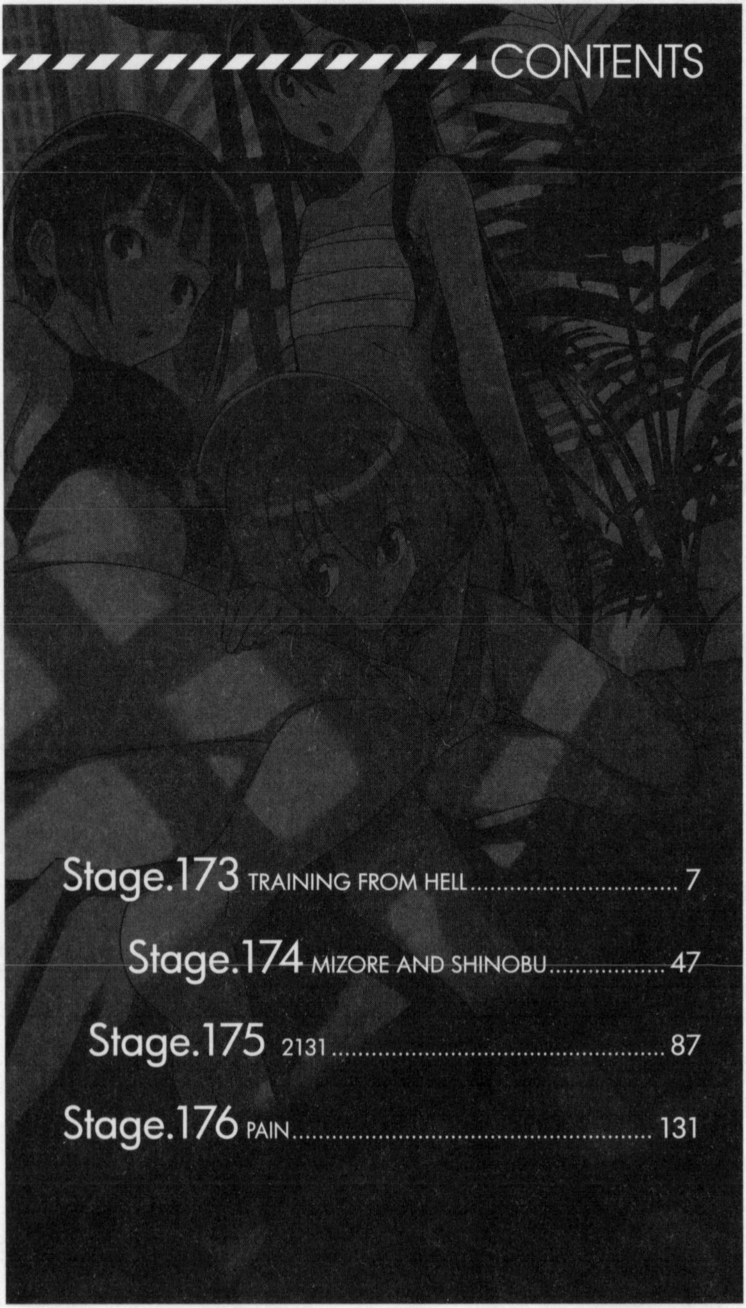

CONTENTS

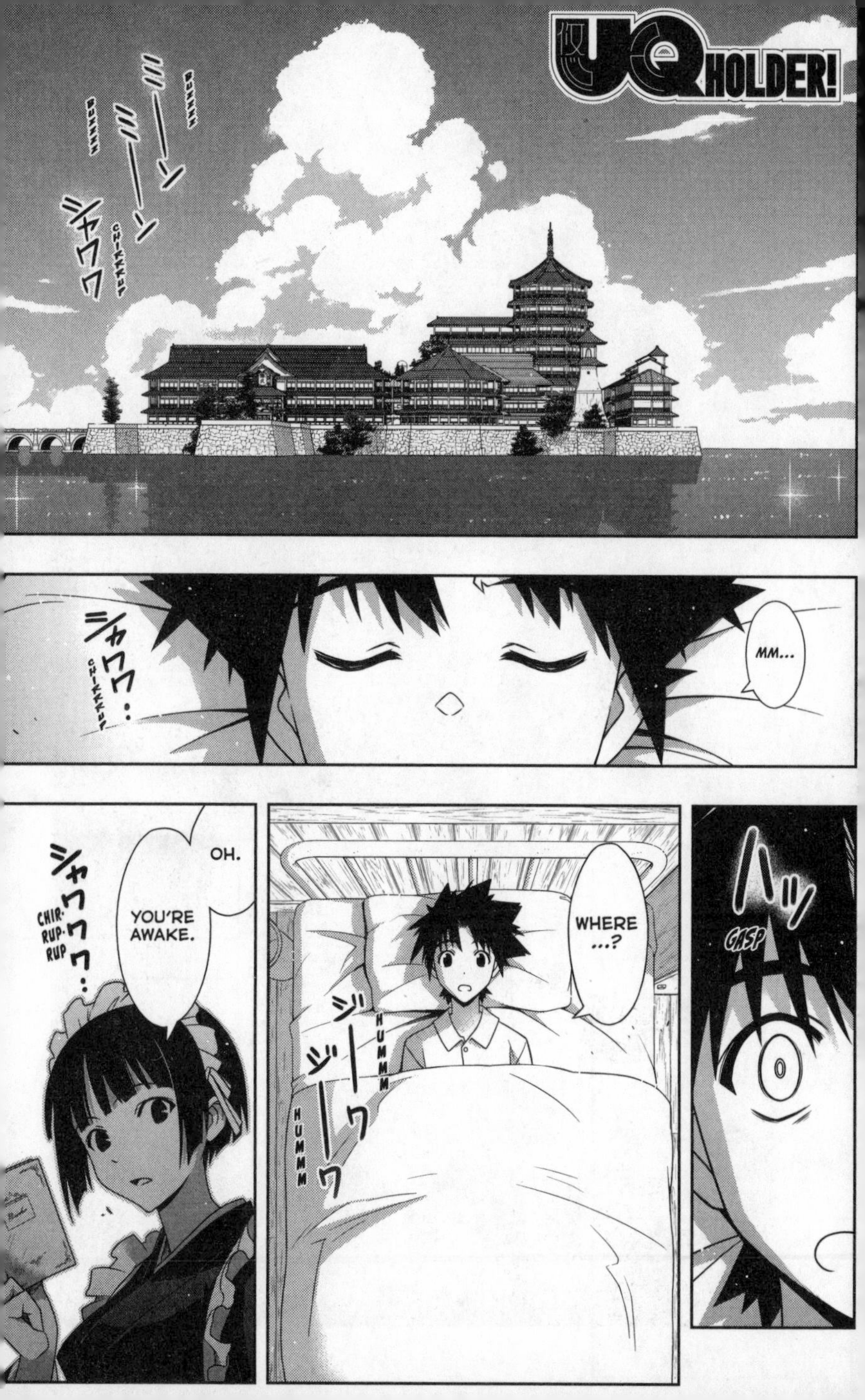
UQ HOLDER!
ミーーン
BUZZZZ
ミーーン
BUZZZZ
シャワワ
CHIRRRUP
シャワワ..
CHIRRRUP
MM...
ハッ
GASP
WHERE ...?
ジーーワ
HUMMM
ジーーワ
HUMMM
OH.
YOU'RE AWAKE.
シャワワワ..
CHIR-RUP-RUP

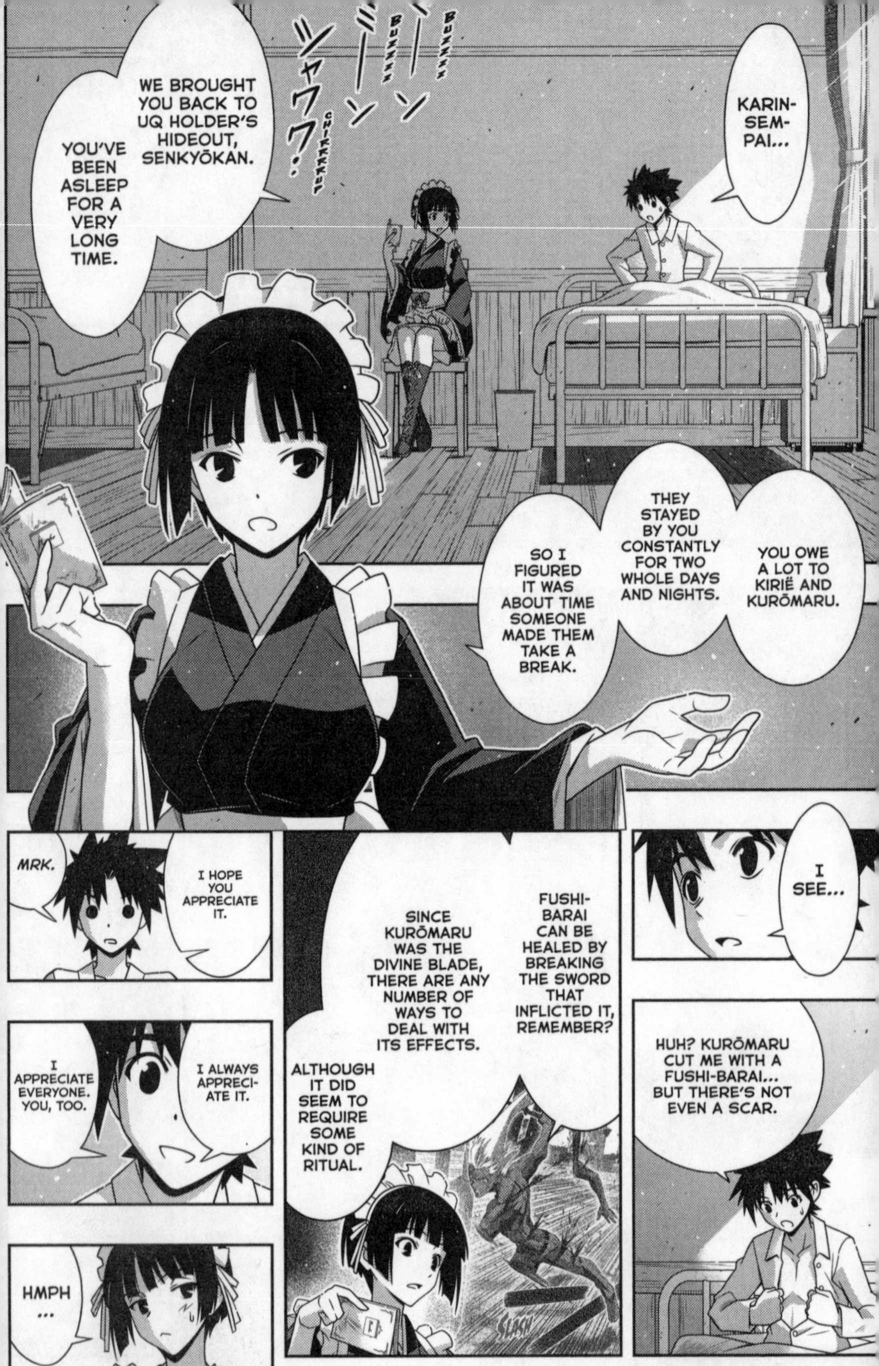
KARIN-SEMPAI...
BUZZZZ
BUZZZZ
CHIRRRUP
WE BROUGHT YOU BACK TO UQ HOLDER'S HIDEOUT, SENKYŌKAN.
YOU'VE BEEN ASLEEP FOR A VERY LONG TIME.
YOU OWE A LOT TO KIRIË AND KURŌMARU.
THEY STAYED BY YOU CONSTANTLY FOR TWO WHOLE DAYS AND NIGHTS.
SO I FIGURED IT WAS ABOUT TIME SOMEONE MADE THEM TAKE A BREAK.
I SEE...
HUH? KURŌMARU CUT ME WITH A FUSHI-BARAI... BUT THERE'S NOT EVEN A SCAR.
FUSHI-BARAI CAN BE HEALED BY BREAKING THE SWORD THAT INFLICTED IT, REMEMBER?
SINCE KURŌMARU WAS THE DIVINE BLADE, THERE ARE ANY NUMBER OF WAYS TO DEAL WITH ITS EFFECTS.
ALTHOUGH IT DID SEEM TO REQUIRE SOME KIND OF RITUAL.
SLASH
I HOPE YOU APPRECIATE IT.
MRK.
I ALWAYS APPRECIATE IT.
I APPRECIATE EVERYONE. YOU, TOO.
HMPH...

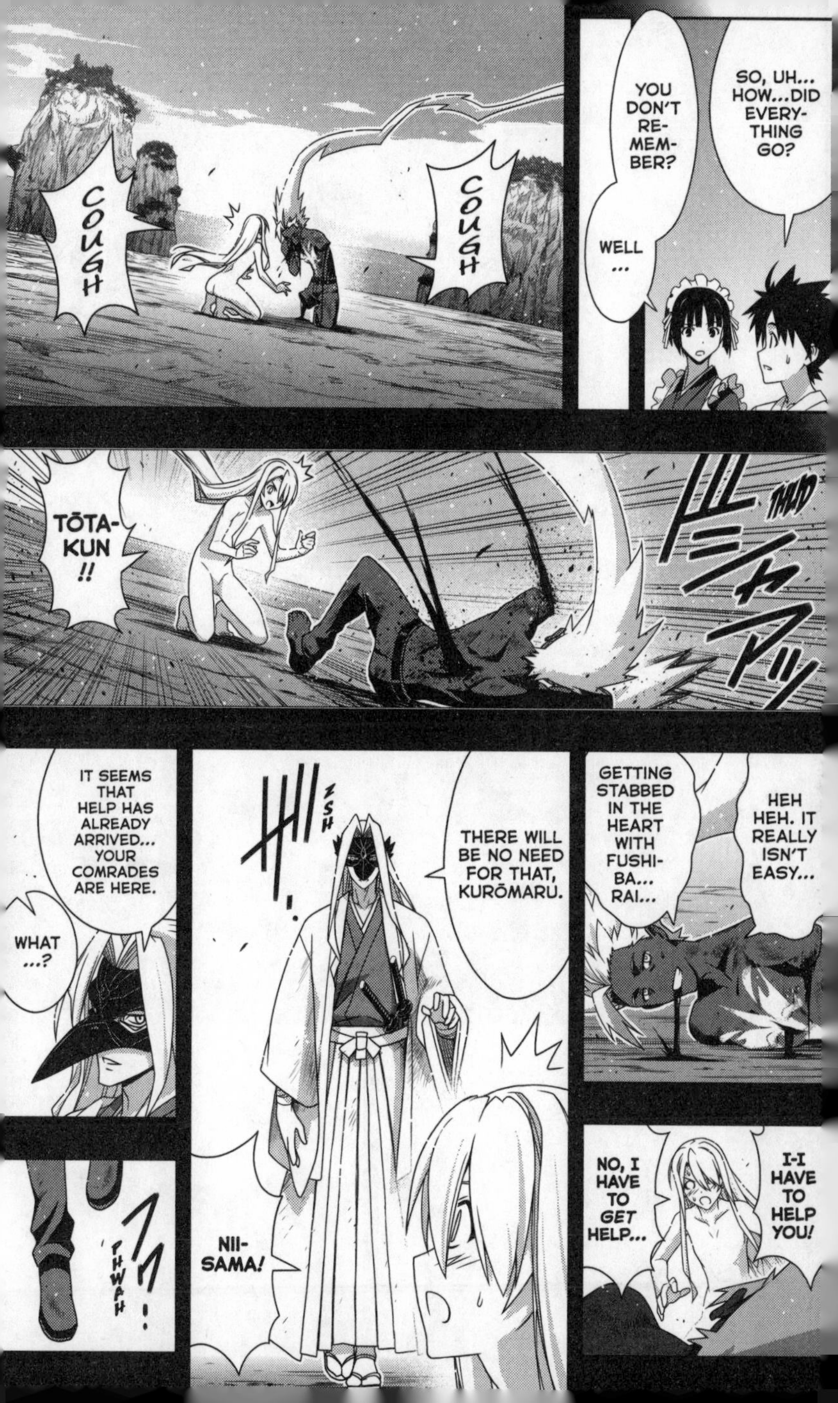
SO, UH... HOW...DID EVERYTHING GO?
YOU DON'T REMEMBER?
WELL...
COUGH
COUGH
THUD
TŌTA-KUN!!
HEH HEH. IT REALLY ISN'T EASY...
GETTING STABBED IN THE HEART WITH FUSHIBA... RAI...
I-I HAVE TO HELP YOU!
NO, I HAVE TO GET HELP...
ZSH
THERE WILL BE NO NEED FOR THAT, KURŌMARU.
NII-SAMA!
IT SEEMS THAT HELP HAS ALREADY ARRIVED... YOUR COMRADES ARE HERE.
WHAT...?
PHWAH

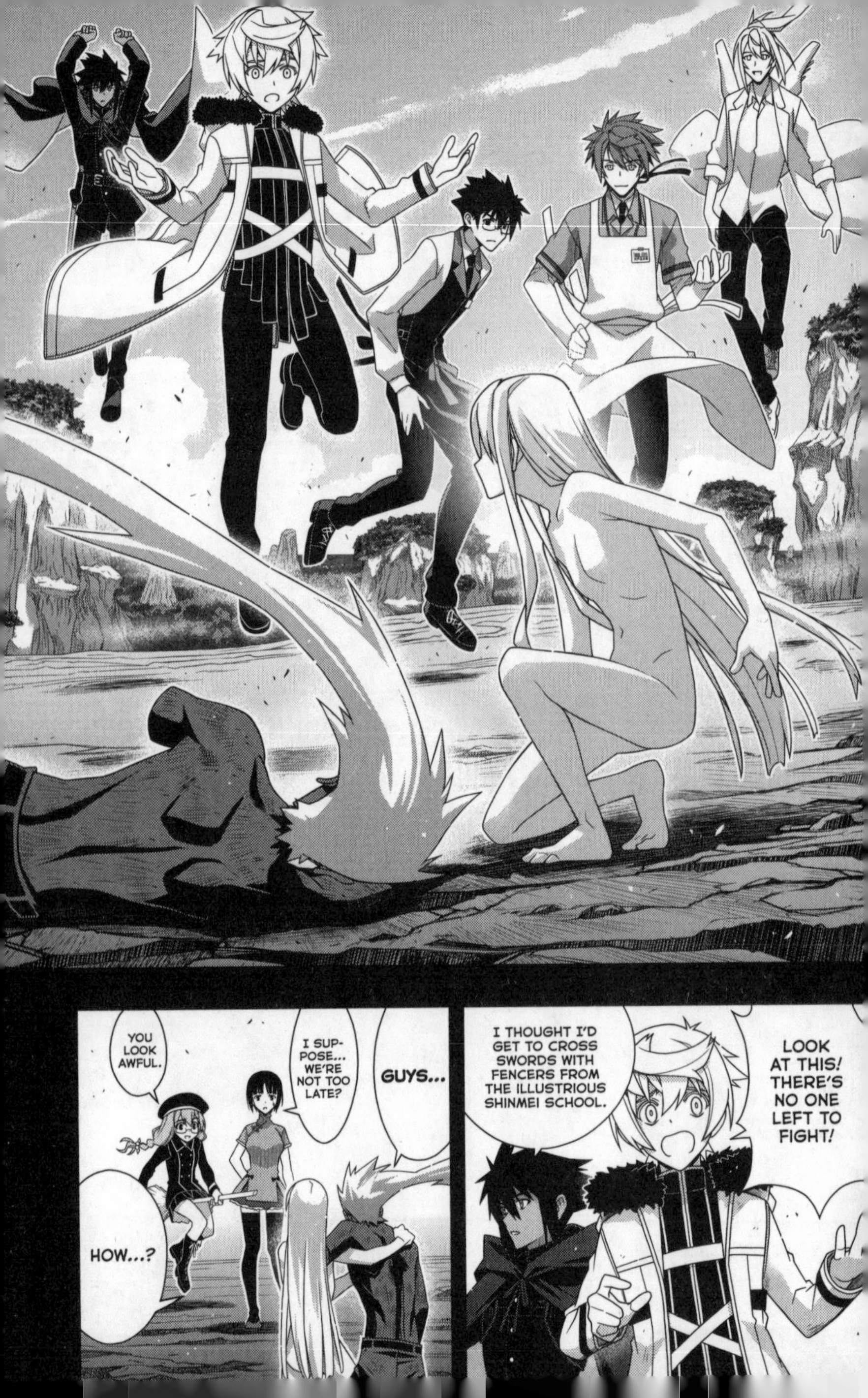
LOOK AT THIS! THERE'S NO ONE LEFT TO FIGHT!
I THOUGHT I'D GET TO CROSS SWORDS WITH FENCERS FROM THE ILLUSTRIOUS SHINMEI SCHOOL.
GUYS...
I SUP-POSE... WE'RE NOT TOO LATE?
YOU LOOK AWFUL.
HOW...?

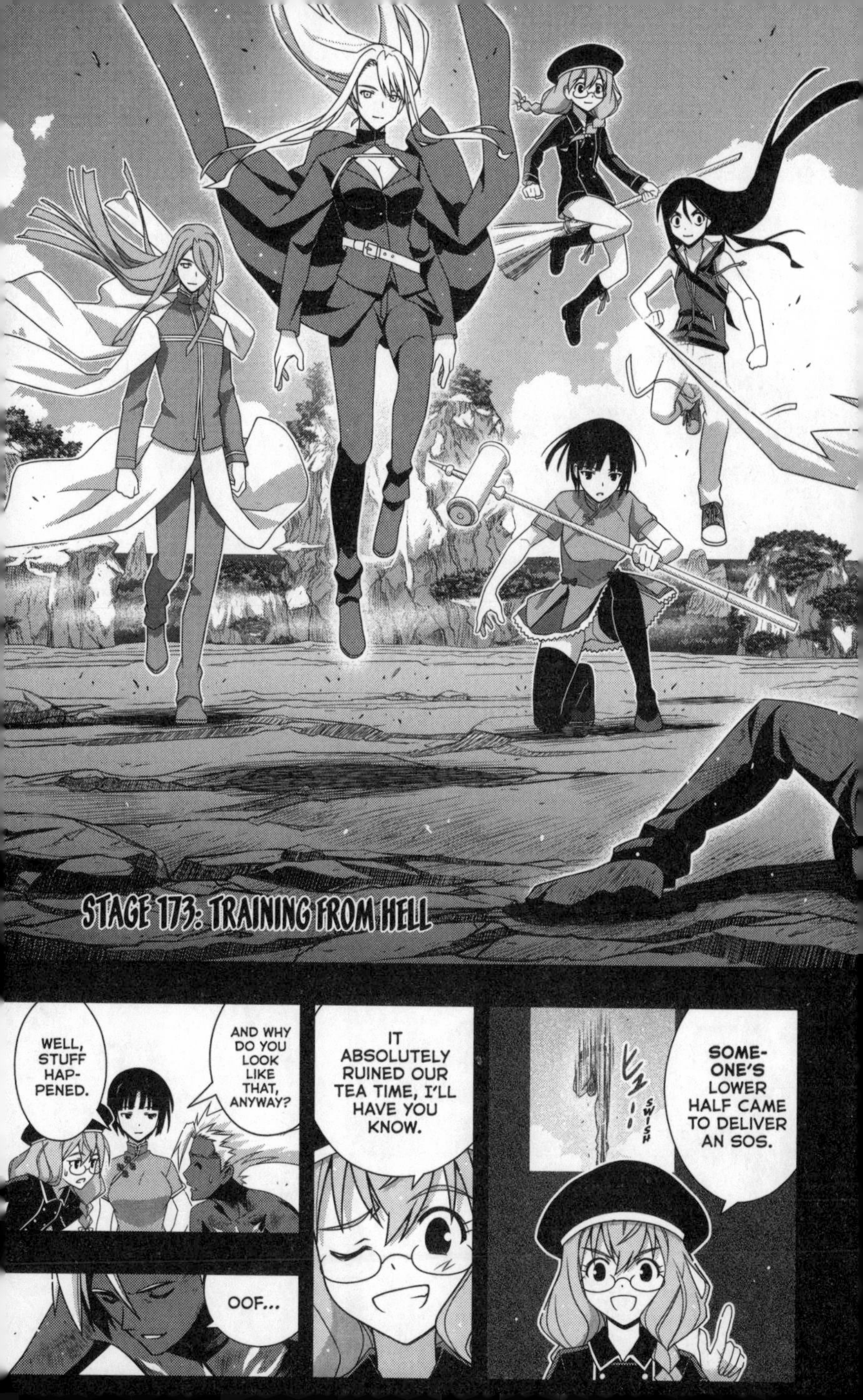
STAGE 173: TRAINING FROM HELL
SWISH
SOME-ONE'S LOWER HALF CAME TO DELIVER AN SOS.
IT ABSOLUTELY RUINED OUR TEA TIME, I'LL HAVE YOU KNOW.
AND WHY DO YOU LOOK LIKE THAT, ANYWAY?
WELL, STUFF HAP-PENED.
OOF...

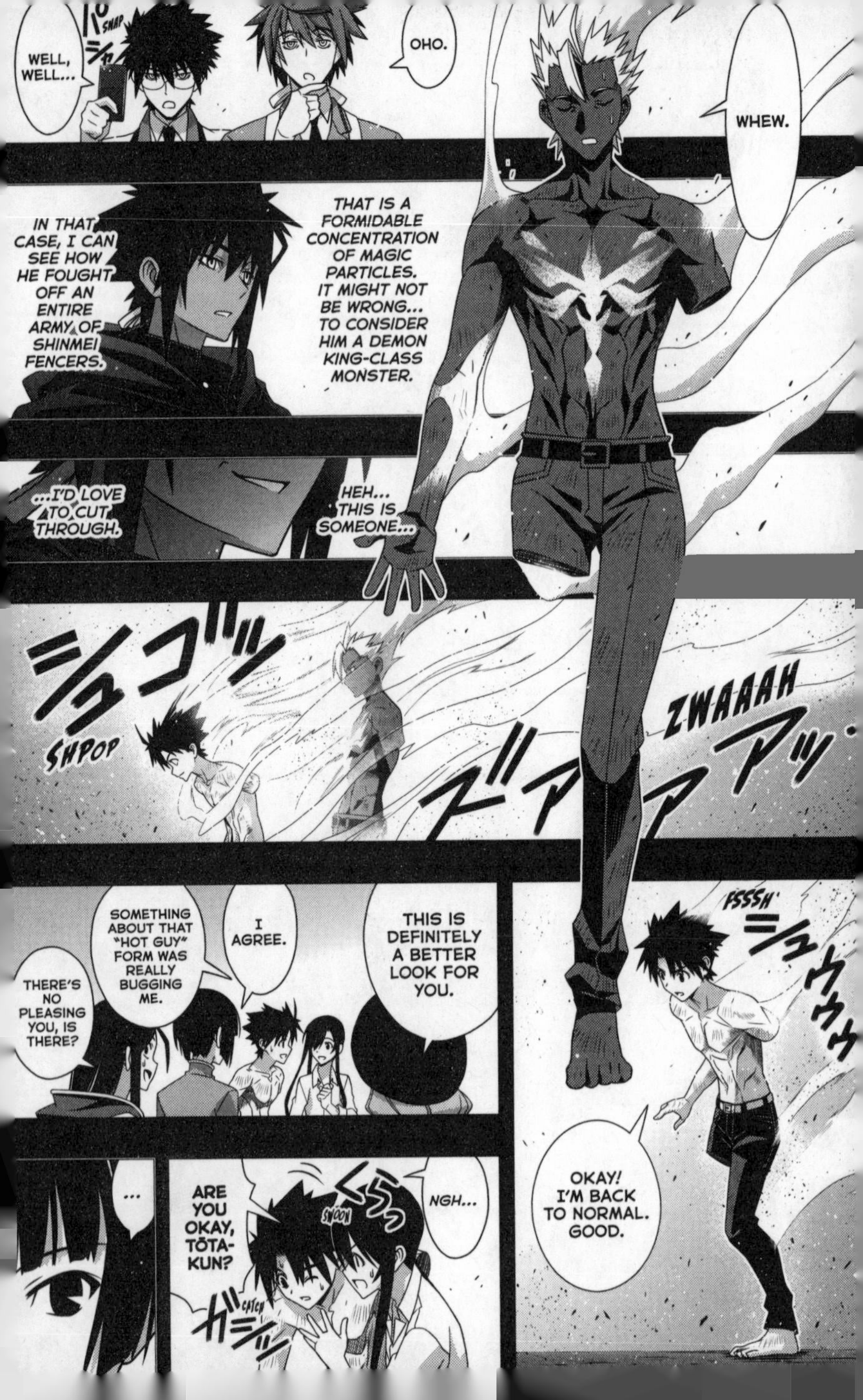
WHEW.
OHO.
SNAP
WELL, WELL...
THAT IS A FORMIDABLE CONCENTRATION OF MAGIC PARTICLES. IT MIGHT NOT BE WRONG... TO CONSIDER HIM A DEMON KING-CLASS MONSTER.
IN THAT CASE, I CAN SEE HOW HE FOUGHT OFF AN ENTIRE ARMY OF SHINMEI FENCERS.
HEH... THIS IS SOMEONE...
...I'D LOVE TO CUT THROUGH.
ZWAAAH
SHPOP
FSSSH
OKAY! I'M BACK TO NORMAL. GOOD.
THIS IS DEFINITELY A BETTER LOOK FOR YOU.
I AGREE.
SOMETHING ABOUT THAT "HOT GUY" FORM WAS REALLY BUGGING ME.
THERE'S NO PLEASING YOU, IS THERE?
NGH...
SWOON
ARE YOU OKAY, TŌTA-KUN?
CATCH
...

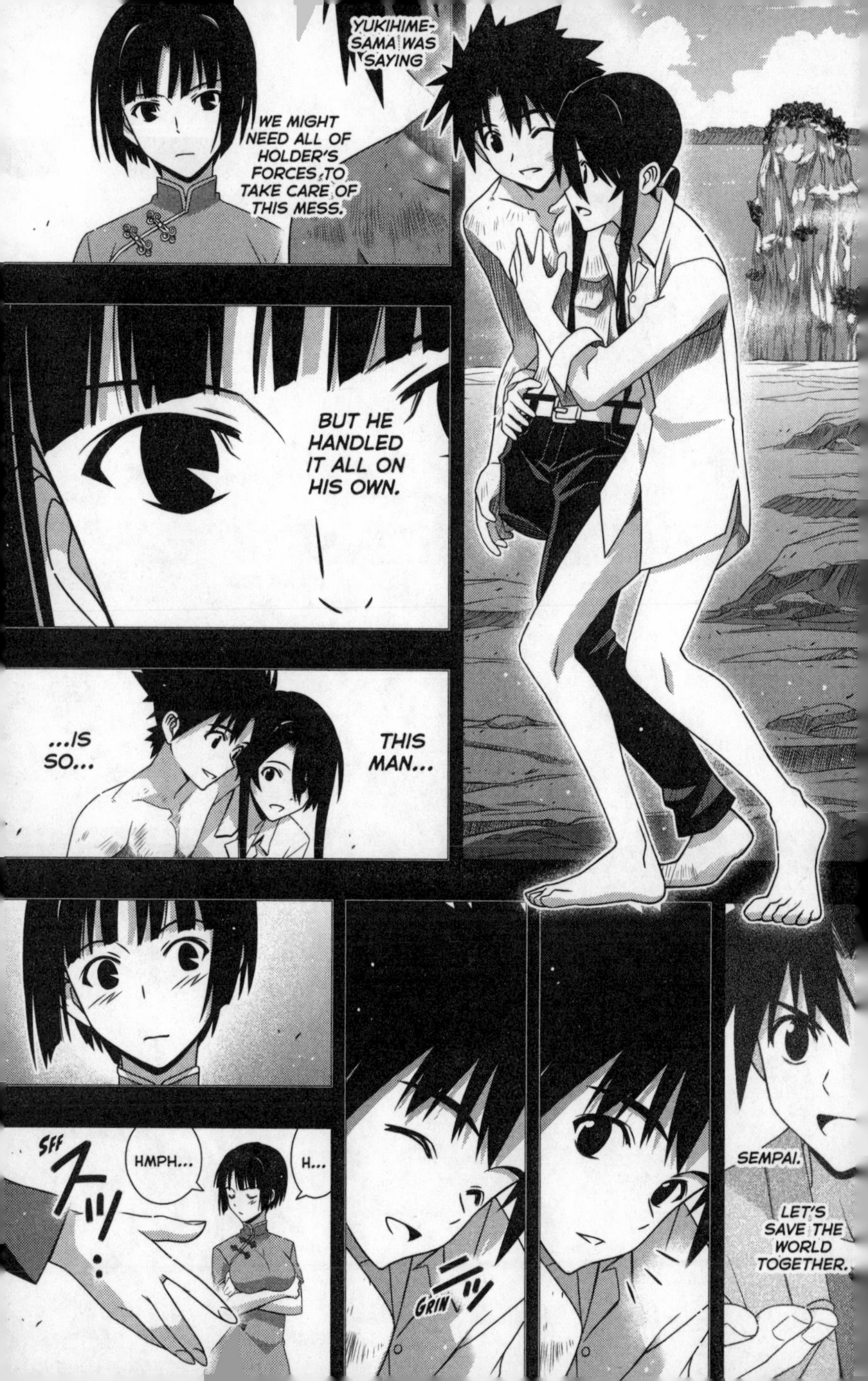
YUKIHIME-SAMA WAS SAYING
WE MIGHT NEED ALL OF HOLDER'S FORCES TO TAKE CARE OF THIS MESS.
BUT HE HANDLED IT ALL ON HIS OWN.
THIS MAN...
...IS SO...
SEMPAI.
LET'S SAVE THE WORLD TOGETHER.
GRIN
H...
HMPH...
SFF

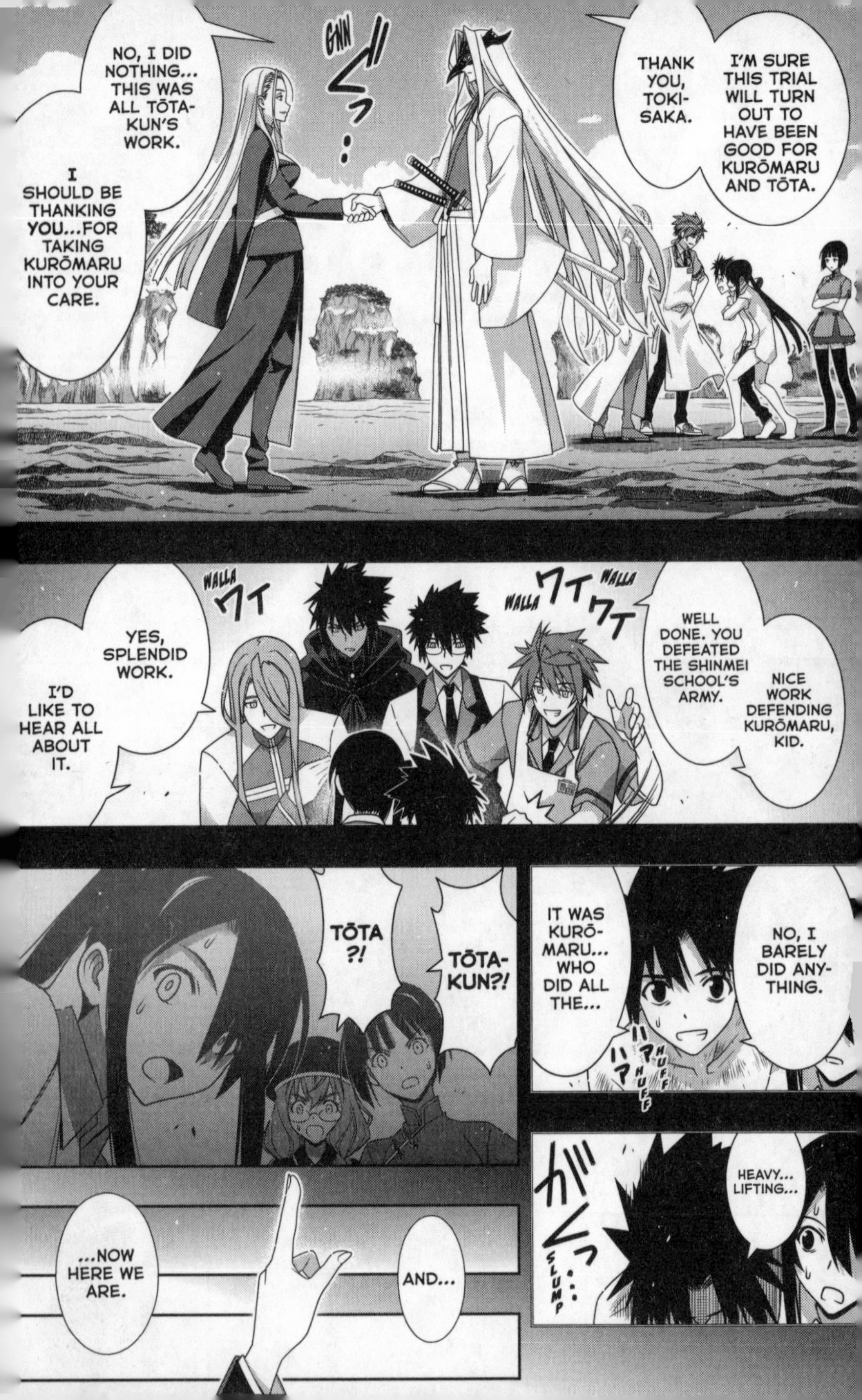
THANK YOU, TOKI-SAKA.
I'M SURE THIS TRIAL WILL TURN OUT TO HAVE BEEN GOOD FOR KURŌMARU AND TŌTA.
GNN
NO, I DID NOTHING... THIS WAS ALL TŌTA-KUN'S WORK.
I SHOULD BE THANKING YOU...FOR TAKING KURŌMARU INTO YOUR CARE.
WELL DONE. YOU DEFEATED THE SHINMEI SCHOOL'S ARMY.
NICE WORK DEFENDING KURŌMARU, KID.
WALLA WALLA
WALLA
YES, SPLENDID WORK.
I'D LIKE TO HEAR ALL ABOUT IT.
NO, I BARELY DID ANY-THING.
IT WAS KURŌ-MARU... WHO DID ALL THE...
HUFF HUFF
HEAVY... LIFTING...
SLUMP
TŌTA-KUN?!
TŌTA ?!
AND...
...NOW HERE WE ARE.

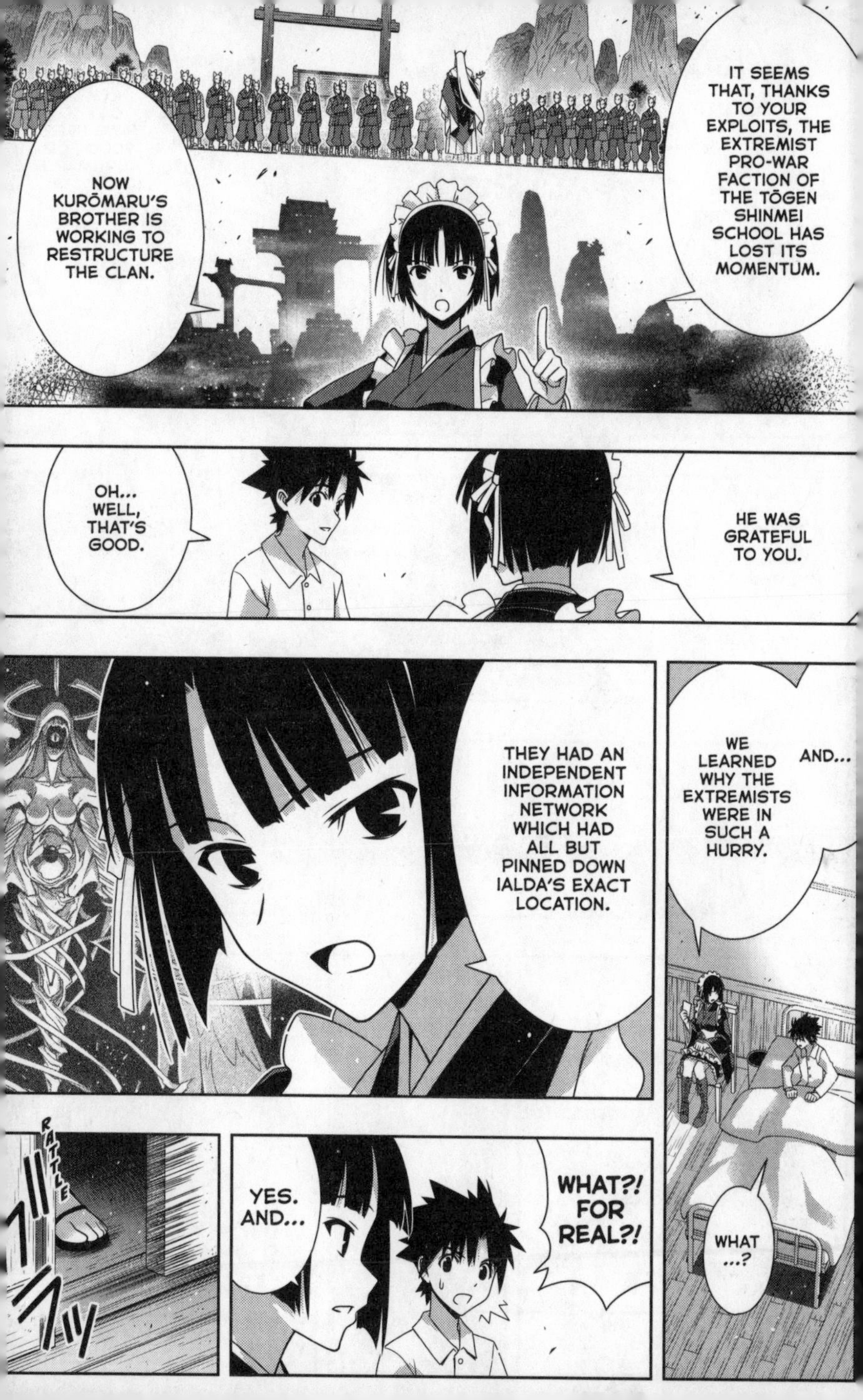
IT SEEMS THAT, THANKS TO YOUR EXPLOITS, THE EXTREMIST PRO-WAR FACTION OF THE TŌGEN SHINMEI SCHOOL HAS LOST ITS MOMENTUM.
NOW KURŌMARU'S BROTHER IS WORKING TO RESTRUCTURE THE CLAN.
HE WAS GRATEFUL TO YOU.
OH... WELL, THAT'S GOOD.
AND...
WE LEARNED WHY THE EXTREMISTS WERE IN SUCH A HURRY.
WHAT ...?
THEY HAD AN INDEPENDENT INFORMATION NETWORK WHICH HAD ALL BUT PINNED DOWN IALDA'S EXACT LOCATION.
WHAT?! FOR REAL?!
YES. AND...
RATTLE

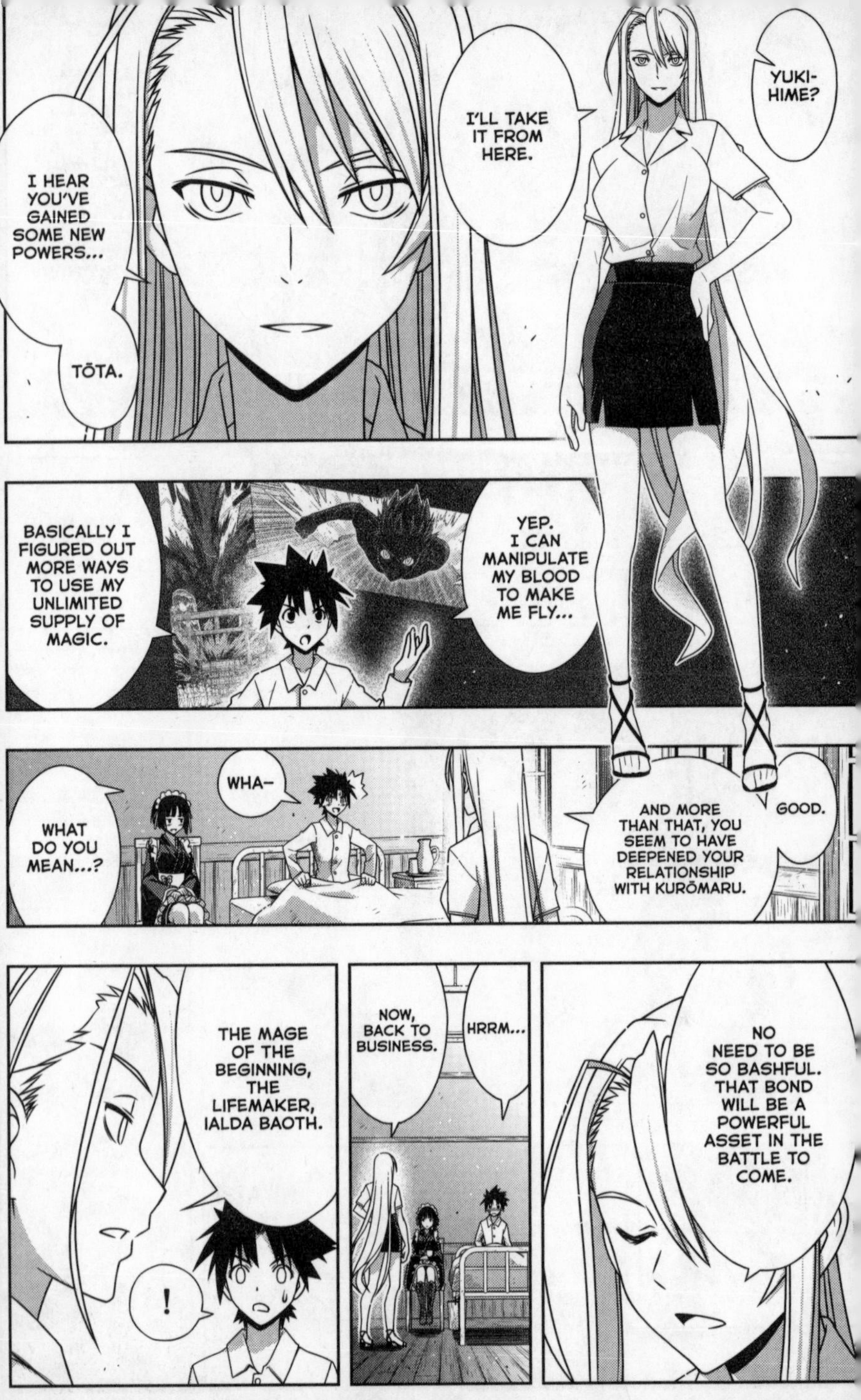
YUKI-HIME?
I'LL TAKE IT FROM HERE.
I HEAR YOU'VE GAINED SOME NEW POWERS...
TŌTA.
YEP. I CAN MANIPULATE MY BLOOD TO MAKE ME FLY...
BASICALLY I FIGURED OUT MORE WAYS TO USE MY UNLIMITED SUPPLY OF MAGIC.
GOOD.
AND MORE THAN THAT, YOU SEEM TO HAVE DEEPENED YOUR RELATIONSHIP WITH KURŌMARU.
WHA–
WHAT DO YOU MEAN...?
NO NEED TO BE SO BASHFUL. THAT BOND WILL BE A POWERFUL ASSET IN THE BATTLE TO COME.
HRRM...
NOW, BACK TO BUSINESS.
THE MAGE OF THE BEGINNING, THE LIFEMAKER, IALDA BAOTH.
!

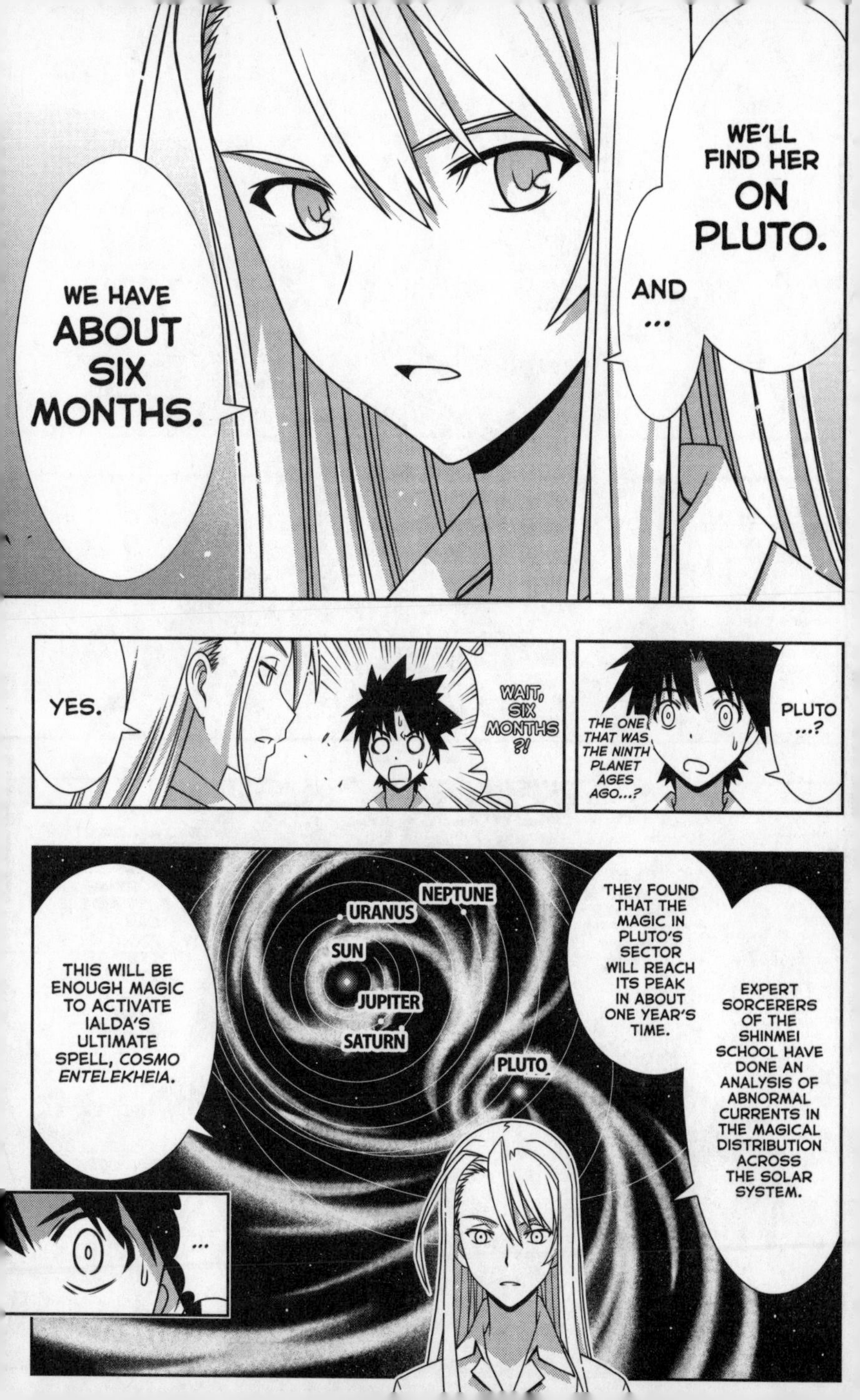
WE'LL FIND HER ON PLUTO.
AND ...
WE HAVE ABOUT SIX MONTHS.
PLUTO ...?
THE ONE THAT WAS THE NINTH PLANET AGES AGO...?
WAIT, SIX MONTHS ?!
YES.
EXPERT SORCERERS OF THE SHINMEI SCHOOL HAVE DONE AN ANALYSIS OF ABNORMAL CURRENTS IN THE MAGICAL DISTRIBUTION ACROSS THE SOLAR SYSTEM.
THEY FOUND THAT THE MAGIC IN PLUTO'S SECTOR WILL REACH ITS PEAK IN ABOUT ONE YEAR'S TIME.
NEPTUNE
URANUS
SUN
JUPITER
SATURN
PLUTO
THIS WILL BE ENOUGH MAGIC TO ACTIVATE IALDA'S ULTIMATE SPELL, *COSMO ENTELEKHEIA*.
...

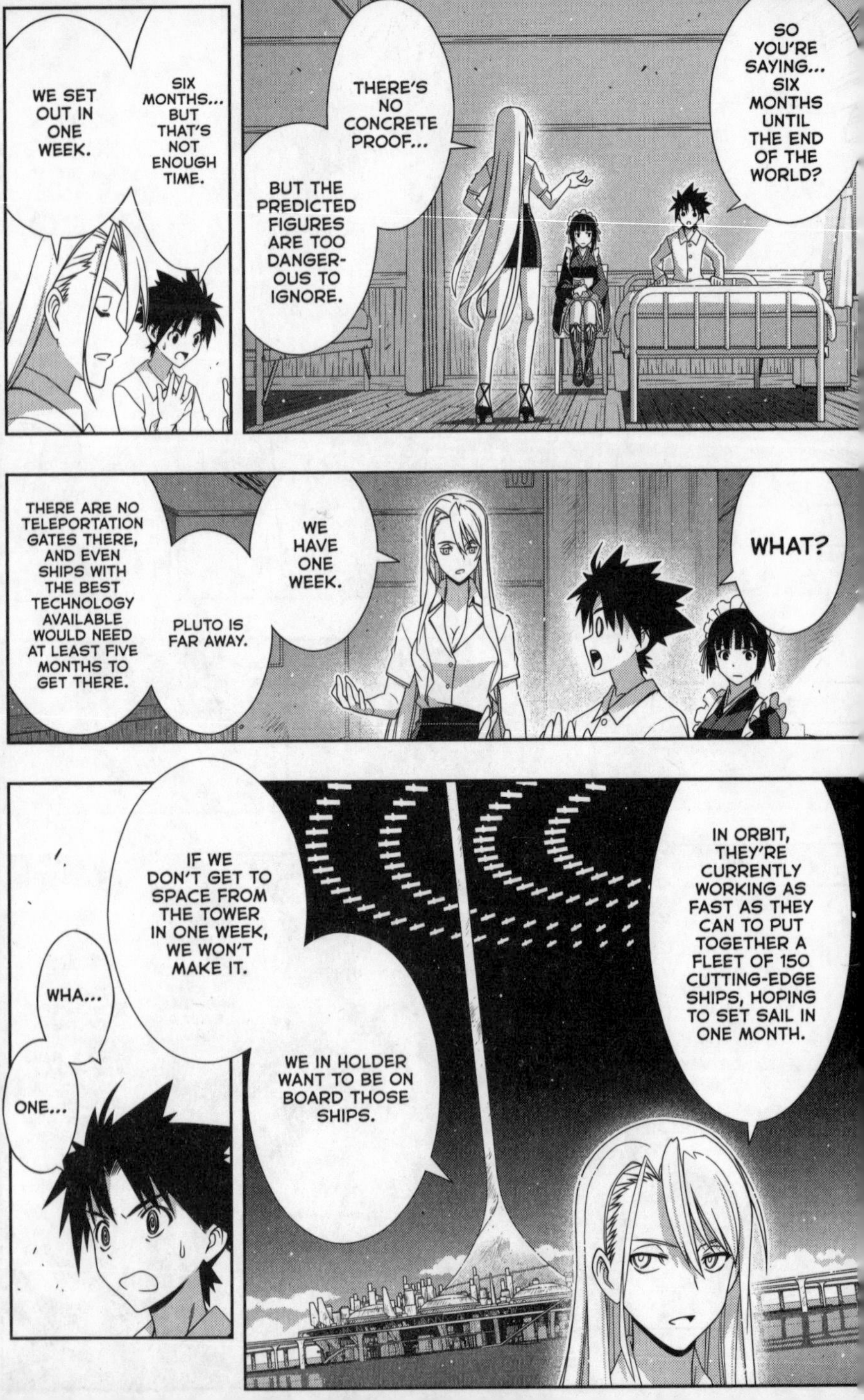
SO YOU'RE SAYING... SIX MONTHS UNTIL THE END OF THE WORLD?
THERE'S NO CONCRETE PROOF...
BUT THE PREDICTED FIGURES ARE TOO DANGER-OUS TO IGNORE.
SIX MONTHS... BUT THAT'S NOT ENOUGH TIME.
WE SET OUT IN ONE WEEK.
WHAT?
WE HAVE ONE WEEK.
PLUTO IS FAR AWAY.
THERE ARE NO TELEPORTATION GATES THERE, AND EVEN SHIPS WITH THE BEST TECHNOLOGY AVAILABLE WOULD NEED AT LEAST FIVE MONTHS TO GET THERE.
IN ORBIT, THEY'RE CURRENTLY WORKING AS FAST AS THEY CAN TO PUT TOGETHER A FLEET OF 150 CUTTING-EDGE SHIPS, HOPING TO SET SAIL IN ONE MONTH.
IF WE DON'T GET TO SPACE FROM THE TOWER IN ONE WEEK, WE WON'T MAKE IT.
WE IN HOLDER WANT TO BE ON BOARD THOSE SHIPS.
WHA...
ONE...

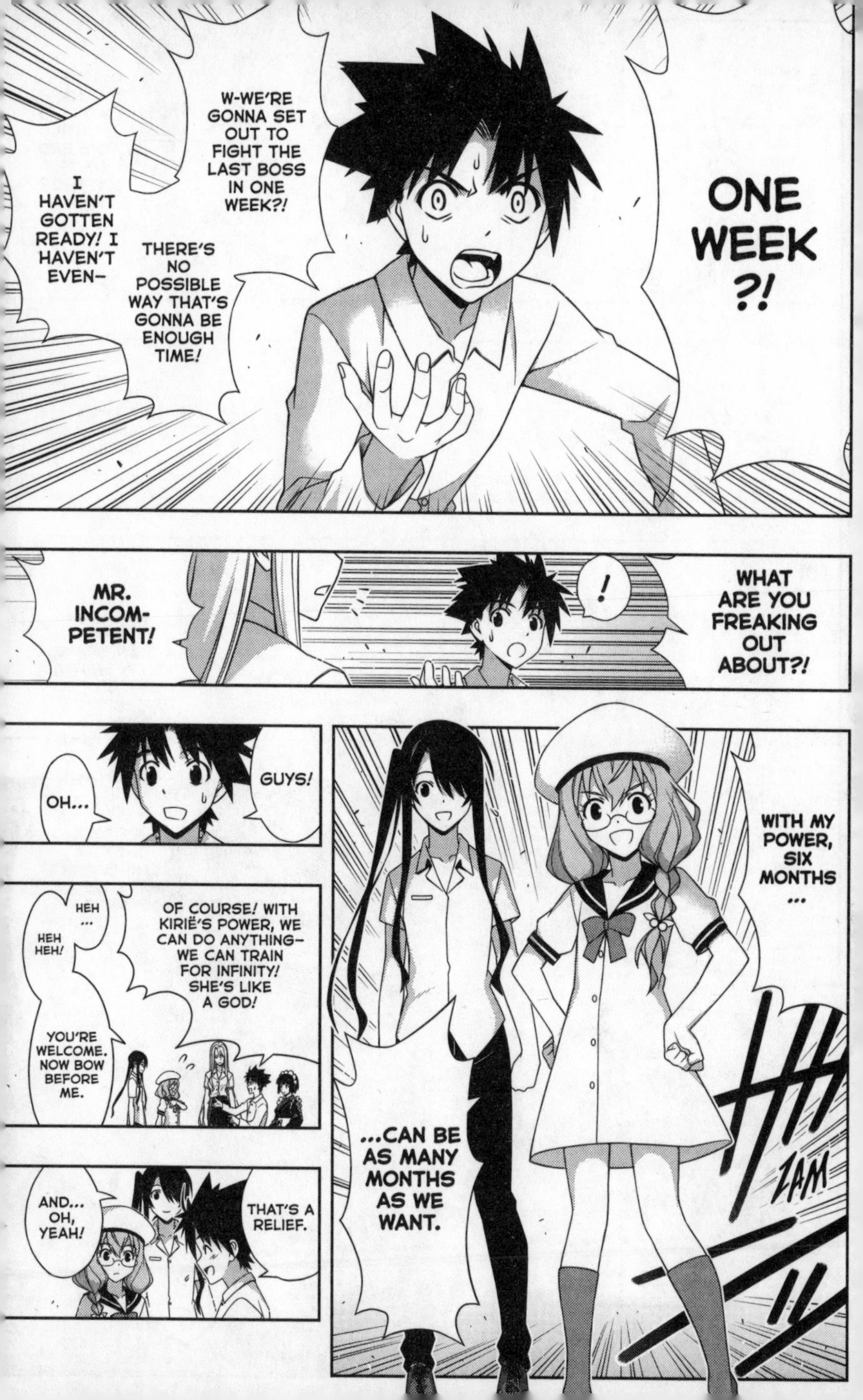
ONE WEEK ?!
W-WE'RE GONNA SET OUT TO FIGHT THE LAST BOSS IN ONE WEEK?!
THERE'S NO POSSIBLE WAY THAT'S GONNA BE ENOUGH TIME!
I HAVEN'T GOTTEN READY! I HAVEN'T EVEN–
WHAT ARE YOU FREAKING OUT ABOUT?!
!
MR. INCOMPETENT!
WITH MY POWER, SIX MONTHS ...
ZAM
...CAN BE AS MANY MONTHS AS WE WANT.
GUYS!
OH...
OF COURSE! WITH KIRIÉ'S POWER, WE CAN DO ANYTHING– WE CAN TRAIN FOR INFINITY! SHE'S LIKE A GOD!
HEH ... HEH HEH!
YOU'RE WELCOME. NOW BOW BEFORE ME.
THAT'S A RELIEF.
AND... OH, YEAH!

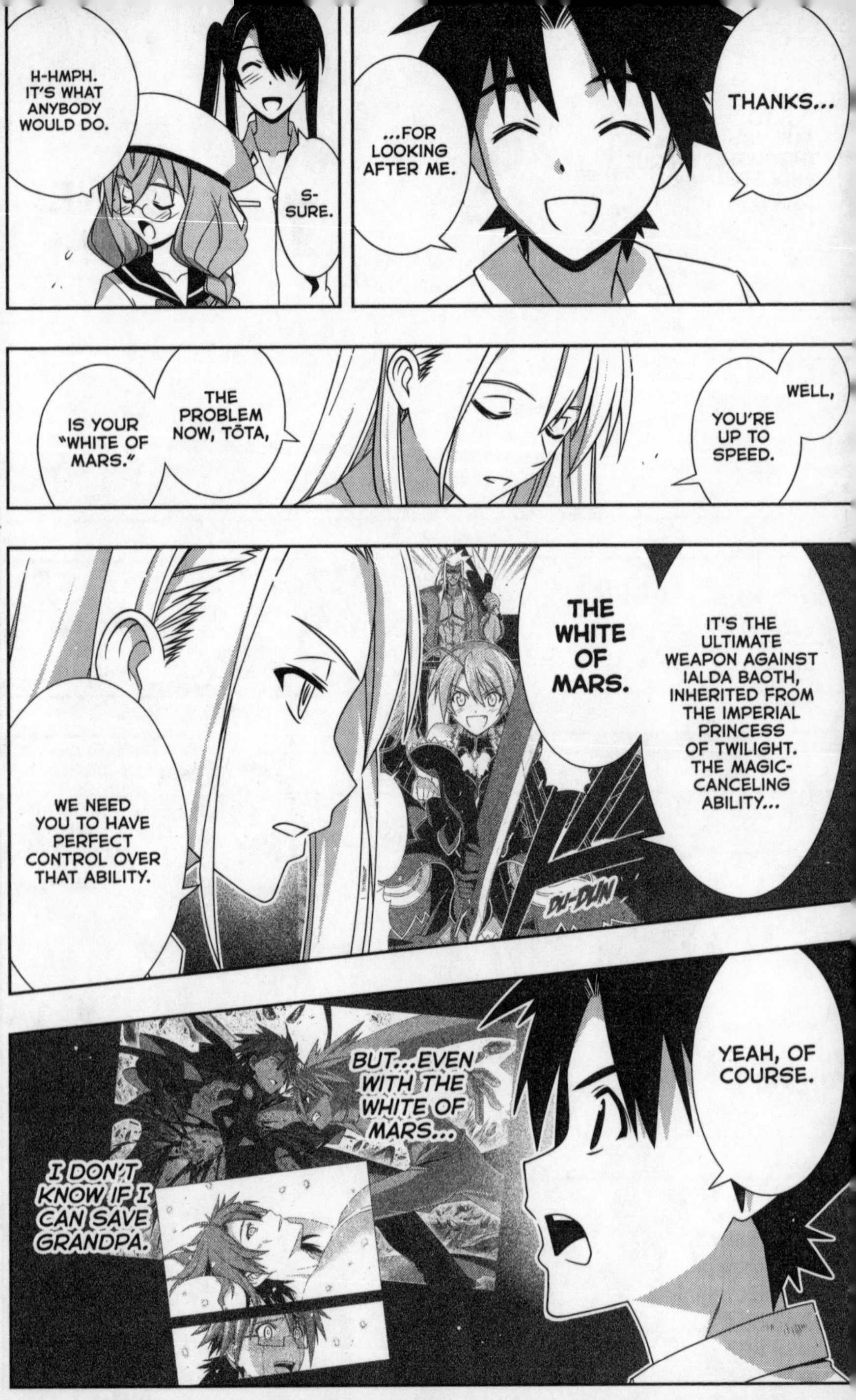
THANKS...
...FOR LOOKING AFTER ME.
H-HMPH. IT'S WHAT ANYBODY WOULD DO.
S-SURE.
WELL, YOU'RE UP TO SPEED.
THE PROBLEM NOW, TŌTA,
IS YOUR "WHITE OF MARS."
IT'S THE ULTIMATE WEAPON AGAINST IALDA BAOTH, INHERITED FROM THE IMPERIAL PRINCESS OF TWILIGHT. THE MAGIC-CANCELING ABILITY...
THE WHITE OF MARS.
DU-DUN
WE NEED YOU TO HAVE PERFECT CONTROL OVER THAT ABILITY.
YEAH, OF COURSE.
BUT...EVEN WITH THE WHITE OF MARS...
I DON'T KNOW IF I CAN SAVE GRANDPA.

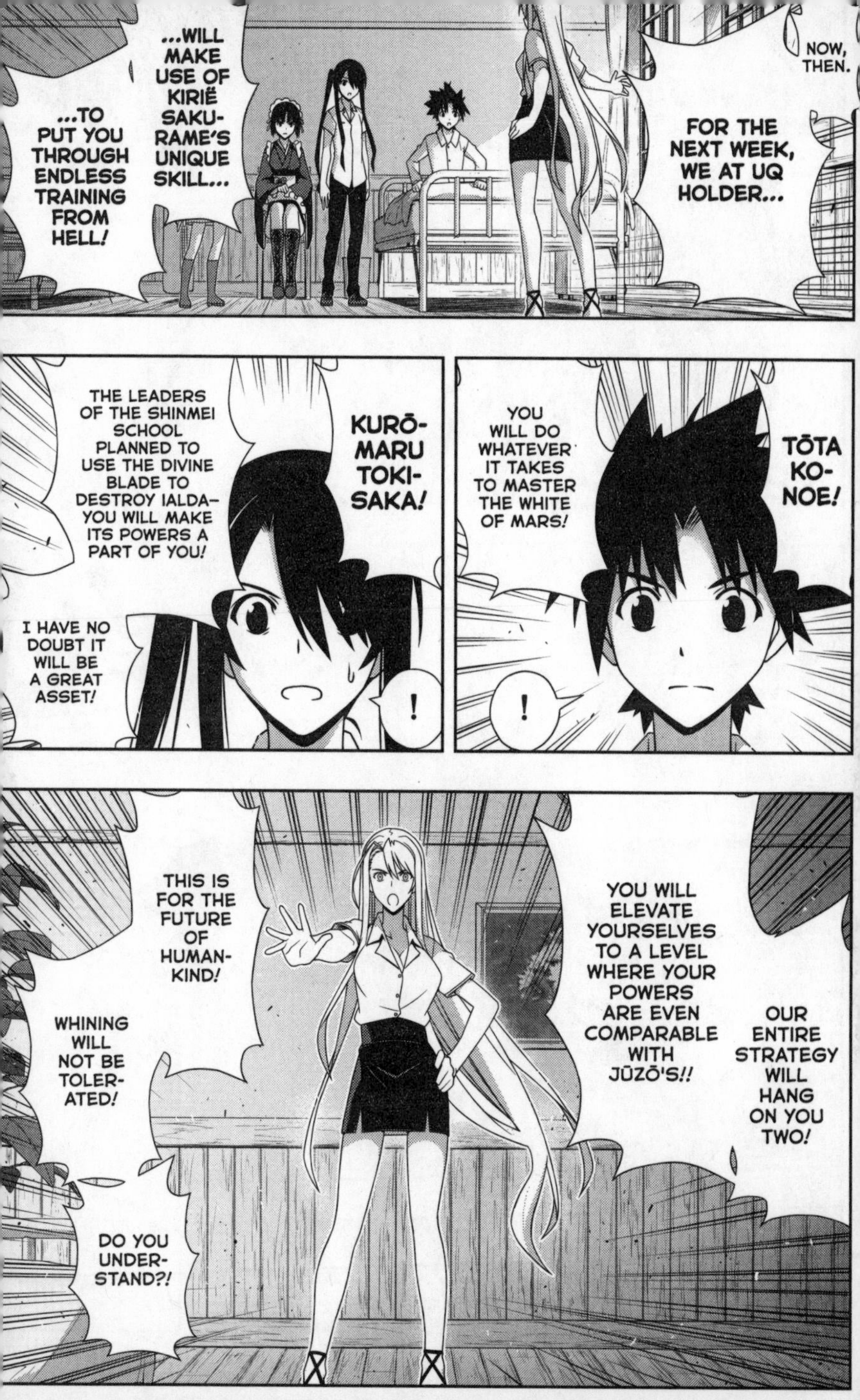
NOW, THEN.
FOR THE NEXT WEEK, WE AT UQ HOLDER...
...WILL MAKE USE OF KIRIË SAKURAME'S UNIQUE SKILL...
...TO PUT YOU THROUGH ENDLESS TRAINING FROM HELL!
TŌTA KONOE!
YOU WILL DO WHATEVER IT TAKES TO MASTER THE WHITE OF MARS!
!
KURŌMARU TOKISAKA!
THE LEADERS OF THE SHINMEI SCHOOL PLANNED TO USE THE DIVINE BLADE TO DESTROY IALDA–YOU WILL MAKE ITS POWERS A PART OF YOU!
I HAVE NO DOUBT IT WILL BE A GREAT ASSET!
!
OUR ENTIRE STRATEGY WILL HANG ON YOU TWO!
YOU WILL ELEVATE YOURSELVES TO A LEVEL WHERE YOUR POWERS ARE EVEN COMPARABLE WITH JŪZŌ'S!!
THIS IS FOR THE FUTURE OF HUMANKIND!
WHINING WILL NOT BE TOLERATED!
DO YOU UNDERSTAND?!

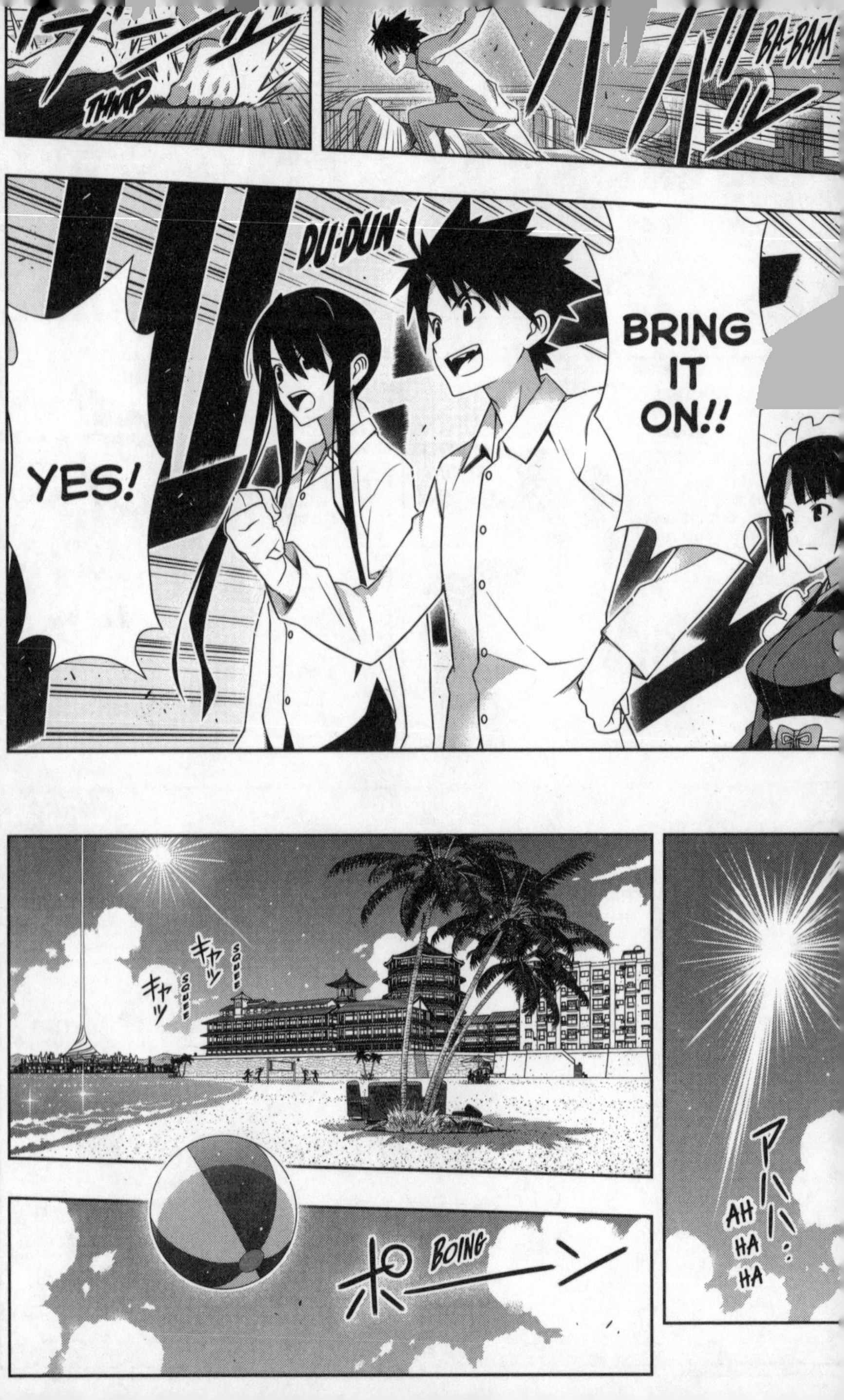
ババッ
BA-BAM
ブンッ
THWAP
BRING IT ON!!
DU-DUN
YES!
アーハハ…
AH HA HA
キャッ
SQUEE
キャッ
SQUEE
ポーン
BOING

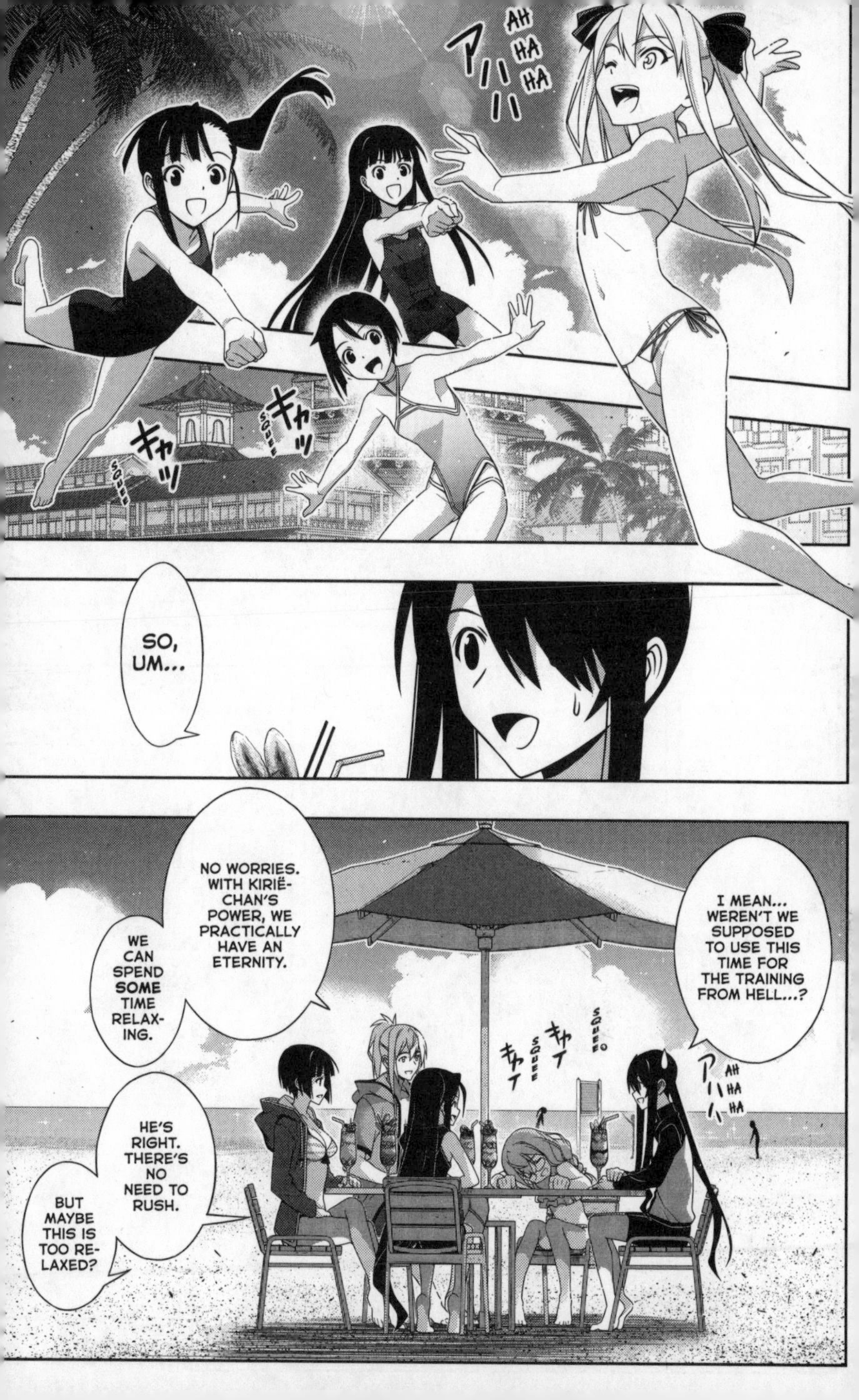
AH HA HA
アハハ
キャッ
SQUEE
キャッ
SQUEE
SO, UM...
I MEAN... WEREN'T WE SUPPOSED TO USE THIS TIME FOR THE TRAINING FROM HELL...?
アハハ
AH HA HA
SQUEE
キャア
SQUEE
キャア
NO WORRIES. WITH KIRIË-CHAN'S POWER, WE PRACTICALLY HAVE AN ETERNITY.
WE CAN SPEND SOME TIME RELAX-ING.
HE'S RIGHT. THERE'S NO NEED TO RUSH.
BUT MAYBE THIS IS TOO RE-LAXED?

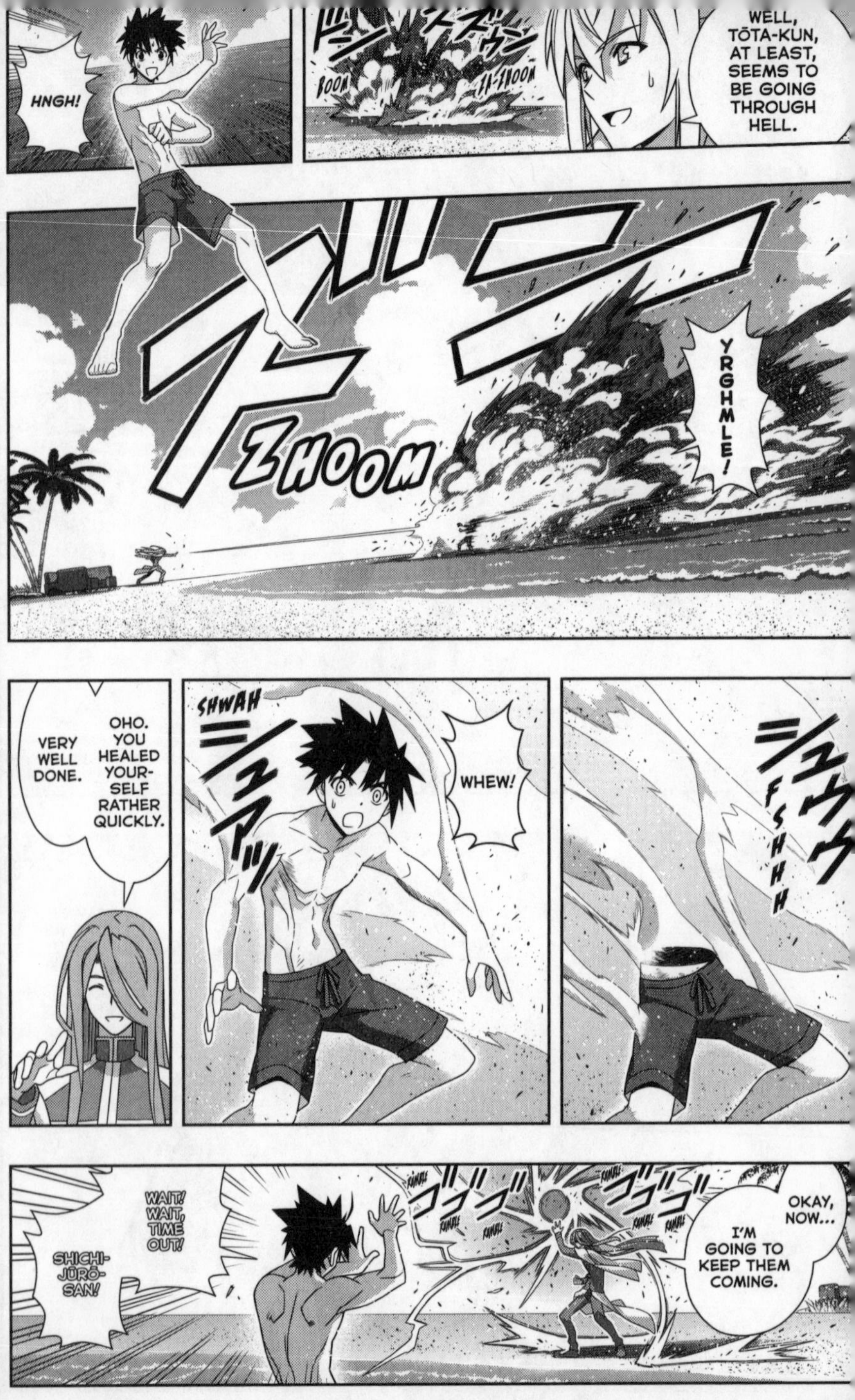
WELL, TŌTA-KUN, AT LEAST, SEEMS TO BE GOING THROUGH HELL.
BOOM
HNGH!
ZHOOM
YRGHMLE!
FSHHH
SHWAH
WHEW!
OHO. YOU HEALED YOUR-SELF RATHER QUICKLY.
VERY WELL DONE.
OKAY, NOW...
I'M GOING TO KEEP THEM COMING.
WAIT! WAIT, TIME OUT!
SHICHI-JŪRŌ-SAN!

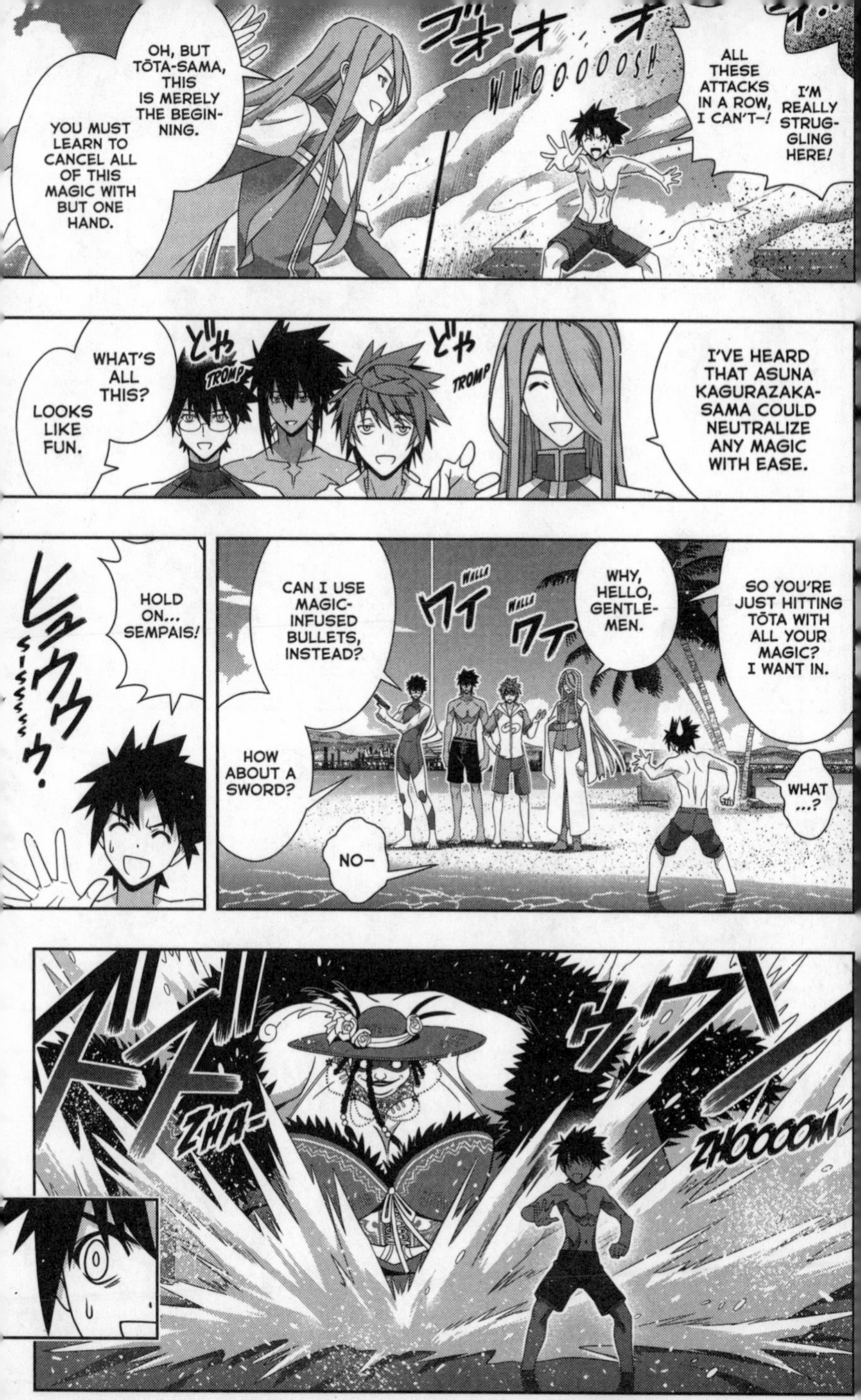
I'M REALLY STRUGGLING HERE!
ALL THESE ATTACKS IN A ROW, I CAN'T–!
WHOOOOOOSH
OH, BUT TŌTA-SAMA, THIS IS MERELY THE BEGINNING.
YOU MUST LEARN TO CANCEL ALL OF THIS MAGIC WITH BUT ONE HAND.
I'VE HEARD THAT ASUNA KAGURAZAKA-SAMA COULD NEUTRALIZE ANY MAGIC WITH EASE.
TROMP
TROMP
WHAT'S ALL THIS?
LOOKS LIKE FUN.
SO YOU'RE JUST HITTING TŌTA WITH ALL YOUR MAGIC? I WANT IN.
WHAT ...?
WHY, HELLO, GENTLEMEN.
WALLA
WALLA
CAN I USE MAGIC-INFUSED BULLETS, INSTEAD?
HOW ABOUT A SWORD?
NO–
HOLD ON... SEMPAIS!
SISSSSSS
ZHOOOOM
ZHA-

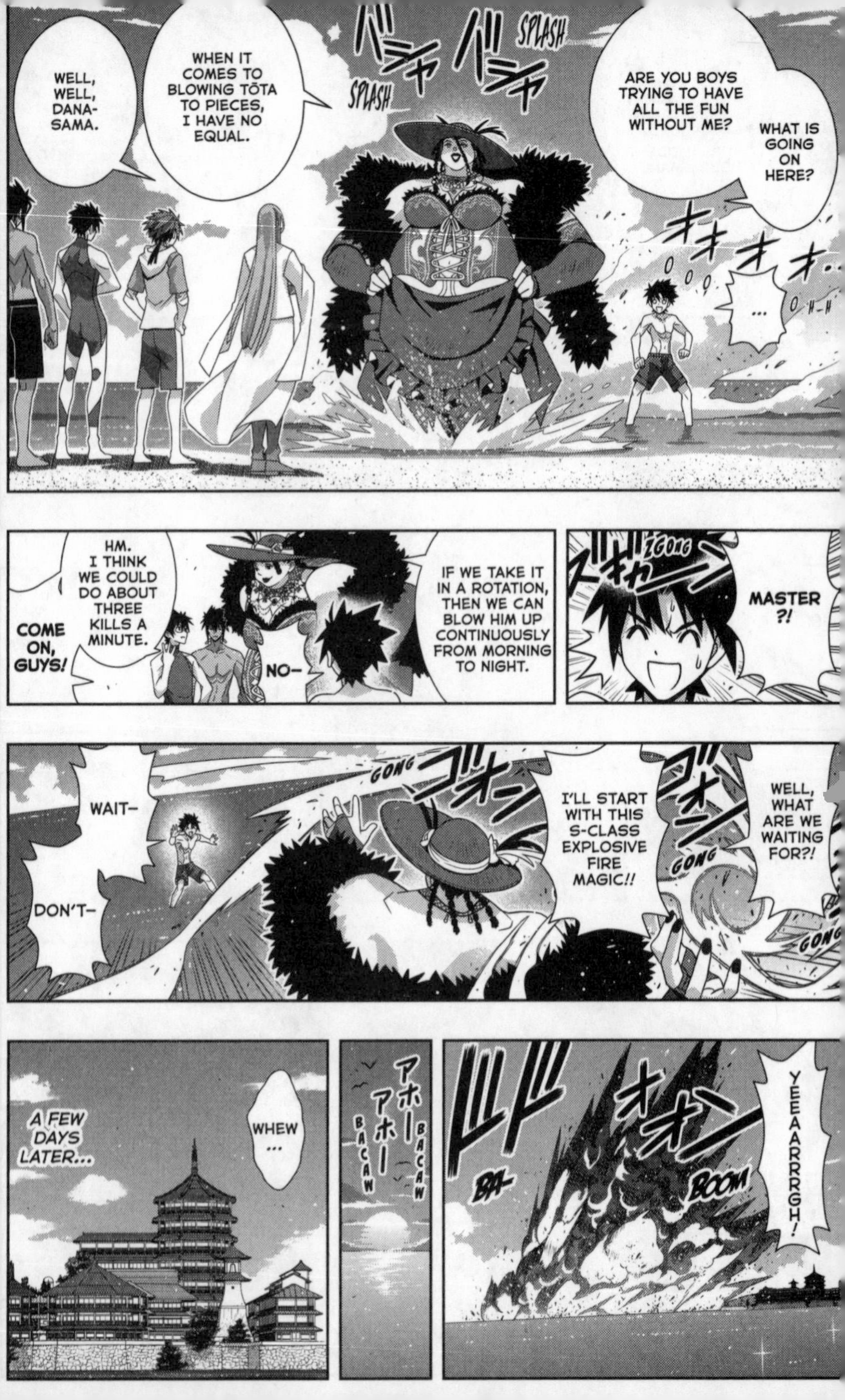

ARE YOU BOYS TRYING TO HAVE ALL THE FUN WITHOUT ME?
WHAT IS GOING ON HERE?
OOO-H-H
...
SPLASH
SPLASH
WHEN IT COMES TO BLOWING TŌTA TO PIECES, I HAVE NO EQUAL.
WELL, WELL, DANA-SAMA.
ZGONG
MASTER?!
IF WE TAKE IT IN A ROTATION, THEN WE CAN BLOW HIM UP CONTINUOUSLY FROM MORNING TO NIGHT.
NO–
HM. I THINK WE COULD DO ABOUT THREE KILLS A MINUTE.
COME ON, GUYS!
WELL, WHAT ARE WE WAITING FOR?!
GONG
GONG
I'LL START WITH THIS S-CLASS EXPLOSIVE FIRE MAGIC!!
GONG
WAIT–
DON'T–
YEEAARRRGH!
BOOM
BA-
BACAW
BACAW
WHEW...
A FEW DAYS LATER...

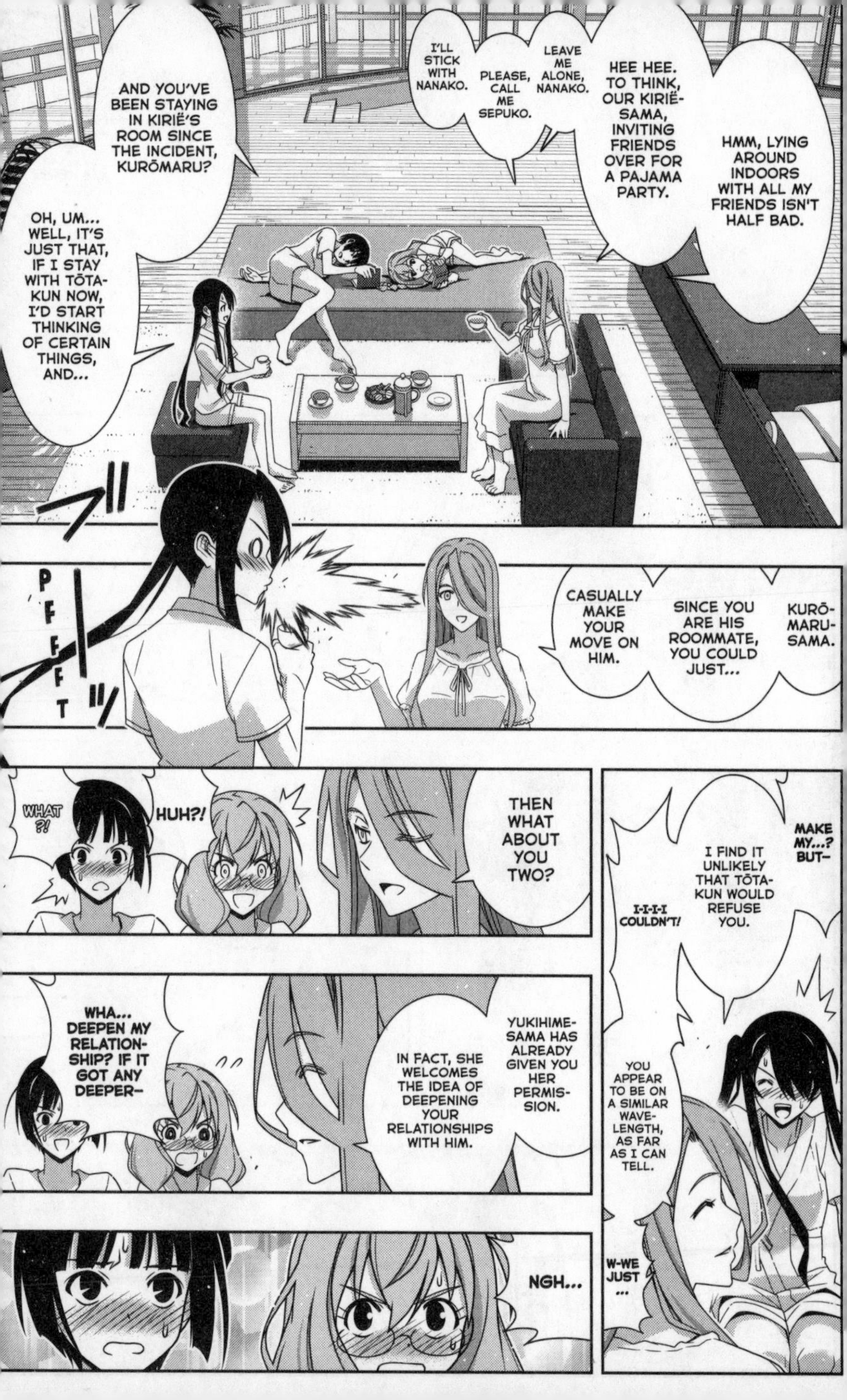
HMM, LYING AROUND INDOORS WITH ALL MY FRIENDS ISN'T HALF BAD.
HEE HEE. TO THINK, OUR KIRIË-SAMA, INVITING FRIENDS OVER FOR A PAJAMA PARTY.
LEAVE ME ALONE, NANAKO.
PLEASE, CALL ME SEPUKO.
I'LL STICK WITH NANAKO.
AND YOU'VE BEEN STAYING IN KIRIË'S ROOM SINCE THE INCIDENT, KURŌMARU?
OH, UM... WELL, IT'S JUST THAT, IF I STAY WITH TŌTA-KUN NOW, I'D START THINKING OF CERTAIN THINGS, AND...
KURŌ-MARU-SAMA.
SINCE YOU ARE HIS ROOMMATE, YOU COULD JUST...
CASUALLY MAKE YOUR MOVE ON HIM.
PFFFFT
MAKE MY...? BUT—
I FIND IT UNLIKELY THAT TŌTA-KUN WOULD REFUSE YOU.
I-I-I-I COULDN'T!
YOU APPEAR TO BE ON A SIMILAR WAVE-LENGTH, AS FAR AS I CAN TELL.
W-WE JUST ...
THEN WHAT ABOUT YOU TWO?
HUH?!
WHAT ?!
YUKIHIME-SAMA HAS ALREADY GIVEN YOU HER PERMIS-SION.
IN FACT, SHE WELCOMES THE IDEA OF DEEPENING YOUR RELATIONSHIPS WITH HIM.
WHA... DEEPEN MY RELATION-SHIP? IF IT GOT ANY DEEPER—
NGH...

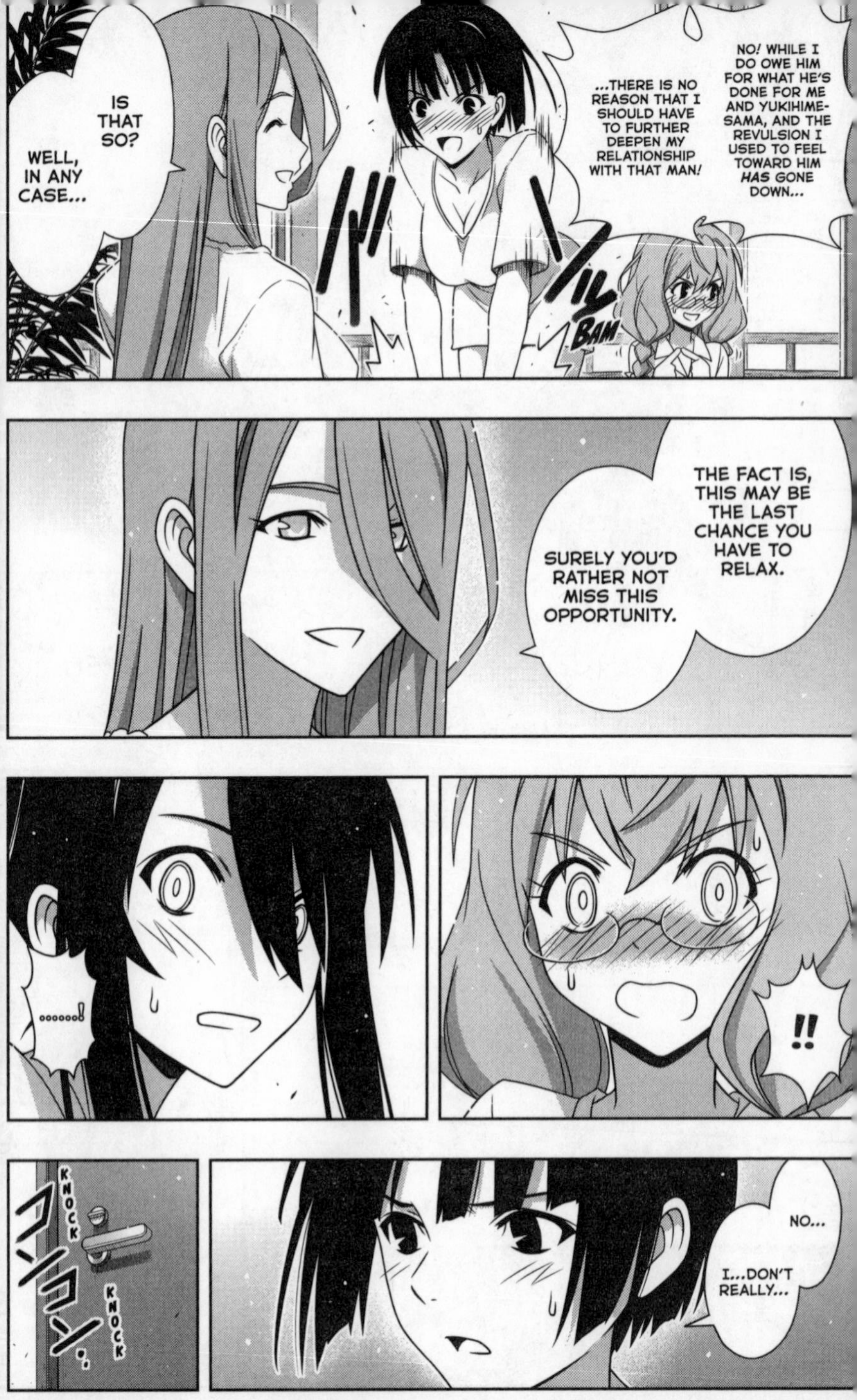
NO! WHILE I DO OWE HIM FOR WHAT HE'S DONE FOR ME AND YUKIHIME-SAMA, AND THE REVULSION I USED TO FEEL TOWARD HIM *HAS* GONE DOWN...
...THERE IS NO REASON THAT I SHOULD HAVE TO FURTHER DEEPEN MY RELATIONSHIP WITH THAT MAN!
BAM
IS THAT SO?
WELL, IN ANY CASE...
THE FACT IS, THIS MAY BE THE LAST CHANCE YOU HAVE TO RELAX.
SURELY YOU'D RATHER NOT MISS THIS OPPORTUNITY.
!!
......!
NO...
I...DON'T REALLY...
KNOCK
KNOCK

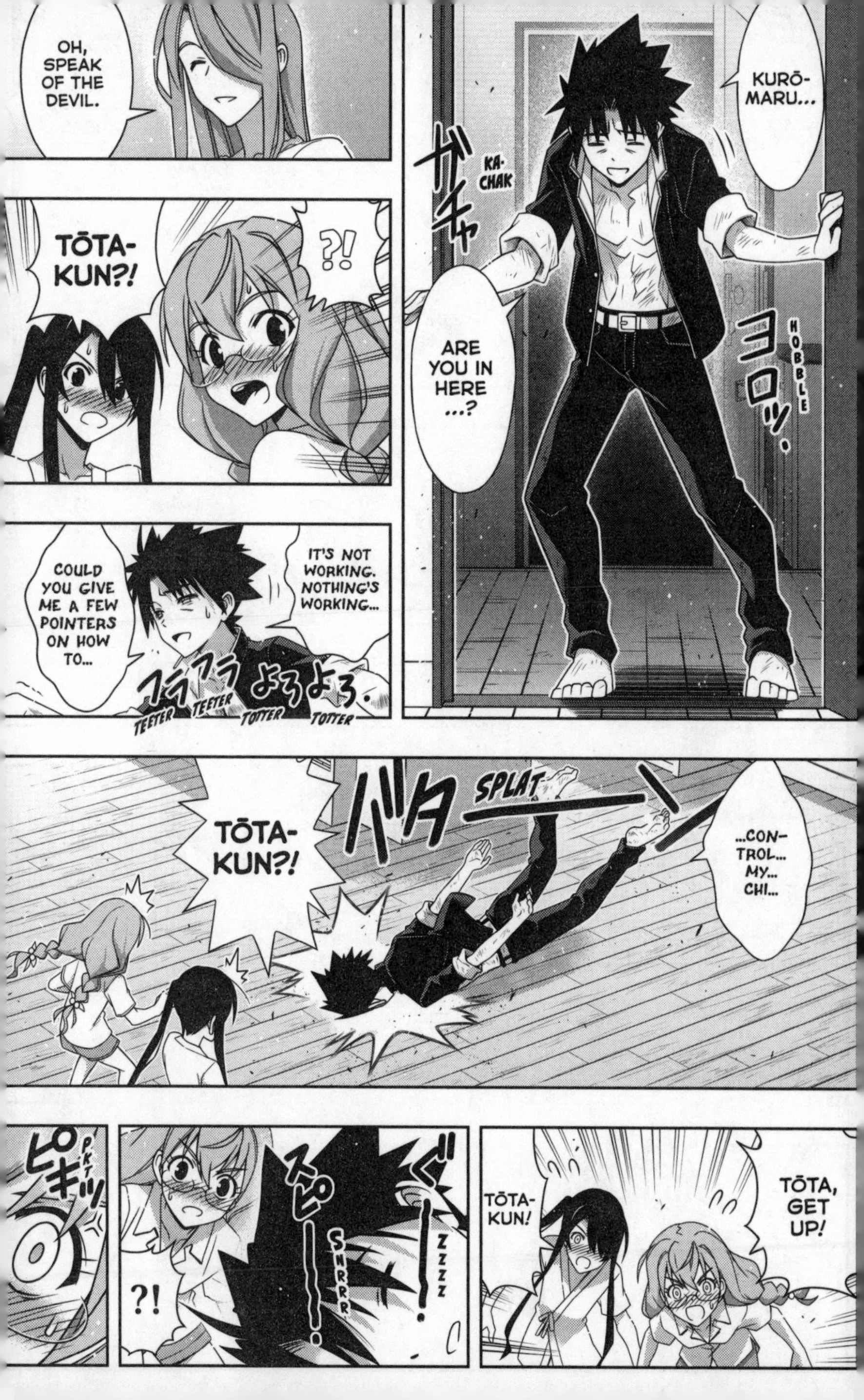
KURŌ-MARU...
ガチャ
KA-CHAK
ARE YOU IN HERE ...?
ヨロッ
HOBBLE
OH, SPEAK OF THE DEVIL.
?!
TŌTA-KUN?!
IT'S NOT WORKING. NOTHING'S WORKING...
COULD YOU GIVE ME A FEW POINTERS ON HOW TO...
フラフラ よろよろ
TEETER TEETER TOTTER TOTTER
...CON-TROL... MY... CHI...
バタ—ン
SPLAT
TŌTA-KUN?!
TŌTA, GET UP!
TŌTA-KUN!
ぐー!
ZZZ
スピー!
SNRRR
?!
ピキッ
PKT

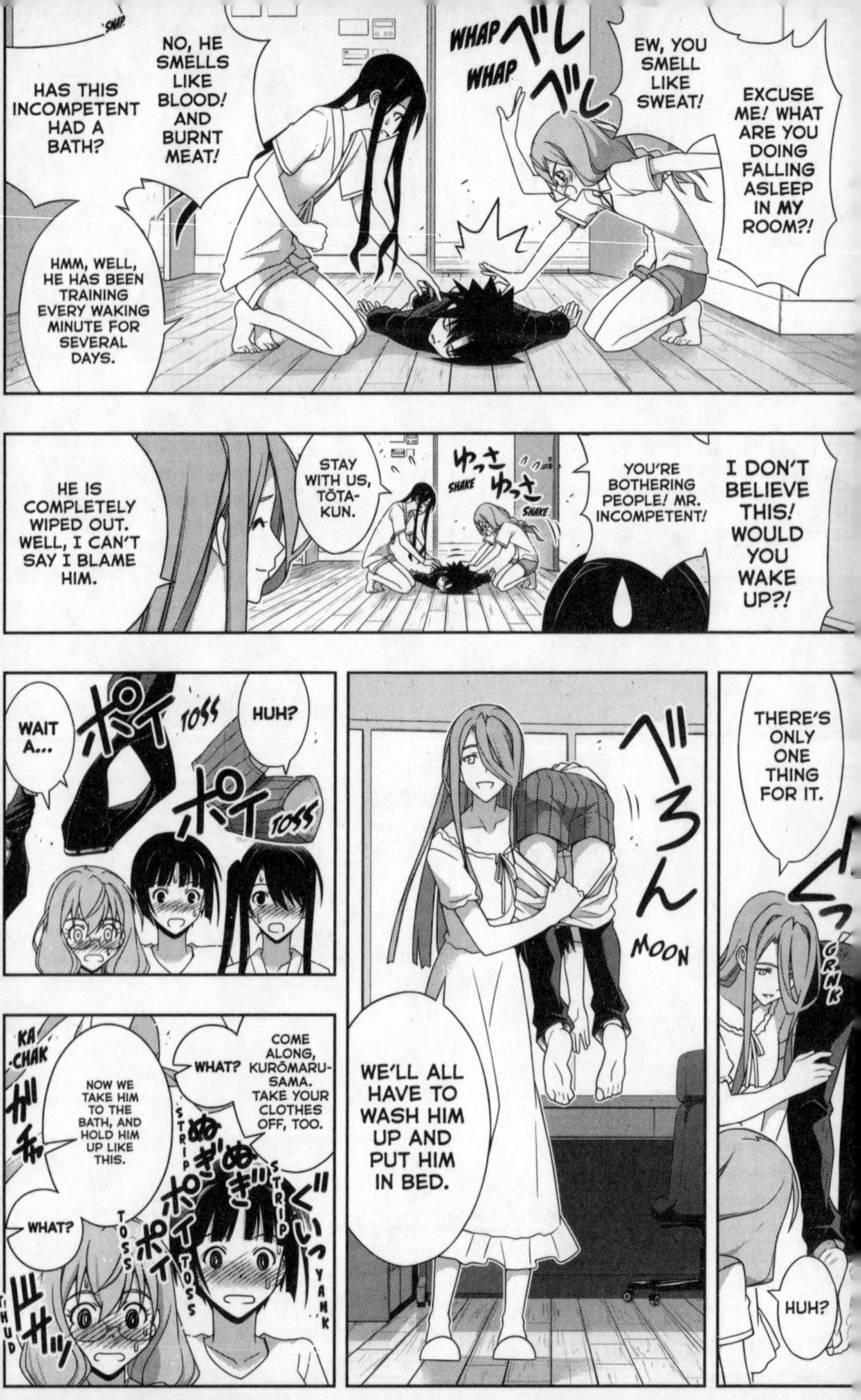
EXCUSE ME! WHAT ARE YOU DOING FALLING ASLEEP IN MY ROOM?!
EW, YOU SMELL LIKE SWEAT!
べし WHAP
べし WHAP
NO, HE SMELLS LIKE BLOOD! AND BURNT MEAT!
SNAP.
HAS THIS INCOMPETENT HAD A BATH?
HMM, WELL, HE HAS BEEN TRAINING EVERY WAKING MINUTE FOR SEVERAL DAYS.
I DON'T BELIEVE THIS! WOULD YOU WAKE UP?!
YOU'RE BOTHERING PEOPLE! MR. INCOMPETENT!
ゆっさ SHAKE
ゆっさ SHAKE
STAY WITH US, TŌTA-KUN.
HE IS COMPLETELY WIPED OUT. WELL, I CAN'T SAY I BLAME HIM.
THERE'S ONLY ONE THING FOR IT.
くっ GRNK
HUH?
べろん MOON
WE'LL ALL HAVE TO WASH HIM UP AND PUT HIM IN BED.
HUH?
ポイ TOSS
ポイ TOSS
WAIT A...
COME ALONG, KURŌMARU-SAMA. TAKE YOUR CLOTHES OFF, TOO.
WHAT?
ガチャ KA-CHAK
NOW WE TAKE HIM TO THE BATH, AND HOLD HIM UP LIKE THIS.
ぬぎ STRIP
ぬぎ STRIP
ぐいっ YANK
ポイ TOSS
ポイ TOSS
WHAT?
ドサッ THUD

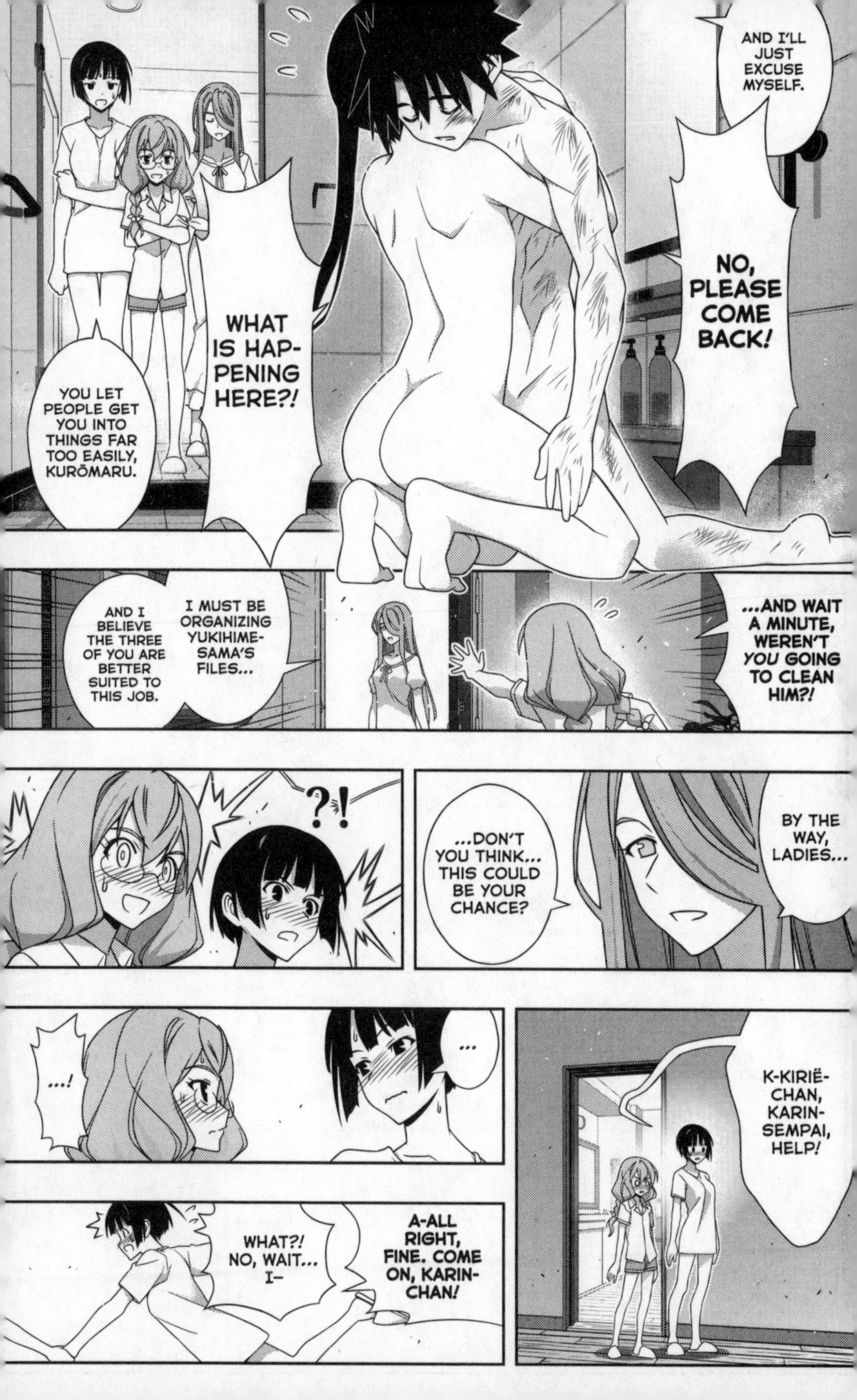
AND I'LL JUST EXCUSE MYSELF.
NO, PLEASE COME BACK!
WHAT IS HAP-PENING HERE?!
YOU LET PEOPLE GET YOU INTO THINGS FAR TOO EASILY, KURŌMARU.
...AND WAIT A MINUTE, WEREN'T *YOU* GOING TO CLEAN HIM?!
I MUST BE ORGANIZING YUKIHIME-SAMA'S FILES...
AND I BELIEVE THE THREE OF YOU ARE BETTER SUITED TO THIS JOB.
BY THE WAY, LADIES...
...DON'T YOU THINK... THIS COULD BE YOUR CHANCE?
?!
K-KIRIË-CHAN, KARIN-SEMPAI, HELP!
...
...!
A-ALL RIGHT, FINE. COME ON, KARIN-CHAN!
WHAT?! NO, WAIT... I–

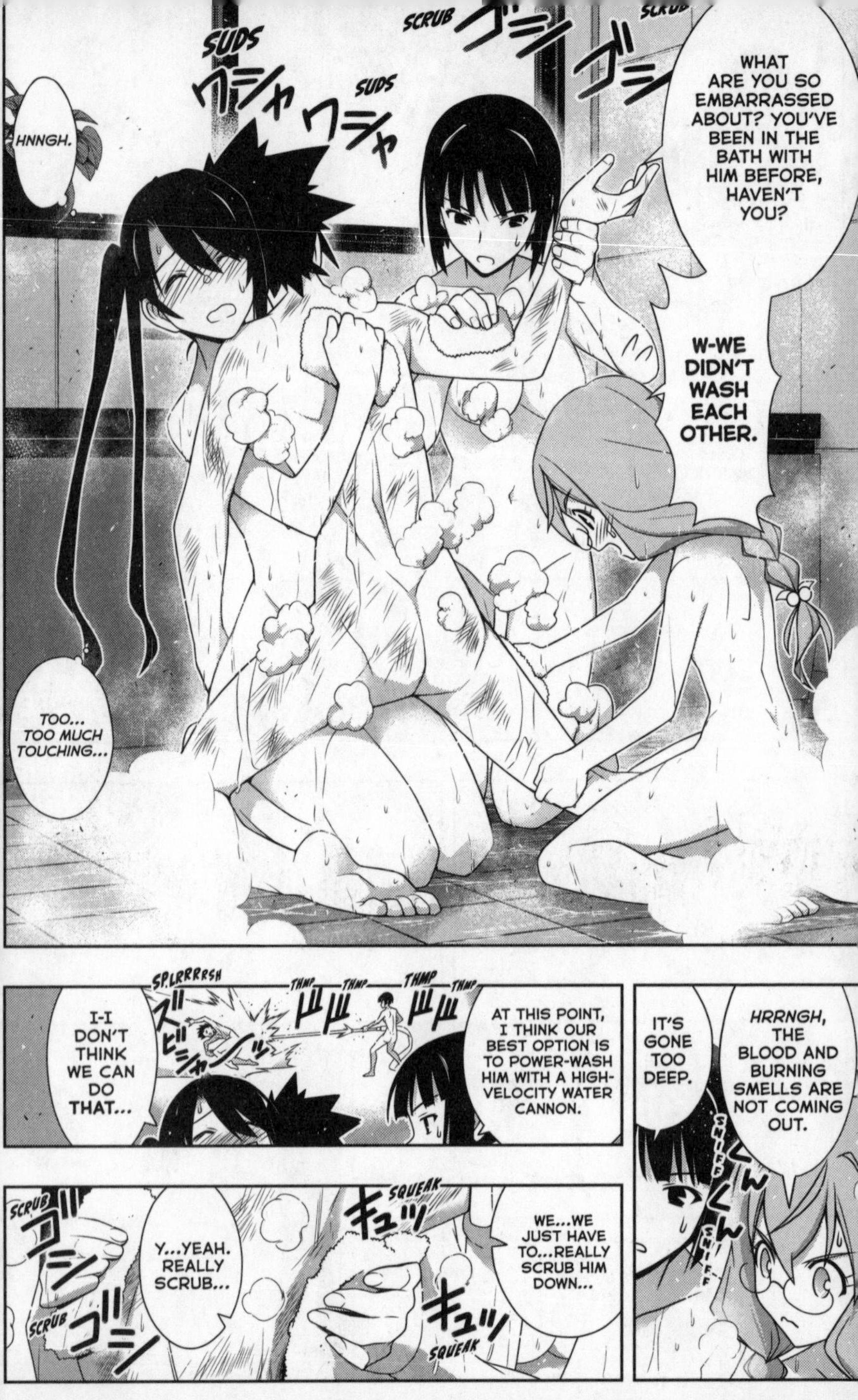
SCRUB
SCRUB
SUDS
SUDS
WHAT ARE YOU SO EMBARRASSED ABOUT? YOU'VE BEEN IN THE BATH WITH HIM BEFORE, HAVEN'T YOU?
W-WE DIDN'T WASH EACH OTHER.
HNNGH.
TOO... TOO MUCH TOUCHING...
HRRNGH, THE BLOOD AND BURNING SMELLS ARE NOT COMING OUT.
SNIFF
SNIFF
IT'S GONE TOO DEEP.
AT THIS POINT, I THINK OUR BEST OPTION IS TO POWER-WASH HIM WITH A HIGH-VELOCITY WATER CANNON.
THMP THMP THMP THMP
SPLRRRRSH
I-I DON'T THINK WE CAN DO THAT...
WE...WE JUST HAVE TO...REALLY SCRUB HIM DOWN...
SQUEAK
SQUEAK
Y...YEAH. REALLY SCRUB...
SCRUB
SCRUB

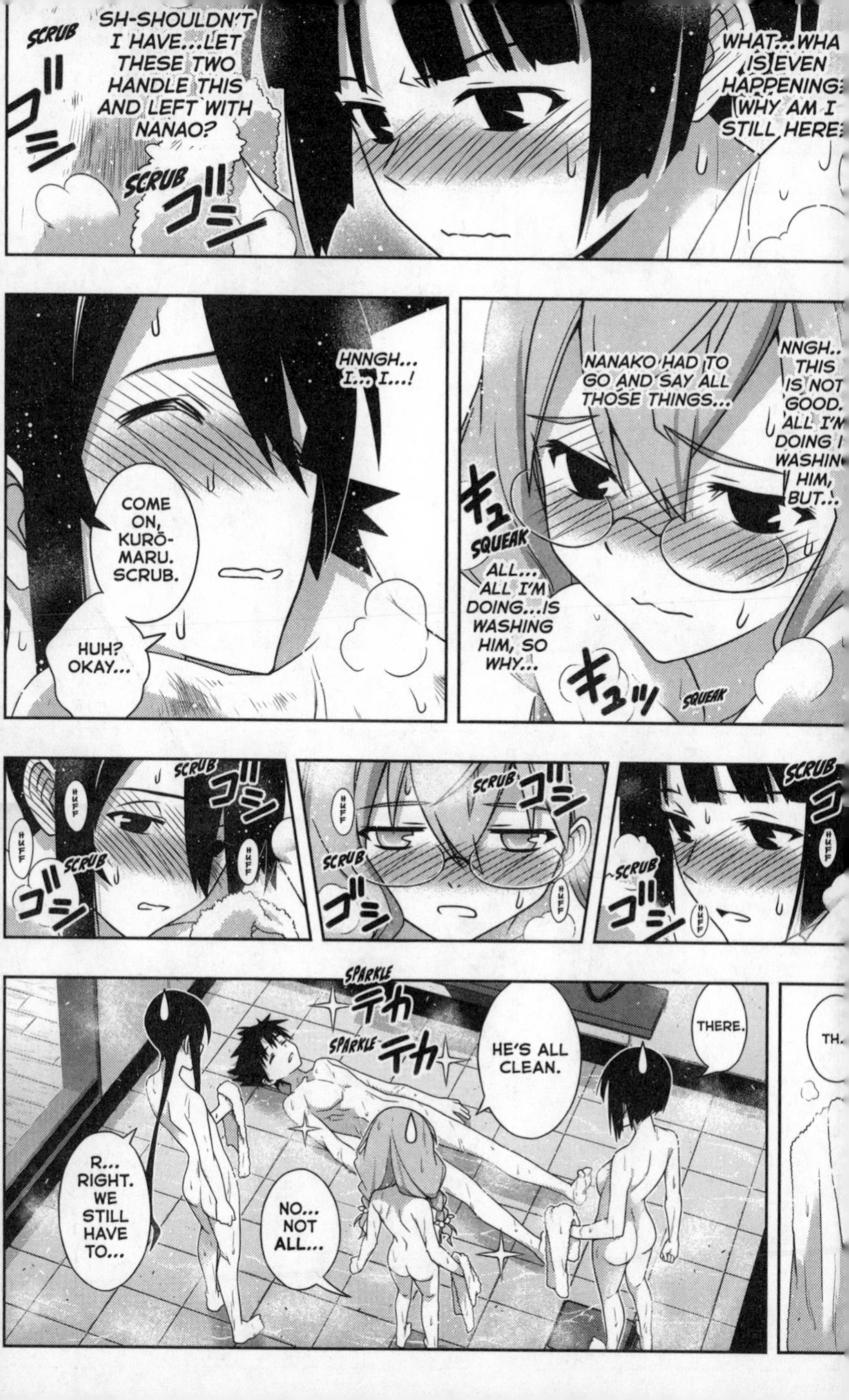

WHAT...WHA IS EVEN HAPPENING? WHY AM I STILL HERE?
SH-SHOULDN'T I HAVE...LET THESE TWO HANDLE THIS AND LEFT WITH NANAO?
SCRUB ゴシ
SCRUB ゴシ
NNGH... THIS IS NOT GOOD. ALL I'M DOING I WASHIN HIM, BUT...
NANAKO HAD TO GO AND SAY ALL THOSE THINGS...
SQUEAK キュ
ALL... ALL I'M DOING...IS WASHING HIM, SO WHY...
SQUEAK キュッ
HNNGH... I... I...!
COME ON, KURO-MARU. SCRUB.
HUH? OKAY...
SCRUB
HUFF
SCRUB ゴシ
HUFF
SCRUB ゴシ
HUFF
SCRUB ゴシ
HUFF
SCRUB ゴシ
HUFF
HUFF
SCRUB ゴシ
TH.
THERE.
HE'S ALL CLEAN.
SPARKLE テカ
SPARKLE テカ
NO... NOT ALL...
R... RIGHT. WE STILL HAVE TO...

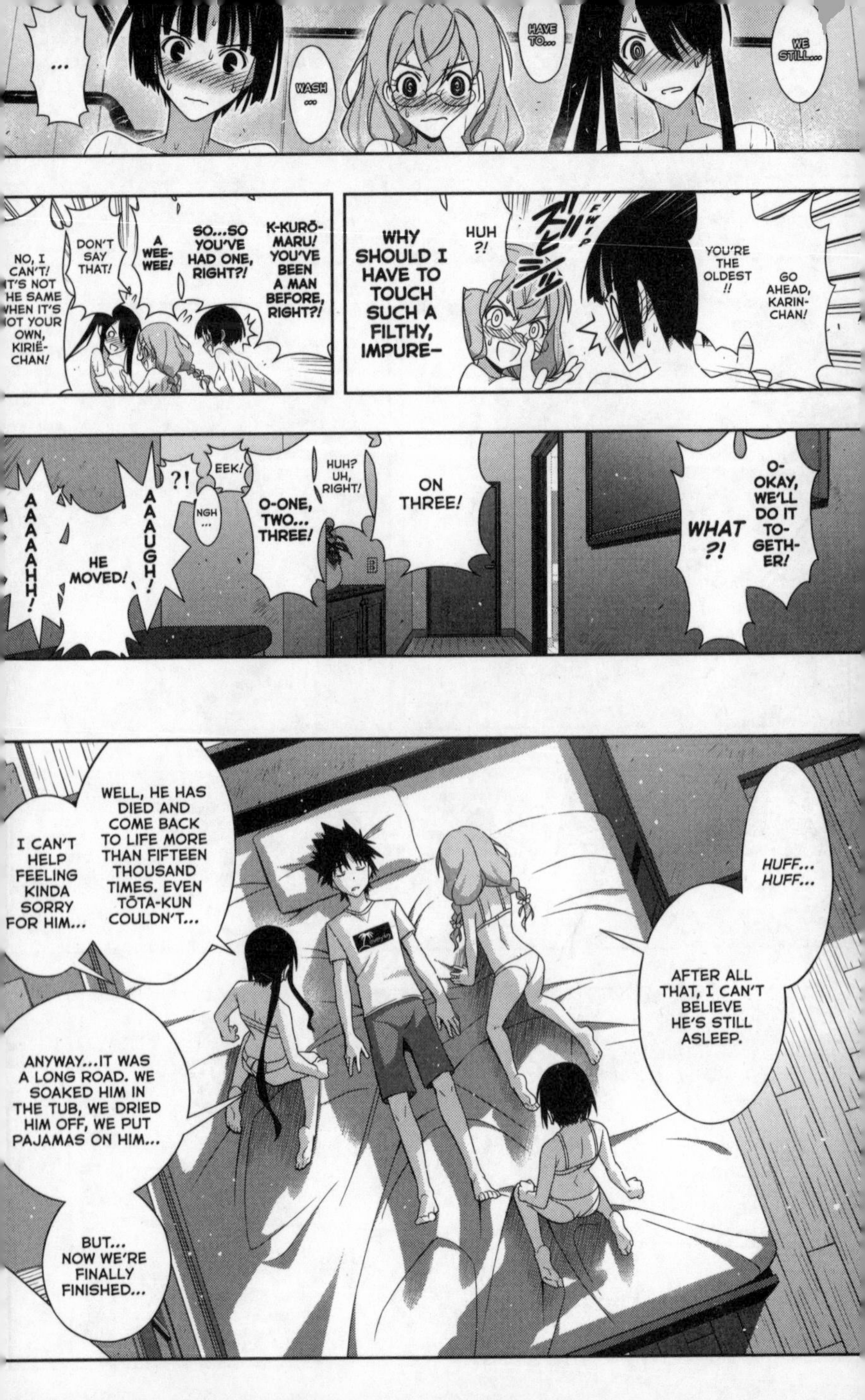

WE STILL...
HAVE TO...
WASH ...
...
GO AHEAD, KARIN-CHAN!
YOU'RE THE OLDEST !!
FWIP
HUH ?!
WHY SHOULD I HAVE TO TOUCH SUCH A FILTHY, IMPURE–
K-KURŌ-MARU! YOU'VE BEEN A MAN BEFORE, RIGHT?!
SO...SO YOU'VE HAD ONE, RIGHT?!
A WEE-WEE!
DON'T SAY THAT!
NO, I CAN'T! T'S NOT HE SAME WHEN IT'S OT YOUR OWN, KIRIĒ-CHAN!
O-OKAY, WE'LL DO IT TO-GETH-ER!
WHAT ?!
ON THREE!
HUH? UH, RIGHT!
O-ONE, TWO... THREE!
EEK!
NGH ...
?!
AAAUGH!
HE MOVED!
AAAAAAHH!
HUFF... HUFF...
AFTER ALL THAT, I CAN'T BELIEVE HE'S STILL ASLEEP.
WELL, HE HAS DIED AND COME BACK TO LIFE MORE THAN FIFTEEN THOUSAND TIMES. EVEN TŌTA-KUN COULDN'T...
I CAN'T HELP FEELING KINDA SORRY FOR HIM...
ANYWAY...IT WAS A LONG ROAD. WE SOAKED HIM IN THE TUB, WE DRIED HIM OFF, WE PUT PAJAMAS ON HIM...
BUT... NOW WE'RE FINALLY FINISHED...

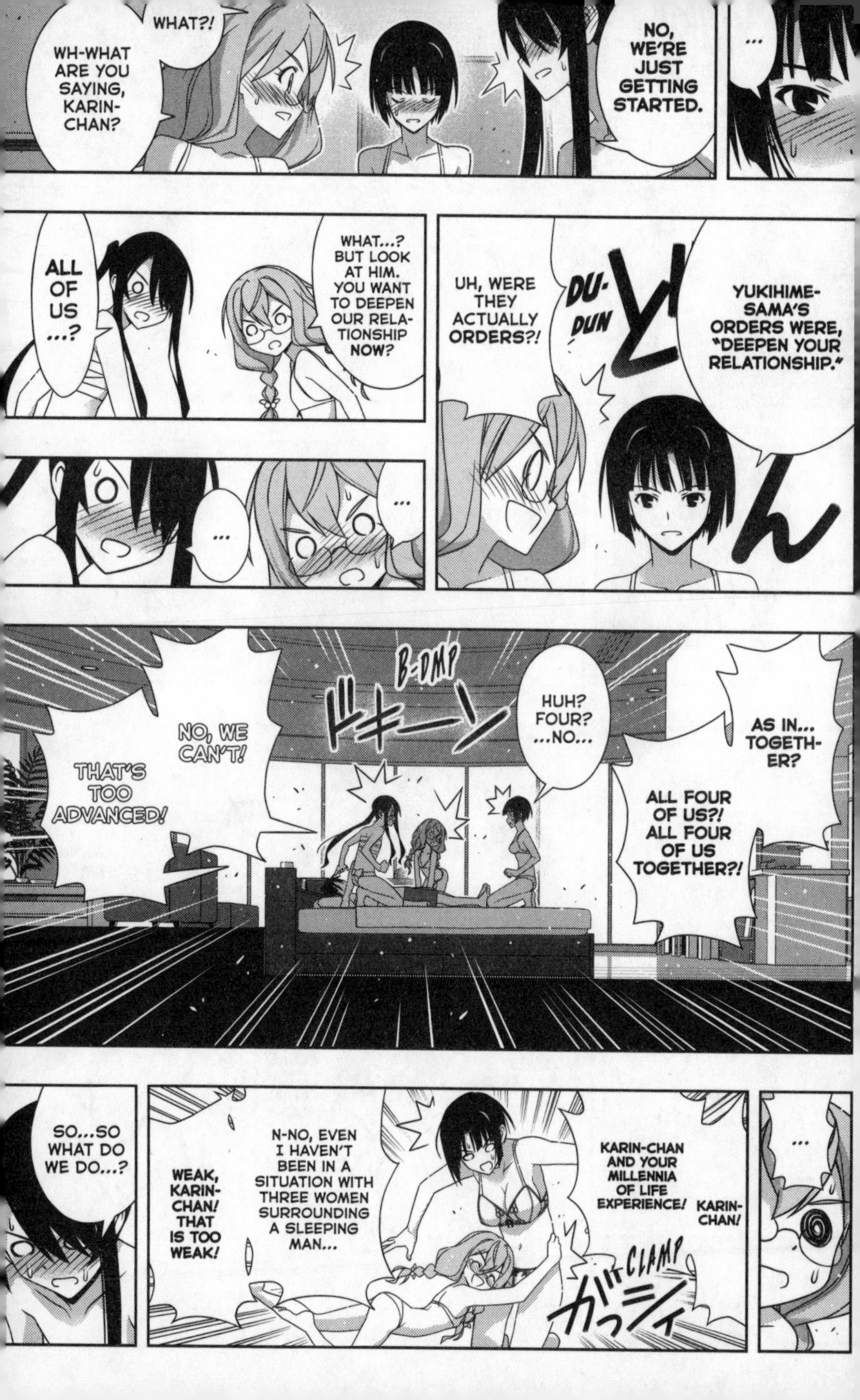
...
NO, WE'RE JUST GETTING STARTED.
WHAT?!
WH-WHAT ARE YOU SAYING, KARIN-CHAN?
YUKIHIME-SAMA'S ORDERS WERE, "DEEPEN YOUR RELATIONSHIP."
DU-DUN
UH, WERE THEY ACTUALLY ORDERS?!
WHAT...? BUT LOOK AT HIM. YOU WANT TO DEEPEN OUR RELATIONSHIP NOW?
ALL OF US ...?
...
...
AS IN... TOGETHER?
ALL FOUR OF US?! ALL FOUR OF US TOGETHER?!
HUH? FOUR? ...NO...
B-DMP
NO, WE CAN'T!
THAT'S TOO ADVANCED!
...
KARIN-CHAN!
KARIN-CHAN AND YOUR MILLENNIA OF LIFE EXPERIENCE!
CLAMP
N-NO, EVEN I HAVEN'T BEEN IN A SITUATION WITH THREE WOMEN SURROUNDING A SLEEPING MAN...
WEAK, KARIN-CHAN! THAT IS TOO WEAK!
SO...SO WHAT DO WE DO...?

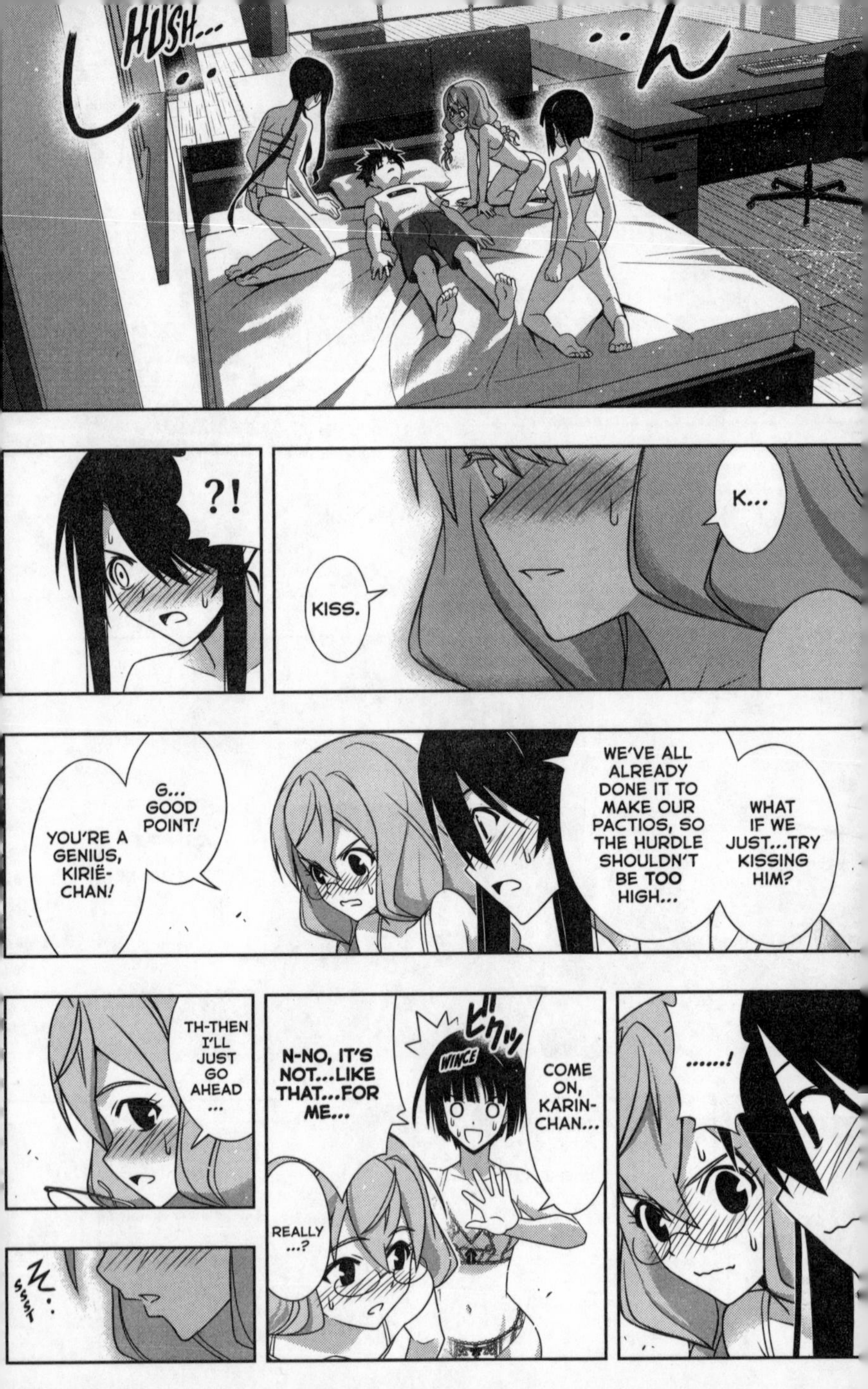

HUSH...
し..
..ん
K...
KISS.
?!
WHAT IF WE JUST...TRY KISSING HIM?
WE'VE ALL ALREADY DONE IT TO MAKE OUR PACTIOS, SO THE HURDLE SHOULDN'T BE TOO HIGH...
G... GOOD POINT!
YOU'RE A GENIUS, KIRIË-CHAN!
......!
COME ON, KARIN-CHAN...
ビクッ
WINCE
N-NO, IT'S NOT...LIKE THAT...FOR ME...
REALLY ...?
TH-THEN I'LL JUST GO AHEAD ...
SSSST

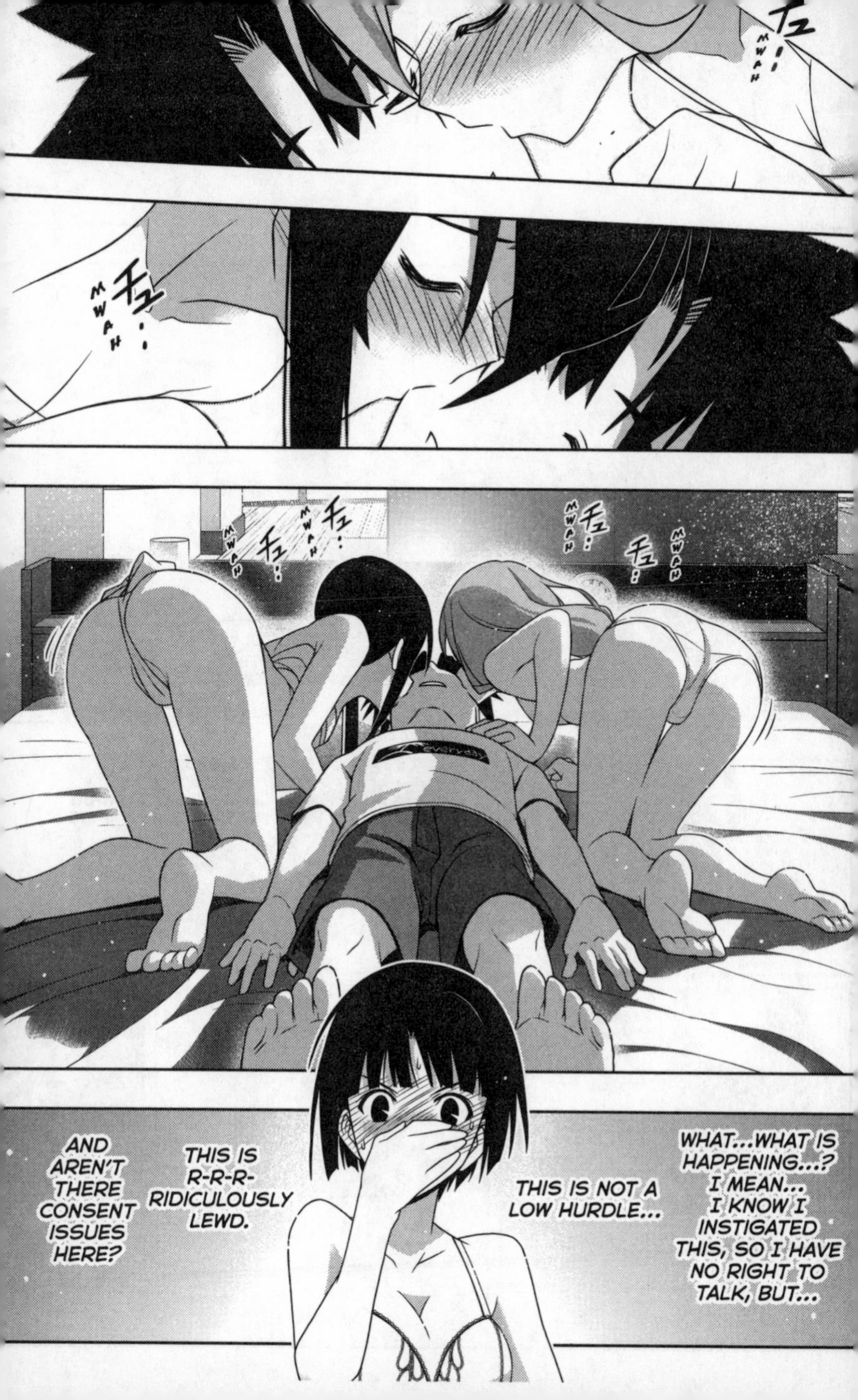
チュ!! MWAH
チュ!! MWAH
チュ!! MWAH
チュ!! MWAH
チュ!! MWAH
チュ!! MWAH
WHAT...WHAT IS HAPPENING...? I MEAN... I KNOW I INSTIGATED THIS, SO I HAVE NO RIGHT TO TALK, BUT...
THIS IS NOT A LOW HURDLE...
THIS IS R-R-R-RIDICULOUSLY LEWD.
AND AREN'T THERE CONSENT ISSUES HERE?

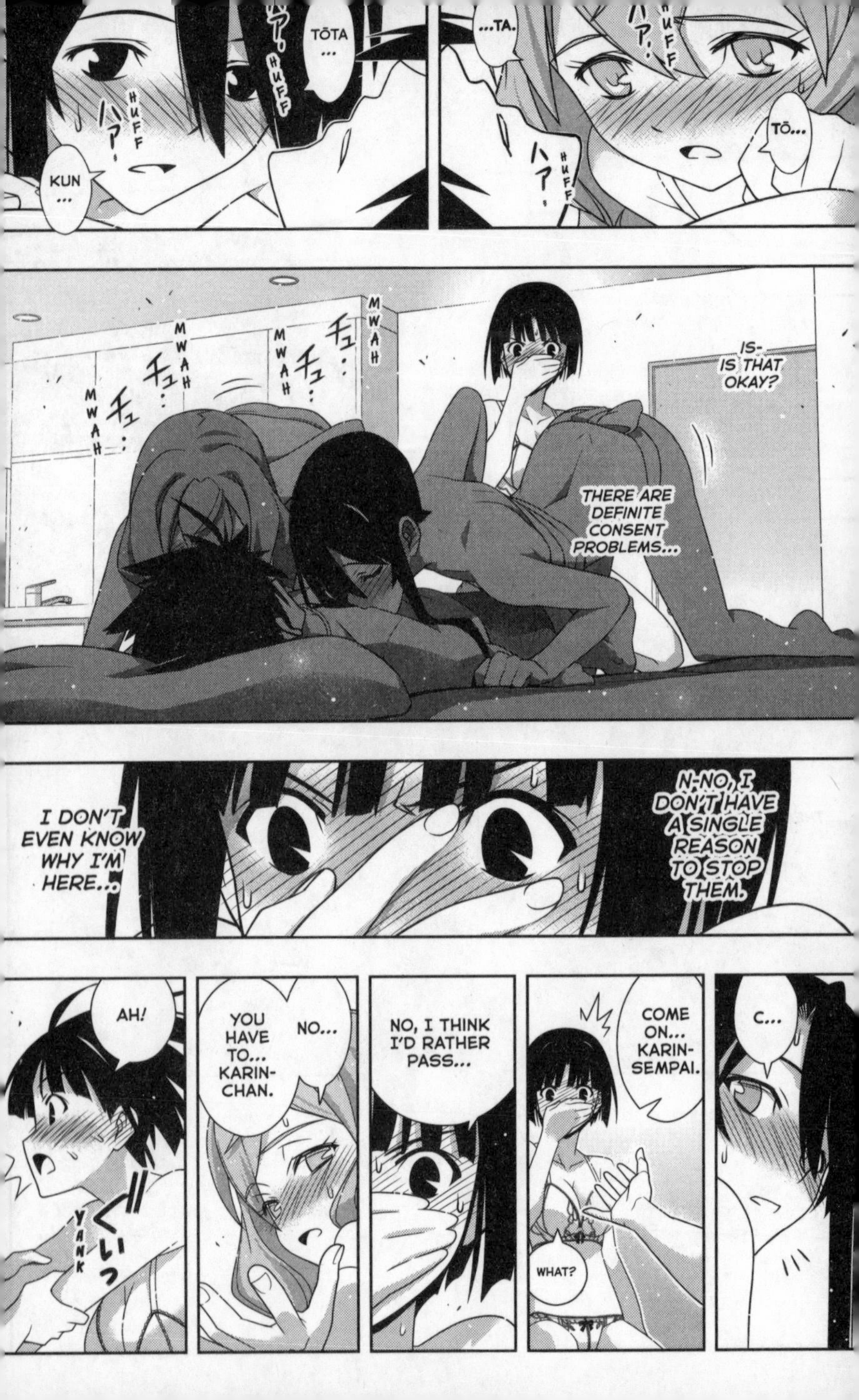
HUFF
TŌ...
...TA.
HUFF
TŌTA ...
HUFF
HUFF
KUN ...
MWAH
MWAH
MWAH
IS- IS THAT OKAY?
THERE ARE DEFINITE CONSENT PROBLEMS...
N-NO, I DON'T HAVE A SINGLE REASON TO STOP THEM.
I DON'T EVEN KNOW WHY I'M HERE...
C...
COME ON... KARIN-SEMPAI.
WHAT?
NO, I THINK I'D RATHER PASS...
NO...
YOU HAVE TO... KARIN-CHAN.
AH!
YANK

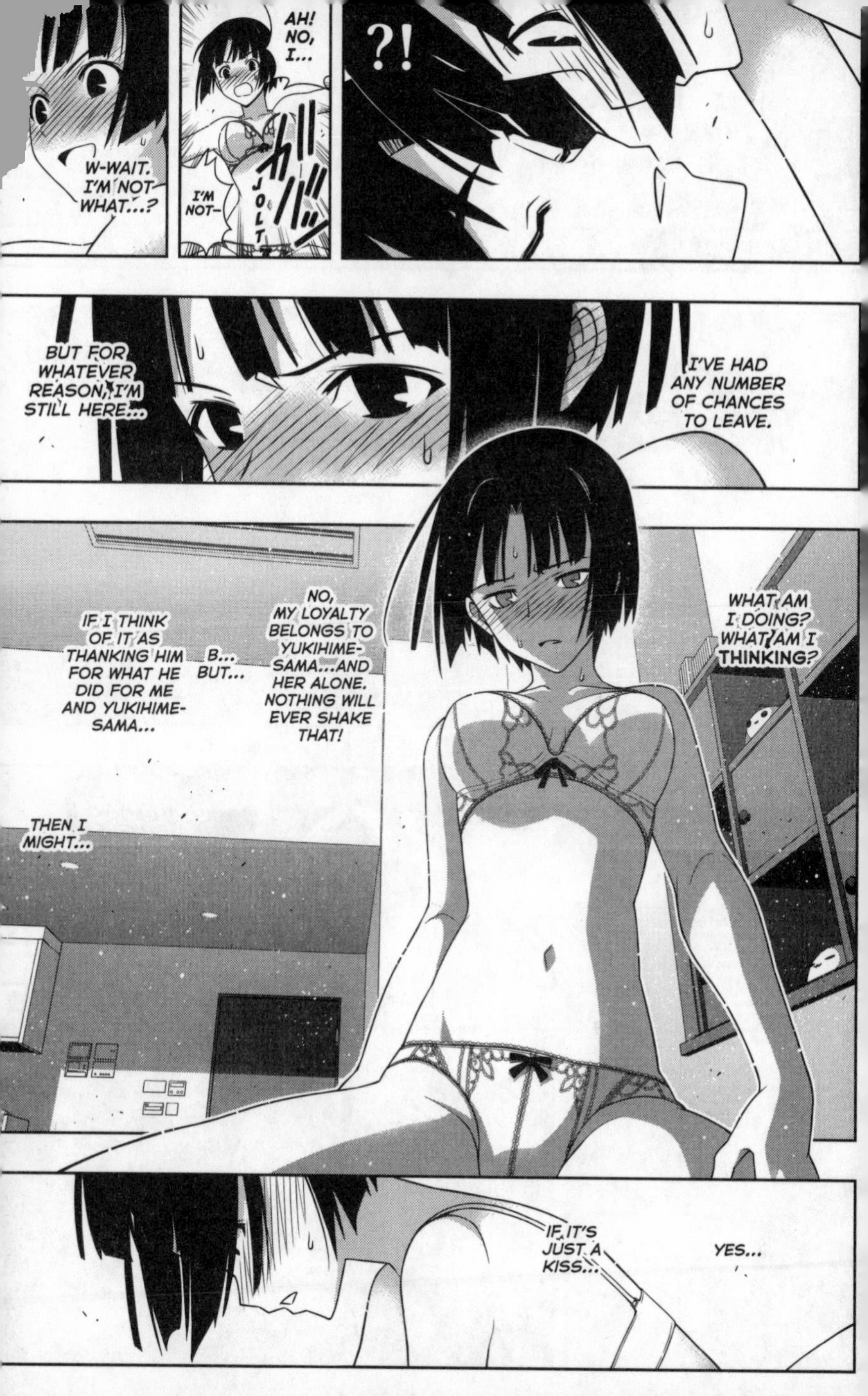
?!
AH! NO, I...
I'M NOT-
JOLT
W-WAIT. I'M NOT WHAT...?
I'VE HAD ANY NUMBER OF CHANCES TO LEAVE.
BUT FOR WHATEVER REASON, I'M STILL HERE...
WHAT AM I DOING? WHAT AM I THINKING?
NO, MY LOYALTY BELONGS TO YUKIHIME-SAMA...AND HER ALONE. NOTHING WILL EVER SHAKE THAT!
B... BUT...
IF I THINK OF IT AS THANKING HIM FOR WHAT HE DID FOR ME AND YUKIHIME-SAMA...
THEN I MIGHT...
YES...
IF IT'S JUST A KISS...

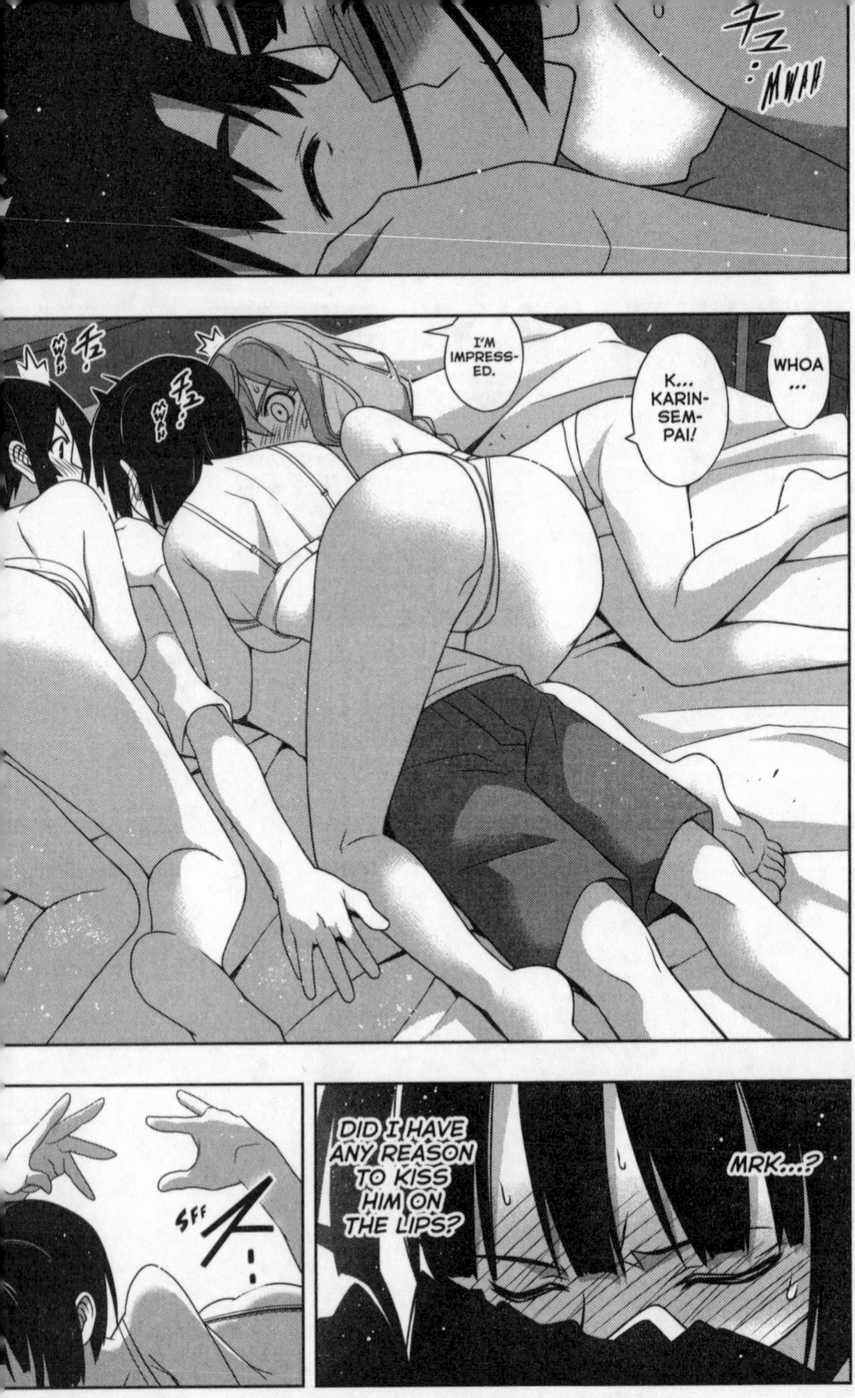
MWAH
WHOA ...
K... KARIN-SEMPAI!
I'M IMPRESSED.
MRK...?
DID I HAVE ANY REASON TO KISS HIM ON THE LIPS?
SFF

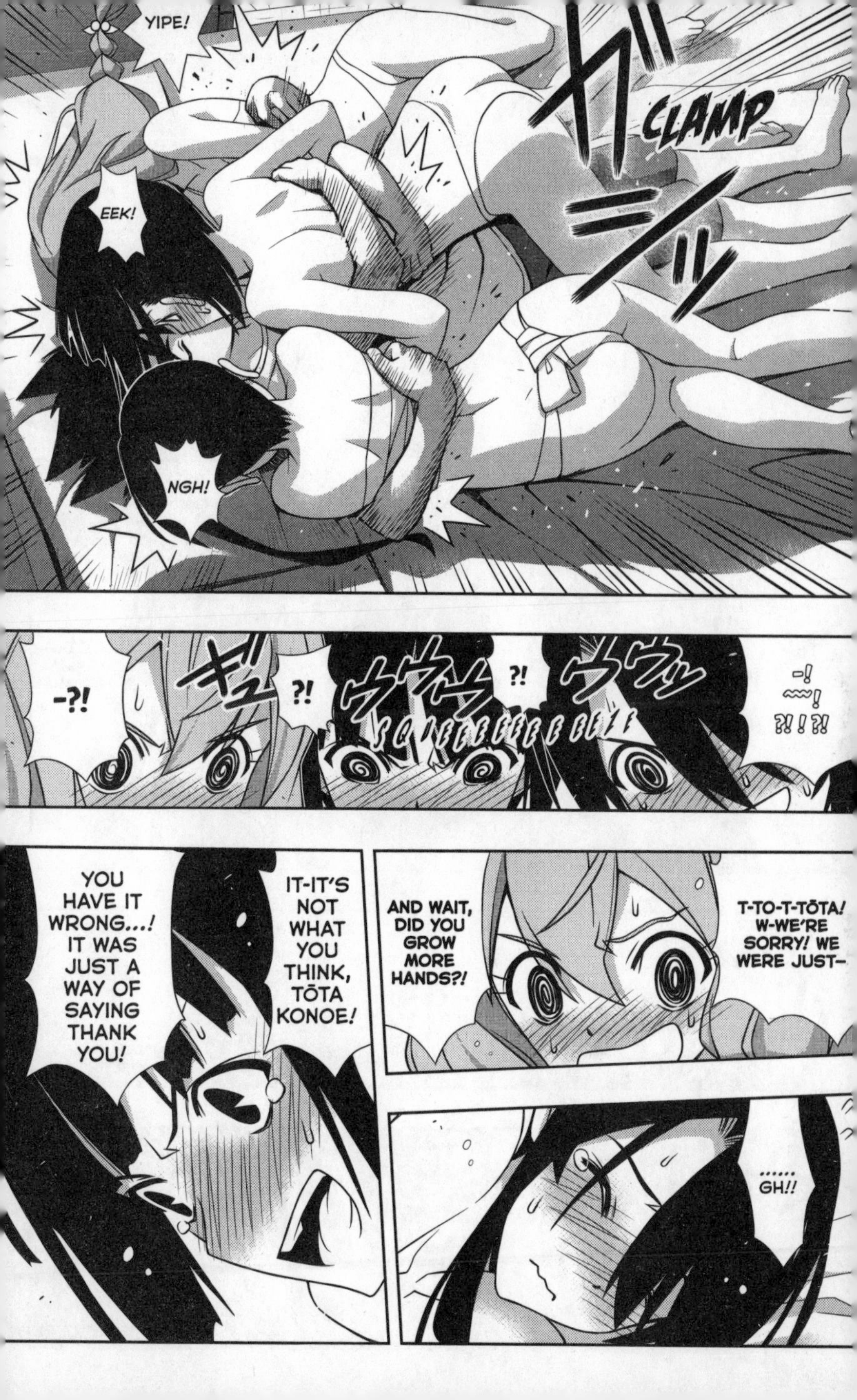
CLAMP
YIPE!
EEK!
NGH!
-!
~~!
?!!?!
?!
?!
-?!
T-TO-T-TŌTA! W-WE'RE SORRY! WE WERE JUST-
AND WAIT, DID YOU GROW MORE HANDS?!
......GH!!
IT-IT'S NOT WHAT YOU THINK, TŌTA KONOE!
YOU HAVE IT WRONG...! IT WAS JUST A WAY OF SAYING THANK YOU!

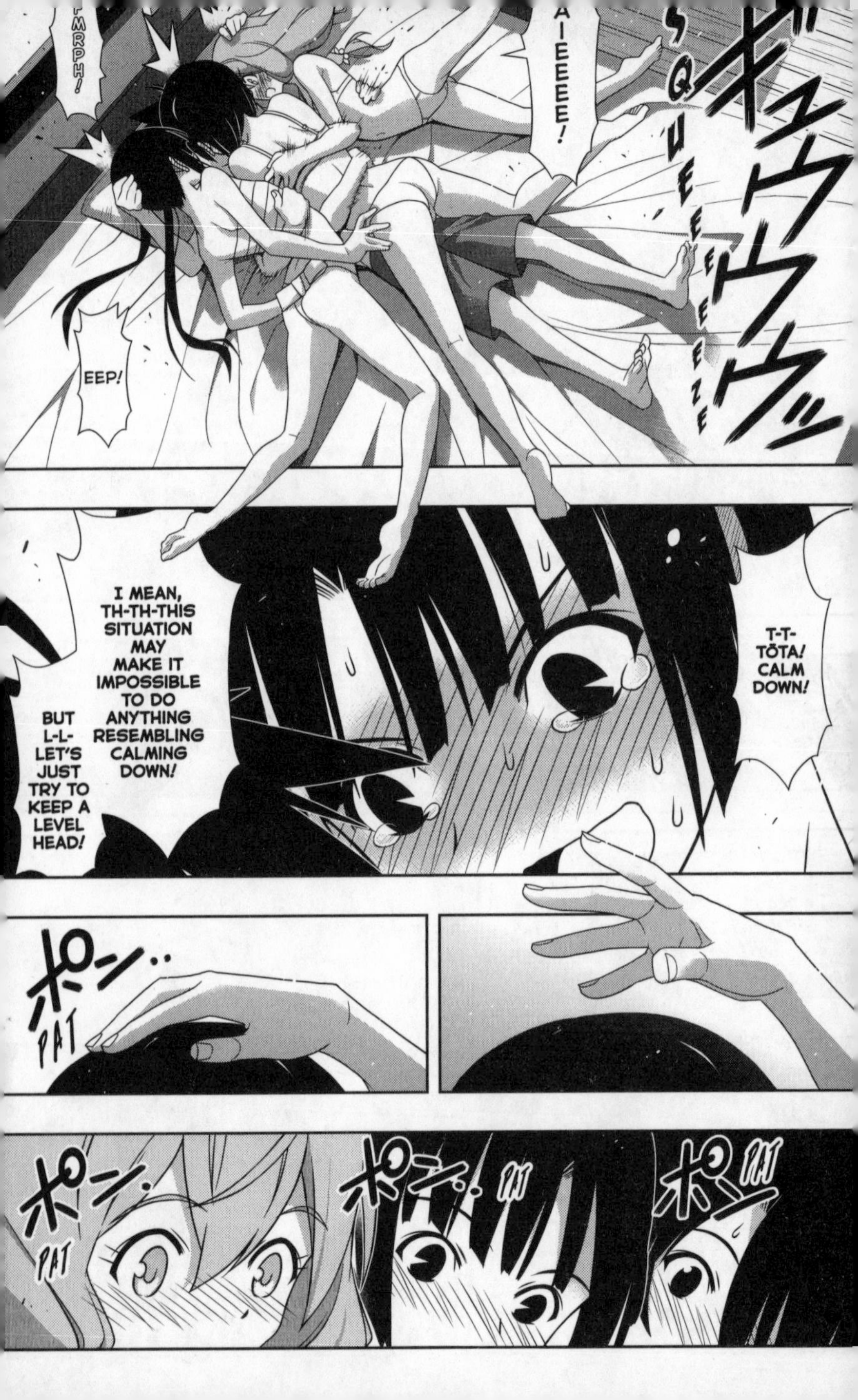
SQUEEEEEZE
AIEEEEE!
MRPH!
EEP!
T-T-TŌTA! CALM DOWN!
I MEAN, TH-TH-THIS SITUATION MAY MAKE IT IMPOSSIBLE TO DO ANYTHING RESEMBLING CALMING DOWN!
BUT L-L-LET'S JUST TRY TO KEEP A LEVEL HEAD!
PAT
PAT
PAT
PAT

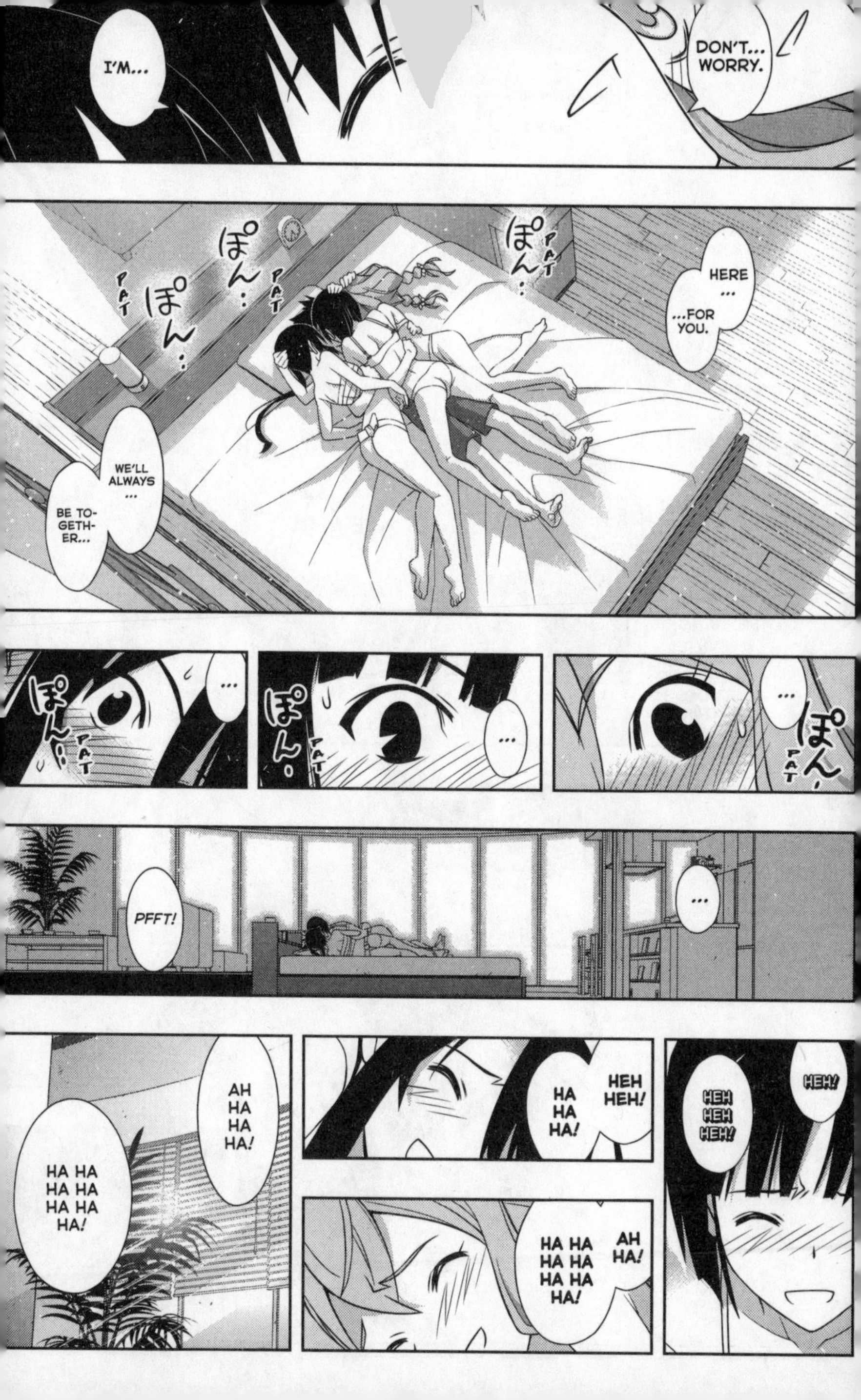
DON'T... WORRY.
I'M...
ぽん… PAT
HERE... ...FOR YOU.
ぽん… PAT
ぽん… PAT
WE'LL ALWAYS... BE TO-GETH-ER...
...
ぽん, PAT
...
ぽん。 PAT
...
ぽん… PAT
...
PFFT!
HEH!
HEH HEH HEH!
HEH HEH!
HA HA HA!
AH HA!
HA HA HA HA HA HA HA!
AH HA HA HA!
HA HA HA HA HA HA HA!

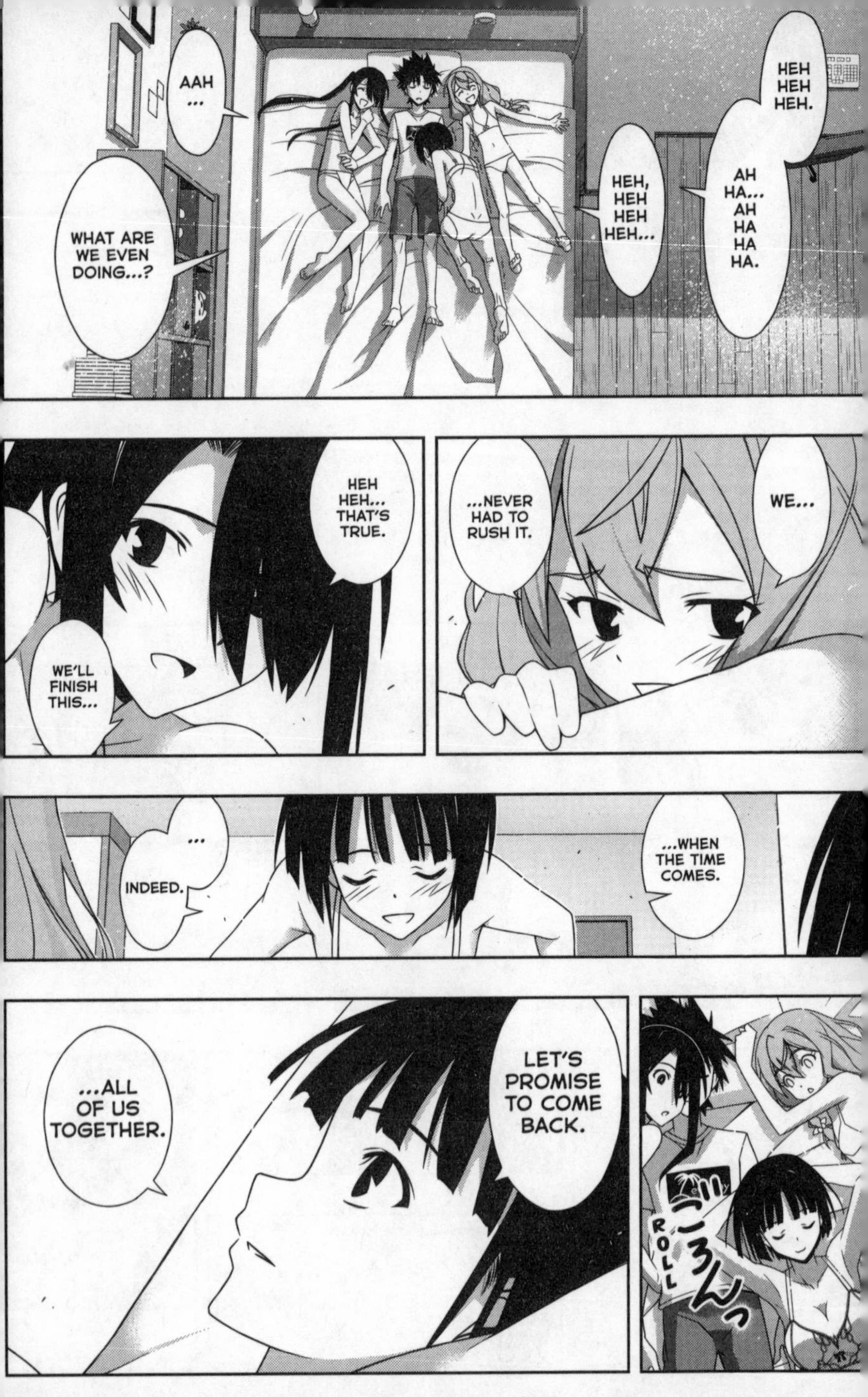
HEH HEH HEH.
AH HA... AH HA HA HA HA.
HEH, HEH HEH HEH...
AAH ...
WHAT ARE WE EVEN DOING...?
WE...
...NEVER HAD TO RUSH IT.
HEH HEH... THAT'S TRUE.
WE'LL FINISH THIS...
...WHEN THE TIME COMES.
... INDEED.
ごろんっ
ROLL
LET'S PROMISE TO COME BACK.
...ALL OF US TOGETHER.

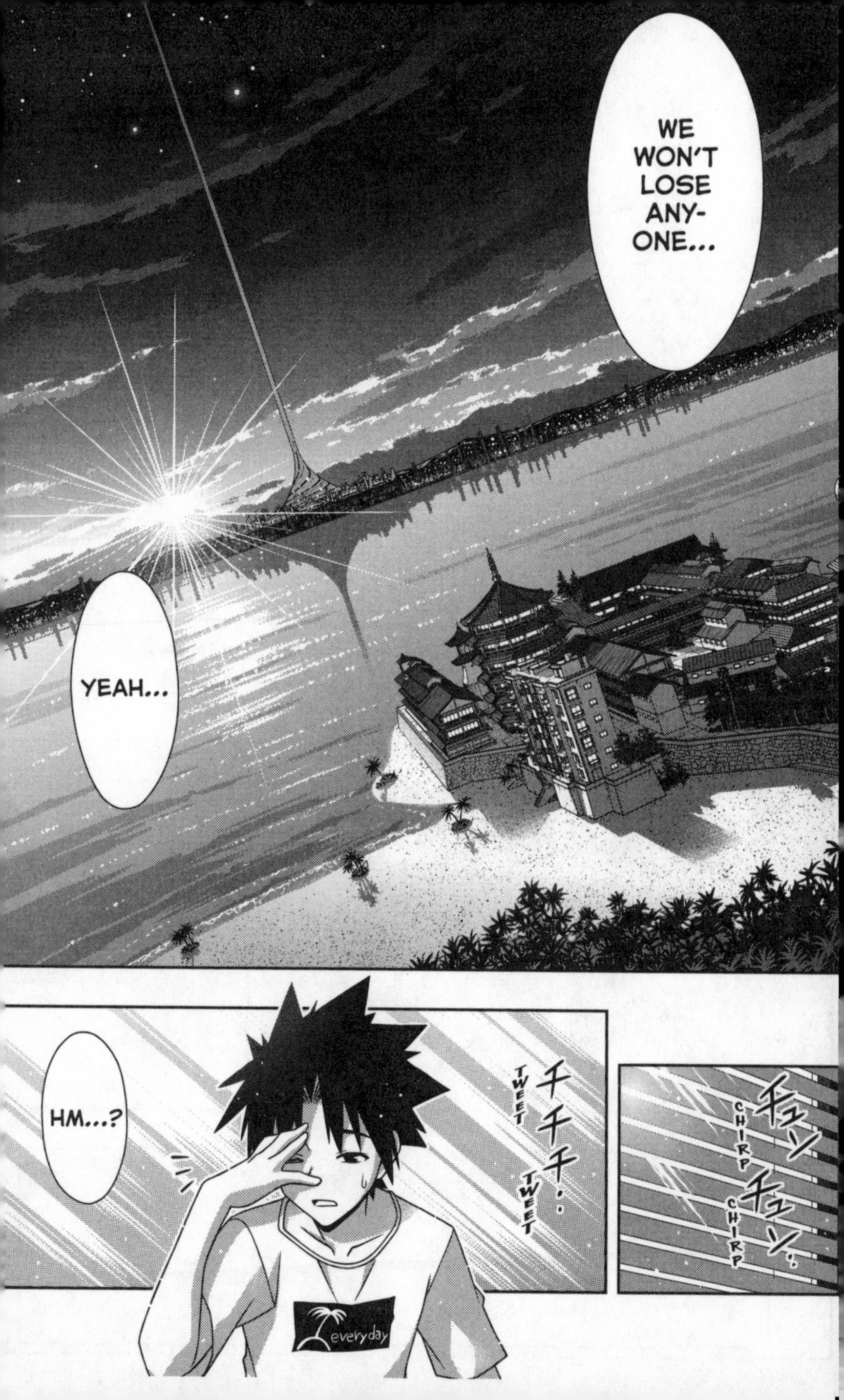

WE WON'T LOSE ANY-ONE...
YEAH...
チュンチュン
CHIRP CHIRP
チチチ..
TWEET TWEET
HM...?
everyday

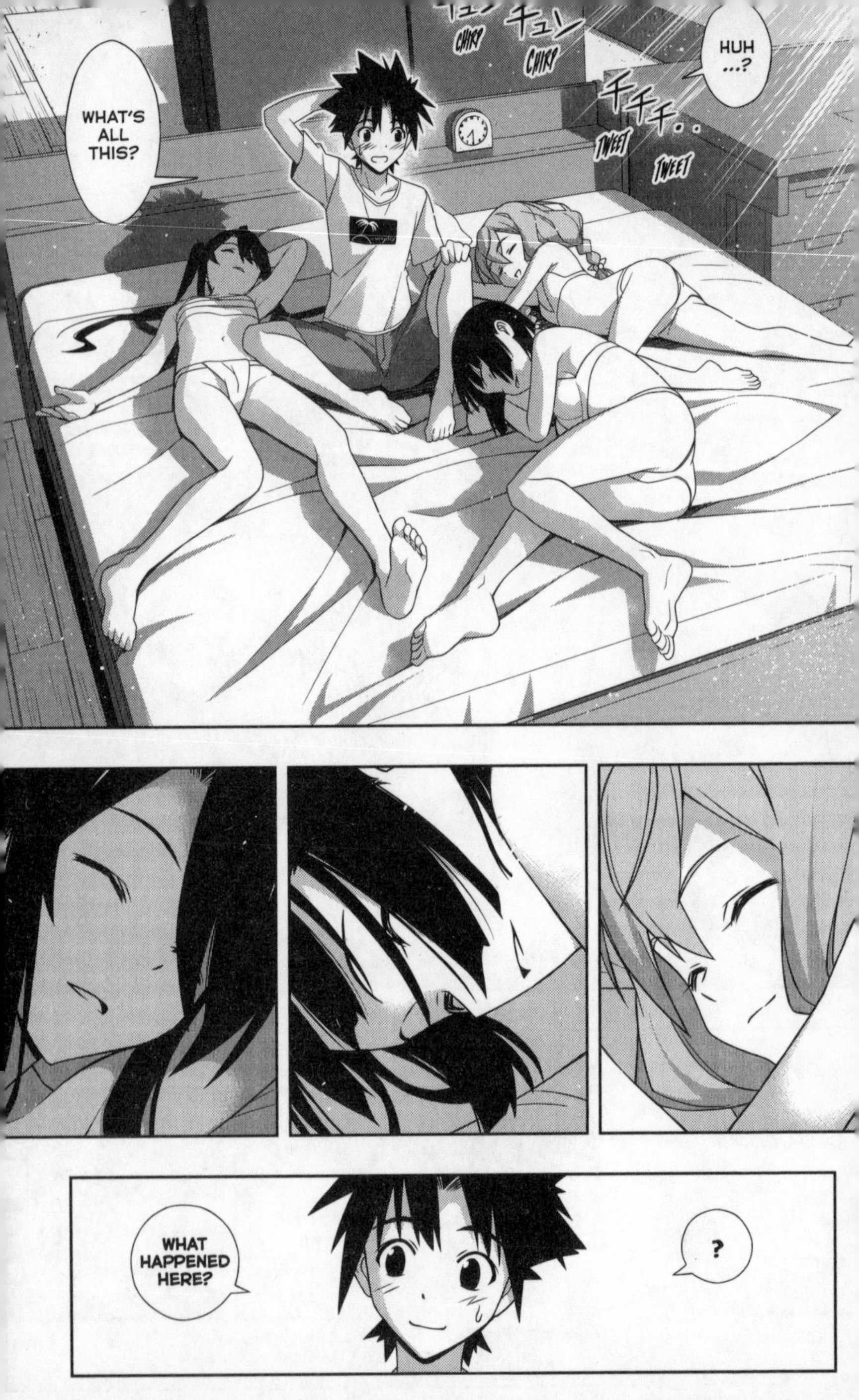
HUH ...?
チュン
CHIRP
CHIRP
チチチ..
TWEET
TWEET
WHAT'S ALL THIS?
?
WHAT HAPPENED HERE?

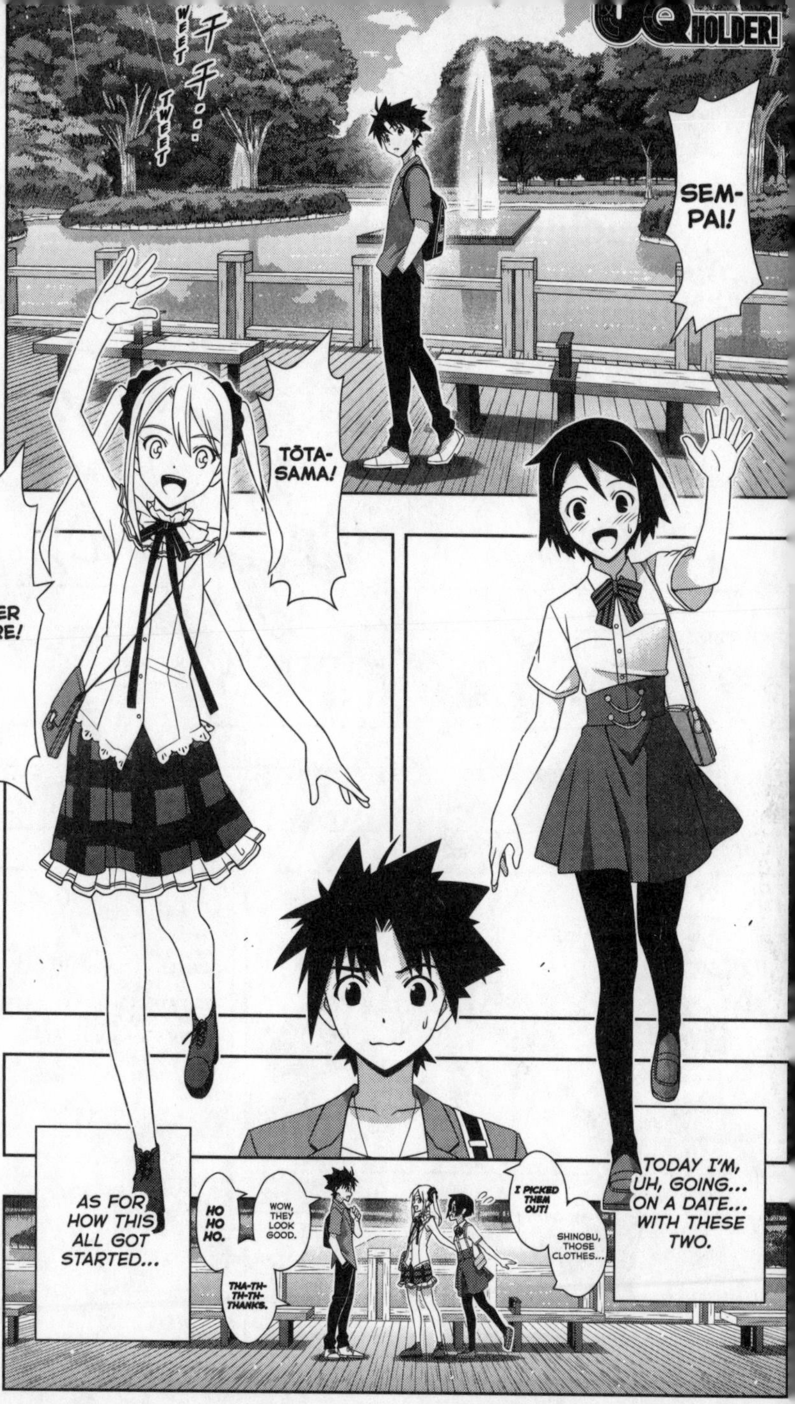
SEM-
PAI!
チチ…
WEET TWEET
TŌTA-
SAMA!
OVER
HERE!
TODAY I'M,
UH, GOING...
ON A DATE...
WITH THESE
TWO.
I PICKED
THEM
OUT!
SHINOBU,
THOSE
CLOTHES...
WOW,
THEY
LOOK
GOOD.
HO
HO
HO.
THA-TH-
TH-TH-
THANKS.
AS FOR
HOW THIS
ALL GOT
STARTED...

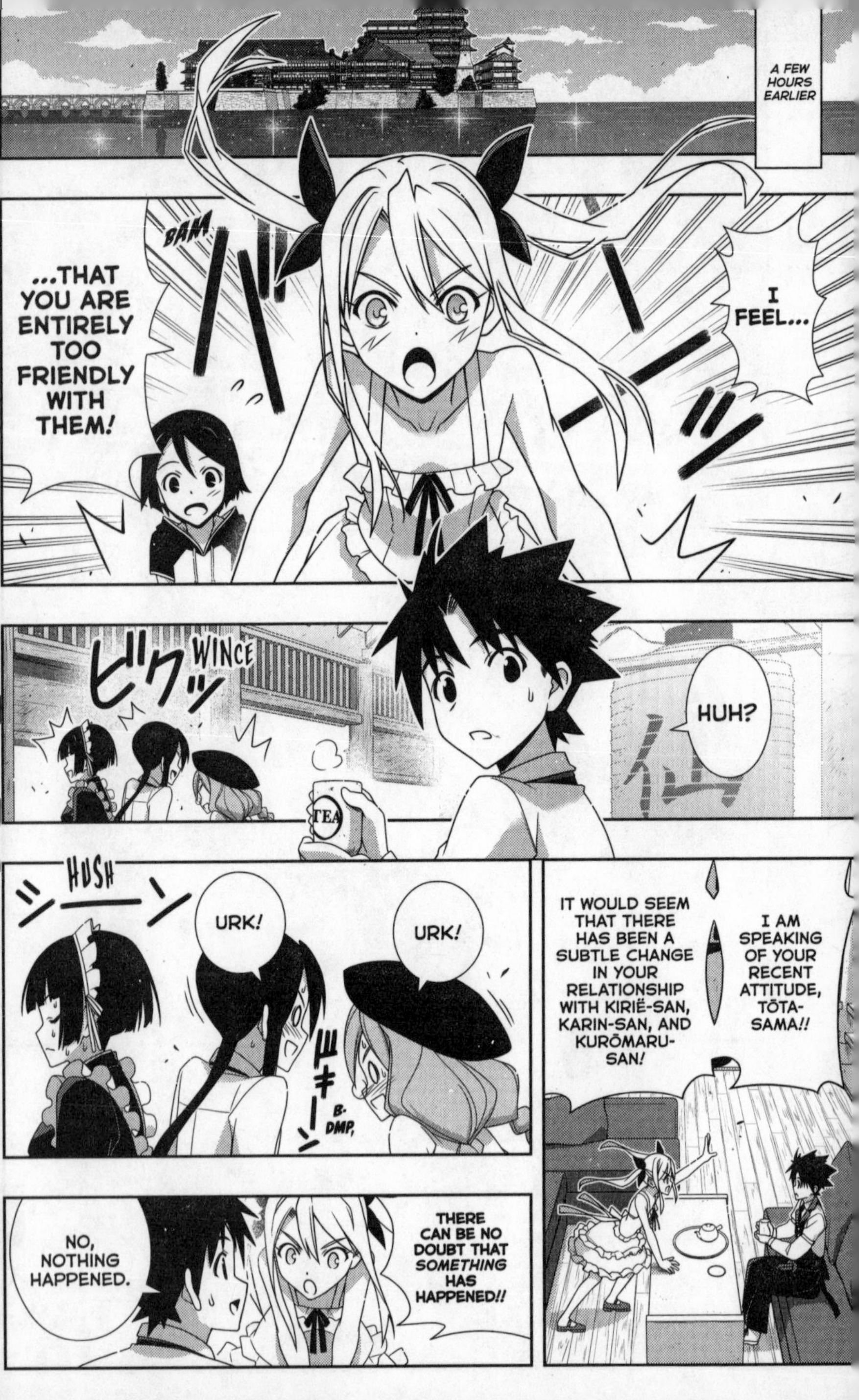
A FEW HOURS EARLIER
I FEEL...
BAM
...THAT YOU ARE ENTIRELY TOO FRIENDLY WITH THEM!
HUH?
WINCE
I AM SPEAKING OF YOUR RECENT ATTITUDE, TŌTA-SAMA!!
IT WOULD SEEM THAT THERE HAS BEEN A SUBTLE CHANGE IN YOUR RELATIONSHIP WITH KIRIË-SAN, KARIN-SAN, AND KURŌMARU-SAN!
URK!
URK!
HUSH
B-DMP,
THERE CAN BE NO DOUBT THAT *SOMETHING* HAS HAPPENED!!
NO, NOTHING HAPPENED.

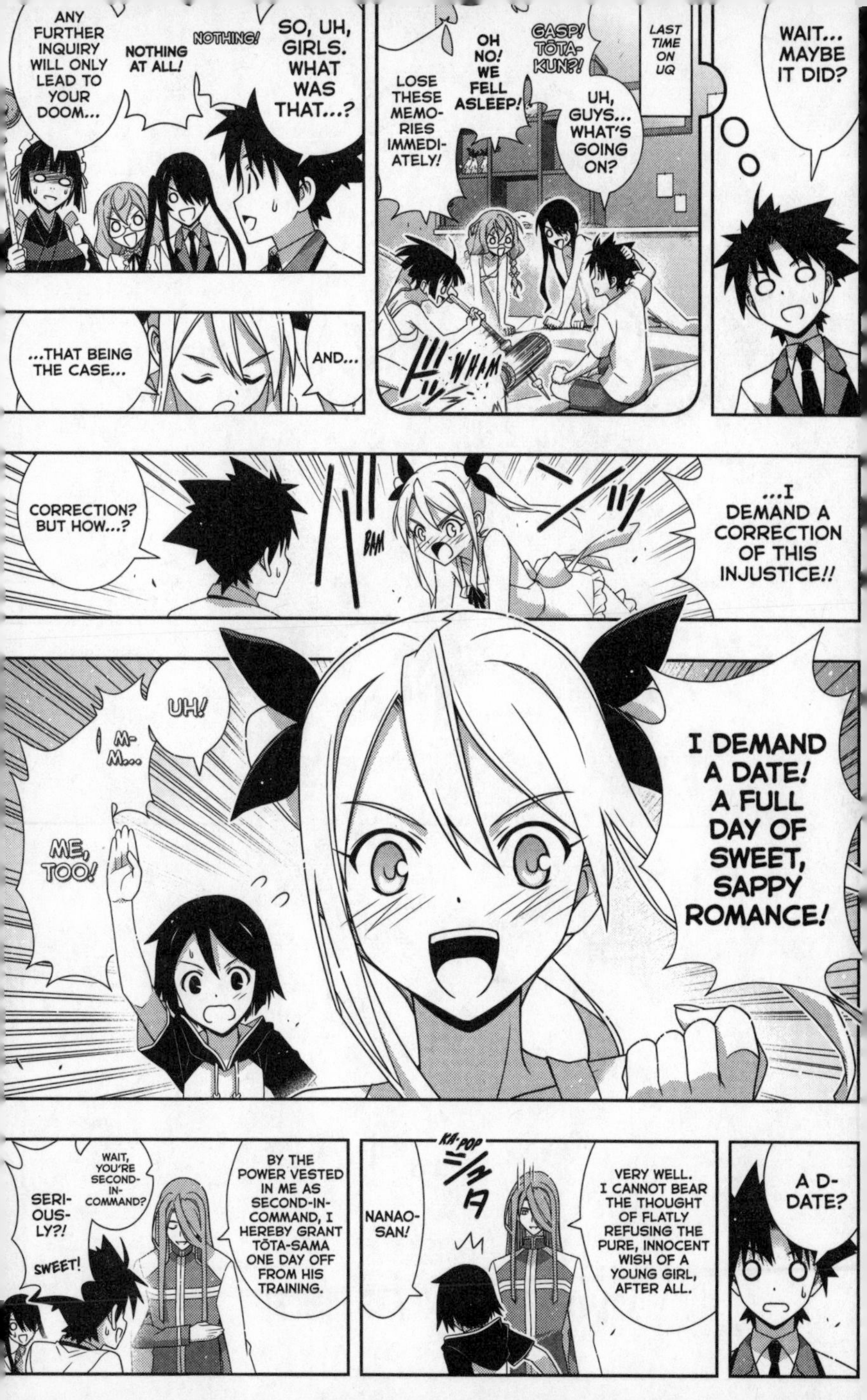
WAIT... MAYBE IT DID?
LAST TIME ON UQ
GASP! TŌTA-KUN?!
UH, GUYS... WHAT'S GOING ON?
OH NO! WE FELL ASLEEP!
LOSE THESE MEMORIES IMMEDIATELY!
WHAM
SO, UH, GIRLS. WHAT WAS THAT...?
NOTHING!
NOTHING AT ALL!
ANY FURTHER INQUIRY WILL ONLY LEAD TO YOUR DOOM...
AND...
...THAT BEING THE CASE...
...I DEMAND A CORRECTION OF THIS INJUSTICE!!
BAM
CORRECTION? BUT HOW...?
I DEMAND A DATE! A FULL DAY OF SWEET, SAPPY ROMANCE!
UH!
M-M...
ME, TOO!
A D-DATE?
VERY WELL. I CANNOT BEAR THE THOUGHT OF FLATLY REFUSING THE PURE, INNOCENT WISH OF A YOUNG GIRL, AFTER ALL.
KA-POP
NANAO-SAN!
BY THE POWER VESTED IN ME AS SECOND-IN-COMMAND, I HEREBY GRANT TŌTA-SAMA ONE DAY OFF FROM HIS TRAINING.
WAIT, YOU'RE SECOND-IN-COMMAND?
SERI-OUS-LY?!
SWEET!

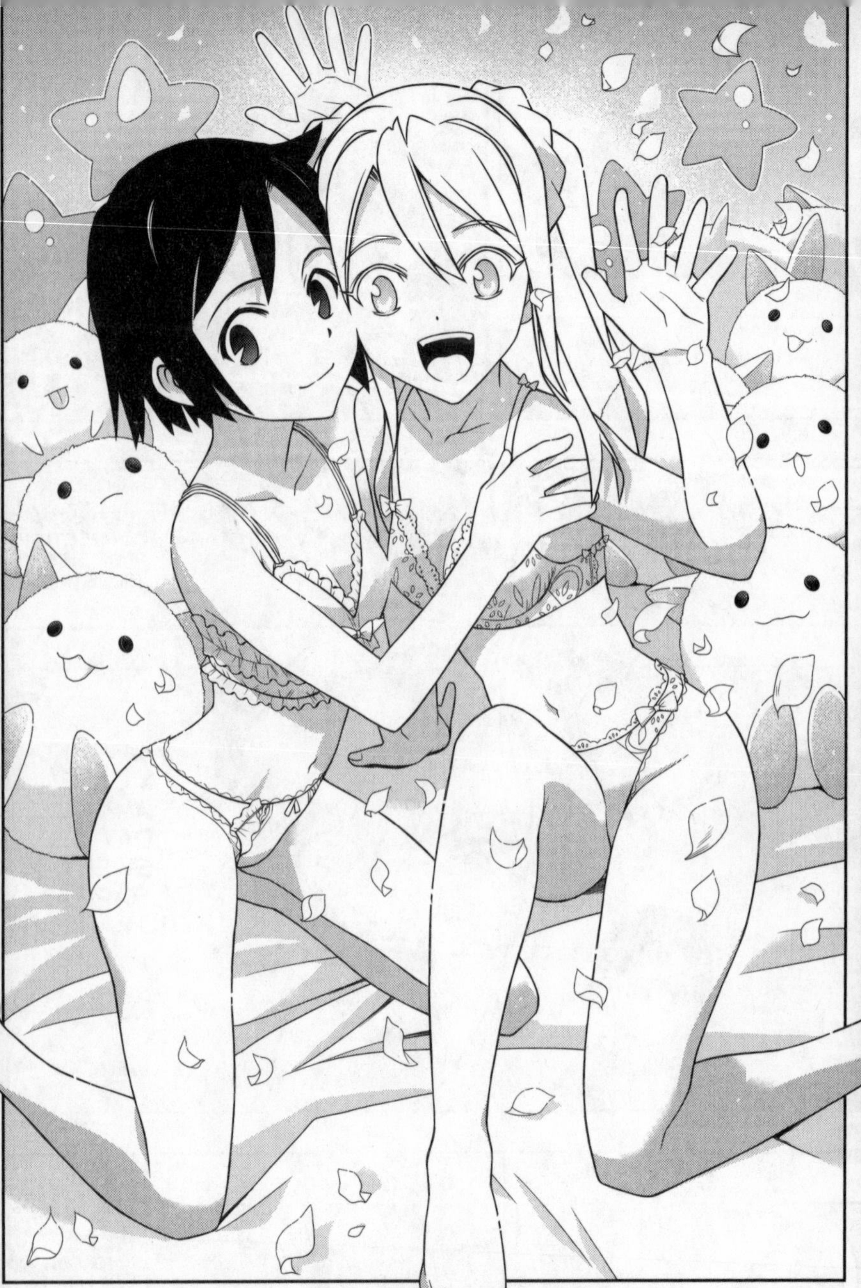

STAGE 174: MIZORE AND SHINOBU

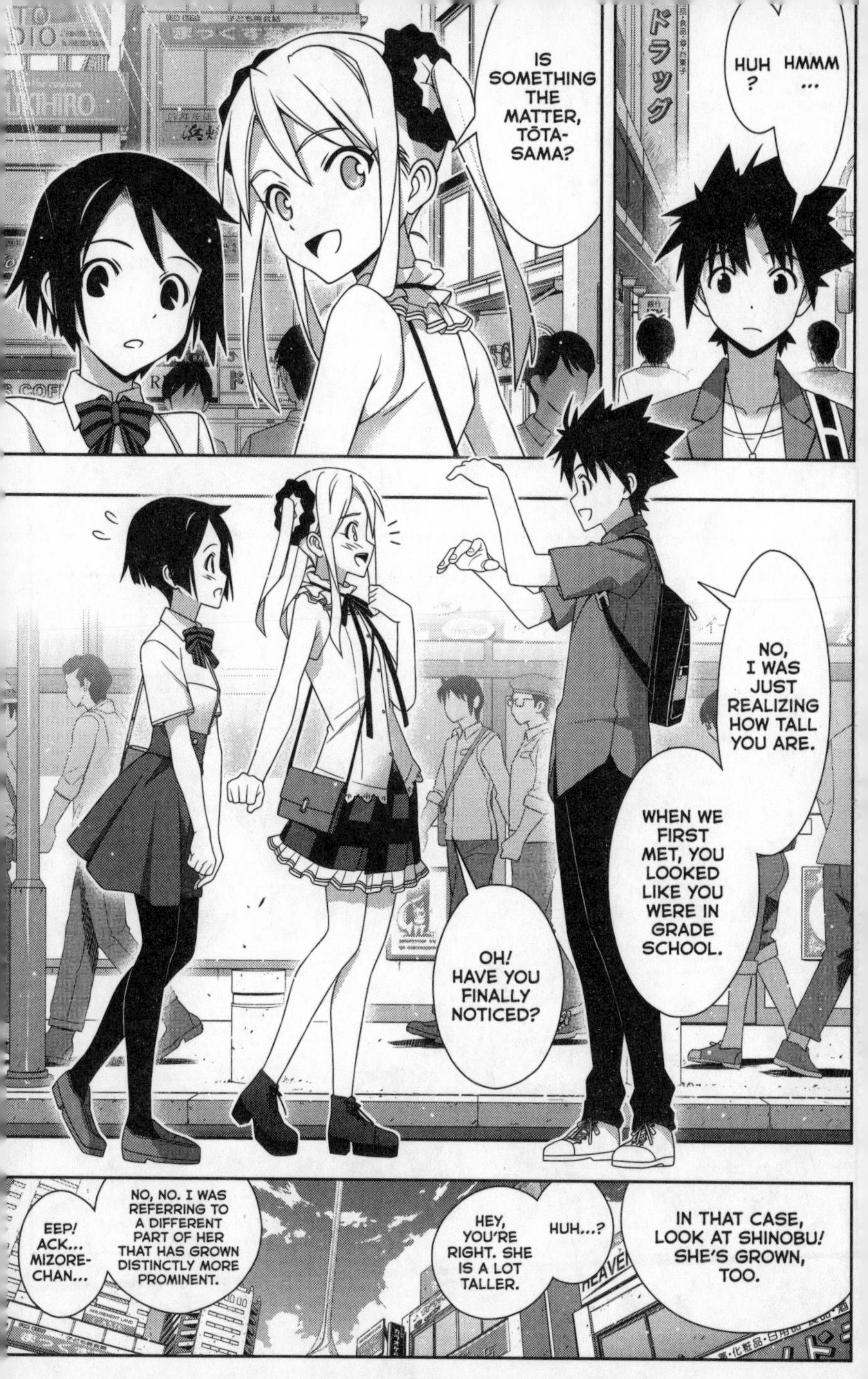
HUH? HMMM...
IS SOMETHING THE MATTER, TŌTA-SAMA?
NO, I WAS JUST REALIZING HOW TALL YOU ARE.
WHEN WE FIRST MET, YOU LOOKED LIKE YOU WERE IN GRADE SCHOOL.
OH! HAVE YOU FINALLY NOTICED?
IN THAT CASE, LOOK AT SHINOBU! SHE'S GROWN, TOO.
HUH...?
HEY, YOU'RE RIGHT. SHE IS A LOT TALLER.
NO, NO. I WAS REFERRING TO A DIFFERENT PART OF HER THAT HAS GROWN DISTINCTLY MORE PROMINENT.
EEP! ACK... MIZORE-CHAN...

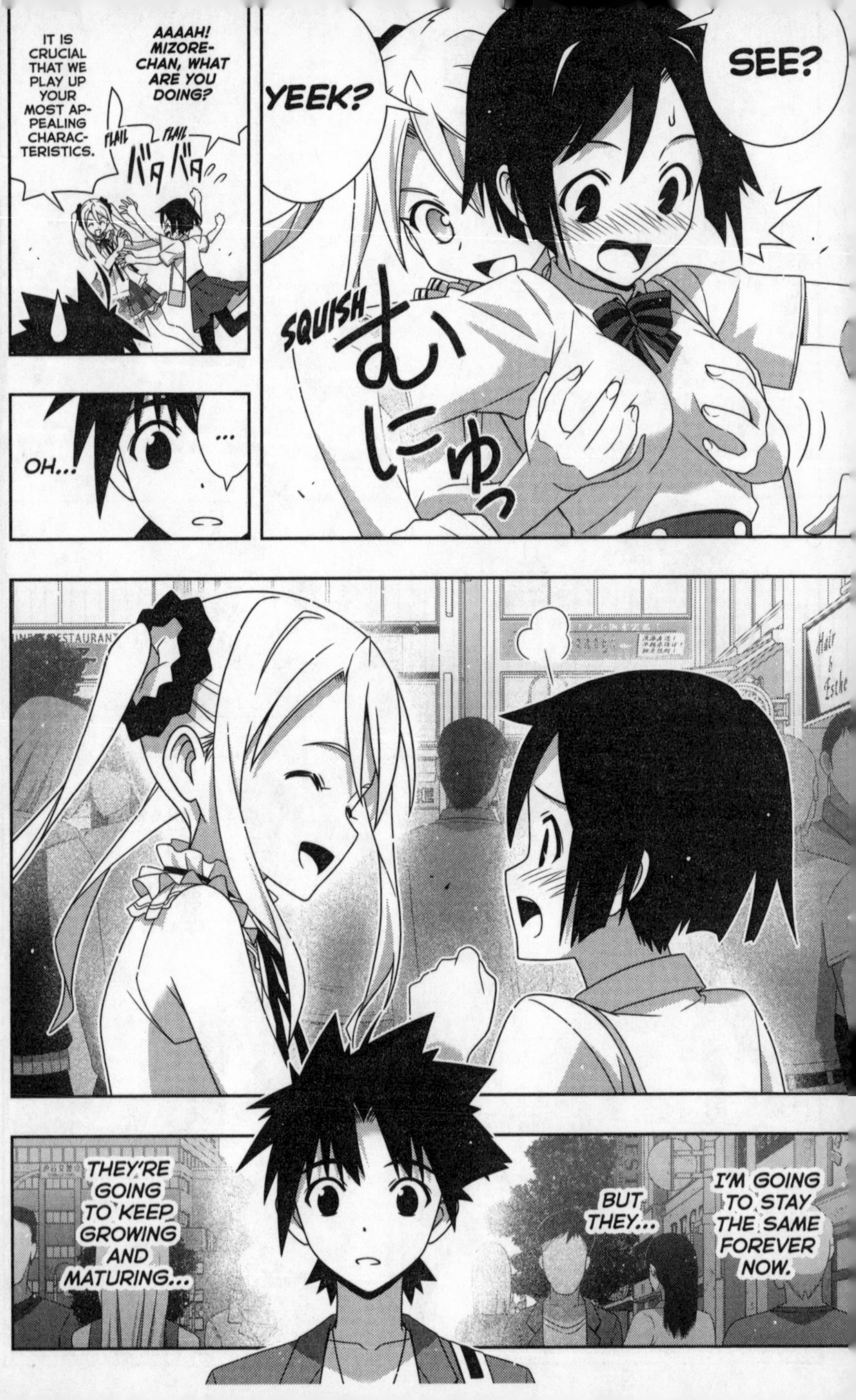
SEE?
YEEK?
SQUISH
むにゅっ
AAAAH! MIZORE-CHAN, WHAT ARE YOU DOING?
IT IS CRUCIAL THAT WE PLAY UP YOUR MOST AP-PEALING CHARAC-TERISTICS.
FLAIL FLAIL
バタバタ
...
OH...
RESTAURANT
Hair & Esthe
I'M GOING TO STAY THE SAME FOREVER NOW.
BUT THEY...
THEY'RE GOING TO KEEP GROWING AND MATURING...

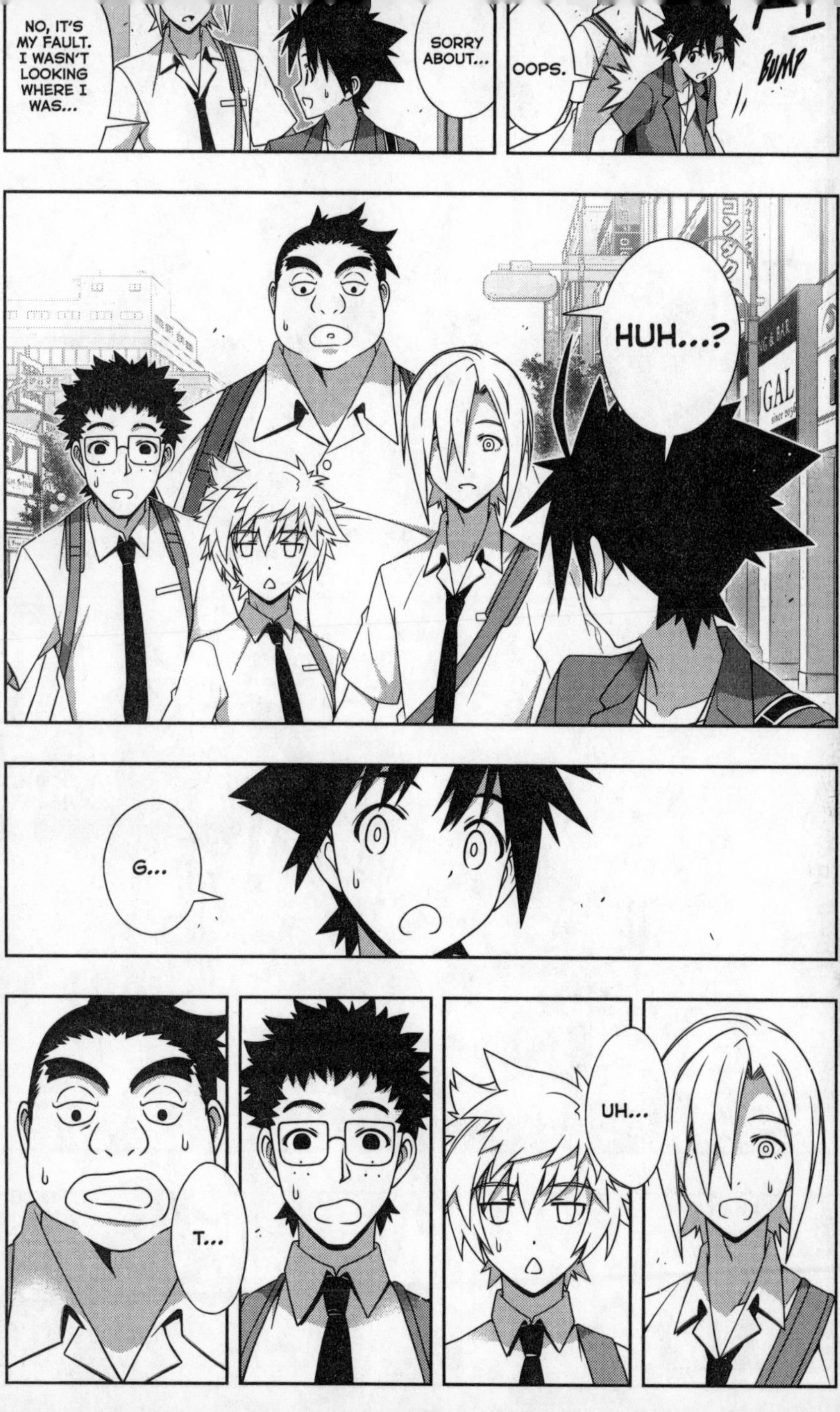
BUMP
OOPS.
SORRY ABOUT...
NO, IT'S MY FAULT. I WASN'T LOOKING WHERE I WAS...
HUH...?
GAL
G...
UH...
T...

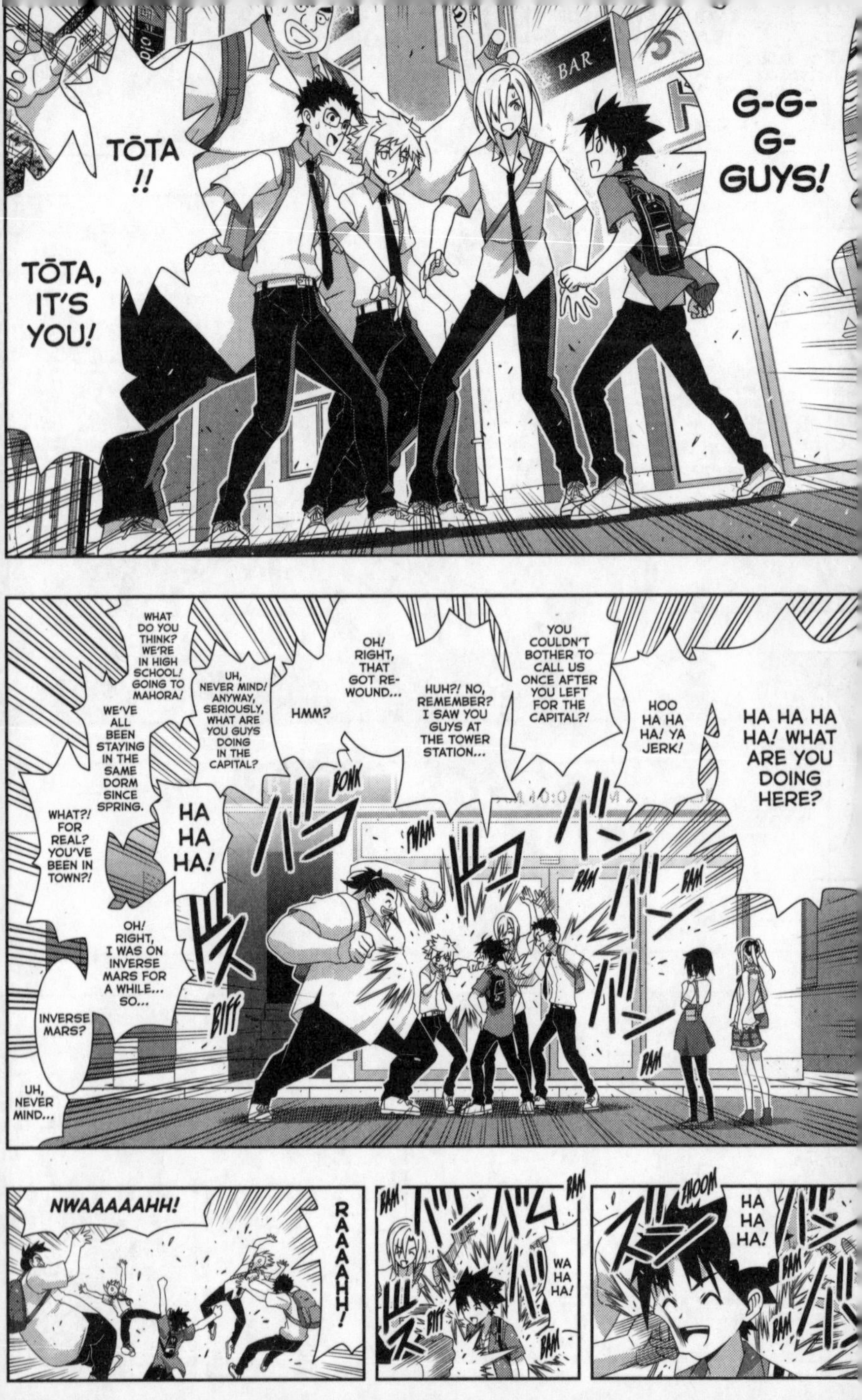
BAR
G-G-G-GUYS!
TŌTA !!
TŌTA, IT'S YOU!
HA HA HA HA! WHAT ARE YOU DOING HERE?
HOO HA HA HA! YA JERK!
YOU COULDN'T BOTHER TO CALL US ONCE AFTER YOU LEFT FOR THE CAPITAL?!
HUH?! NO, REMEMBER? I SAW YOU GUYS AT THE TOWER STATION...
OH! RIGHT, THAT GOT RE-WOUND...
HMM?
UH, NEVER MIND! ANYWAY, SERIOUSLY, WHAT ARE YOU GUYS DOING IN THE CAPITAL?
WHAT DO YOU THINK? WE'RE IN HIGH SCHOOL! GOING TO MAHORA! WE'VE ALL BEEN STAYING IN THE SAME DORM SINCE SPRING.
HA HA HA!
WHAT?! FOR REAL? YOU'VE BEEN IN TOWN?!
OH! RIGHT, I WAS ON INVERSE MARS FOR A WHILE... SO...
INVERSE MARS?
UH, NEVER MIND...
BAM
BAM
BONK
FWAM
BAM
BIFF
BAM
FHOOM
HA HA HA!
BAM
BAM
BAM
BAM
WA HA HA!
BIFF
BAM
RAAAAHH!
NWAAAAAAH!

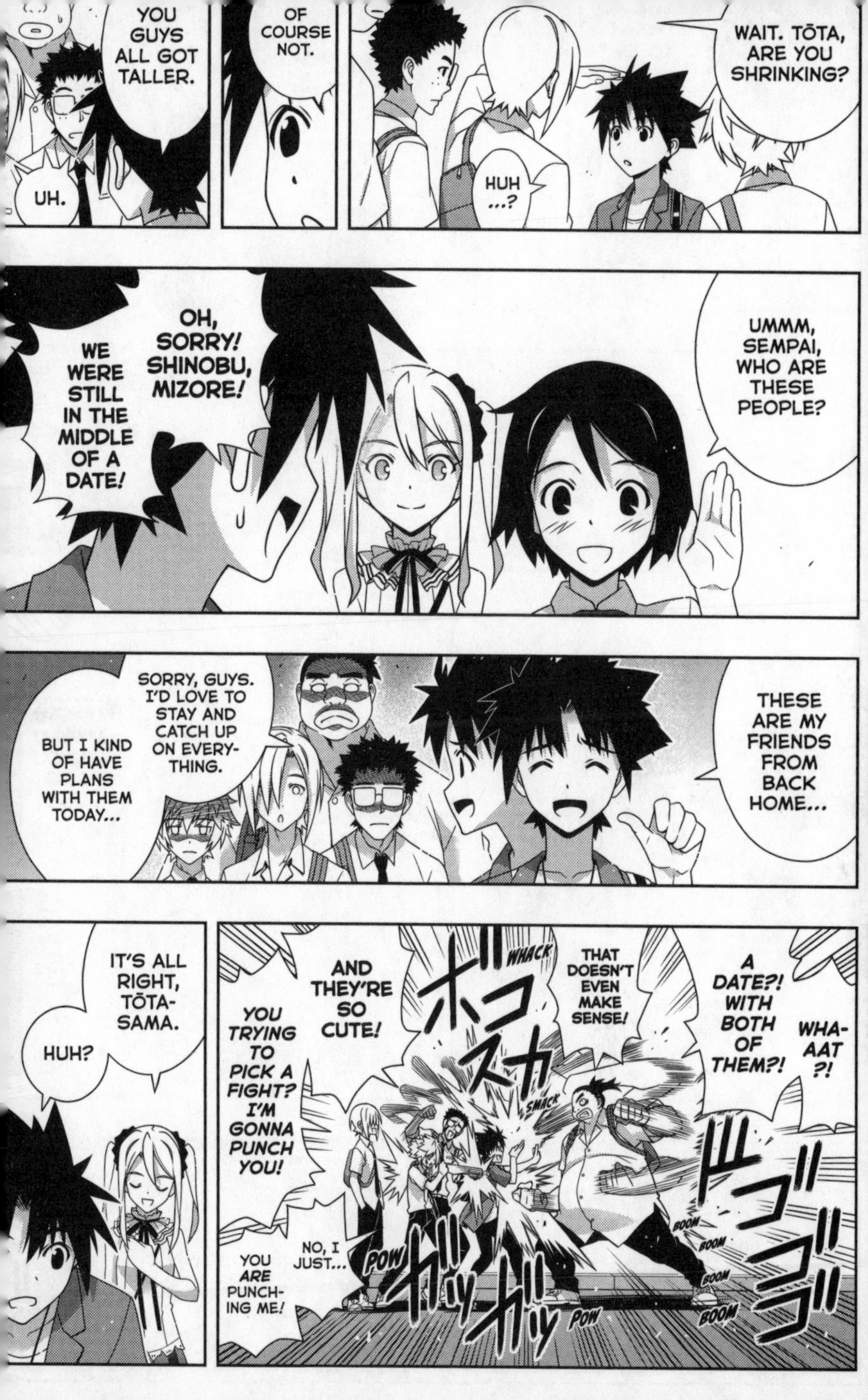
WAIT. TŌTA, ARE YOU SHRINKING?
HUH ...?
OF COURSE NOT.
YOU GUYS ALL GOT TALLER.
UH.
UMMM, SEMPAI, WHO ARE THESE PEOPLE?
OH, SORRY! SHINOBU, MIZORE!
WE WERE STILL IN THE MIDDLE OF A DATE!
THESE ARE MY FRIENDS FROM BACK HOME...
SORRY, GUYS. I'D LOVE TO STAY AND CATCH UP ON EVERY-THING.
BUT I KIND OF HAVE PLANS WITH THEM TODAY...
WHA-AAT?!
A DATE?! WITH BOTH OF THEM?!
ドゴゴゴ
BOOM
BOOM
BOOM
BOOM
THAT DOESN'T EVEN MAKE SENSE!
ボコスカ
WHACK
SMACK
AND THEY'RE SO CUTE!
YOU TRYING TO PICK A FIGHT? I'M GONNA PUNCH YOU!
ガッガッ
POW
POW
NO, I JUST...
YOU ARE PUNCH-ING ME!
IT'S ALL RIGHT, TŌTA-SAMA.
HUH?

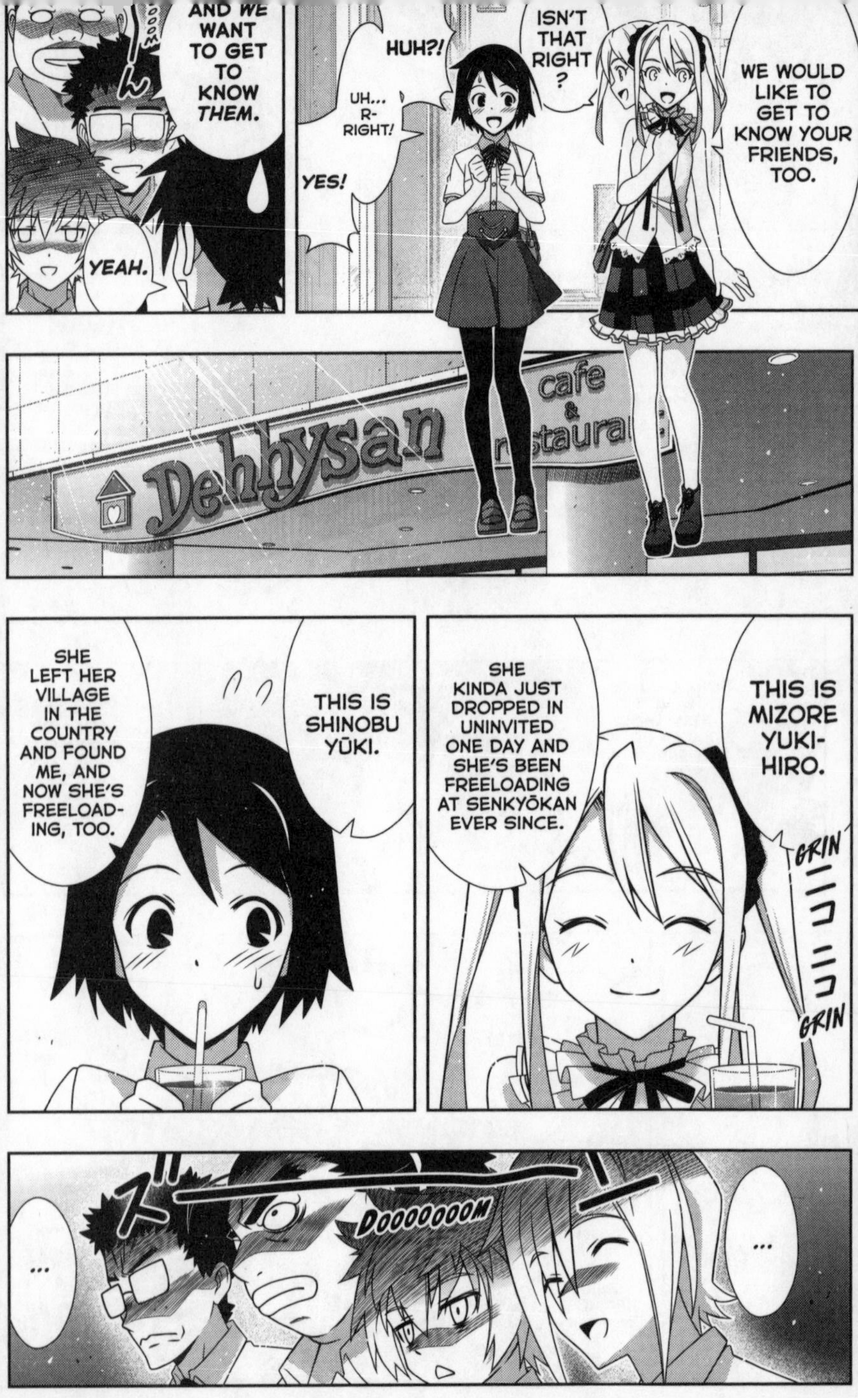
WE WOULD LIKE TO GET TO KNOW YOUR FRIENDS, TOO.
ISN'T THAT RIGHT?
HUH?!
UH... R-RIGHT!
YES!
AND WE WANT TO GET TO KNOW THEM.
YEAH.
cafe
&
Dehhysan
THIS IS MIZORE YUKI-HIRO.
SHE KINDA JUST DROPPED IN UNINVITED ONE DAY AND SHE'S BEEN FREELOADING AT SENKYŌKAN EVER SINCE.
GRIN
GRIN
THIS IS SHINOBU YŪKI.
SHE LEFT HER VILLAGE IN THE COUNTRY AND FOUND ME, AND NOW SHE'S FREELOAD-ING, TOO.
...
DOOOOOOOM
...

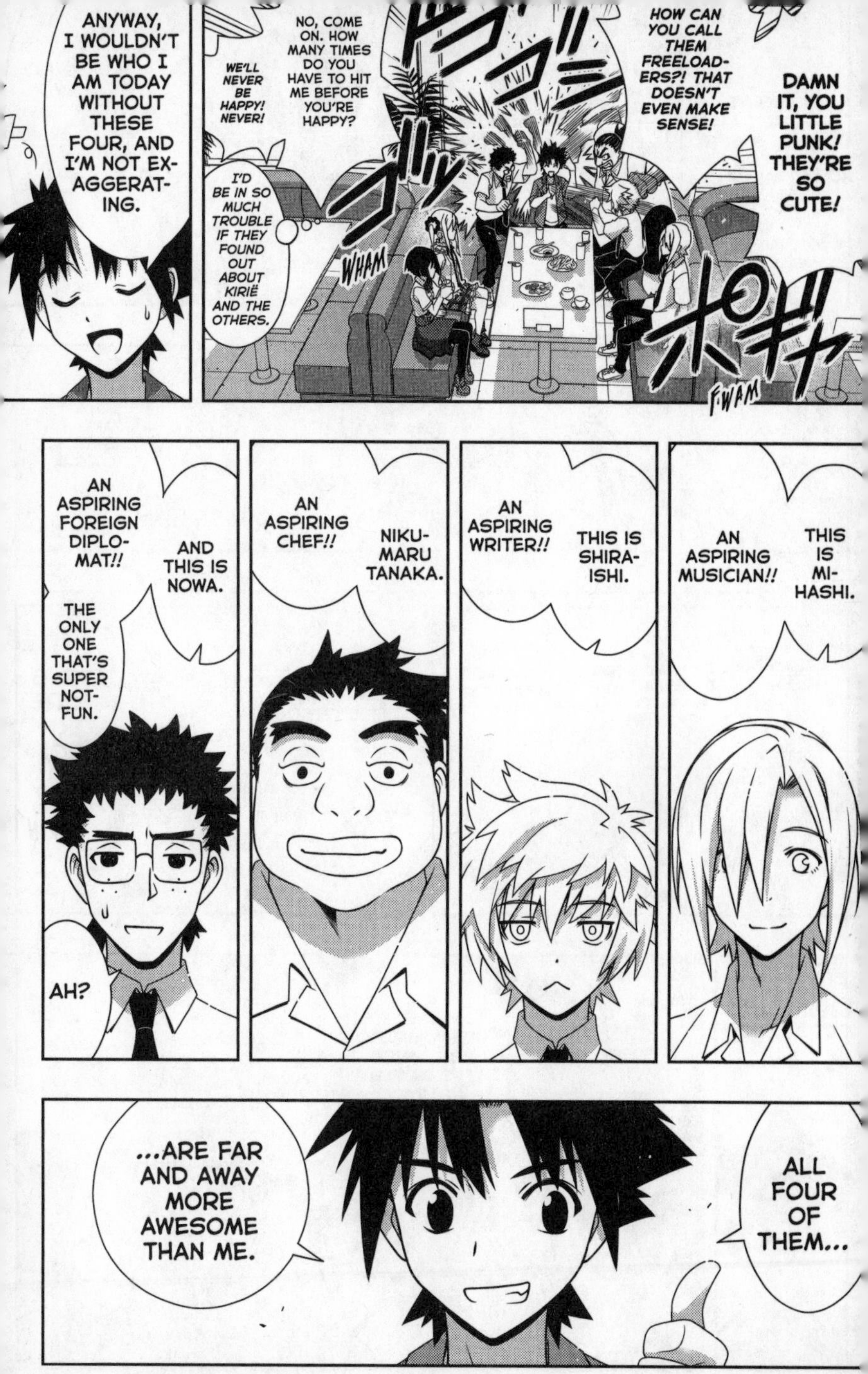
DAMN IT, YOU LITTLE PUNK! THEY'RE SO CUTE!
HOW CAN YOU CALL THEM FREELOAD-ERS?! THAT DOESN'T EVEN MAKE SENSE!
NO, COME ON. HOW MANY TIMES DO YOU HAVE TO HIT ME BEFORE YOU'RE HAPPY?
WE'LL NEVER BE HAPPY! NEVER!
I'D BE IN SO MUCH TROUBLE IF THEY FOUND OUT ABOUT KIRIË AND THE OTHERS.
WHAM
F-WAM
ANYWAY, I WOULDN'T BE WHO I AM TODAY WITHOUT THESE FOUR, AND I'M NOT EX-AGGERAT-ING.
THIS IS MI-HASHI.
AN ASPIRING MUSICIAN!!
THIS IS SHIRA-ISHI.
AN ASPIRING WRITER!!
NIKU-MARU TANAKA.
AN ASPIRING CHEF!!
AND THIS IS NOWA.
AN ASPIRING FOREIGN DIPLO-MAT!!
THE ONLY ONE THAT'S SUPER NOT-FUN.
AH?
ALL FOUR OF THEM...
...ARE FAR AND AWAY MORE AWESOME THAN ME.

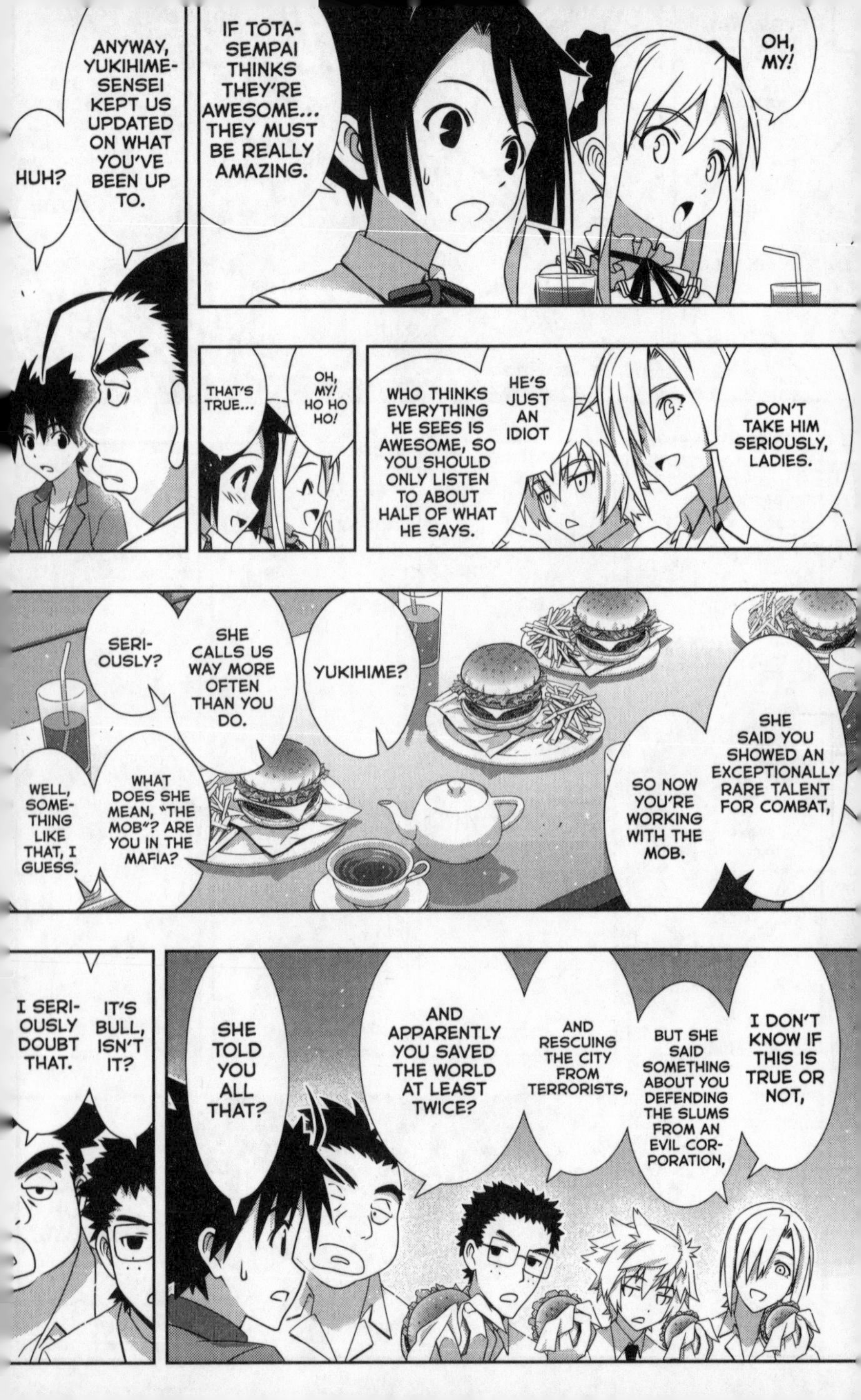
OH, MY!
IF TŌTA-SEMPAI THINKS THEY'RE AWESOME... THEY MUST BE REALLY AMAZING.
DON'T TAKE HIM SERIOUSLY, LADIES.
HE'S JUST AN IDIOT
WHO THINKS EVERYTHING HE SEES IS AWESOME, SO YOU SHOULD ONLY LISTEN TO ABOUT HALF OF WHAT HE SAYS.
OH, MY! HO HO HO!
THAT'S TRUE...
ANYWAY, YUKIHIME-SENSEI KEPT US UPDATED ON WHAT YOU'VE BEEN UP TO.
HUH?
SHE SAID YOU SHOWED AN EXCEPTIONALLY RARE TALENT FOR COMBAT,
SO NOW YOU'RE WORKING WITH THE MOB.
YUKIHIME?
SHE CALLS US WAY MORE OFTEN THAN YOU DO.
SERI-OUSLY?
WHAT DOES SHE MEAN, "THE MOB"? ARE YOU IN THE MAFIA?
WELL, SOME-THING LIKE THAT, I GUESS.
I DON'T KNOW IF THIS IS TRUE OR NOT,
BUT SHE SAID SOMETHING ABOUT YOU DEFENDING THE SLUMS FROM AN EVIL COR-PORATION,
AND RESCUING THE CITY FROM TERRORISTS,
AND APPARENTLY YOU SAVED THE WORLD AT LEAST TWICE?
SHE TOLD YOU ALL THAT?
IT'S BULL, ISN'T IT?
I SERI-OUSLY DOUBT THAT.

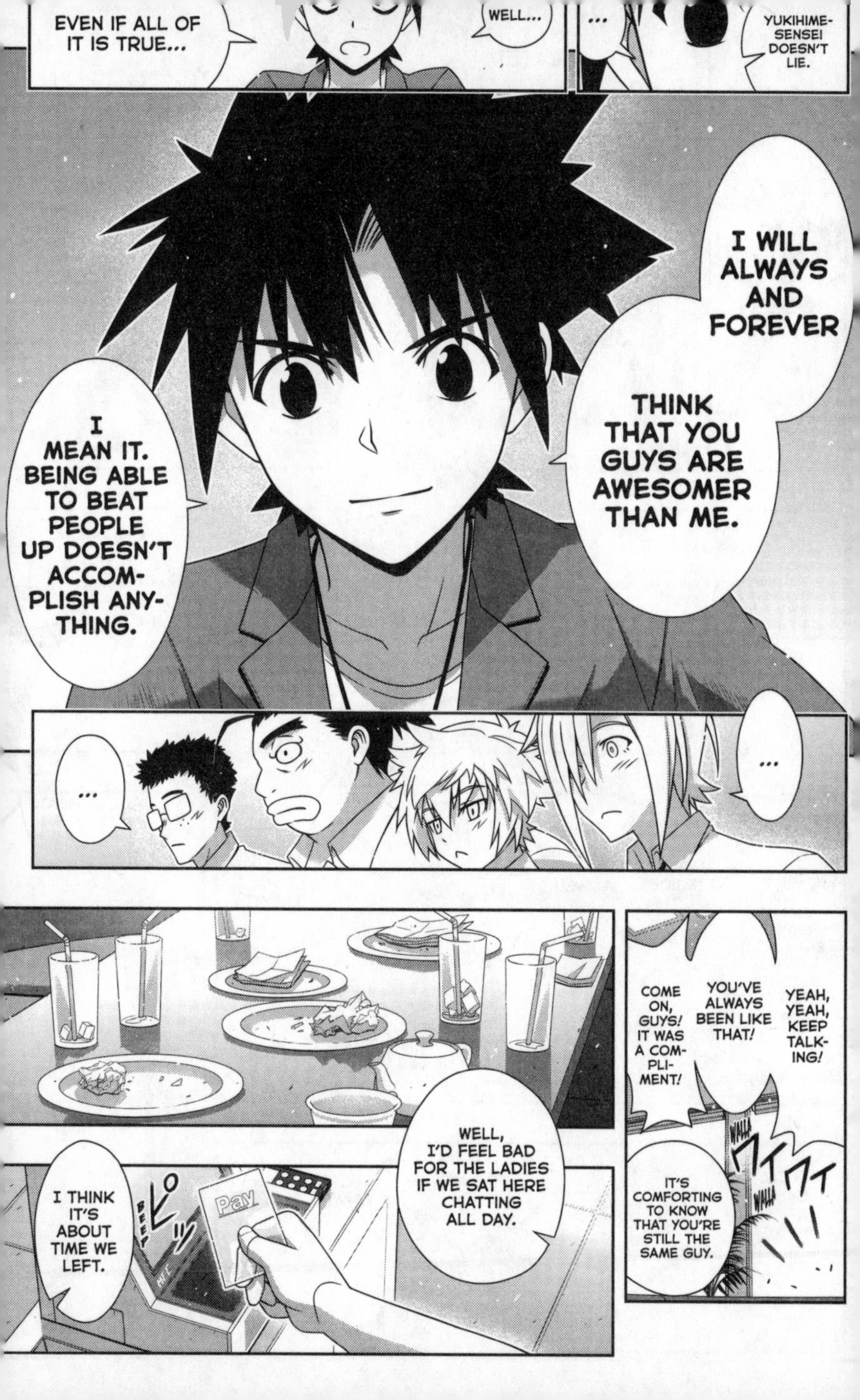
YUKIHIME-SENSEI DOESN'T LIE.
...
WELL...
EVEN IF ALL OF IT IS TRUE...
I WILL ALWAYS AND FOREVER
THINK THAT YOU GUYS ARE AWESOMER THAN ME.
I MEAN IT. BEING ABLE TO BEAT PEOPLE UP DOESN'T ACCOMPLISH ANYTHING.
...
...
YEAH, YEAH, KEEP TALKING!
YOU'VE ALWAYS BEEN LIKE THAT!
COME ON, GUYS! IT WAS A COMPLIMENT!
WALLA
WALLA
IT'S COMFORTING TO KNOW THAT YOU'RE STILL THE SAME GUY.
WELL, I'D FEEL BAD FOR THE LADIES IF WE SAT HERE CHATTING ALL DAY.
BEEP
Pay
I THINK IT'S ABOUT TIME WE LEFT.

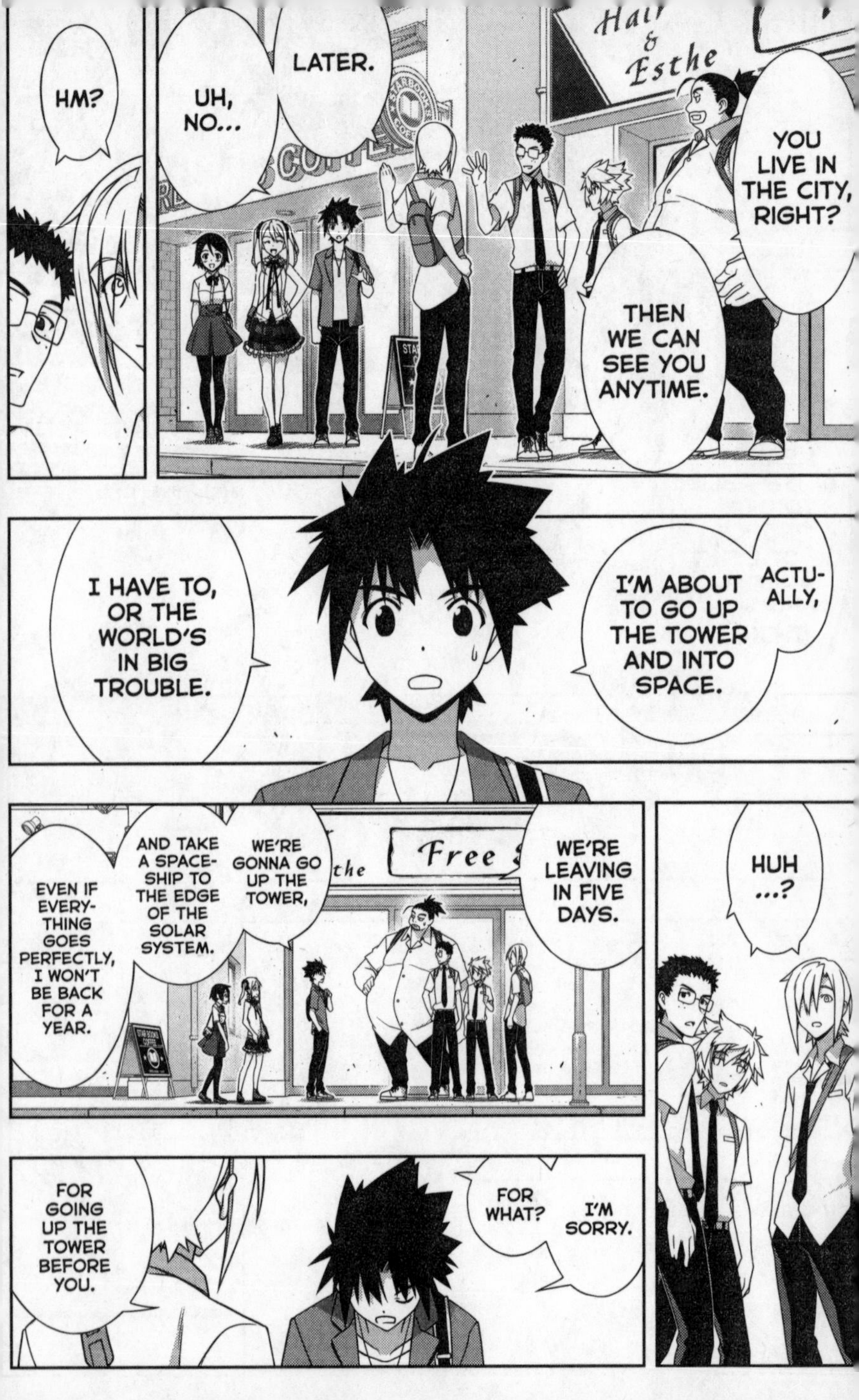
Hair & Esthe
YOU LIVE IN THE CITY, RIGHT?
THEN WE CAN SEE YOU ANYTIME.
LATER.
UH, NO...
HM?
ACTU-ALLY,
I'M ABOUT TO GO UP THE TOWER AND INTO SPACE.
I HAVE TO, OR THE WORLD'S IN BIG TROUBLE.
HUH ...?
WE'RE LEAVING IN FIVE DAYS.
WE'RE GONNA GO UP THE TOWER,
AND TAKE A SPACE-SHIP TO THE EDGE OF THE SOLAR SYSTEM.
EVEN IF EVERY-THING GOES PERFECTLY, I WON'T BE BACK FOR A YEAR.
I'M SORRY.
FOR WHAT?
FOR GOING UP THE TOWER BEFORE YOU.

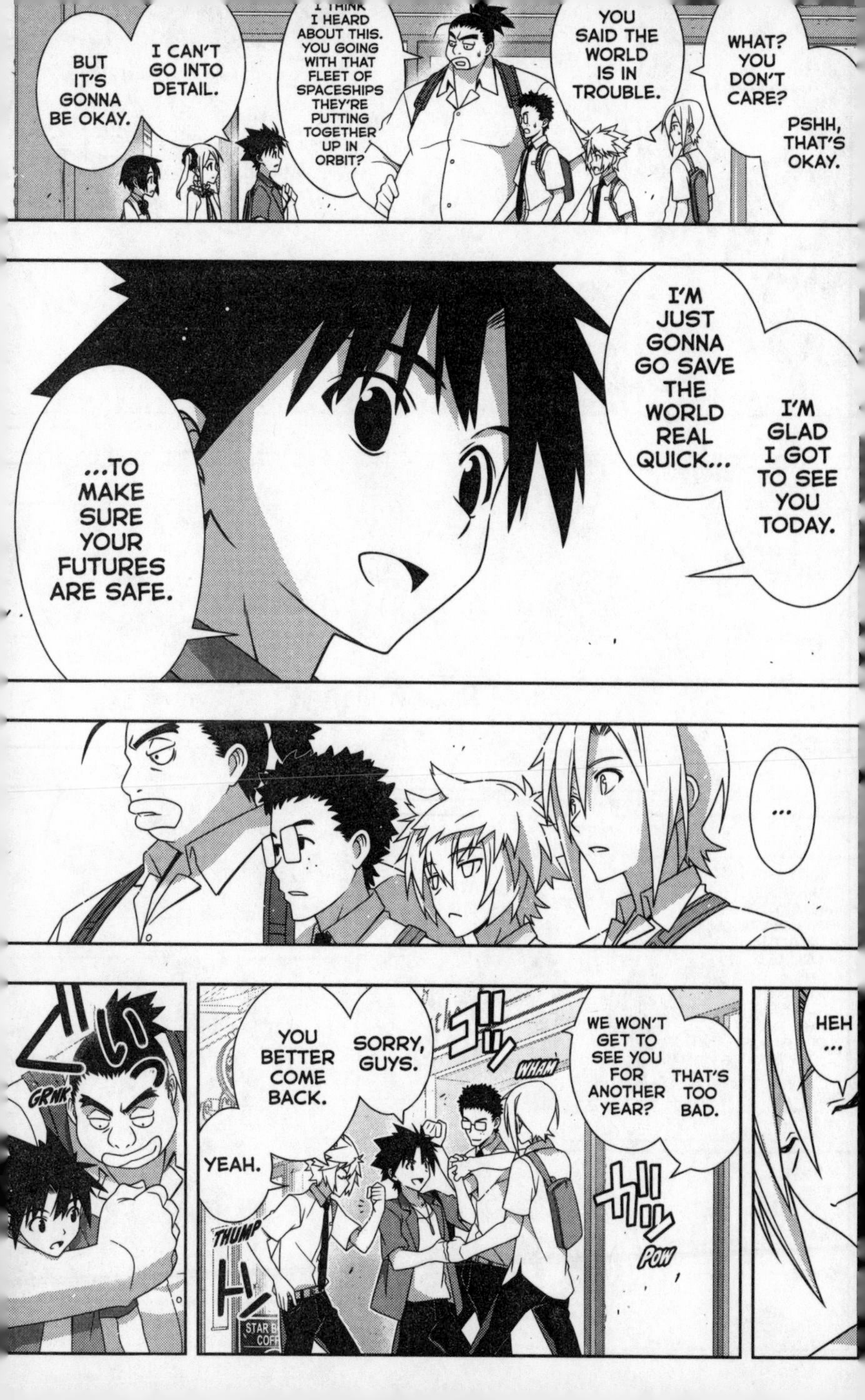
WHAT? YOU DON'T CARE?
PSHH, THAT'S OKAY.
YOU SAID THE WORLD IS IN TROUBLE.
I THINK I HEARD ABOUT THIS. YOU GOING WITH THAT FLEET OF SPACESHIPS THEY'RE PUTTING TOGETHER UP IN ORBIT?
I CAN'T GO INTO DETAIL.
BUT IT'S GONNA BE OKAY.
I'M JUST GONNA GO SAVE THE WORLD REAL QUICK...
I'M GLAD I GOT TO SEE YOU TODAY.
...TO MAKE SURE YOUR FUTURES ARE SAFE.
...
HEH ...
WE WON'T GET TO SEE YOU FOR ANOTHER YEAR?
THAT'S TOO BAD.
WHAM
POW
SORRY, GUYS.
YOU BETTER COME BACK.
YEAH.
THUMP
GRNK

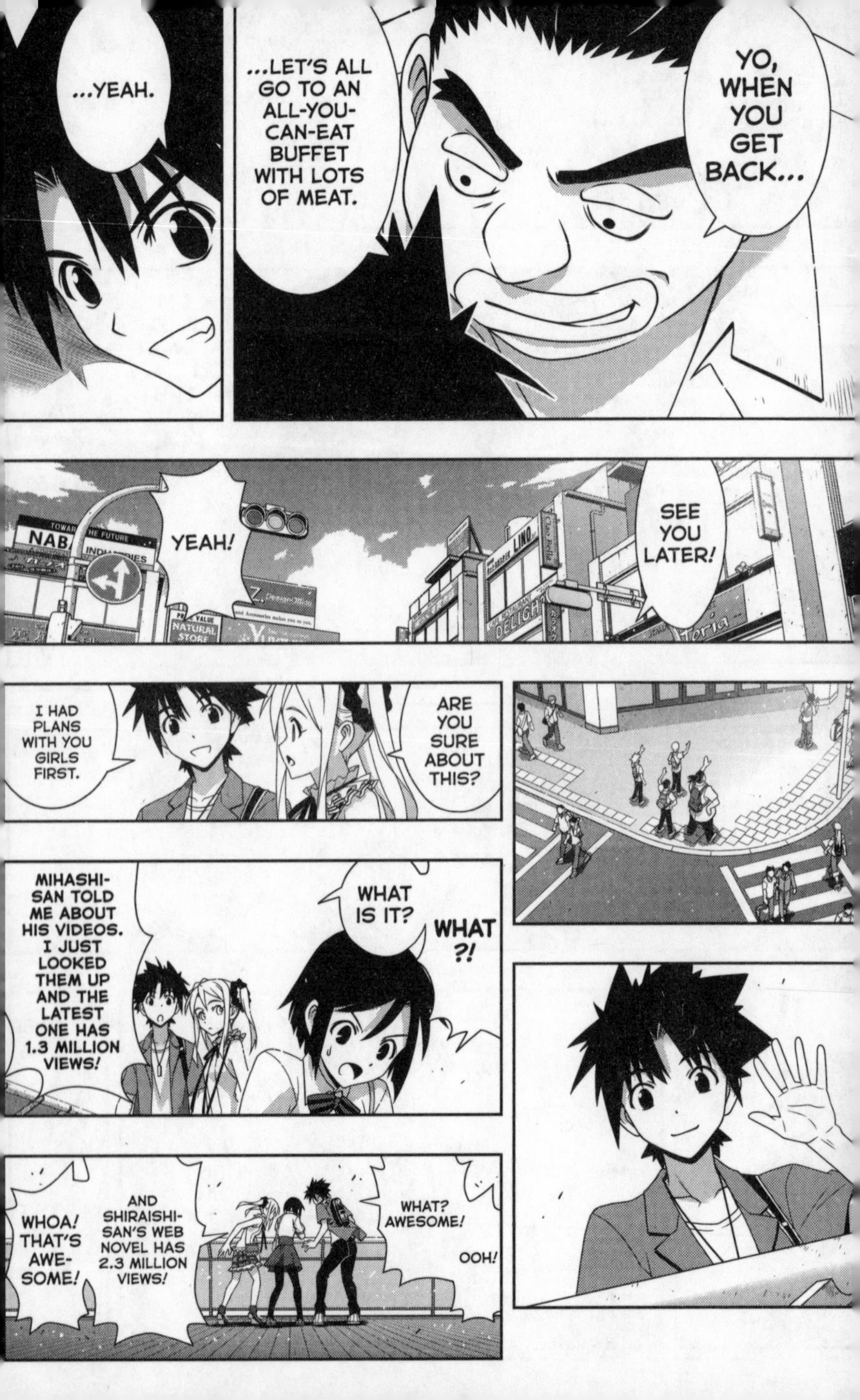

YO, WHEN YOU GET BACK...
...LET'S ALL GO TO AN ALL-YOU-CAN-EAT BUFFET WITH LOTS OF MEAT.
...YEAH.
SEE YOU LATER!
YEAH!
ARE YOU SURE ABOUT THIS?
I HAD PLANS WITH YOU GIRLS FIRST.
WHAT ?!
WHAT IS IT?
MIHASHI-SAN TOLD ME ABOUT HIS VIDEOS. I JUST LOOKED THEM UP AND THE LATEST ONE HAS 1.3 MILLION VIEWS!
OOH!
WHAT? AWESOME!
AND SHIRAISHI-SAN'S WEB NOVEL HAS 2.3 MILLION VIEWS!
WHOA! THAT'S AWE-SOME!

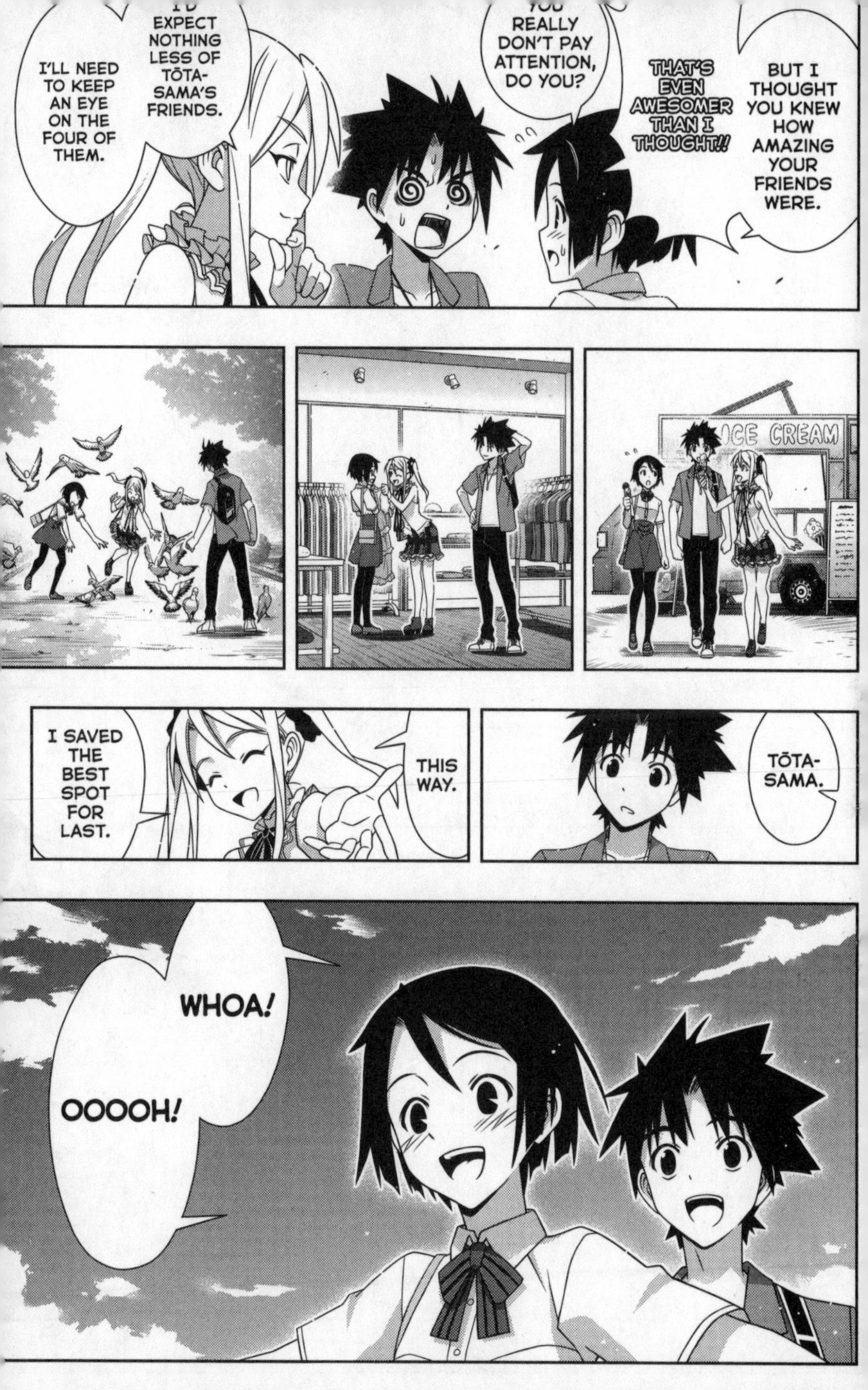

BUT I THOUGHT YOU KNEW HOW AMAZING YOUR FRIENDS WERE.
THAT'S EVEN AWESOMER THAN I THOUGHT!!
YOU REALLY DON'T PAY ATTENTION, DO YOU?
I'D EXPECT NOTHING LESS OF TŌTA-SAMA'S FRIENDS.
I'LL NEED TO KEEP AN EYE ON THE FOUR OF THEM.
ICE CREAM
TŌTA-SAMA.
THIS WAY.
I SAVED THE BEST SPOT FOR LAST.
WHOA!
OOOOH!

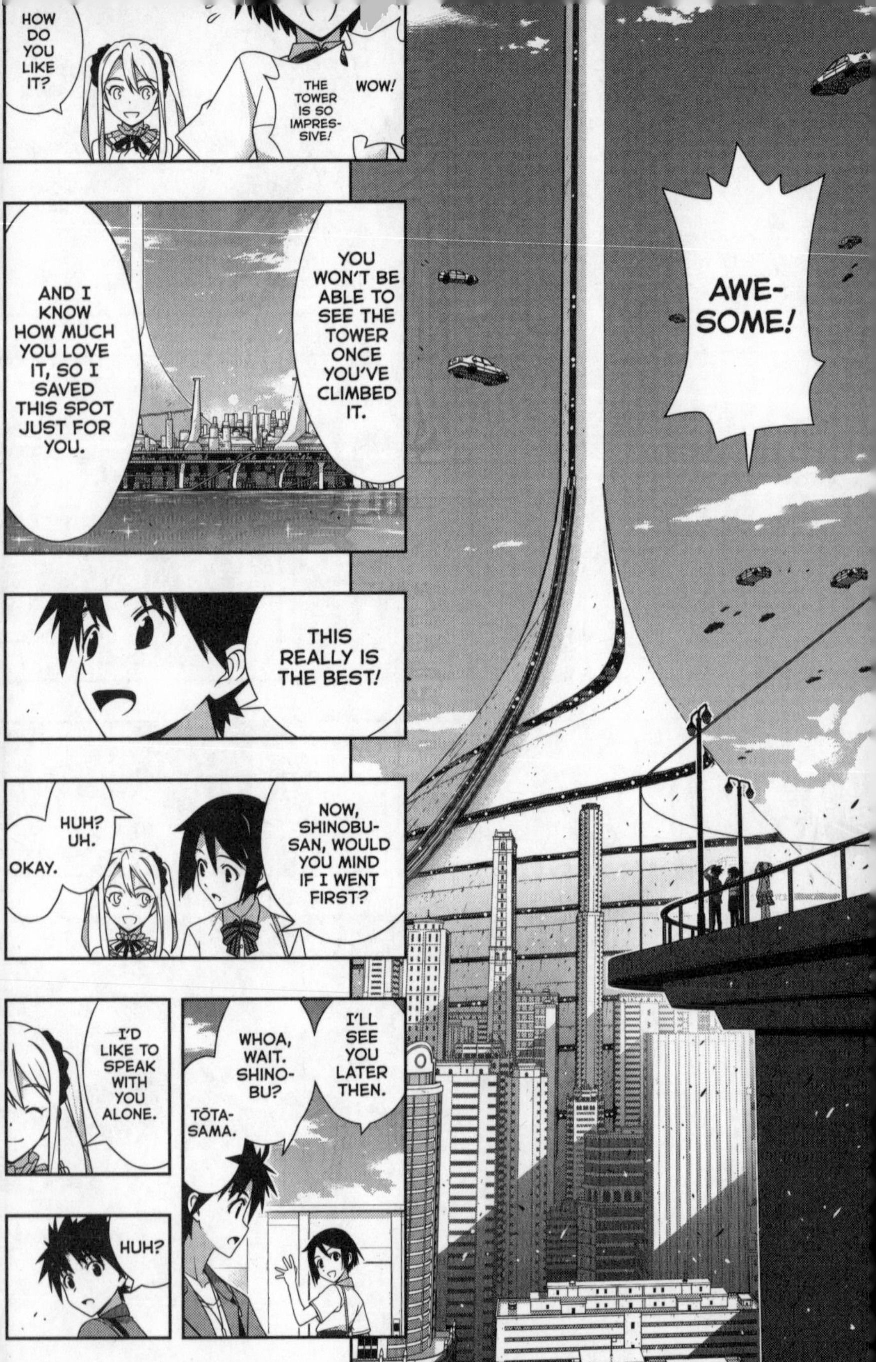
AWE-SOME!
WOW!
THE TOWER IS SO IMPRESSIVE!
HOW DO YOU LIKE IT?
YOU WON'T BE ABLE TO SEE THE TOWER ONCE YOU'VE CLIMBED IT.
AND I KNOW HOW MUCH YOU LOVE IT, SO I SAVED THIS SPOT JUST FOR YOU.
THIS REALLY IS THE BEST!
NOW, SHINOBU-SAN, WOULD YOU MIND IF I WENT FIRST?
HUH? UH.
OKAY.
I'LL SEE YOU LATER THEN.
WHOA, WAIT. SHINOBU?
TŌTA-SAMA.
I'D LIKE TO SPEAK WITH YOU ALONE.
HUH?

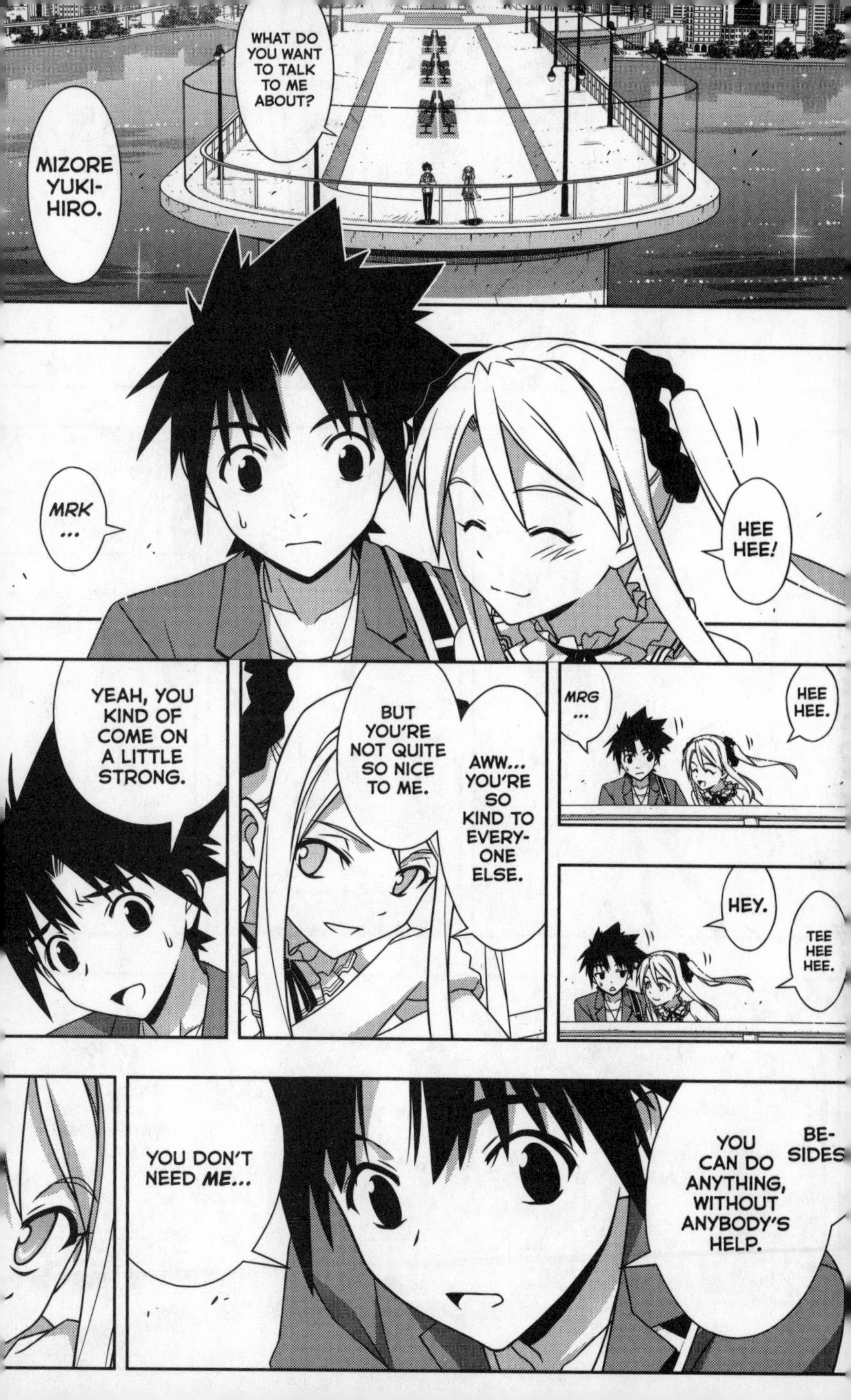
WHAT DO YOU WANT TO TALK TO ME ABOUT?
MIZORE YUKI-HIRO.
HEE HEE!
MRK ...
HEE HEE.
MRG ...
HEY.
TEE HEE HEE.
AWW... YOU'RE SO KIND TO EVERY-ONE ELSE.
BUT YOU'RE NOT QUITE SO NICE TO ME.
YEAH, YOU KIND OF COME ON A LITTLE STRONG.
BE-SIDES
YOU CAN DO ANYTHING, WITHOUT ANYBODY'S HELP.
YOU DON'T NEED *ME*...

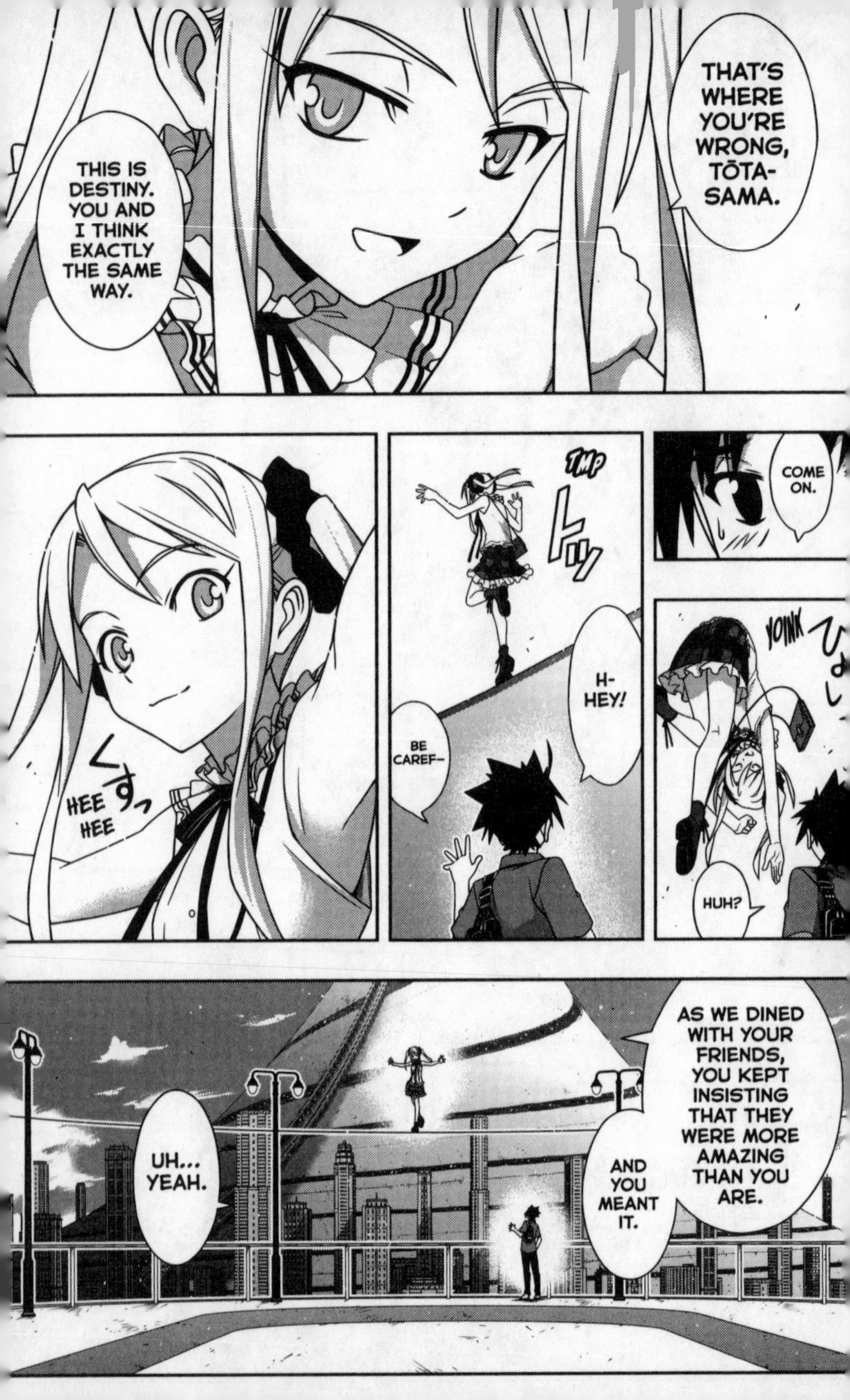

THAT'S WHERE YOU'RE WRONG, TŌTA-SAMA.
THIS IS DESTINY. YOU AND I THINK EXACTLY THE SAME WAY.
COME ON.
YOINK
ひょい
HUH?
TMP
トッ
H-HEY!
BE CAREF—
HEE HEE
くすっ
AS WE DINED WITH YOUR FRIENDS, YOU KEPT INSISTING THAT THEY WERE MORE AMAZING THAN YOU ARE.
AND YOU MEANT IT.
UH... YEAH.

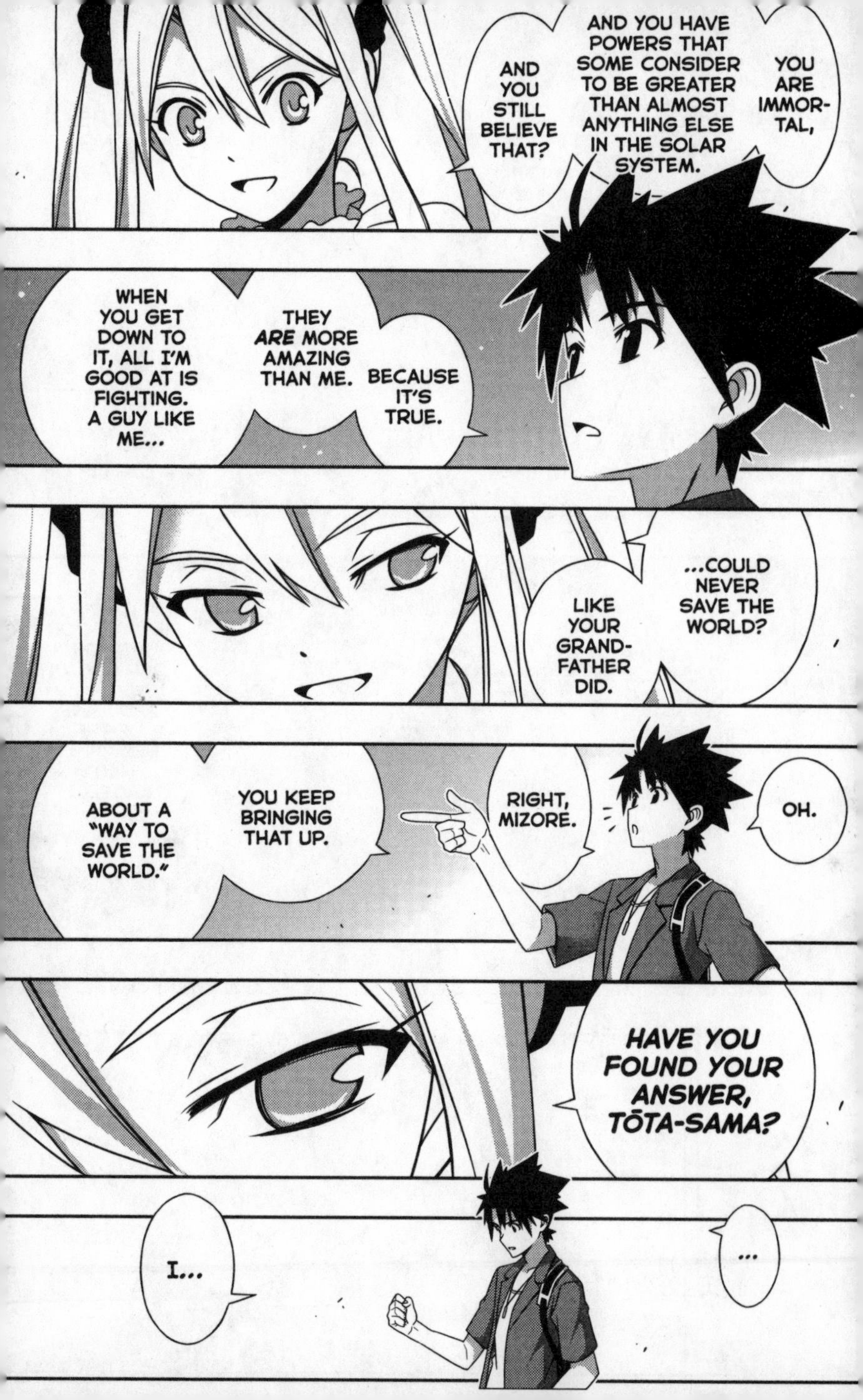
YOU ARE IMMORTAL,
AND YOU HAVE POWERS THAT SOME CONSIDER TO BE GREATER THAN ALMOST ANYTHING ELSE IN THE SOLAR SYSTEM.
AND YOU STILL BELIEVE THAT?
BECAUSE IT'S TRUE.
THEY *ARE* MORE AMAZING THAN ME.
WHEN YOU GET DOWN TO IT, ALL I'M GOOD AT IS FIGHTING. A GUY LIKE ME...
...COULD NEVER SAVE THE WORLD?
LIKE YOUR GRAND-FATHER DID.
OH.
RIGHT, MIZORE.
YOU KEEP BRINGING THAT UP.
ABOUT A "WAY TO SAVE THE WORLD."
HAVE YOU FOUND YOUR ANSWER, TŌTA-SAMA?
...
I...

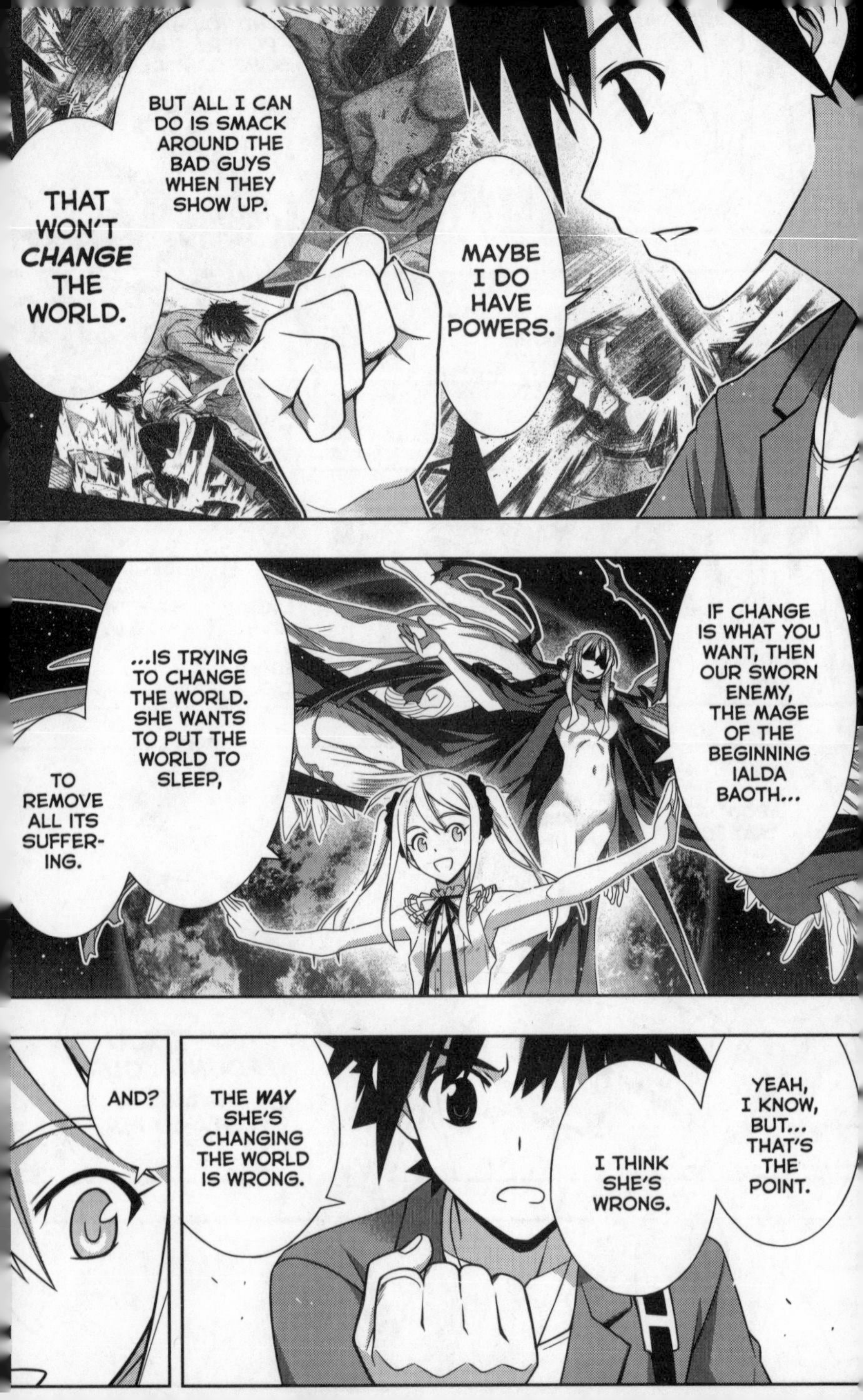
MAYBE I DO HAVE POWERS.
BUT ALL I CAN DO IS SMACK AROUND THE BAD GUYS WHEN THEY SHOW UP.
THAT WON'T *CHANGE* THE WORLD.
IF CHANGE IS WHAT YOU WANT, THEN OUR SWORN ENEMY, THE MAGE OF THE BEGINNING IALDA BAOTH...
...IS TRYING TO CHANGE THE WORLD. SHE WANTS TO PUT THE WORLD TO SLEEP,
TO REMOVE ALL ITS SUFFER-ING.
YEAH, I KNOW, BUT... THAT'S THE POINT.
I THINK SHE'S WRONG.
THE *WAY* SHE'S CHANGING THE WORLD IS WRONG.
AND?

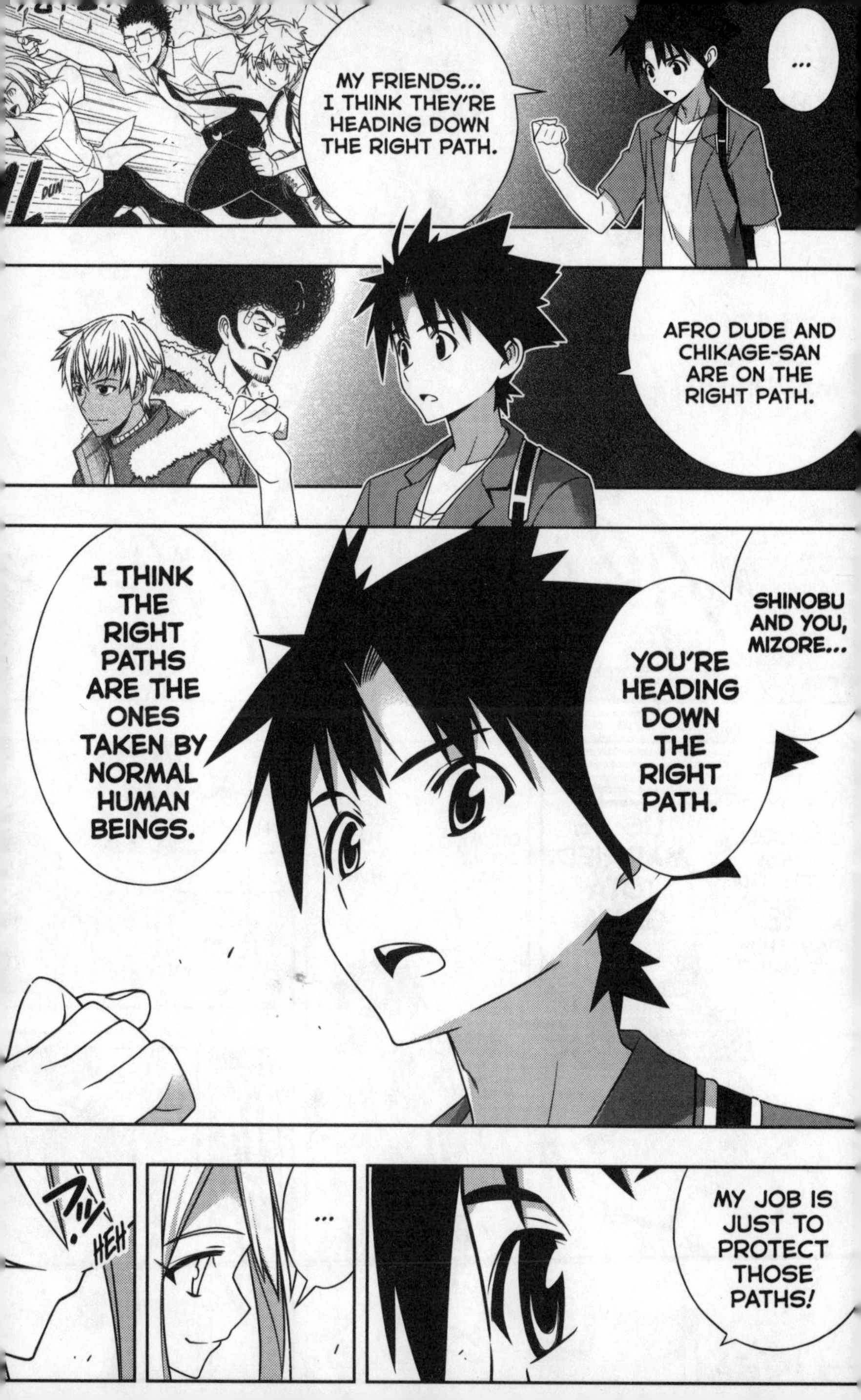
...
MY FRIENDS... I THINK THEY'RE HEADING DOWN THE RIGHT PATH.
DUN
AFRO DUDE AND CHIKAGE-SAN ARE ON THE RIGHT PATH.
SHINOBU AND YOU, MIZORE...
YOU'RE HEADING DOWN THE RIGHT PATH.
I THINK THE RIGHT PATHS ARE THE ONES TAKEN BY NORMAL HUMAN BEINGS.
MY JOB IS JUST TO PROTECT THOSE PATHS!
...
HEH

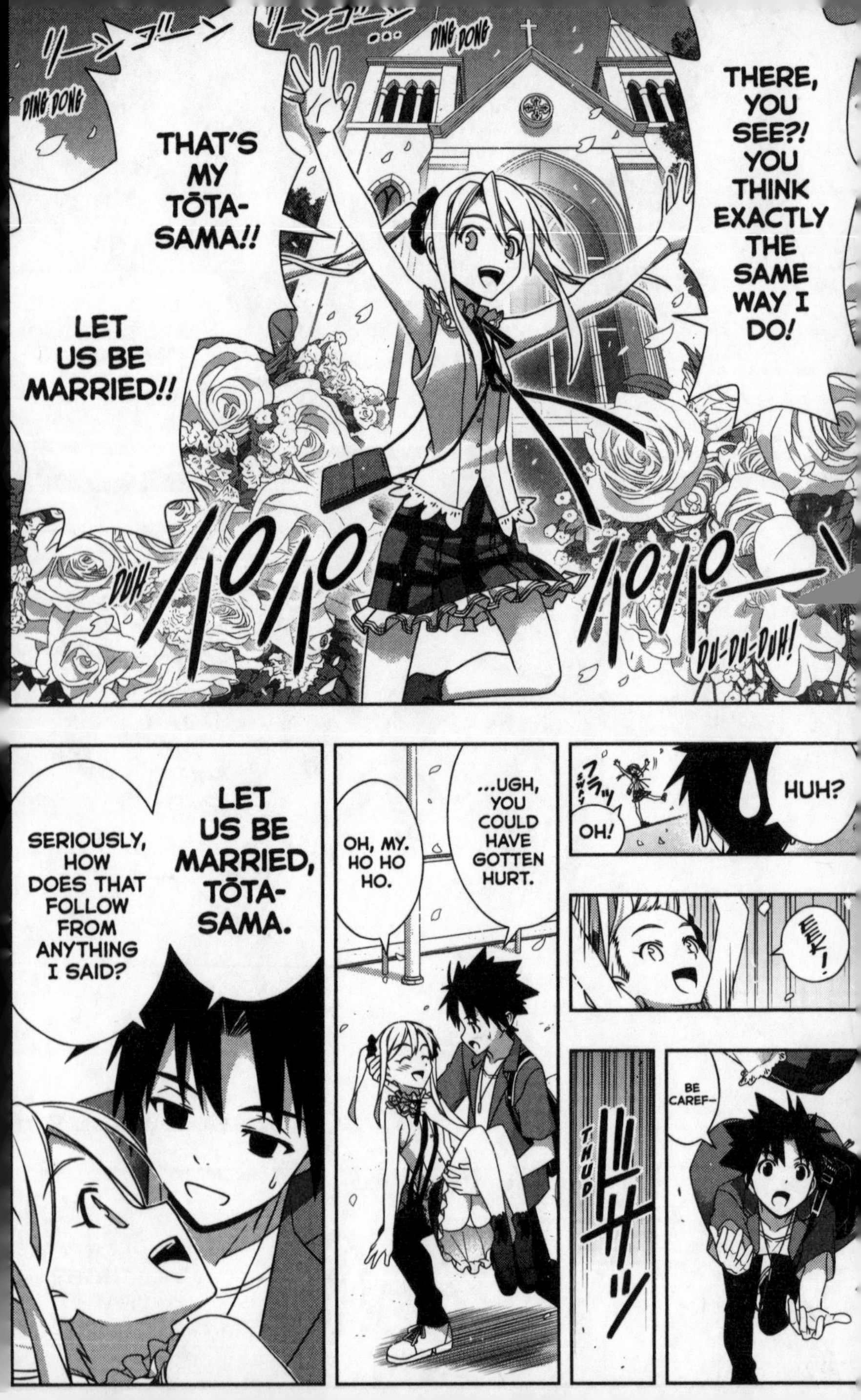
DING DONG
DING DONG
THERE, YOU SEE?! YOU THINK EXACTLY THE SAME WAY I DO!
THAT'S MY TŌTA-SAMA!!
LET US BE MARRIED!!
DU-DU-DUH!
DUH
HUH?
SWAY
OH!
EEEK!
BE CAREF-
THUD
...UGH, YOU COULD HAVE GOTTEN HURT.
OH, MY. HO HO HO.
LET US BE MARRIED, TŌTA-SAMA.
SERIOUSLY, HOW DOES THAT FOLLOW FROM ANYTHING I SAID?

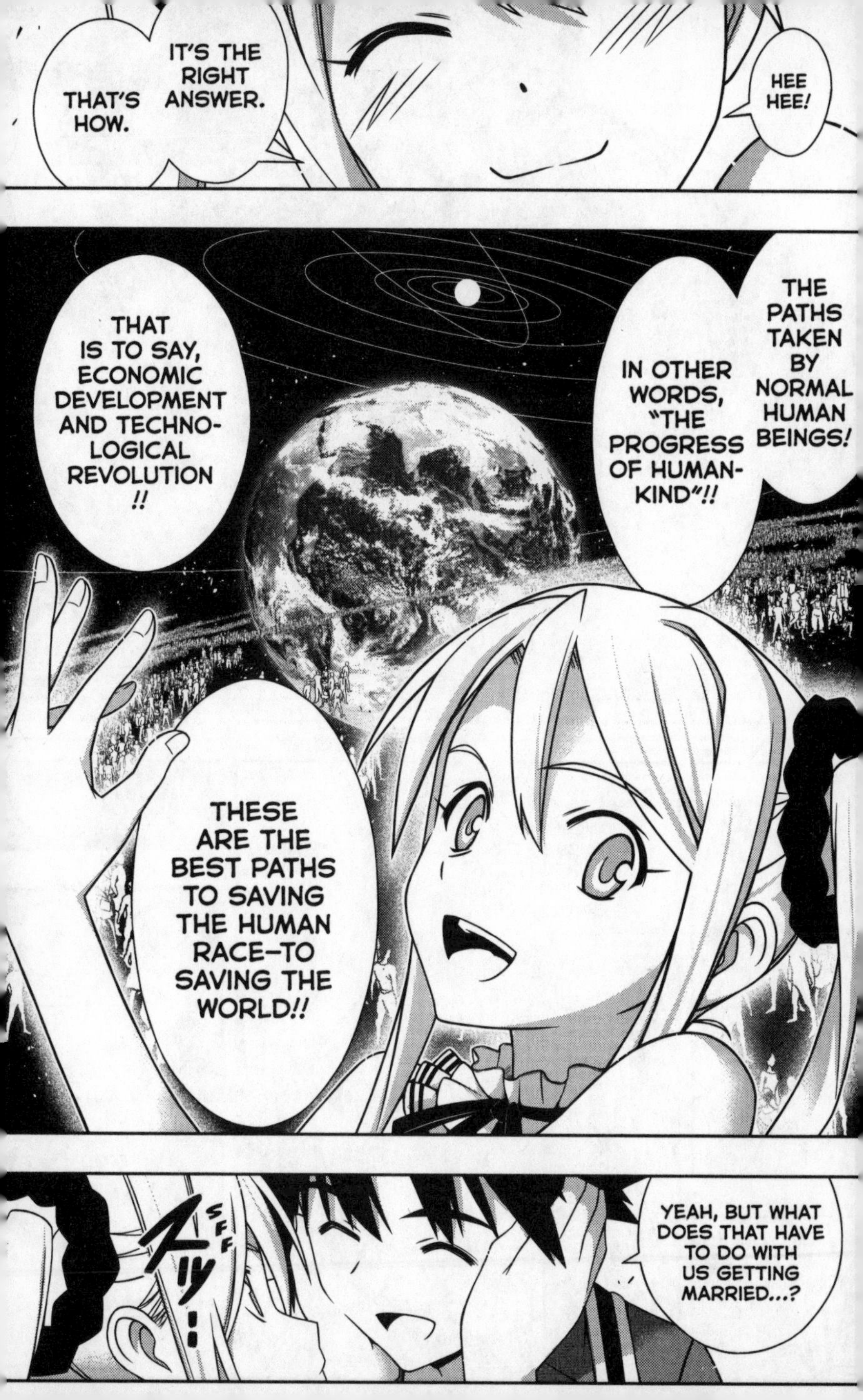
HEE HEE!
IT'S THE RIGHT ANSWER.
THAT'S HOW.
THE PATHS TAKEN BY NORMAL HUMAN BEINGS!
IN OTHER WORDS, "THE PROGRESS OF HUMAN-KIND"!!
THAT IS TO SAY, ECONOMIC DEVELOPMENT AND TECHNO-LOGICAL REVOLUTION!!
THESE ARE THE BEST PATHS TO SAVING THE HUMAN RACE—TO SAVING THE WORLD!!
YEAH, BUT WHAT DOES THAT HAVE TO DO WITH US GETTING MARRIED...?
SFF

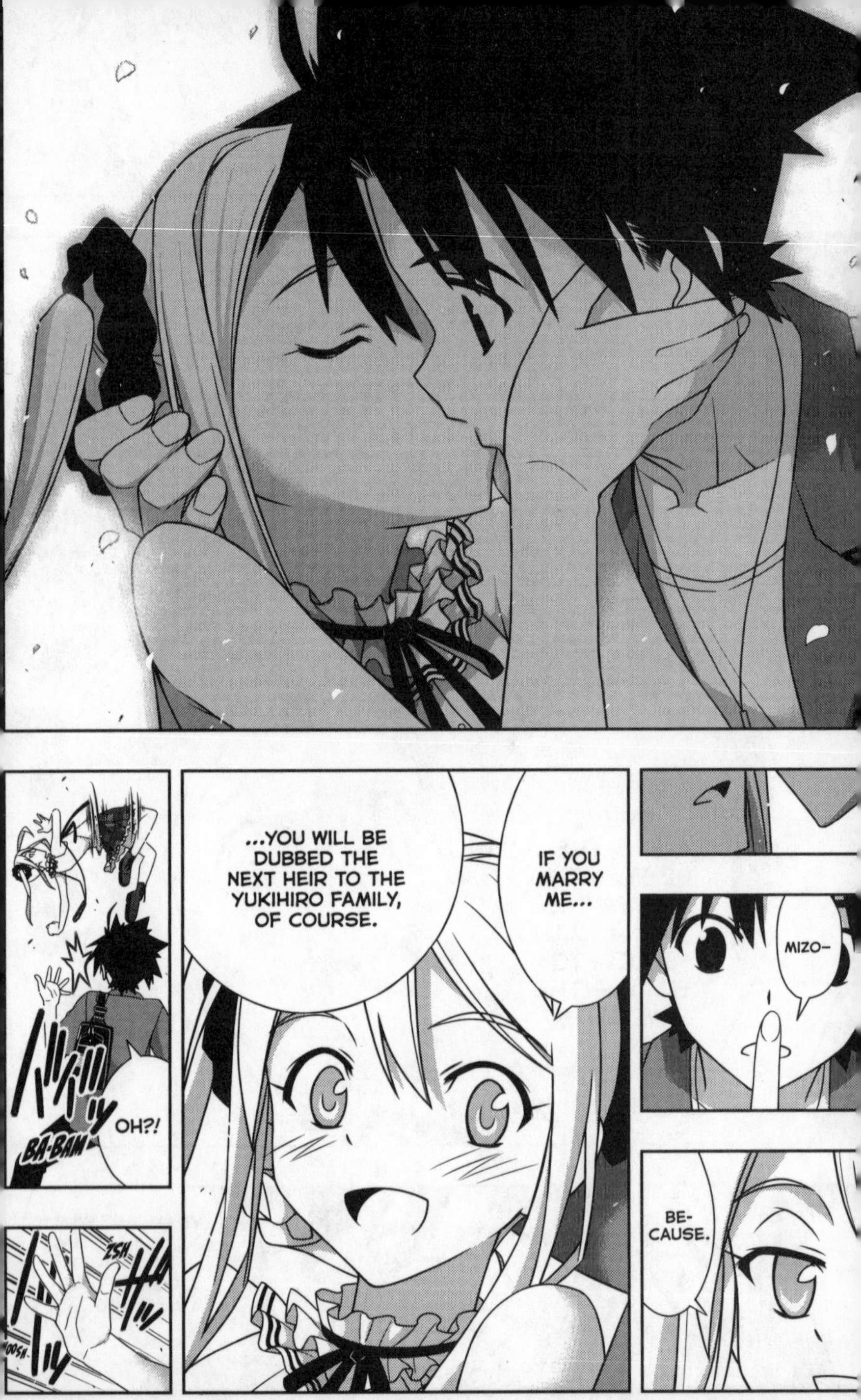
MIZO–
BE-CAUSE.
IF YOU MARRY ME...
...YOU WILL BE DUBBED THE NEXT HEIR TO THE YUKIHIRO FAMILY, OF COURSE.
OH?!
BA-BAM
ZSH

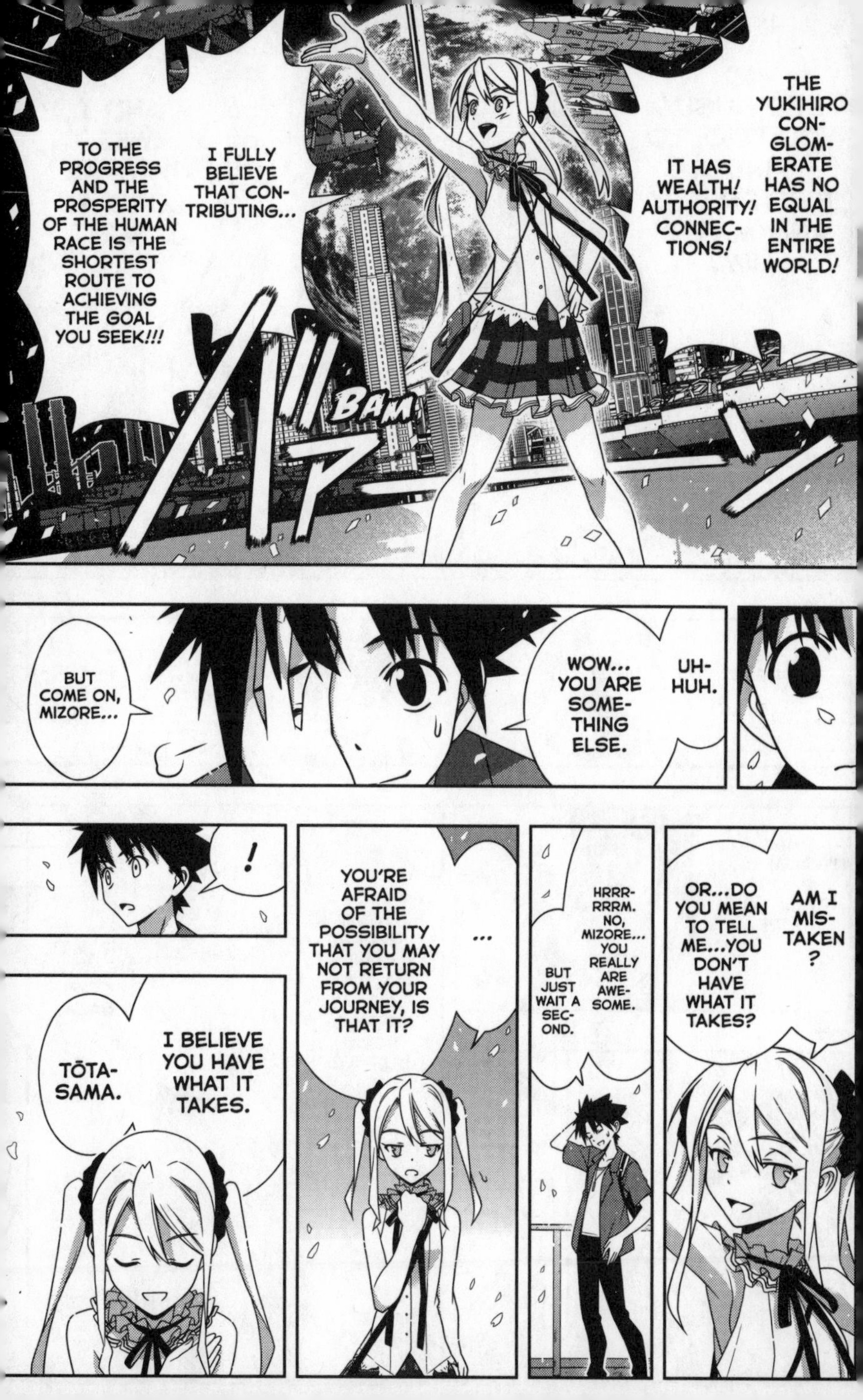
THE YUKIHIRO CON-GLOM-ERATE HAS NO EQUAL IN THE ENTIRE WORLD!
IT HAS WEALTH! AUTHORITY! CONNEC-TIONS!
I FULLY BELIEVE THAT CON-TRIBUTING...
TO THE PROGRESS AND THE PROSPERITY OF THE HUMAN RACE IS THE SHORTEST ROUTE TO ACHIEVING THE GOAL YOU SEEK!!!
BAM
UH-HUH.
WOW... YOU ARE SOME-THING ELSE.
BUT COME ON, MIZORE...
AM I MIS-TAKEN?
OR...DO YOU MEAN TO TELL ME...YOU DON'T HAVE WHAT IT TAKES?
HRRR-RRRM. NO, MIZORE... YOU REALLY ARE AWE-SOME.
BUT JUST WAIT A SEC-OND.
...
YOU'RE AFRAID OF THE POSSIBILITY THAT YOU MAY NOT RETURN FROM YOUR JOURNEY, IS THAT IT?
!
I BELIEVE YOU HAVE WHAT IT TAKES.
TŌTA-SAMA.

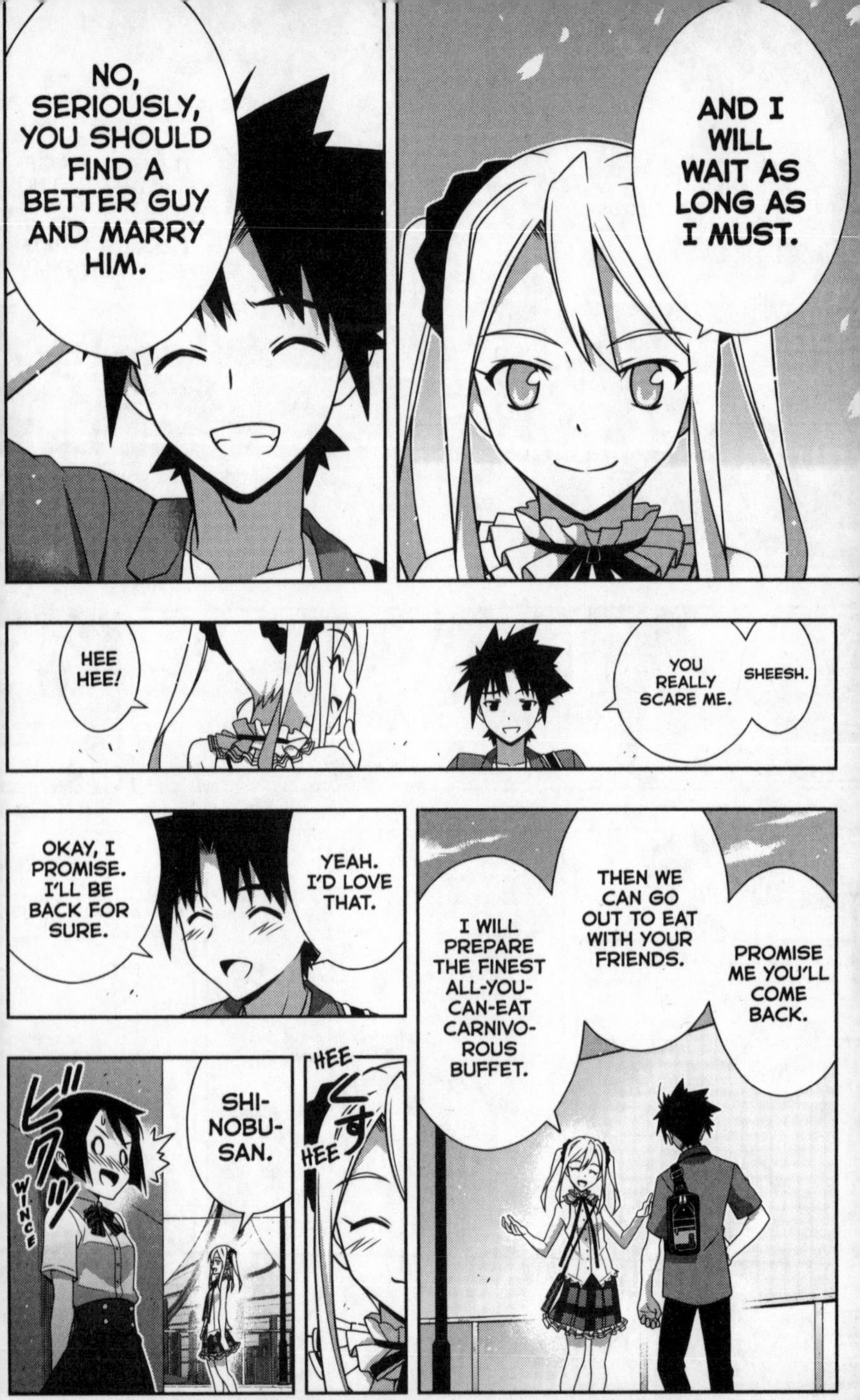
AND I WILL WAIT AS LONG AS I MUST.
NO, SERIOUSLY, YOU SHOULD FIND A BETTER GUY AND MARRY HIM.
SHEESH.
YOU REALLY SCARE ME.
HEE HEE!
PROMISE ME YOU'LL COME BACK.
THEN WE CAN GO OUT TO EAT WITH YOUR FRIENDS.
I WILL PREPARE THE FINEST ALL-YOU-CAN-EAT CARNIVOROUS BUFFET.
YEAH. I'D LOVE THAT.
OKAY, I PROMISE. I'LL BE BACK FOR SURE.
HEE
HEE
SHI-NOBU-SAN.
WINCE

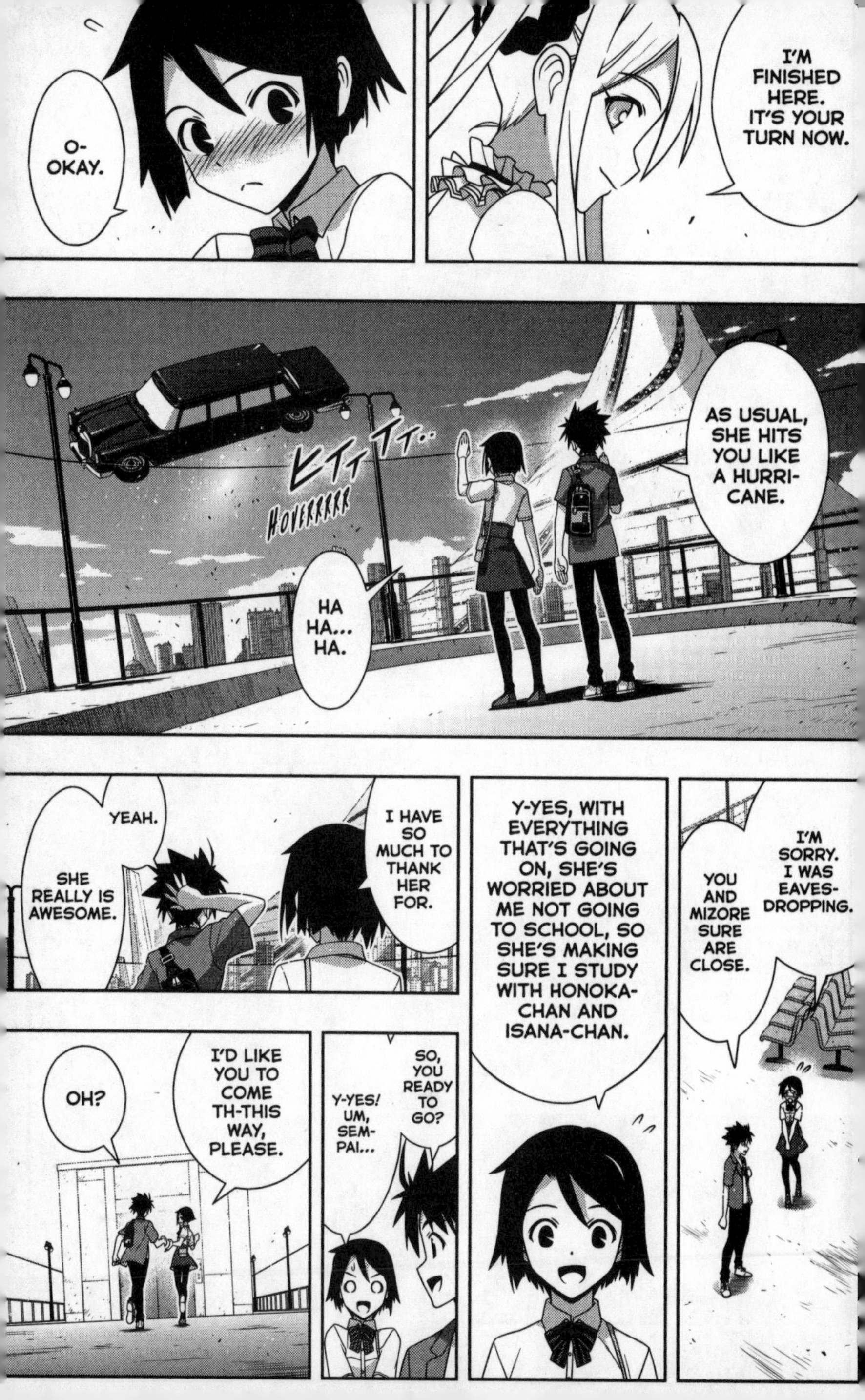
I'M FINISHED HERE. IT'S YOUR TURN NOW.
O-OKAY.
AS USUAL, SHE HITS YOU LIKE A HURRI-CANE.
HOVERRRRR
HA HA... HA.
I'M SORRY. I WAS EAVES-DROPPING.
YOU AND MIZORE SURE ARE CLOSE.
Y-YES, WITH EVERYTHING THAT'S GOING ON, SHE'S WORRIED ABOUT ME NOT GOING TO SCHOOL, SO SHE'S MAKING SURE I STUDY WITH HONOKA-CHAN AND ISANA-CHAN.
I HAVE SO MUCH TO THANK HER FOR.
YEAH.
SHE REALLY IS AWESOME.
SO, YOU READY TO GO?
Y-YES! UM, SEM-PAI...
I'D LIKE YOU TO COME TH-THIS WAY, PLEASE.
OH?

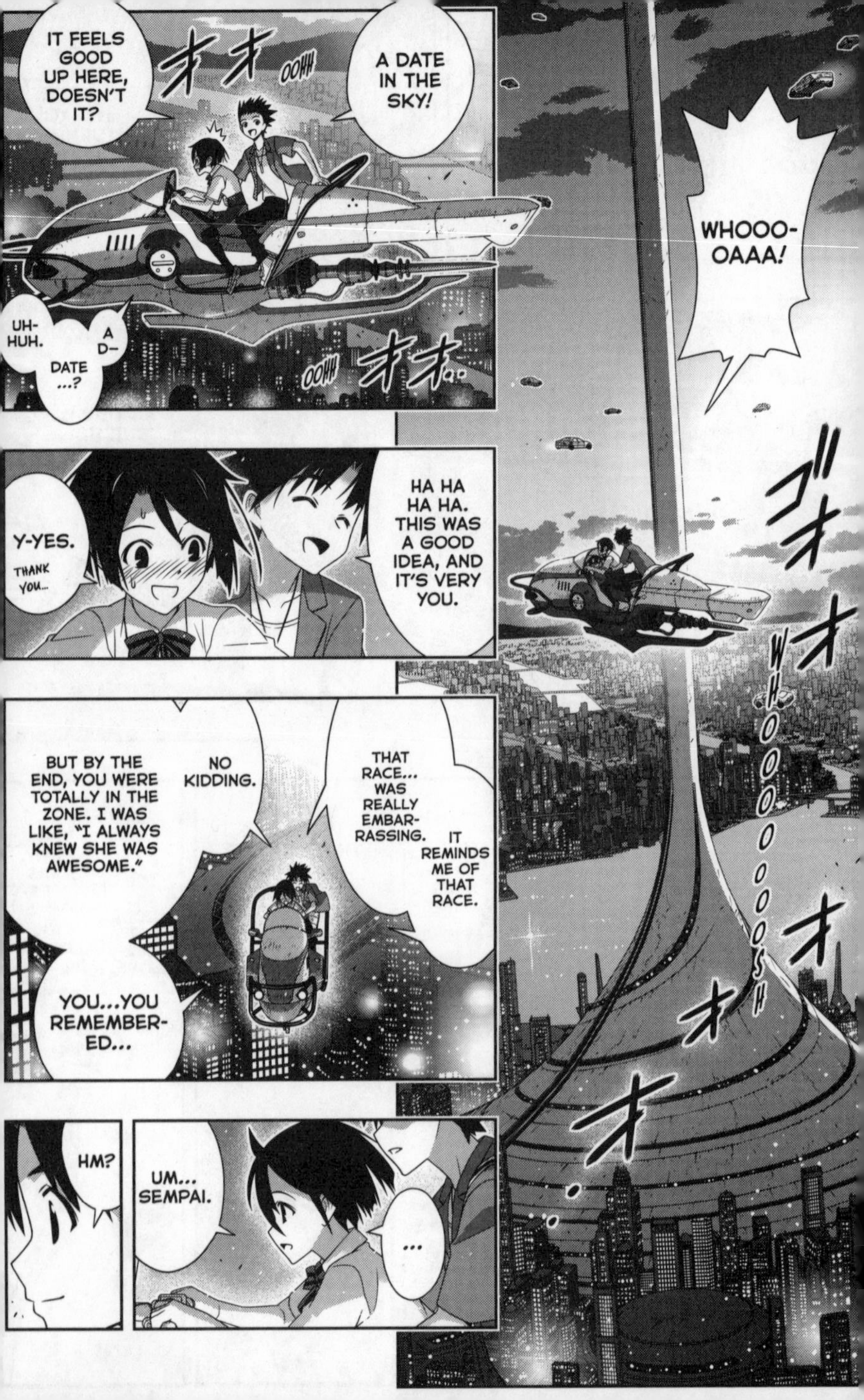
WHOOO-OAAA!
ゴオオオオ
WHOOOOOOOOOOSH
A DATE IN THE SKY!
IT FEELS GOOD UP HERE, DOESN'T IT?
オオ
OOHH
A D— DATE ...?
UH-HUH.
オオ..
OOHH
HA HA HA HA. THIS WAS A GOOD IDEA, AND IT'S VERY YOU.
Y-YES.
THANK YOU...
IT REMINDS ME OF THAT RACE.
THAT RACE... WAS REALLY EMBARRASSING.
NO KIDDING.
BUT BY THE END, YOU WERE TOTALLY IN THE ZONE. I WAS LIKE, "I ALWAYS KNEW SHE WAS AWESOME."
YOU...YOU REMEMBERED...
...
UM... SEMPAI.
HM?

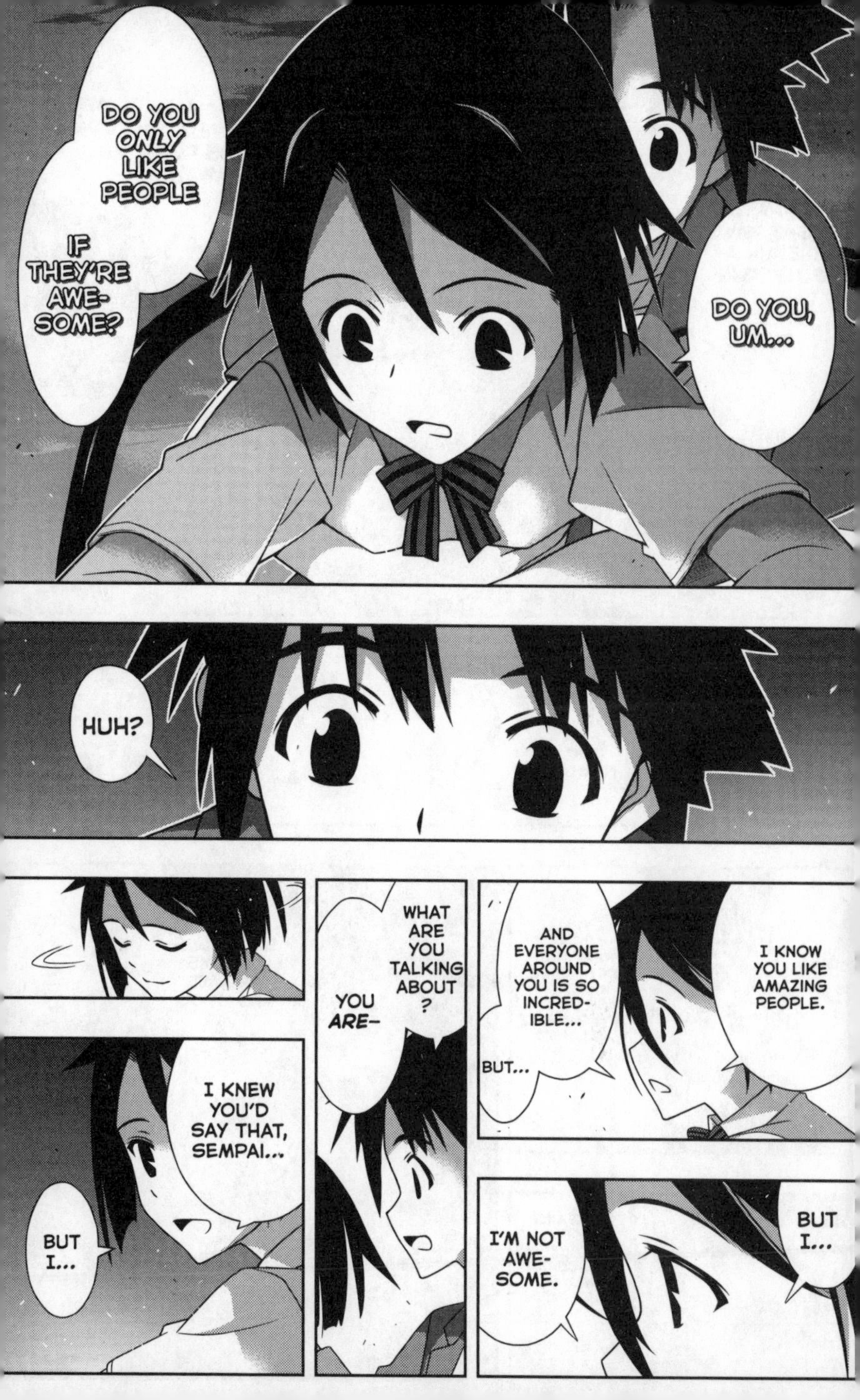
DO YOU, UM...
DO YOU ONLY LIKE PEOPLE
IF THEY'RE AWESOME?
HUH?
I KNOW YOU LIKE AMAZING PEOPLE.
AND EVERYONE AROUND YOU IS SO INCRED-IBLE...
BUT...
BUT I...
I'M NOT AWE-SOME.
WHAT ARE YOU TALKING ABOUT?
YOU *ARE*–
I KNEW YOU'D SAY THAT, SEMPAI...
BUT I...

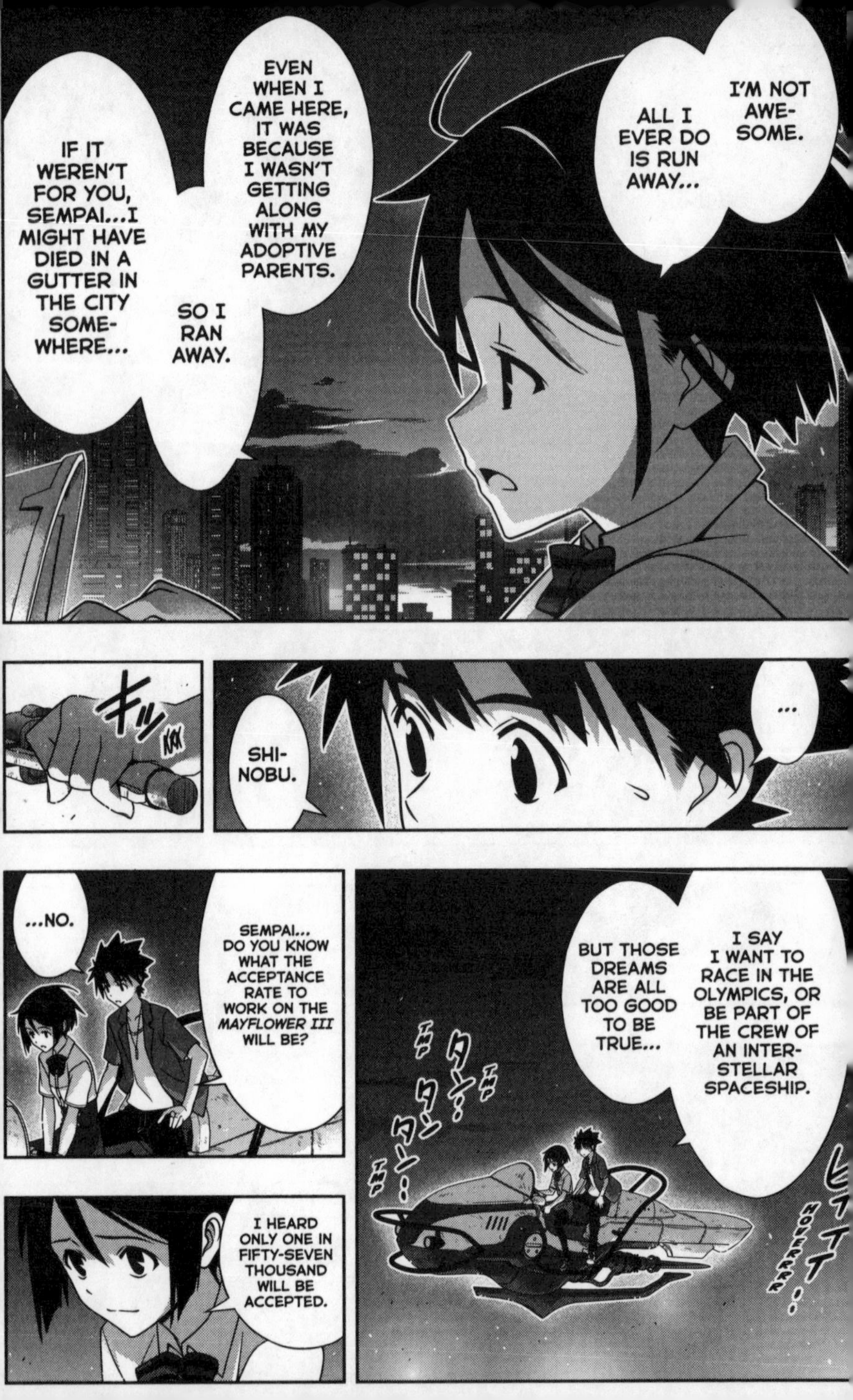
I'M NOT AWESOME.
ALL I EVER DO IS RUN AWAY...
EVEN WHEN I CAME HERE, IT WAS BECAUSE I WASN'T GETTING ALONG WITH MY ADOPTIVE PARENTS.
SO I RAN AWAY.
IF IT WEREN'T FOR YOU, SEMPAI...I MIGHT HAVE DIED IN A GUTTER IN THE CITY SOMEWHERE...
...
SHINOBU.
ギッ
KKK
I SAY I WANT TO RACE IN THE OLYMPICS, OR BE PART OF THE CREW OF AN INTERSTELLAR SPACESHIP.
BUT THOSE DREAMS ARE ALL TOO GOOD TO BE TRUE...
HOVERRR
SEMPAI... DO YOU KNOW WHAT THE ACCEPTANCE RATE TO WORK ON THE *MAYFLOWER III* WILL BE?
...NO.
I HEARD ONLY ONE IN FIFTY-SEVEN THOUSAND WILL BE ACCEPTED.

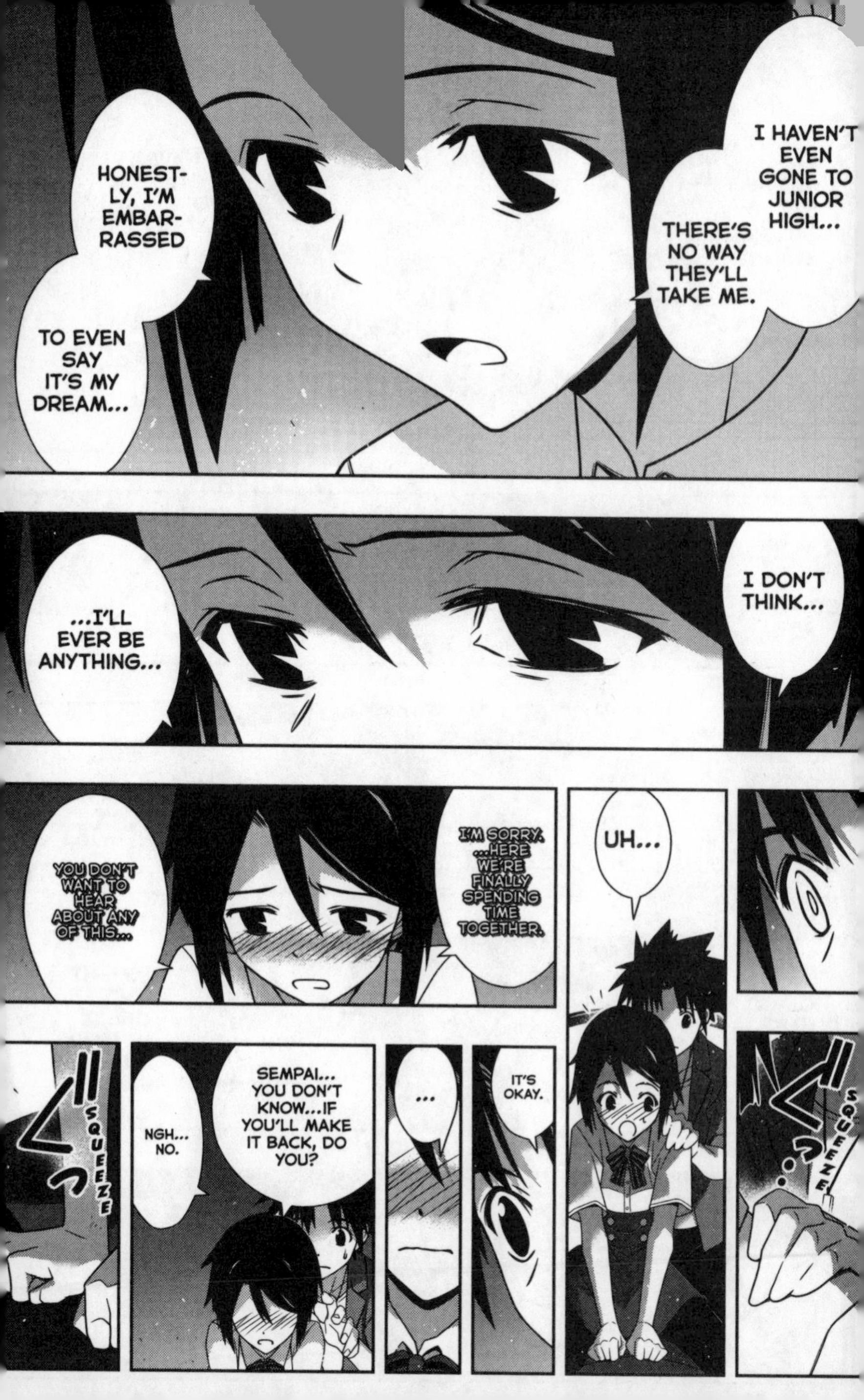
I HAVEN'T EVEN GONE TO JUNIOR HIGH...
THERE'S NO WAY THEY'LL TAKE ME.
HONESTLY, I'M EMBARRASSED
TO EVEN SAY IT'S MY DREAM...
I DON'T THINK...
...I'LL EVER BE ANYTHING...
SQUEEZE
UH...
I'M SORRY. ...HERE WE'RE FINALLY SPENDING TIME TOGETHER.
YOU DON'T WANT TO HEAR ABOUT ANY OF THIS...
IT'S OKAY.
...
SEMPAI... YOU DON'T KNOW...IF YOU'LL MAKE IT BACK, DO YOU?
NGH... NO.
SQUEEZE

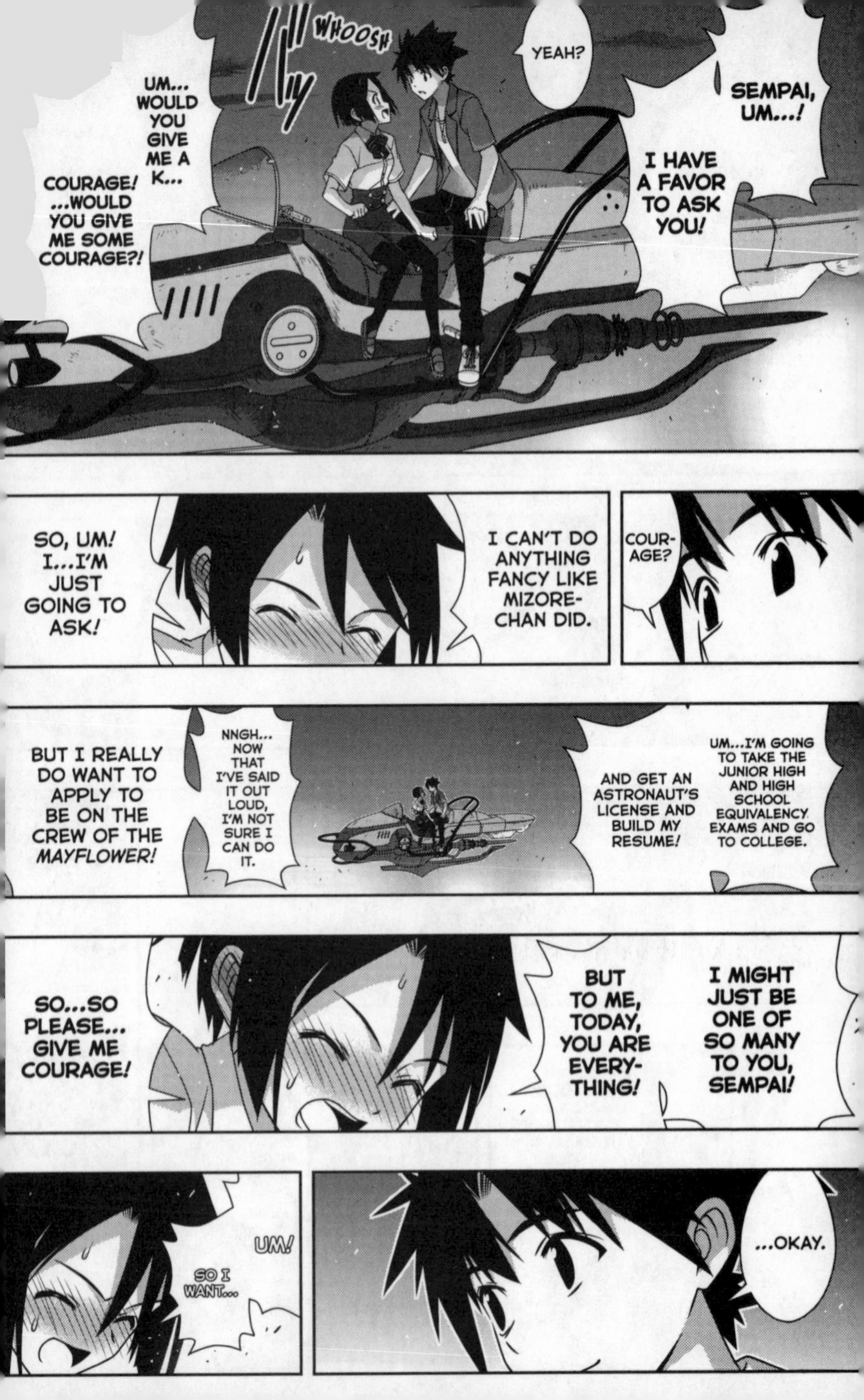
SEMPAI, UM...!
I HAVE A FAVOR TO ASK YOU!
YEAH?
WHOOSH
UM... WOULD YOU GIVE ME A K...
COURAGE! ...WOULD YOU GIVE ME SOME COURAGE?!
COUR-AGE?
I CAN'T DO ANYTHING FANCY LIKE MIZORE-CHAN DID.
SO, UM! I...I'M JUST GOING TO ASK!
UM...I'M GOING TO TAKE THE JUNIOR HIGH AND HIGH SCHOOL EQUIVALENCY EXAMS AND GO TO COLLEGE.
AND GET AN ASTRONAUT'S LICENSE AND BUILD MY RESUME!
NNGH... NOW THAT I'VE SAID IT OUT LOUD, I'M NOT SURE I CAN DO IT.
BUT I REALLY DO WANT TO APPLY TO BE ON THE CREW OF THE *MAYFLOWER*!
I MIGHT JUST BE ONE OF SO MANY TO YOU, SEMPAI!
BUT TO ME, TODAY, YOU ARE EVERY-THING!
SO...SO PLEASE... GIVE ME COURAGE!
...OKAY.
UM!
SO I WANT...

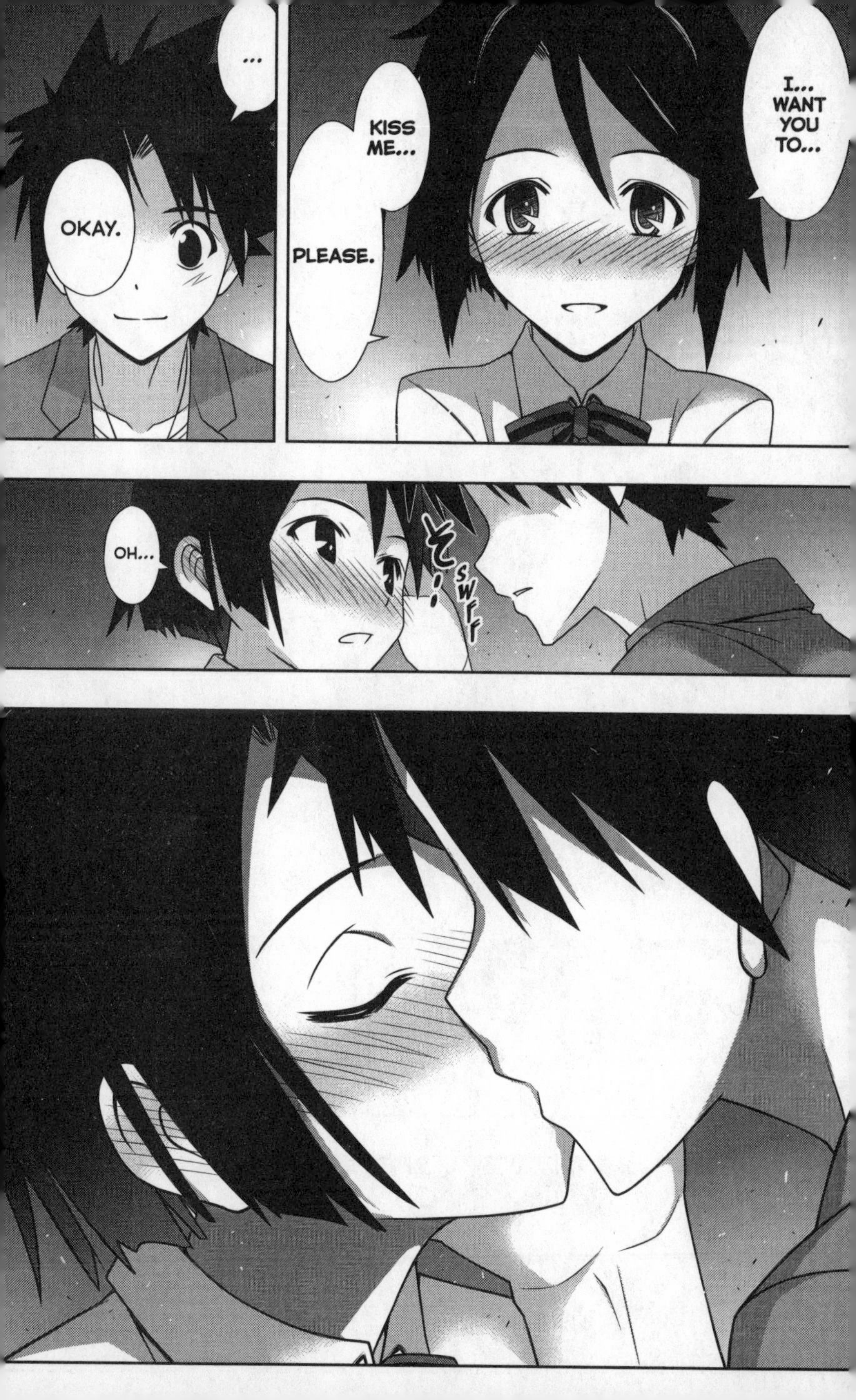
I... WANT YOU TO...
KISS ME...
PLEASE.
...
OKAY.
SWFF
OH...

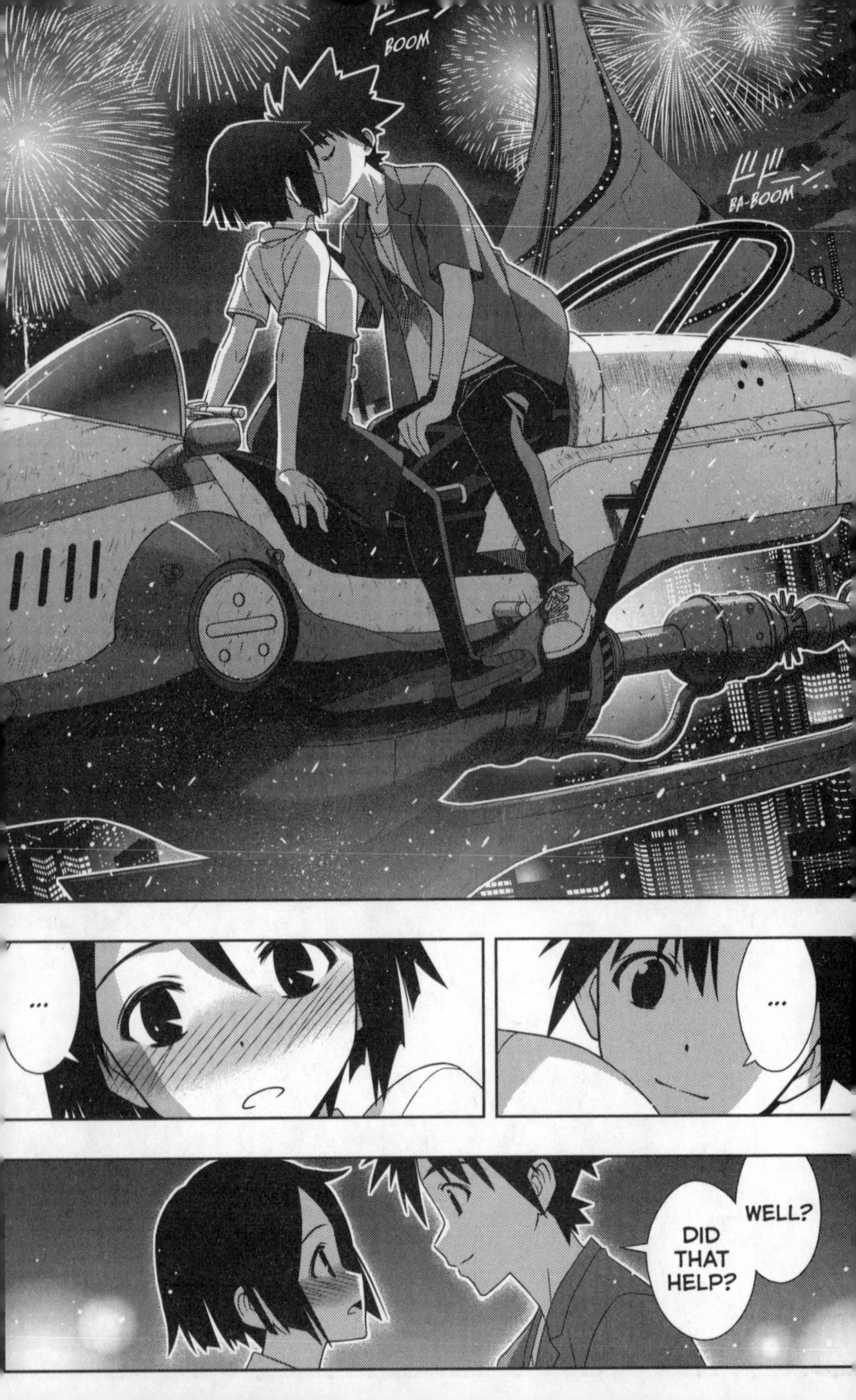

BOOM
BA-BOOM
...
...
WELL?
DID THAT HELP?

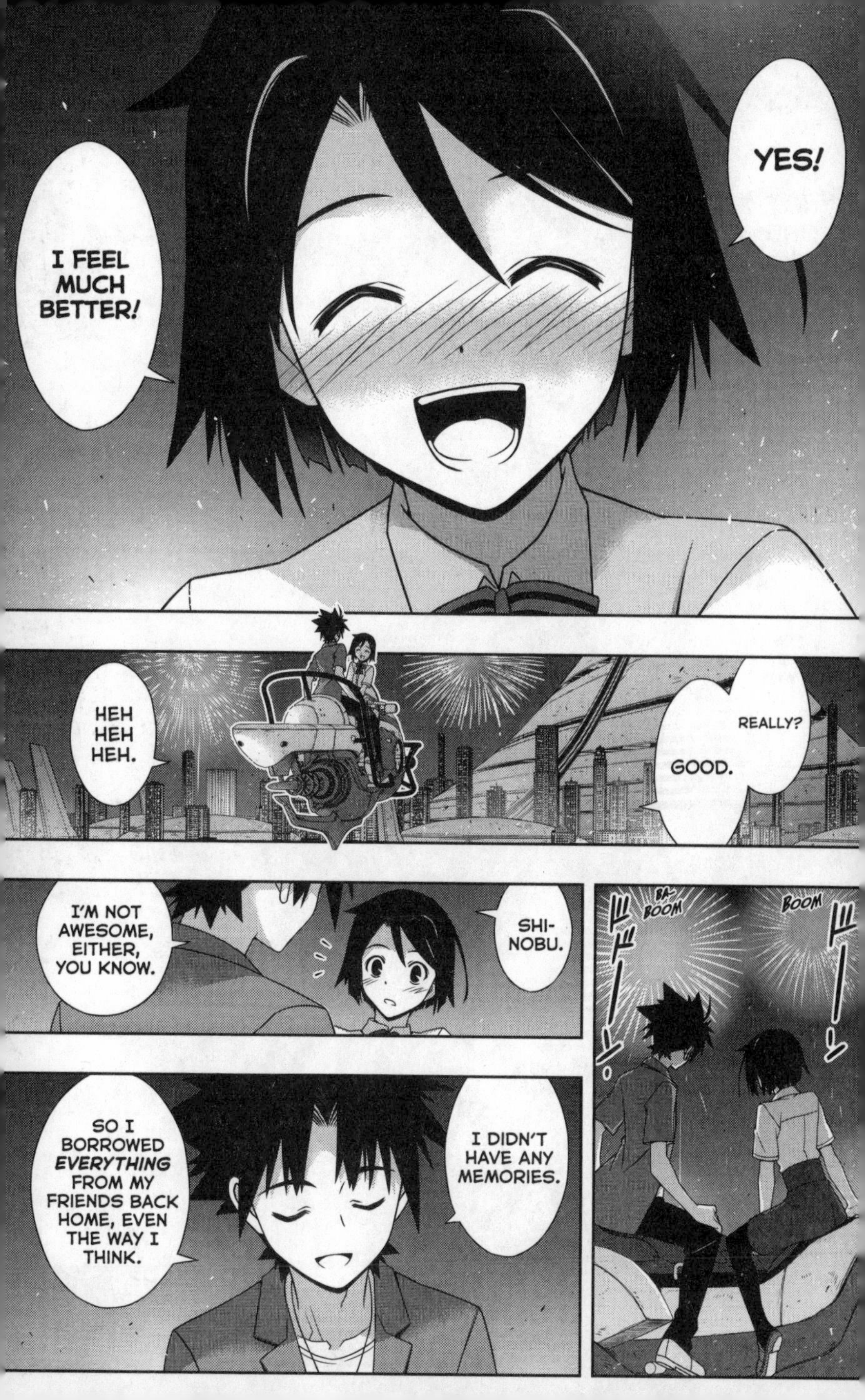
YES!
I FEEL MUCH BETTER!
REALLY?
GOOD.
HEH HEH HEH.
BOOM
BA-BOOM
SHI-NOBU.
I'M NOT AWESOME, EITHER, YOU KNOW.
I DIDN'T HAVE ANY MEMORIES.
SO I BORROWED *EVERYTHING* FROM MY FRIENDS BACK HOME, EVEN THE WAY I THINK.

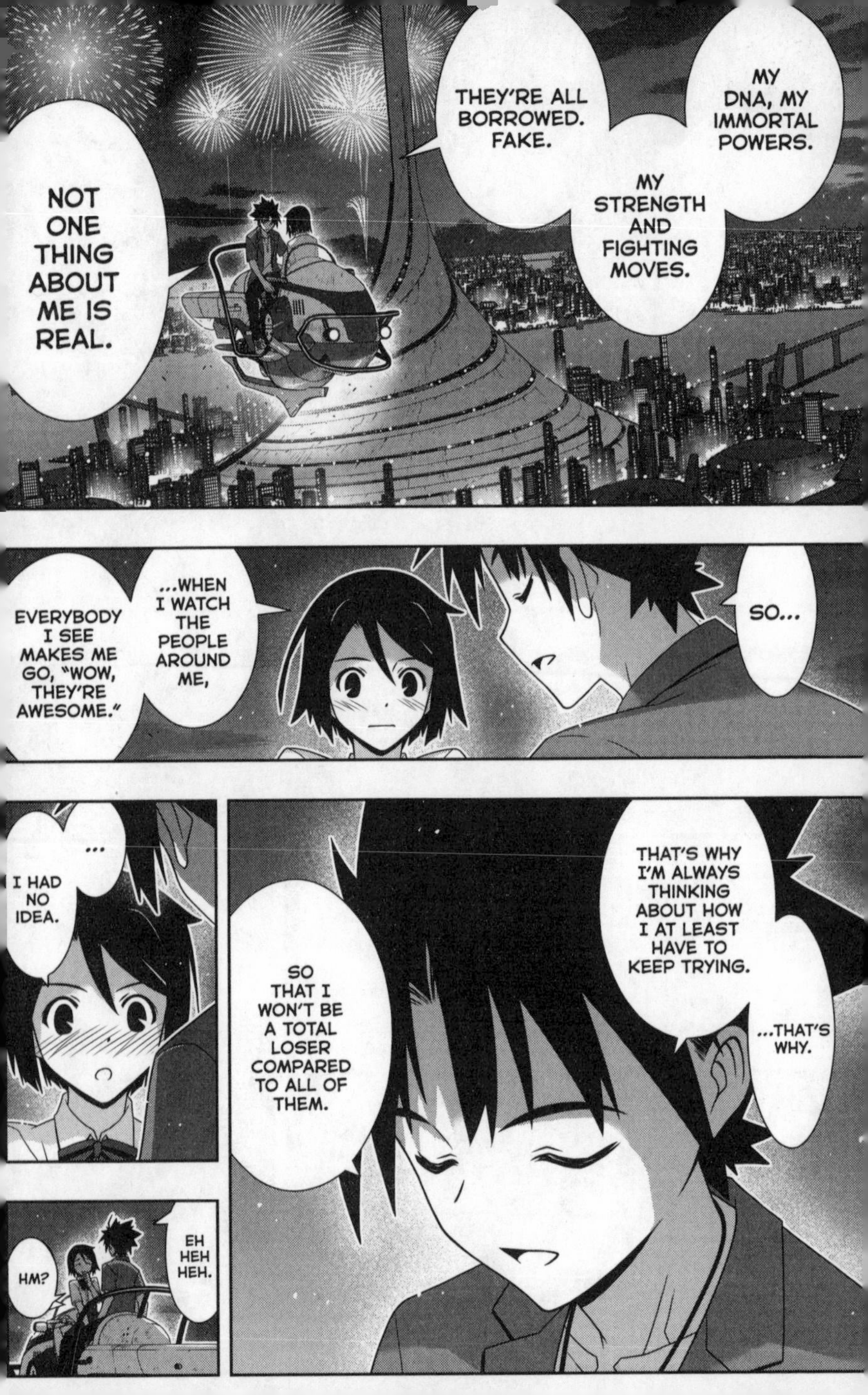
MY DNA, MY IMMORTAL POWERS.
MY STRENGTH AND FIGHTING MOVES.
THEY'RE ALL BORROWED. FAKE.
NOT ONE THING ABOUT ME IS REAL.
SO...
...WHEN I WATCH THE PEOPLE AROUND ME,
EVERYBODY I SEE MAKES ME GO, "WOW, THEY'RE AWESOME."
THAT'S WHY I'M ALWAYS THINKING ABOUT HOW I AT LEAST HAVE TO KEEP TRYING.
...THAT'S WHY.
SO THAT I WON'T BE A TOTAL LOSER COMPARED TO ALL OF THEM.
...
I HAD NO IDEA.
EH HEH HEH.
HM?

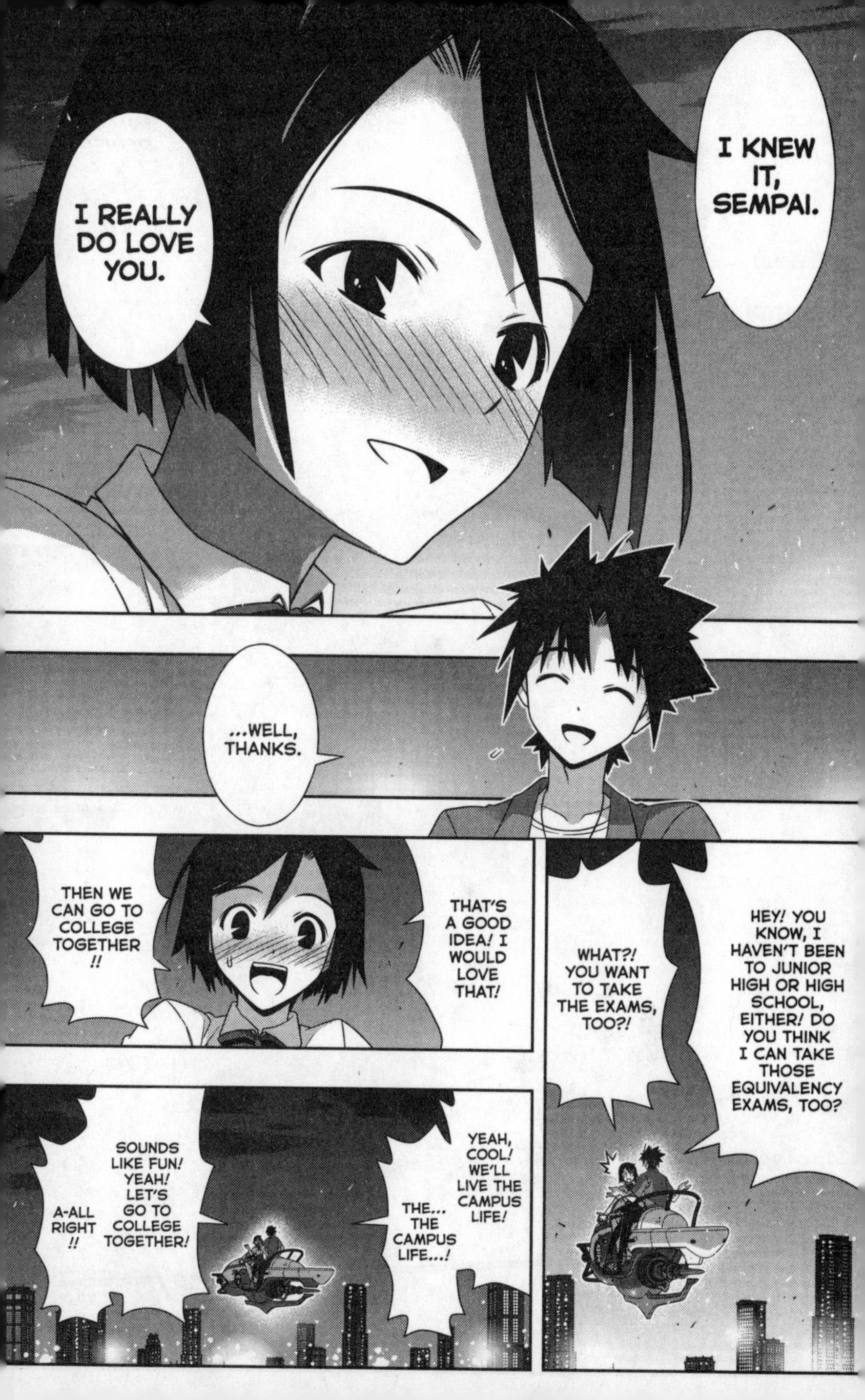
I KNEW IT, SEMPAI.
I REALLY DO LOVE YOU.
...WELL, THANKS.
HEY! YOU KNOW, I HAVEN'T BEEN TO JUNIOR HIGH OR HIGH SCHOOL, EITHER! DO YOU THINK I CAN TAKE THOSE EQUIVALENCY EXAMS, TOO?
WHAT?! YOU WANT TO TAKE THE EXAMS, TOO?!
THAT'S A GOOD IDEA! I WOULD LOVE THAT!
THEN WE CAN GO TO COLLEGE TOGETHER!!
YEAH, COOL! WE'LL LIVE THE CAMPUS LIFE!
THE... THE CAMPUS LIFE...!
SOUNDS LIKE FUN! YEAH! LET'S GO TO COLLEGE TOGETHER!
A-ALL RIGHT!!

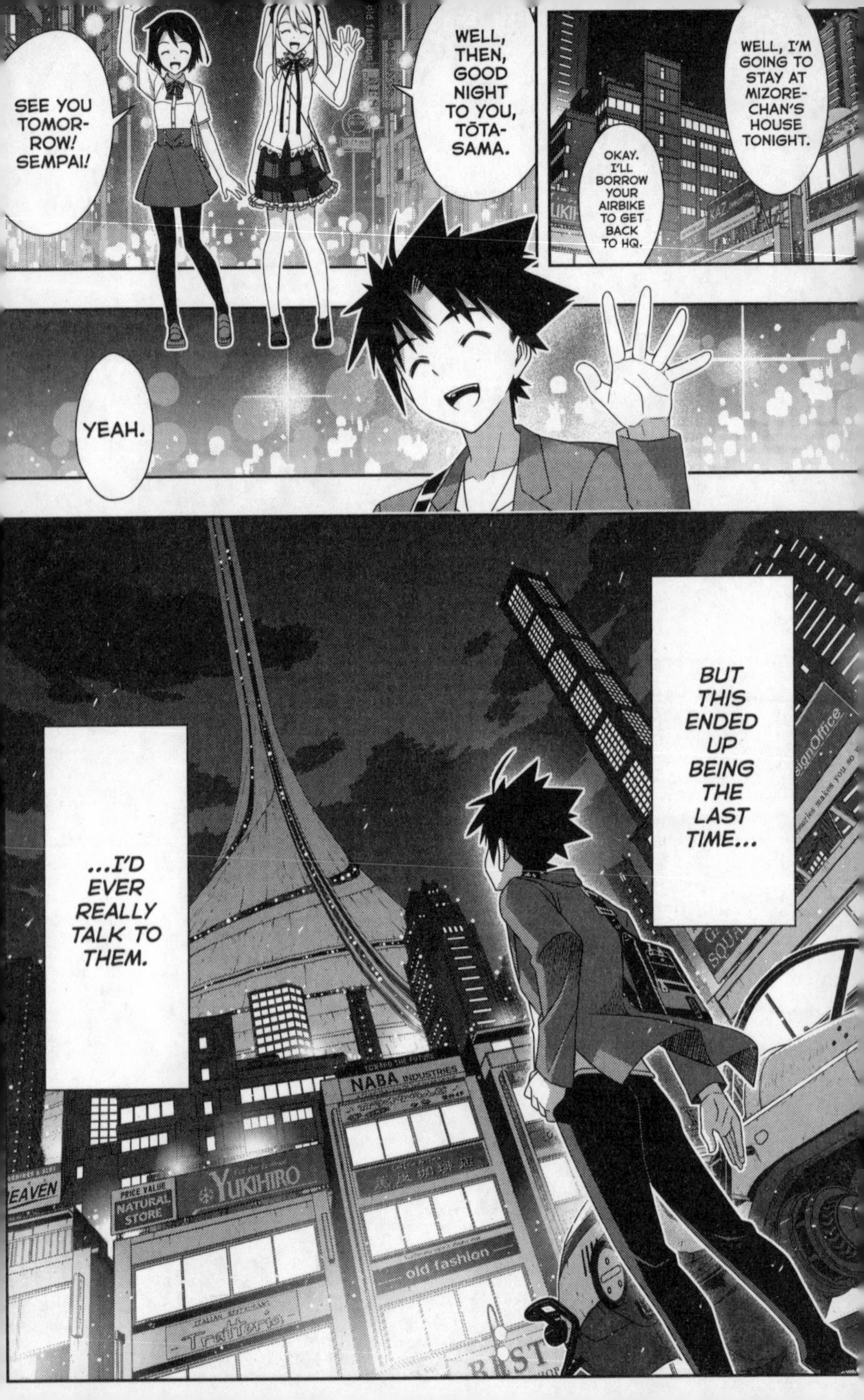
WELL, I'M GOING TO STAY AT MIZORE-CHAN'S HOUSE TONIGHT.
OKAY. I'LL BORROW YOUR AIRBIKE TO GET BACK TO HQ.
WELL, THEN, GOOD NIGHT TO YOU, TŌTA-SAMA.
SEE YOU TOMOR-ROW! SEMPAI!
YEAH.
BUT THIS ENDED UP BEING THE LAST TIME...
...I'D EVER REALLY TALK TO THEM.
NABA INDUSTRIES
YUKIHIRO
PRICE VALUE NATURAL STORE
EAVEN
old fashion

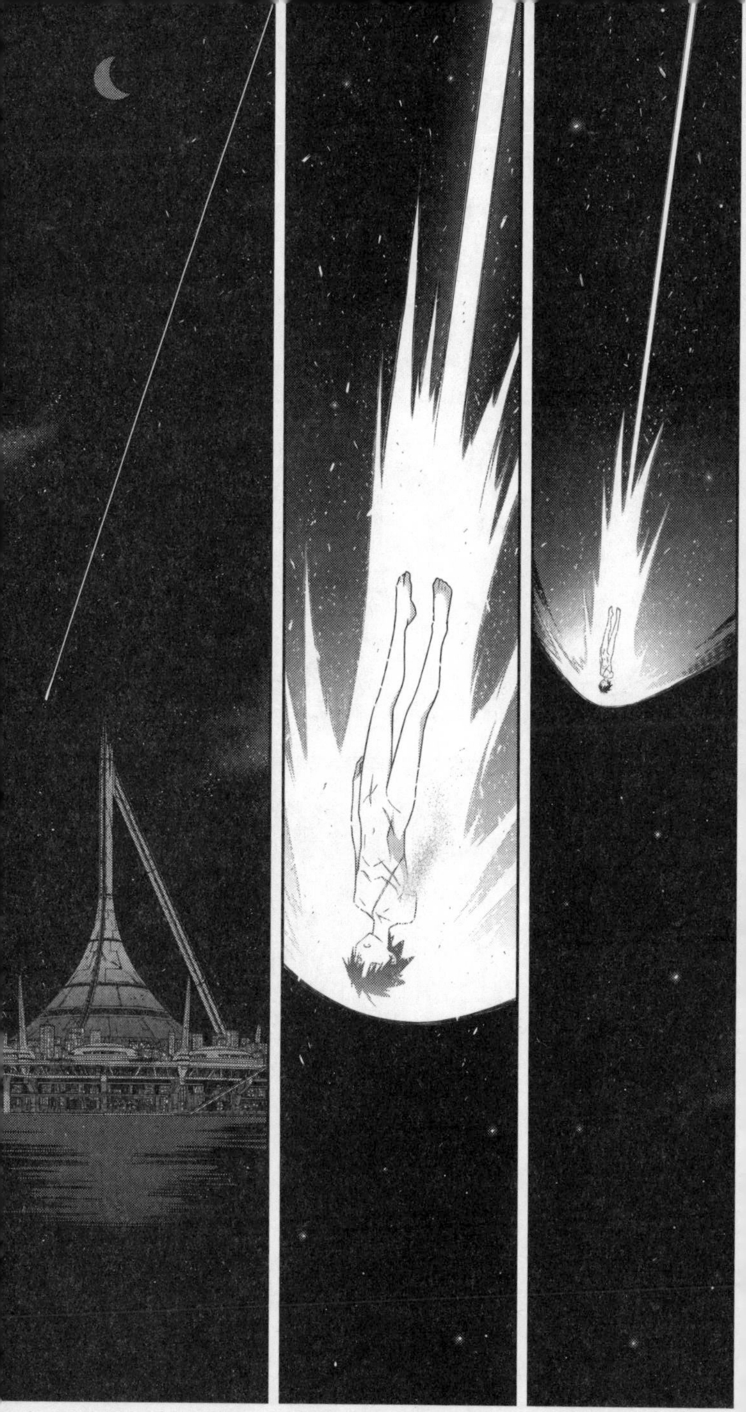

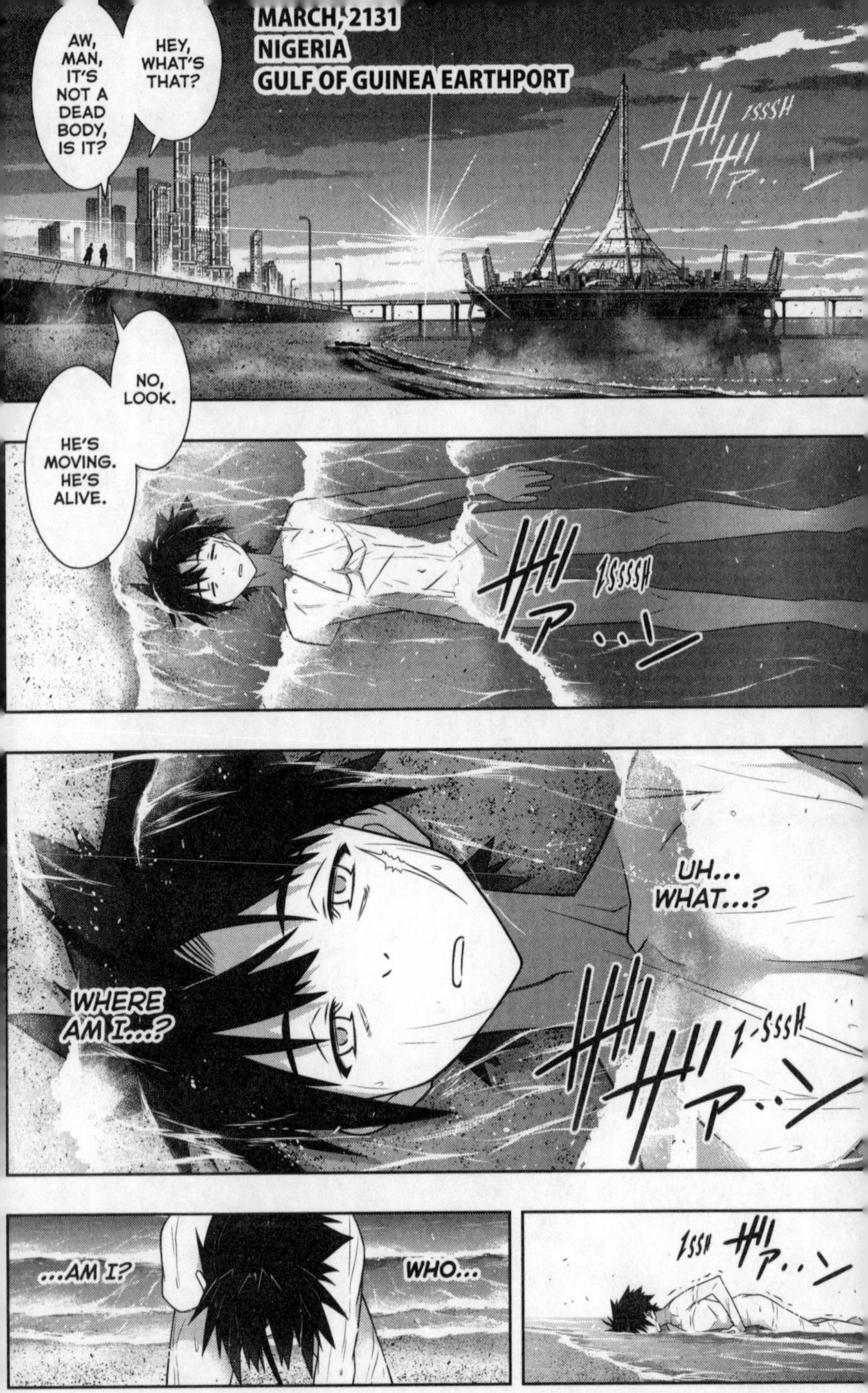
MARCH, 2131
NIGERIA
GULF OF GUINEA EARTHPORT
HEY, WHAT'S THAT?
AW, MAN, IT'S NOT A DEAD BODY, IS IT?
NO, LOOK.
HE'S MOVING. HE'S ALIVE.
UH... WHAT...?
WHERE AM I...?
WHO...
...AM I?

STAGE 175: 2131

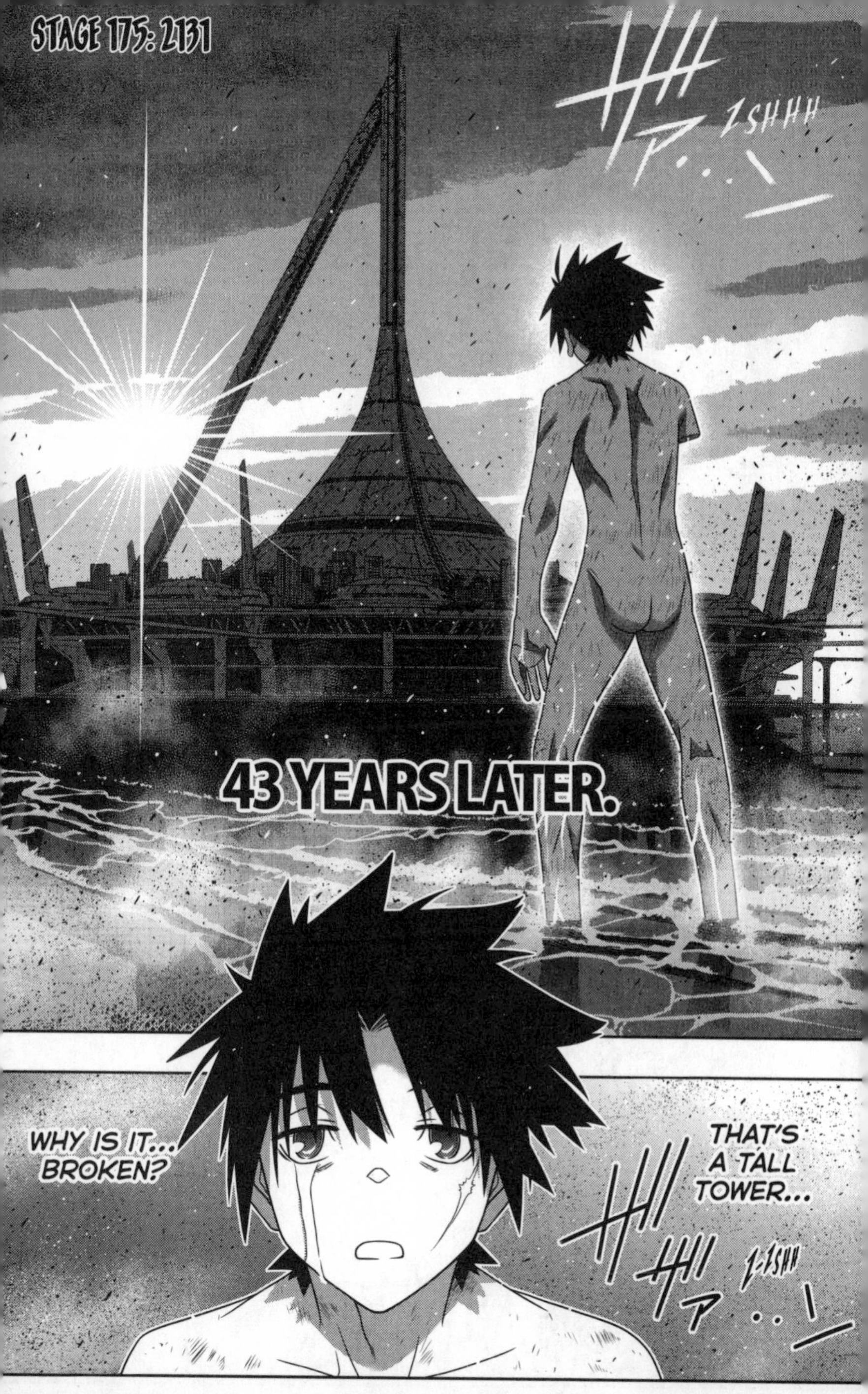

ZSHHH
43 YEARS LATER.
THAT'S A TALL TOWER...
Z-ZSHH
WHY IS IT... BROKEN?

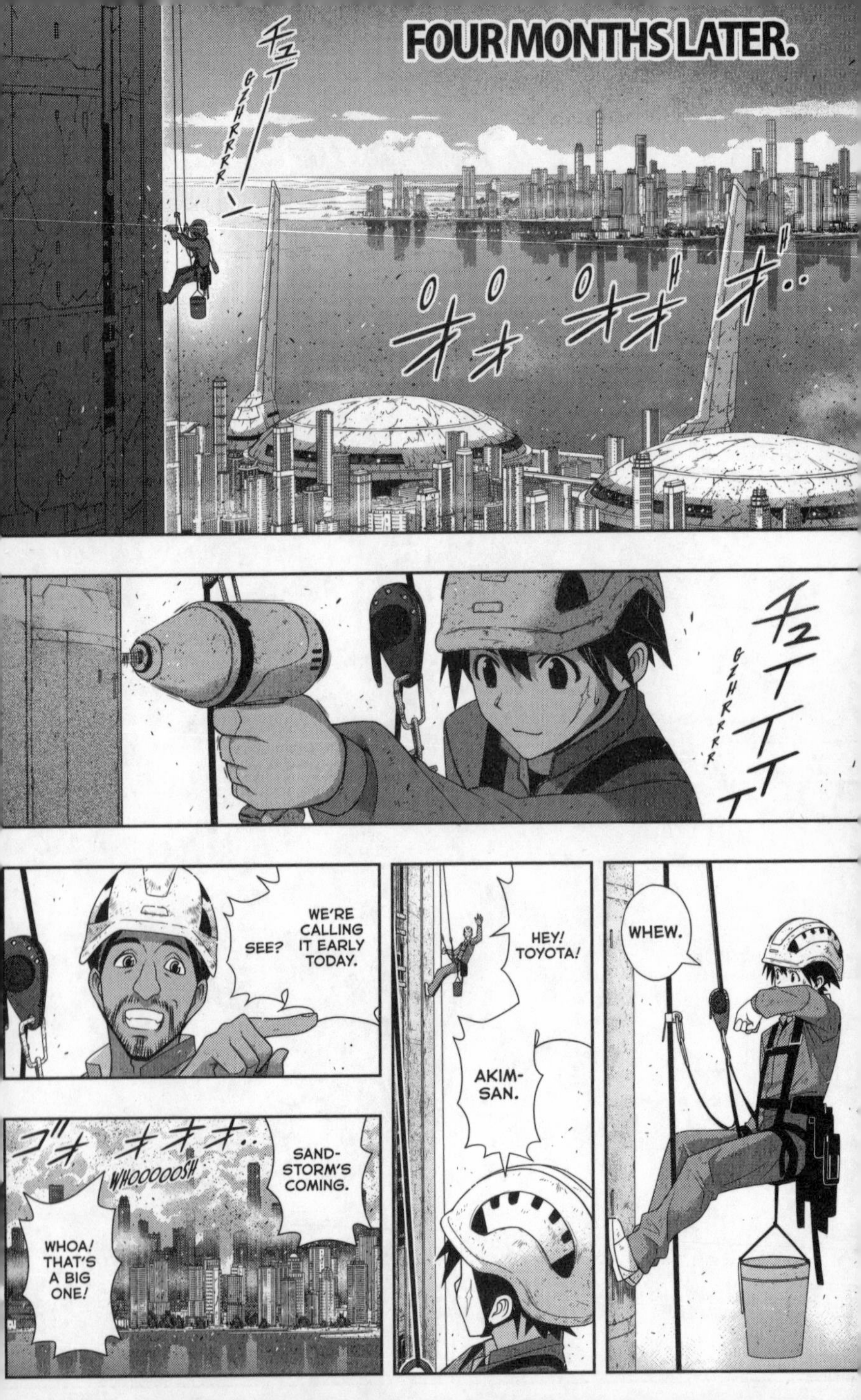

FOUR MONTHS LATER.
GZHRRRR
GZHRRRR
WHEW.
HEY! TOYOTA!
AKIM-SAN.
WE'RE CALLING IT EARLY TODAY.
SEE?
SAND-STORM'S COMING.
WHOOOOOSH
WHOA! THAT'S A BIG ONE!

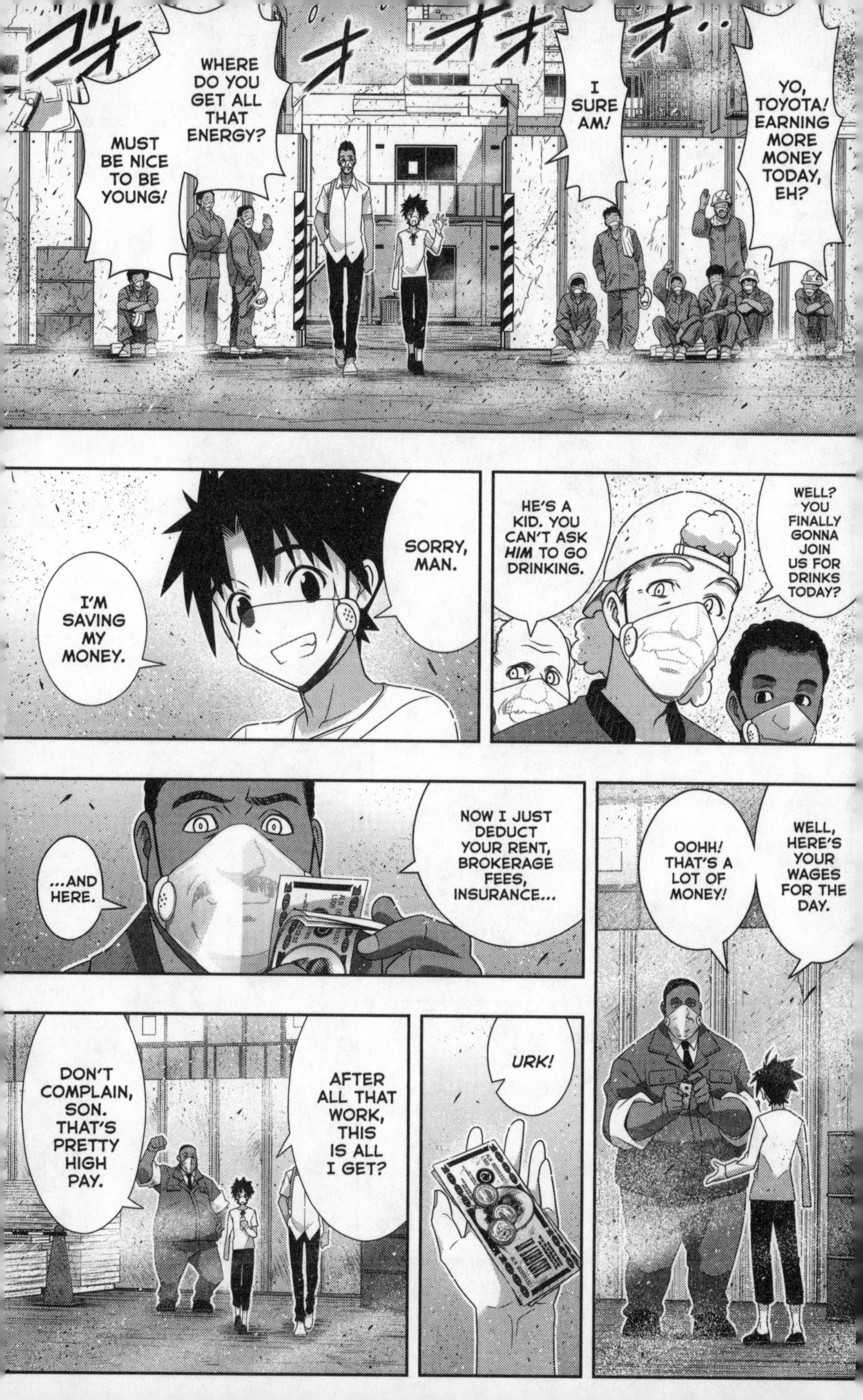

ゴオオオオオ‥
YO, TOYOTA! EARNING MORE MONEY TODAY, EH?
I SURE AM!
WHERE DO YOU GET ALL THAT ENERGY?
MUST BE NICE TO BE YOUNG!
WELL? YOU FINALLY GONNA JOIN US FOR DRINKS TODAY?
HE'S A KID. YOU CAN'T ASK *HIM* TO GO DRINKING.
SORRY, MAN.
I'M SAVING MY MONEY.
WELL, HERE'S YOUR WAGES FOR THE DAY.
OOHH! THAT'S A LOT OF MONEY!
NOW I JUST DEDUCT YOUR RENT, BROKERAGE FEES, INSURANCE...
...AND HERE.
URK!
AFTER ALL THAT WORK, THIS IS ALL I GET?
DON'T COMPLAIN, SON. THAT'S PRETTY HIGH PAY.

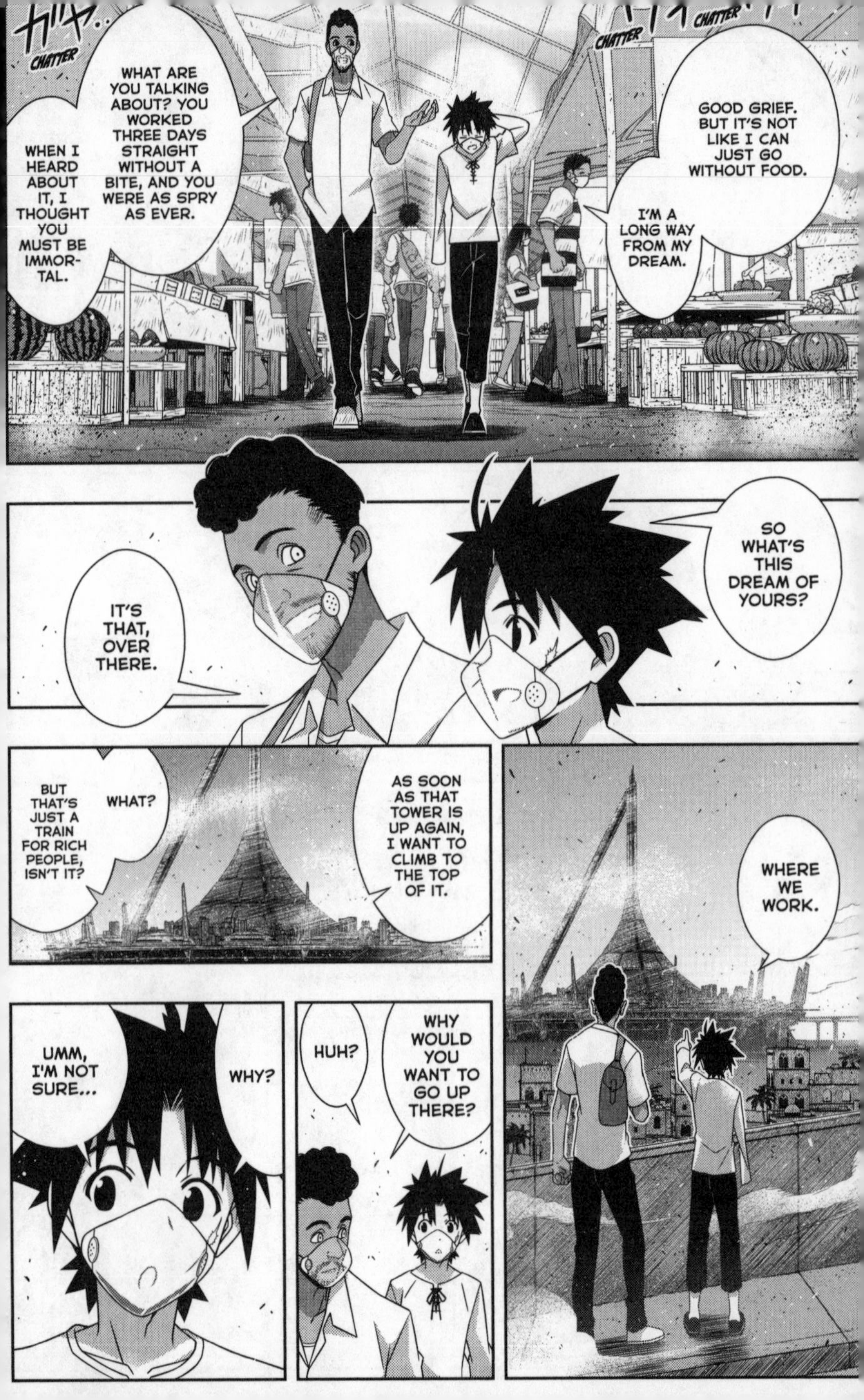
CHATTER
CHATTER
GOOD GRIEF. BUT IT'S NOT LIKE I CAN JUST GO WITHOUT FOOD.
I'M A LONG WAY FROM MY DREAM.
WHAT ARE YOU TALKING ABOUT? YOU WORKED THREE DAYS STRAIGHT WITHOUT A BITE, AND YOU WERE AS SPRY AS EVER.
WHEN I HEARD ABOUT IT, I THOUGHT YOU MUST BE IMMORTAL.
CHATTER
SO WHAT'S THIS DREAM OF YOURS?
IT'S THAT, OVER THERE.
WHERE WE WORK.
AS SOON AS THAT TOWER IS UP AGAIN, I WANT TO CLIMB TO THE TOP OF IT.
WHAT?
BUT THAT'S JUST A TRAIN FOR RICH PEOPLE, ISN'T IT?
WHY WOULD YOU WANT TO GO UP THERE?
HUH?
WHY?
UMM, I'M NOT SURE...

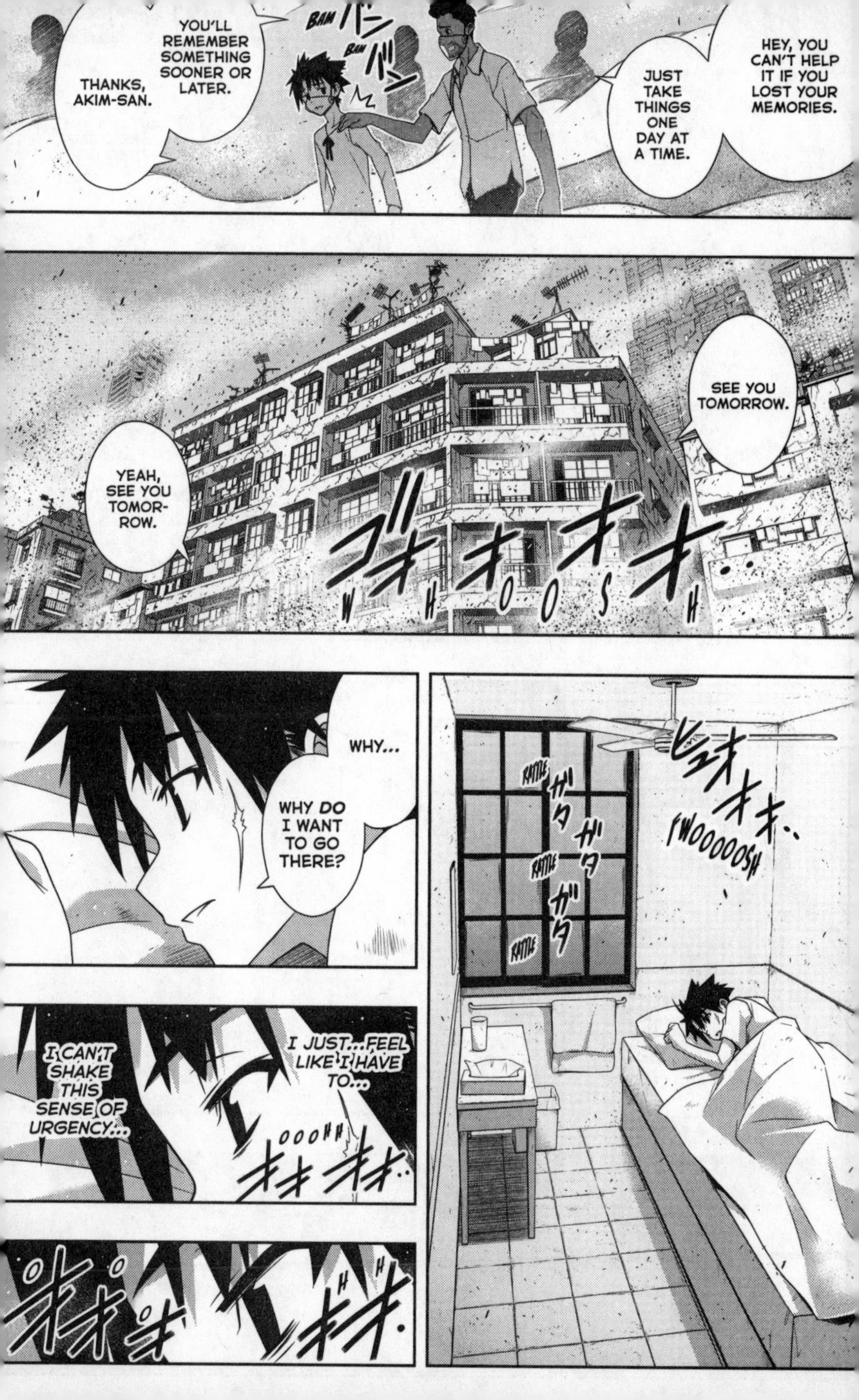
HEY, YOU CAN'T HELP IT IF YOU LOST YOUR MEMORIES.
JUST TAKE THINGS ONE DAY AT A TIME.
BAM
BAM
YOU'LL REMEMBER SOMETHING SOONER OR LATER.
THANKS, AKIM-SAN.
SEE YOU TOMORROW.
YEAH, SEE YOU TOMOR-ROW.
WHOOSH
WOOOOOOSH
RATTLE
RATTLE
RATTLE
WHY...
WHY DO I WANT TO GO THERE?
I JUST...FEEL LIKE I HAVE TO...
I CAN'T SHAKE THIS SENSE OF URGENCY...
OOOOHH

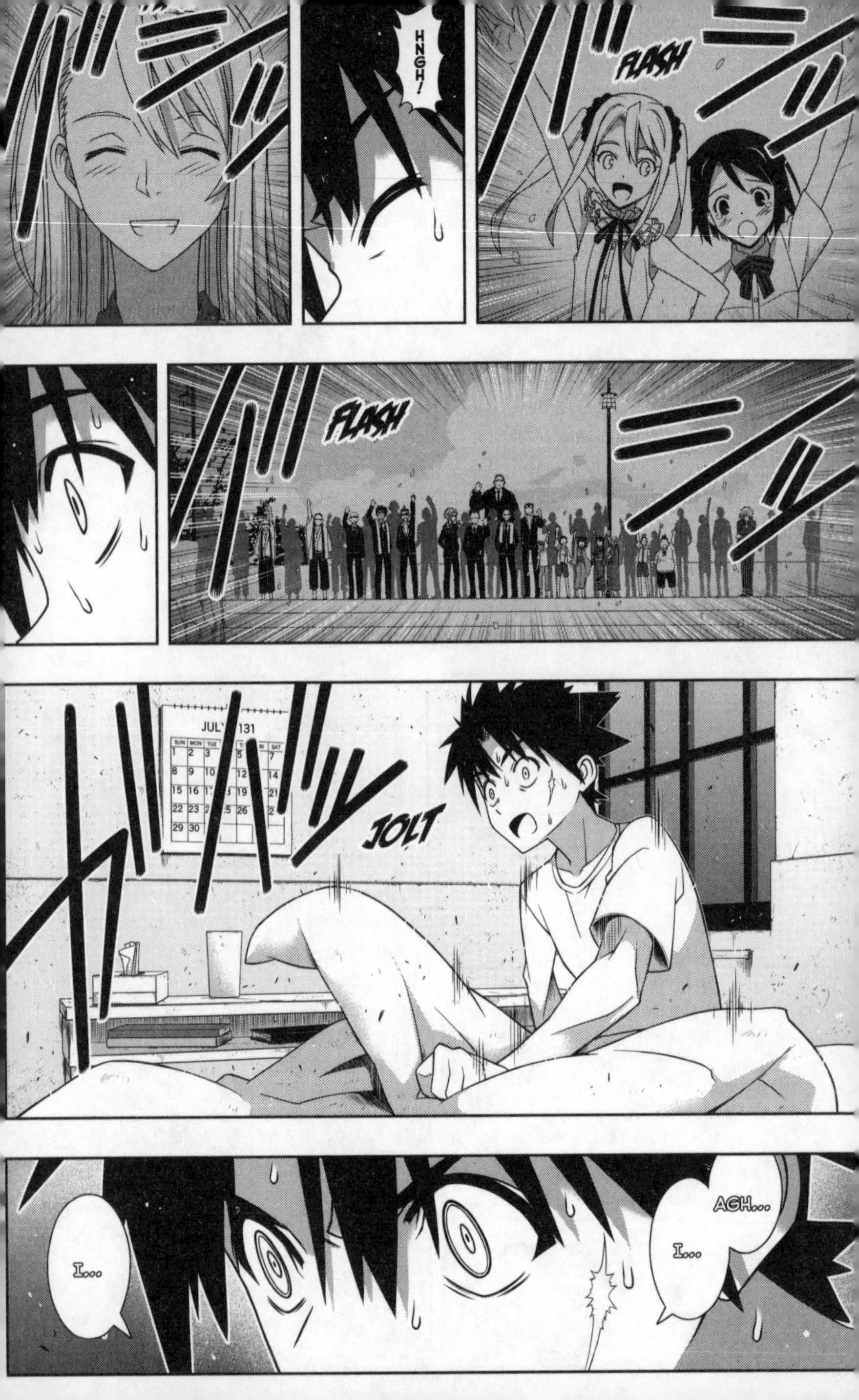
FLASH
HNGH!
FLASH
JOLT
AGH...
I...
I...

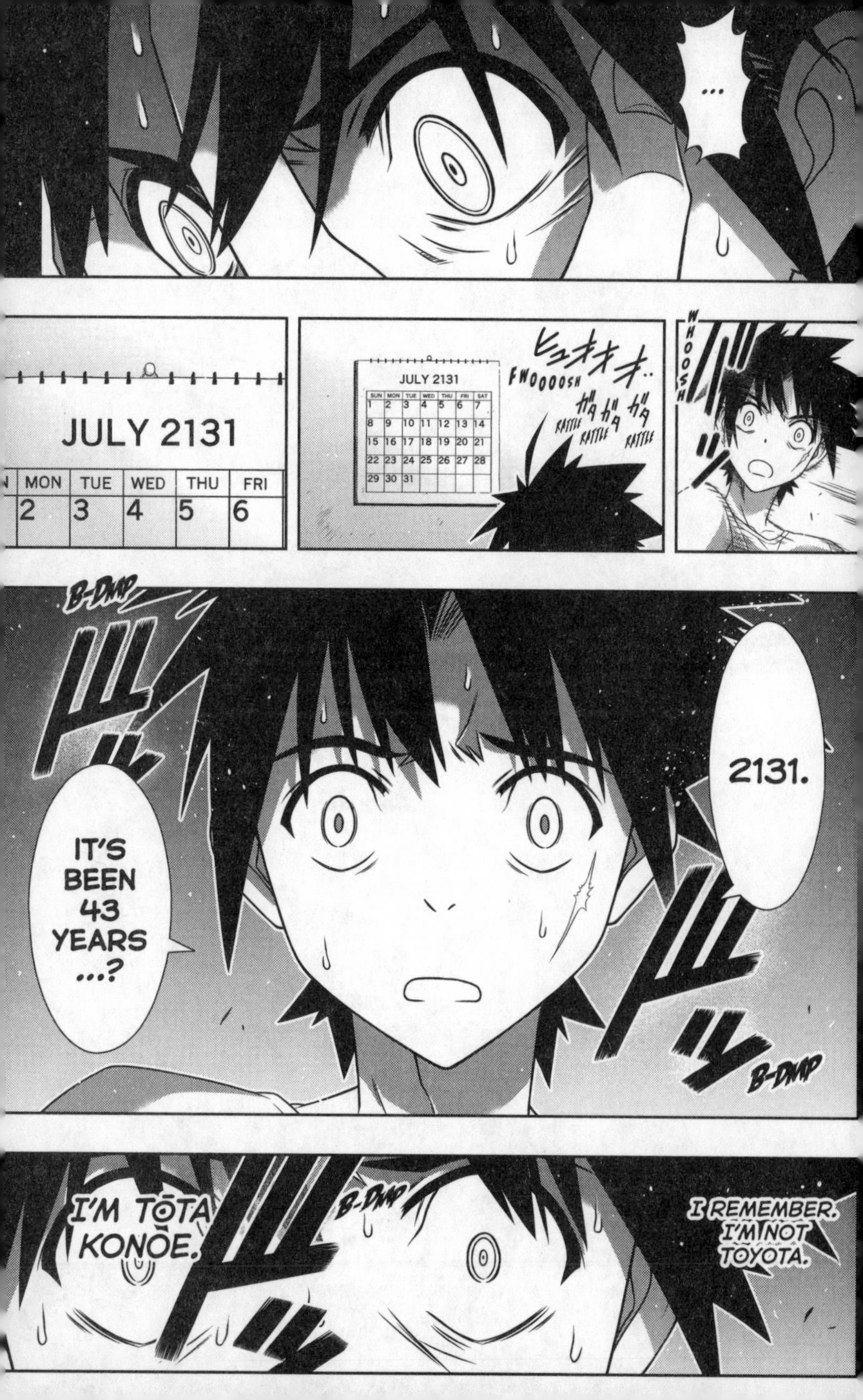
...
WHOOSH
ヒュオオオ…
FWOOOOSH
ガタガタガタ
RATTLE RATTLE RATTLE
JULY 2131
SUN MON TUE WED THU FRI SAT
1 2 3 4 5 6 7
8 9 10 11 12 13 14
15 16 17 18 19 20 21
22 23 24 25 26 27 28
29 30 31
JULY 2131
MON TUE WED THU FRI
2 3 4 5 6
B-DMP
2131.
IT'S BEEN 43 YEARS ...?
B-DMP
I REMEMBER. I'M NOT TOYOTA.
B-DMP
I'M TŌTA KONOE.

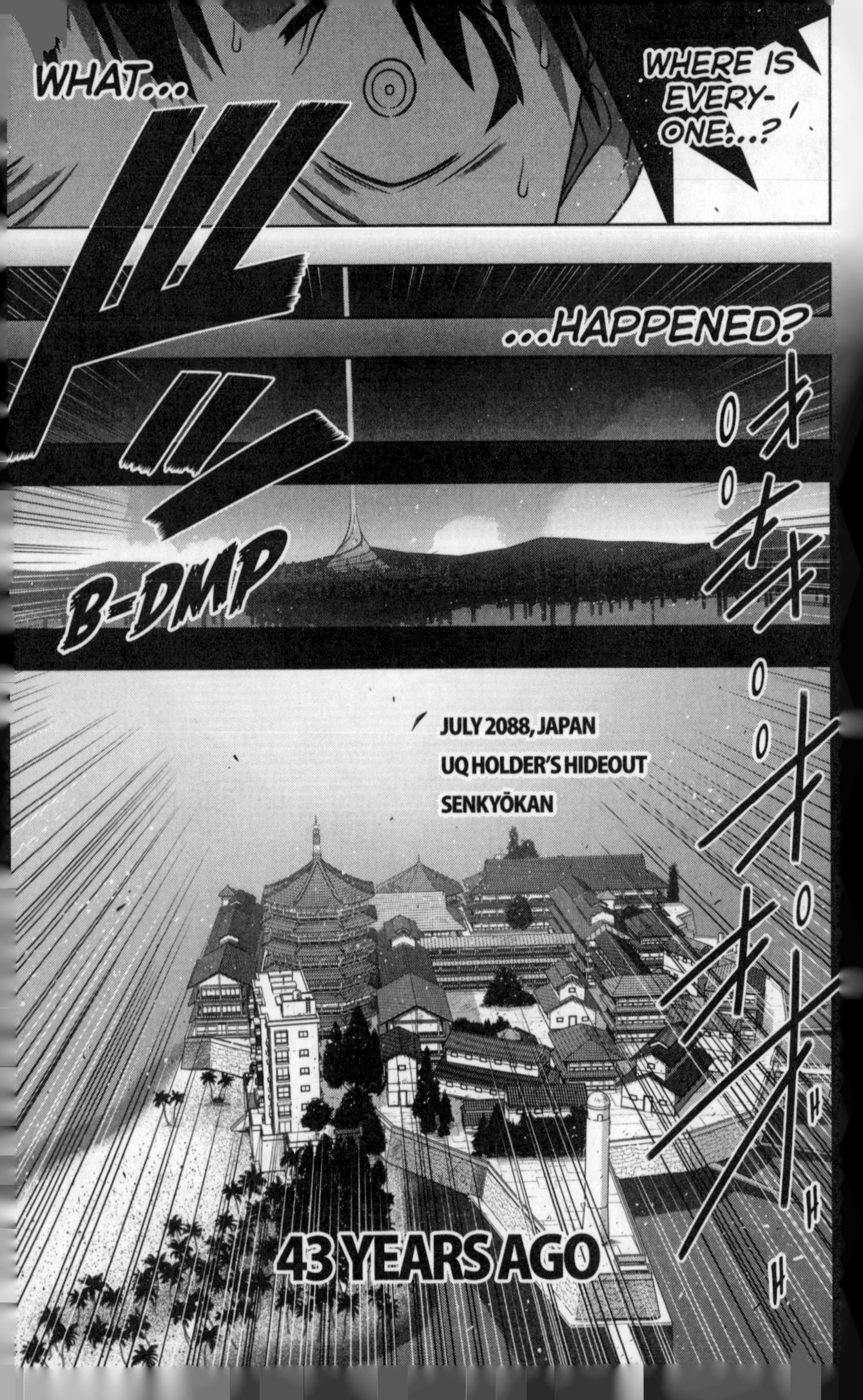
WHERE IS EVERY-ONE...?
WHAT...
...HAPPENED?
B-DMP
JULY 2088, JAPAN
UQ HOLDER'S HIDEOUT
SENKYŌKAN
43 YEARS AGO

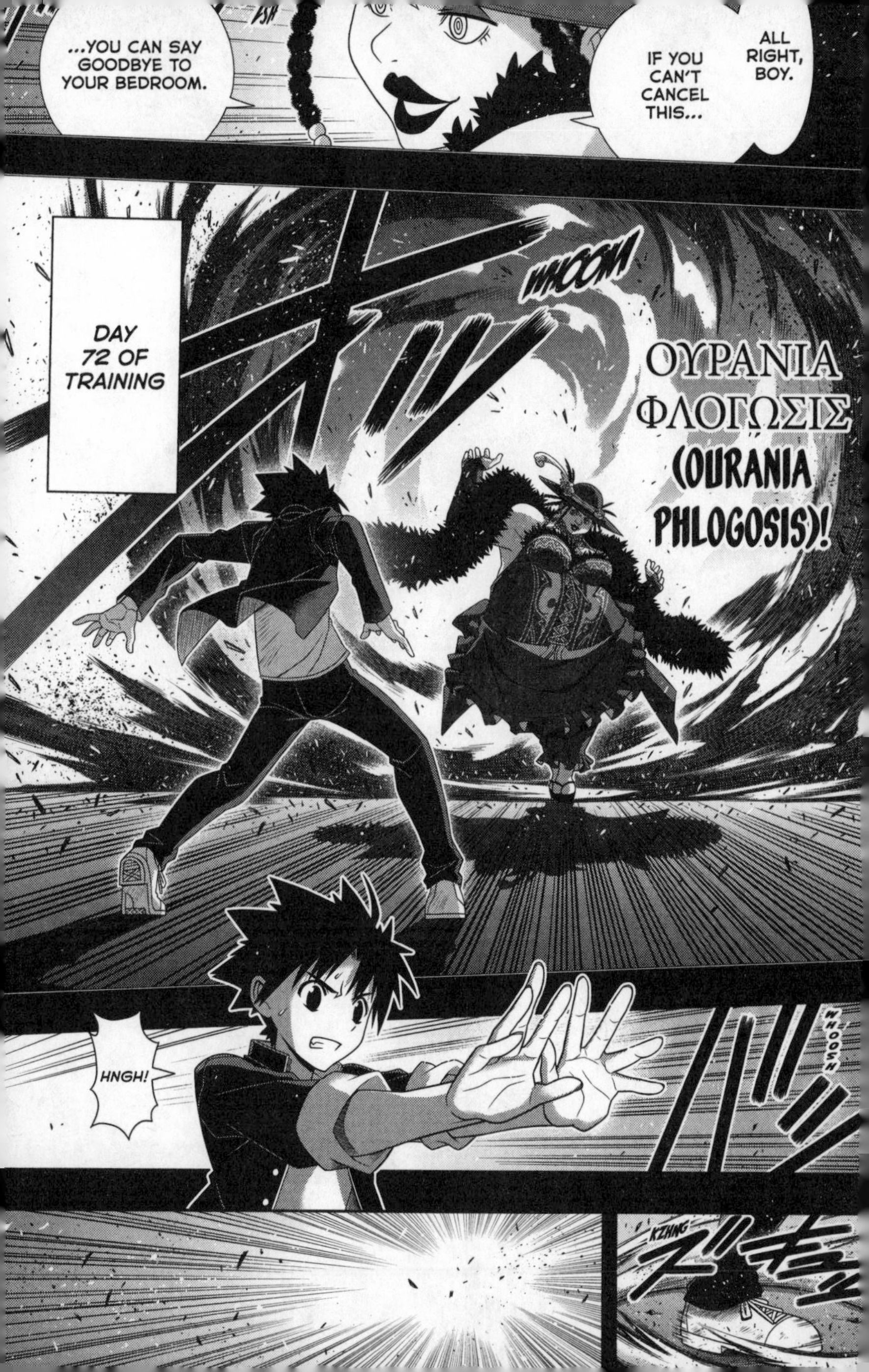
ALL RIGHT, BOY.
IF YOU CAN'T CANCEL THIS...
FSH
...YOU CAN SAY GOODBYE TO YOUR BEDROOM.
WHOOM
ΟΥΡΑΝΙΑ ΦΛΟΓΩΣΙΣ (OURANIA PHLOGOSIS)!
DAY 72 OF TRAINING
WHOOSH
HNGH!
KZHNG

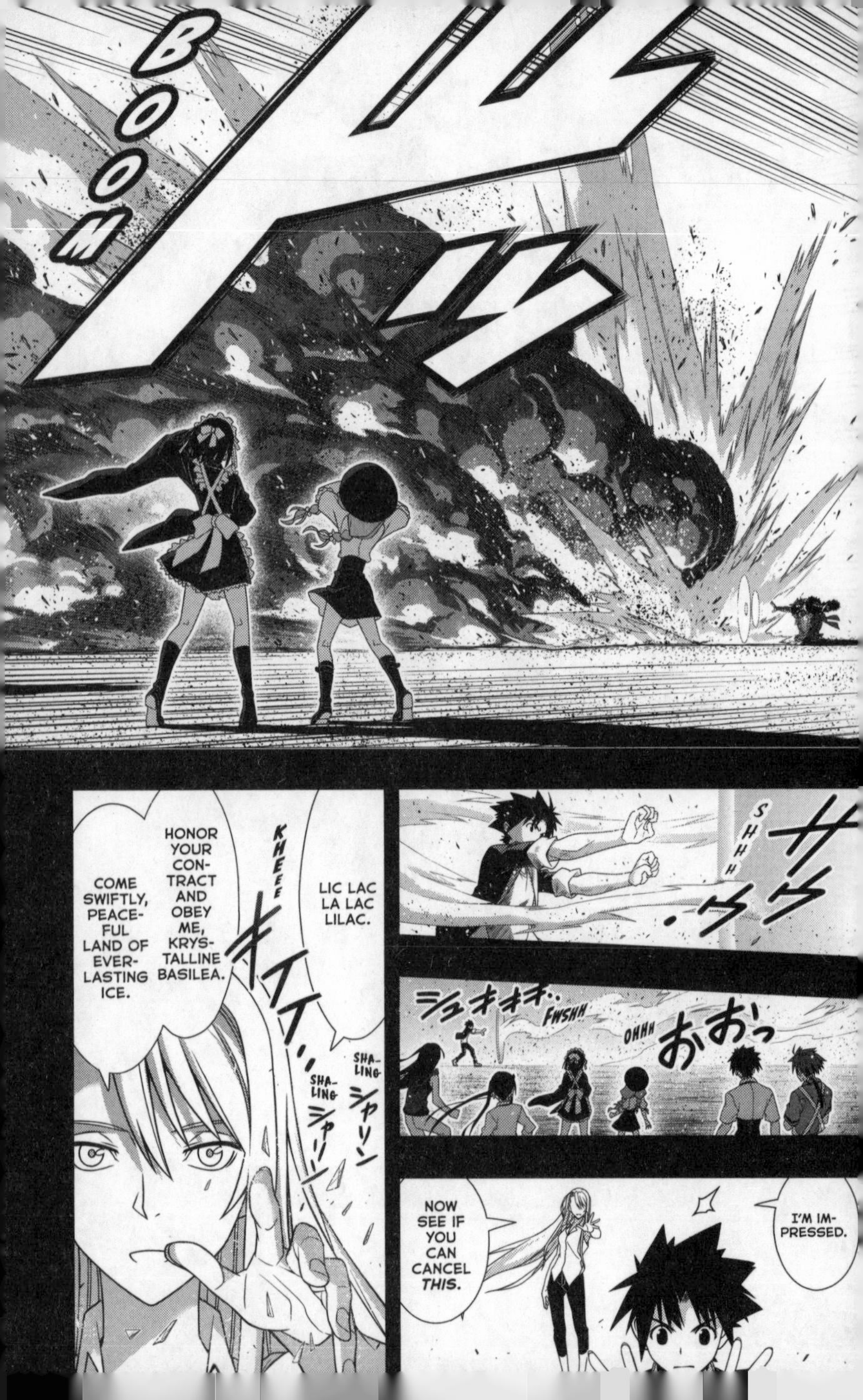
BOOM
SHHH
FWSHH
シュオオオ..
OHHH
おおっ
I'M IMPRESSED.
NOW SEE IF YOU CAN CANCEL *THIS*.
LIC LAC LA LAC LILAC.
HONOR YOUR CONTRACT AND OBEY ME, KRYSTALLINE BASILEA.
COME SWIFTLY, PEACEFUL LAND OF EVERLASTING ICE.
KHEEE
SHA-LING
シャリン
SHA-LING
シャリーン

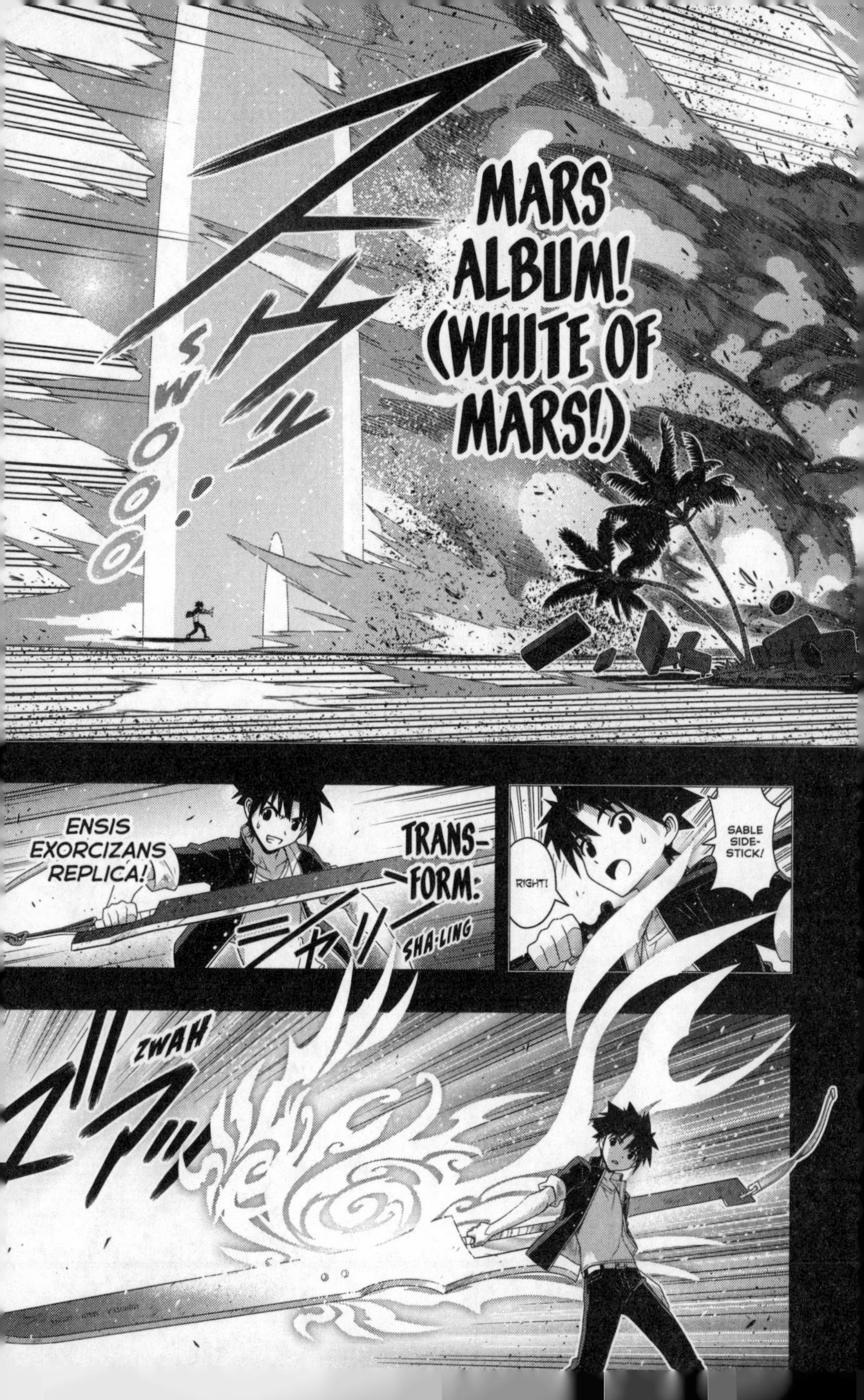
MARS ALBUM! (WHITE OF MARS!)
SWOOOOO
SABLE SIDE-STICK!
RIGHT!
ENSIS EXORCIZANS REPLICA!
TRANS-FORM.
SHA-LING
ZWAH

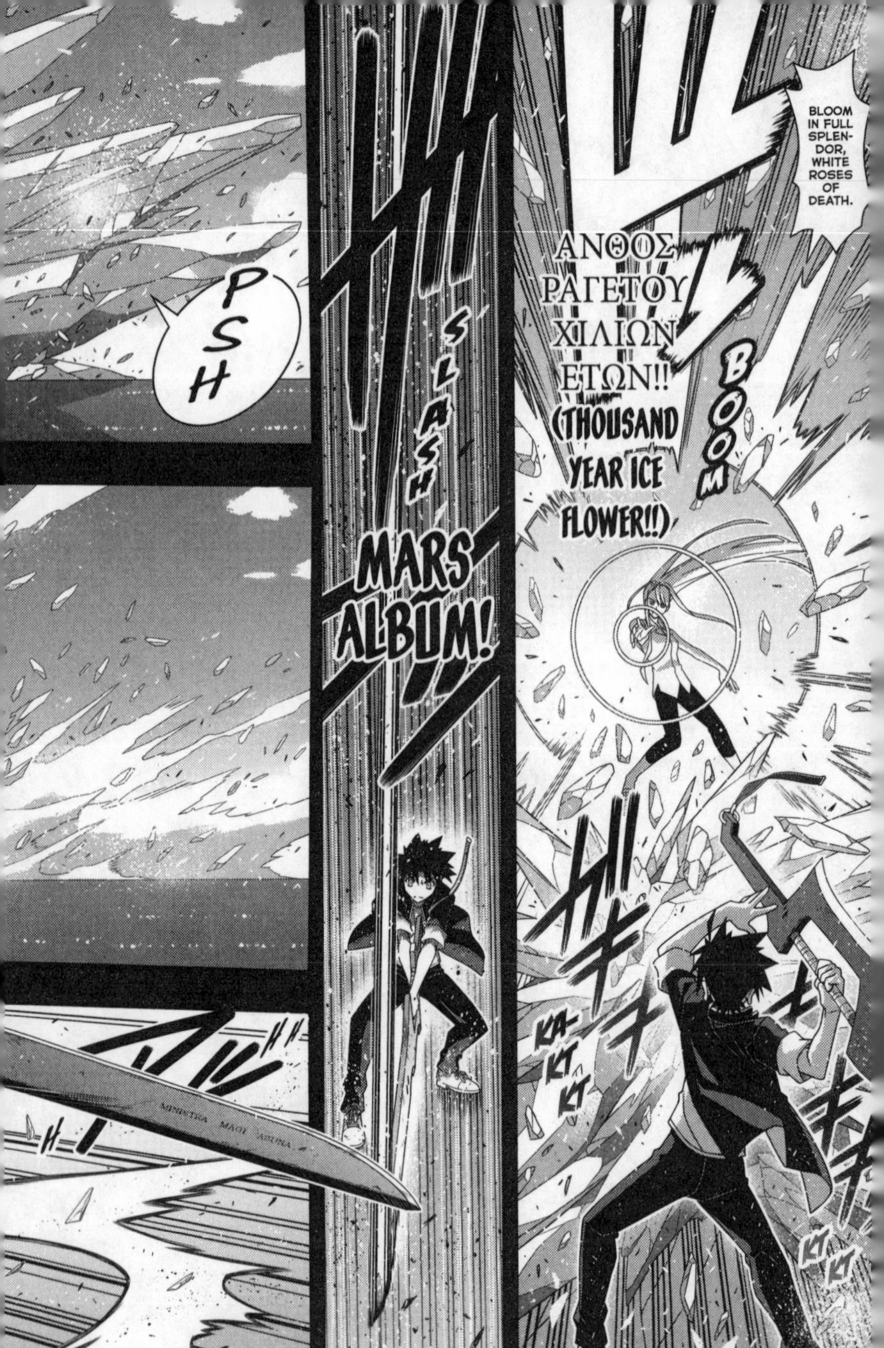
BLOOM IN FULL SPLEN-DOR, WHITE ROSES OF DEATH.
ΑΝΘΟΣ ΡΑΓΕΤΟΥ ΧΙΛΙΩΝ ΕΤΩΝ!! (THOUSAND YEAR ICE FLOWER!!)
BOOOM
KA-KT KT
KT KT
SLASH
MARS ALBUM!
PSH
MINISTRA MAGI ASUNA

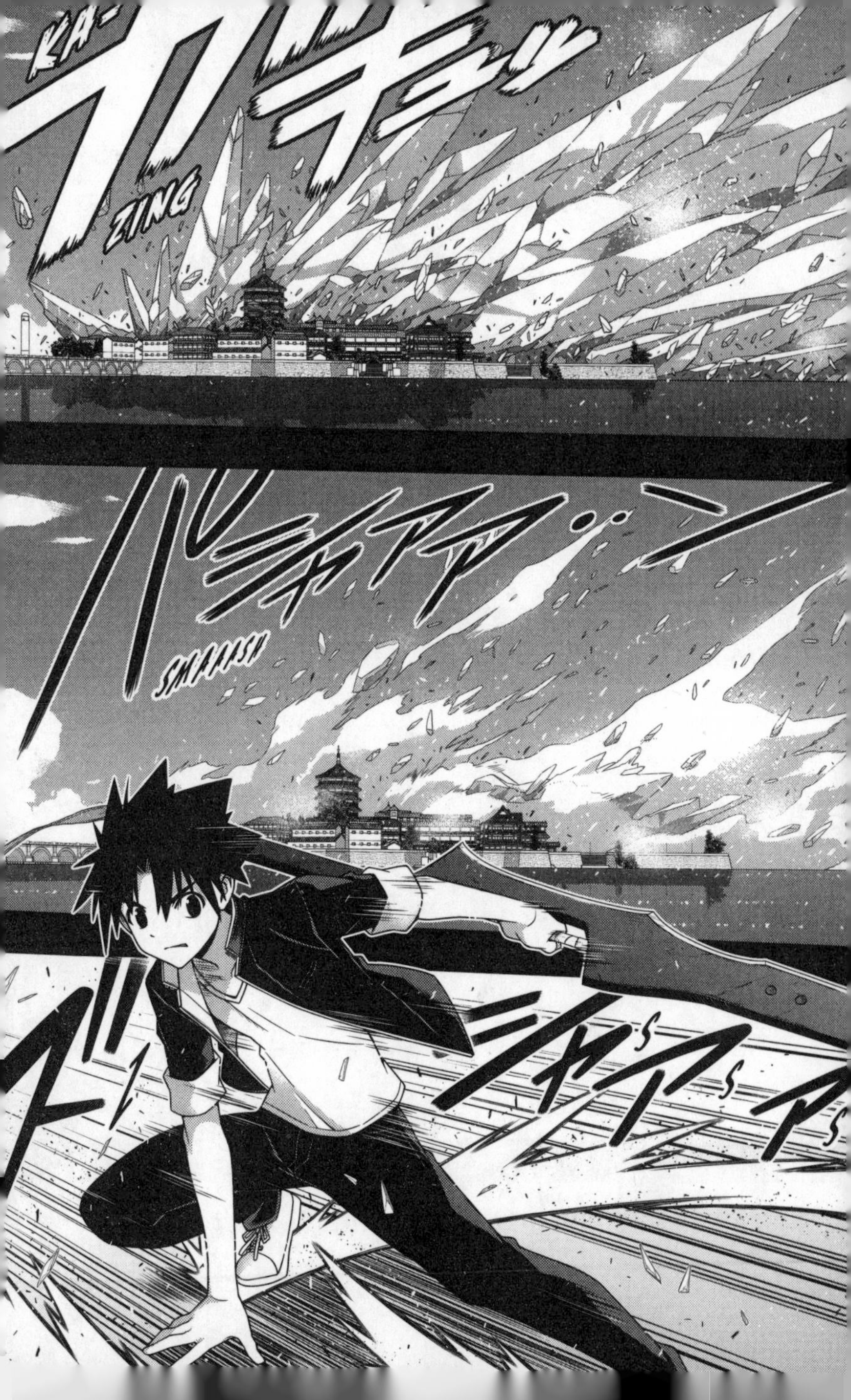
KA-
ZING
SMAAASH
SSSS

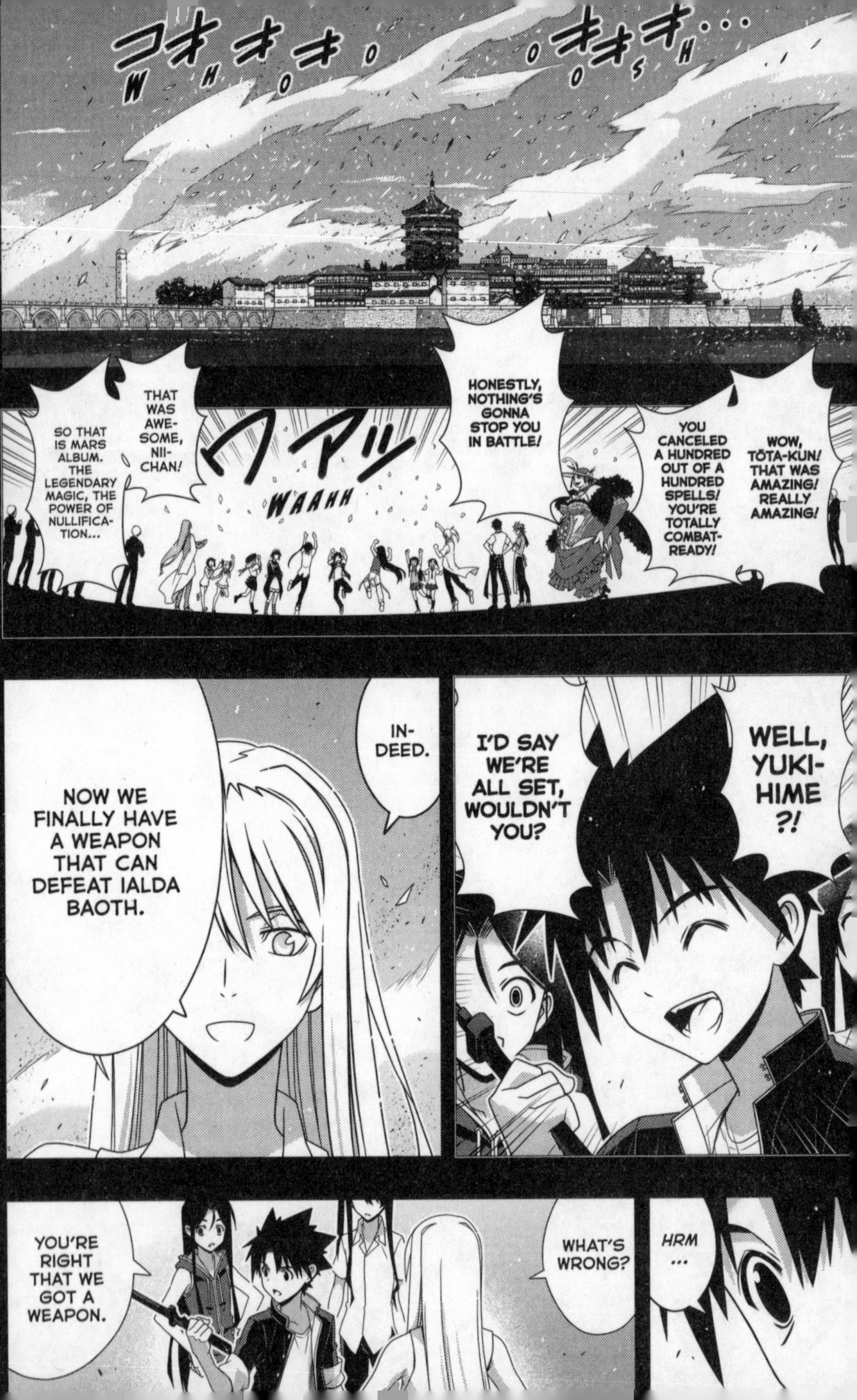
WHOOOOSH
WOW, TŌTA-KUN! THAT WAS AMAZING! REALLY AMAZING!
YOU CANCELED A HUNDRED OUT OF A HUNDRED SPELLS! YOU'RE TOTALLY COMBAT-READY!
HONESTLY, NOTHING'S GONNA STOP YOU IN BATTLE!
WAAHH
THAT WAS AWE-SOME, NII-CHAN!
SO THAT IS MARS ALBUM. THE LEGENDARY MAGIC, THE POWER OF NULLIFICA-TION...
WELL, YUKI-HIME?!
I'D SAY WE'RE ALL SET, WOULDN'T YOU?
IN-DEED.
NOW WE FINALLY HAVE A WEAPON THAT CAN DEFEAT IALDA BAOTH.
HRM ...
WHAT'S WRONG?
YOU'RE RIGHT THAT WE GOT A WEAPON.

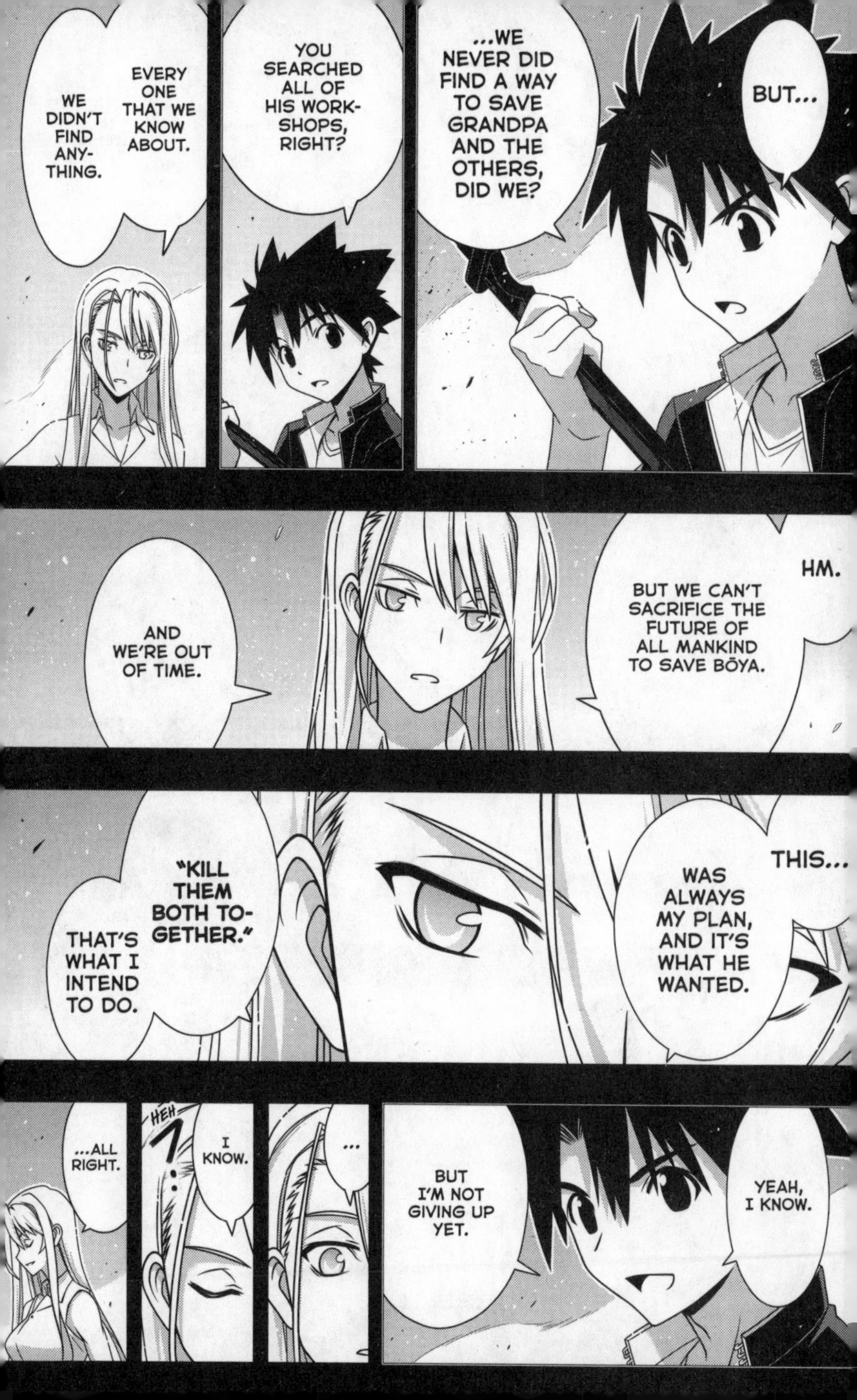
BUT...
...WE NEVER DID FIND A WAY TO SAVE GRANDPA AND THE OTHERS, DID WE?
YOU SEARCHED ALL OF HIS WORK-SHOPS, RIGHT?
EVERY ONE THAT WE KNOW ABOUT.
WE DIDN'T FIND ANY-THING.
HM.
BUT WE CAN'T SACRIFICE THE FUTURE OF ALL MANKIND TO SAVE BŌYA.
AND WE'RE OUT OF TIME.
THIS...
WAS ALWAYS MY PLAN, AND IT'S WHAT HE WANTED.
"KILL THEM BOTH TO-GETHER."
THAT'S WHAT I INTEND TO DO.
YEAH, I KNOW.
BUT I'M NOT GIVING UP YET.
...
HEH
I KNOW.
...ALL RIGHT.

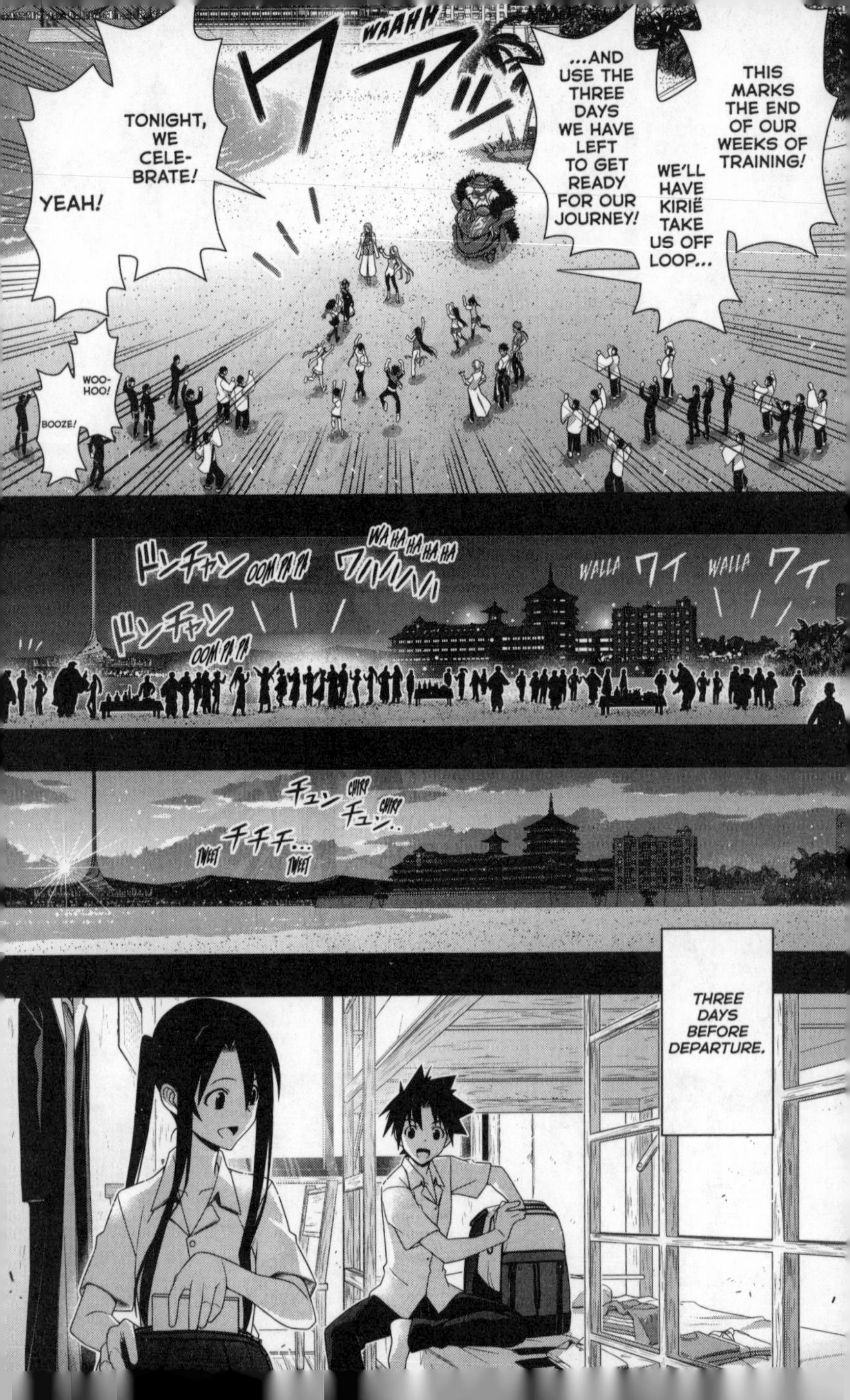
THIS MARKS THE END OF OUR WEEKS OF TRAINING!
WE'LL HAVE KIRIË TAKE US OFF LOOP...
...AND USE THE THREE DAYS WE HAVE LEFT TO GET READY FOR OUR JOURNEY!
ワアッ WAAHH
TONIGHT, WE CELEBRATE!
YEAH!
WOO-HOO!
BOOZE!
ワイ WALLA
ワイ WALLA
ワハハハハ WA HA HA HA HA
ドンチャン OOM PA PA
ドンチャン OOM PA PA
チュン CHIRP
チュン… CHIRP
チチチ… TWEET TWEET
THREE DAYS BEFORE DEPARTURE.

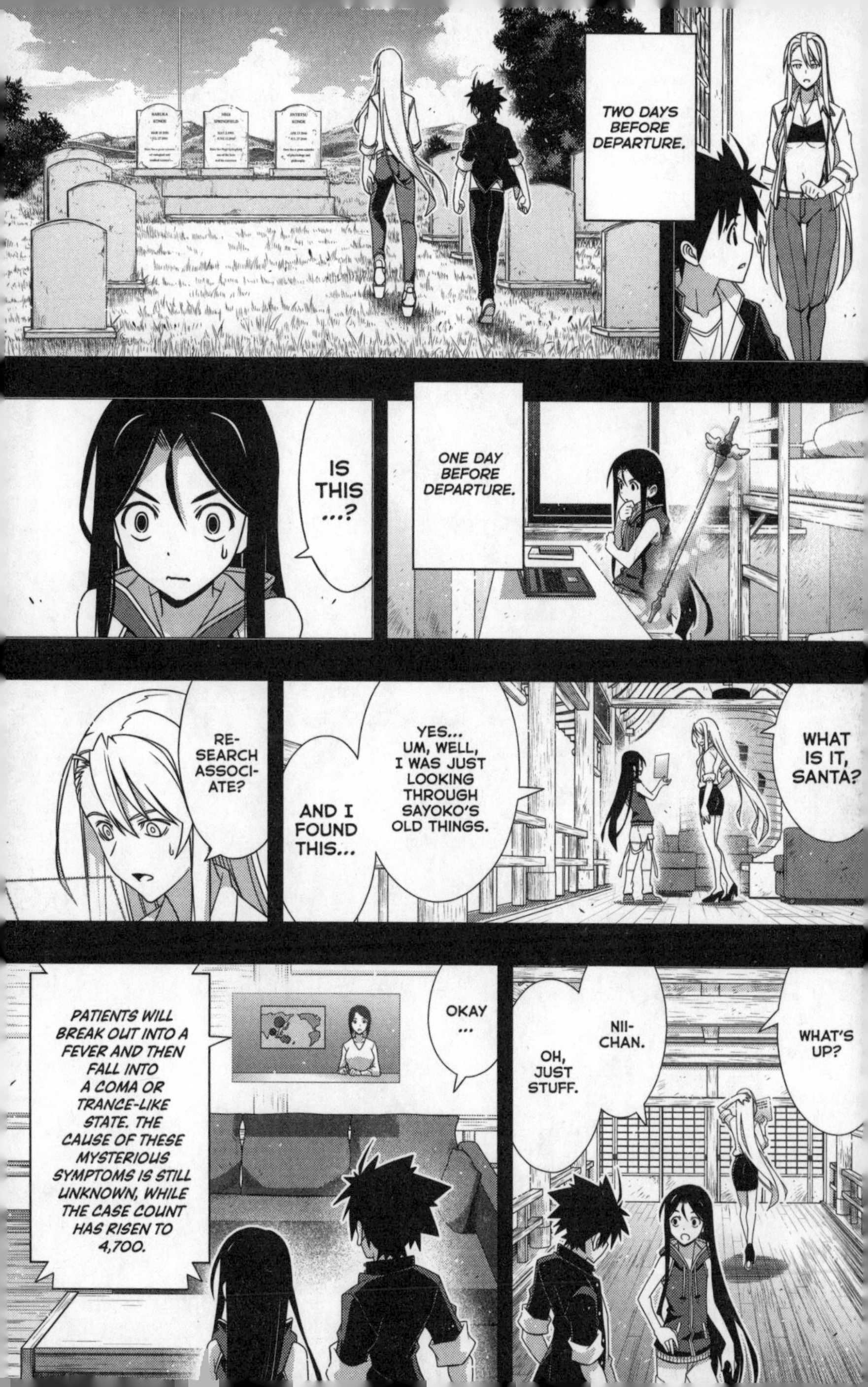
TWO DAYS BEFORE DEPARTURE.
ONE DAY BEFORE DEPARTURE.
IS THIS ...?
WHAT IS IT, SANTA?
YES... UM, WELL, I WAS JUST LOOKING THROUGH SAYOKO'S OLD THINGS.
AND I FOUND THIS...
RE-SEARCH ASSOCI-ATE?
WHAT'S UP?
NII-CHAN.
OH, JUST STUFF.
OKAY ...
PATIENTS WILL BREAK OUT INTO A FEVER AND THEN FALL INTO A COMA OR TRANCE-LIKE STATE. THE CAUSE OF THESE MYSTERIOUS SYMPTOMS IS STILL UNKNOWN, WHILE THE CASE COUNT HAS RISEN TO 4,700.

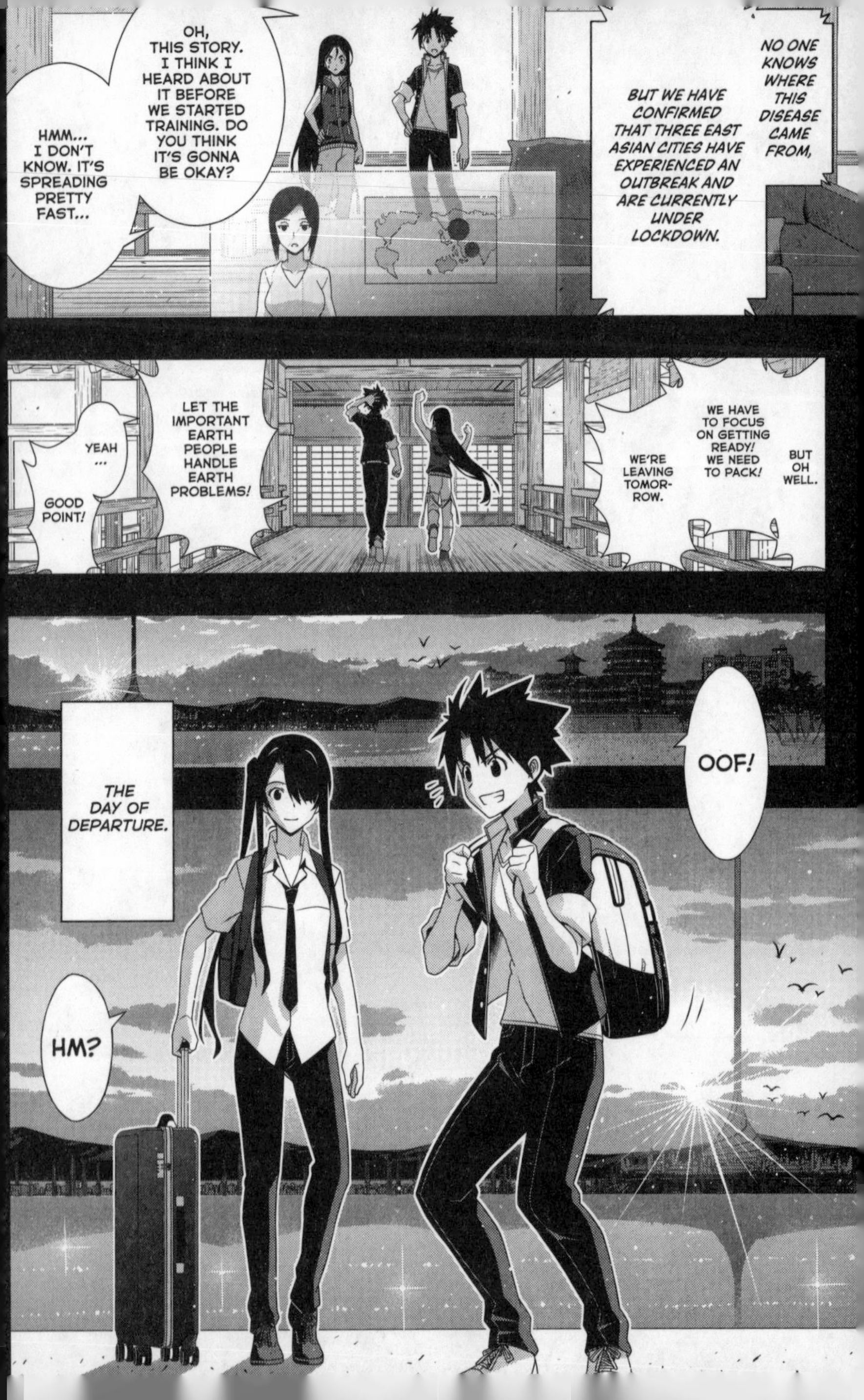
NO ONE KNOWS WHERE THIS DISEASE CAME FROM,
BUT WE HAVE CONFIRMED THAT THREE EAST ASIAN CITIES HAVE EXPERIENCED AN OUTBREAK AND ARE CURRENTLY UNDER LOCKDOWN.
OH, THIS STORY. I THINK I HEARD ABOUT IT BEFORE WE STARTED TRAINING. DO YOU THINK IT'S GONNA BE OKAY?
HMM... I DON'T KNOW. IT'S SPREADING PRETTY FAST...
BUT OH WELL.
WE HAVE TO FOCUS ON GETTING READY! WE NEED TO PACK!
WE'RE LEAVING TOMOR-ROW.
LET THE IMPORTANT EARTH PEOPLE HANDLE EARTH PROBLEMS!
YEAH ...
GOOD POINT!
OOF!
THE DAY OF DEPARTURE.
HM?

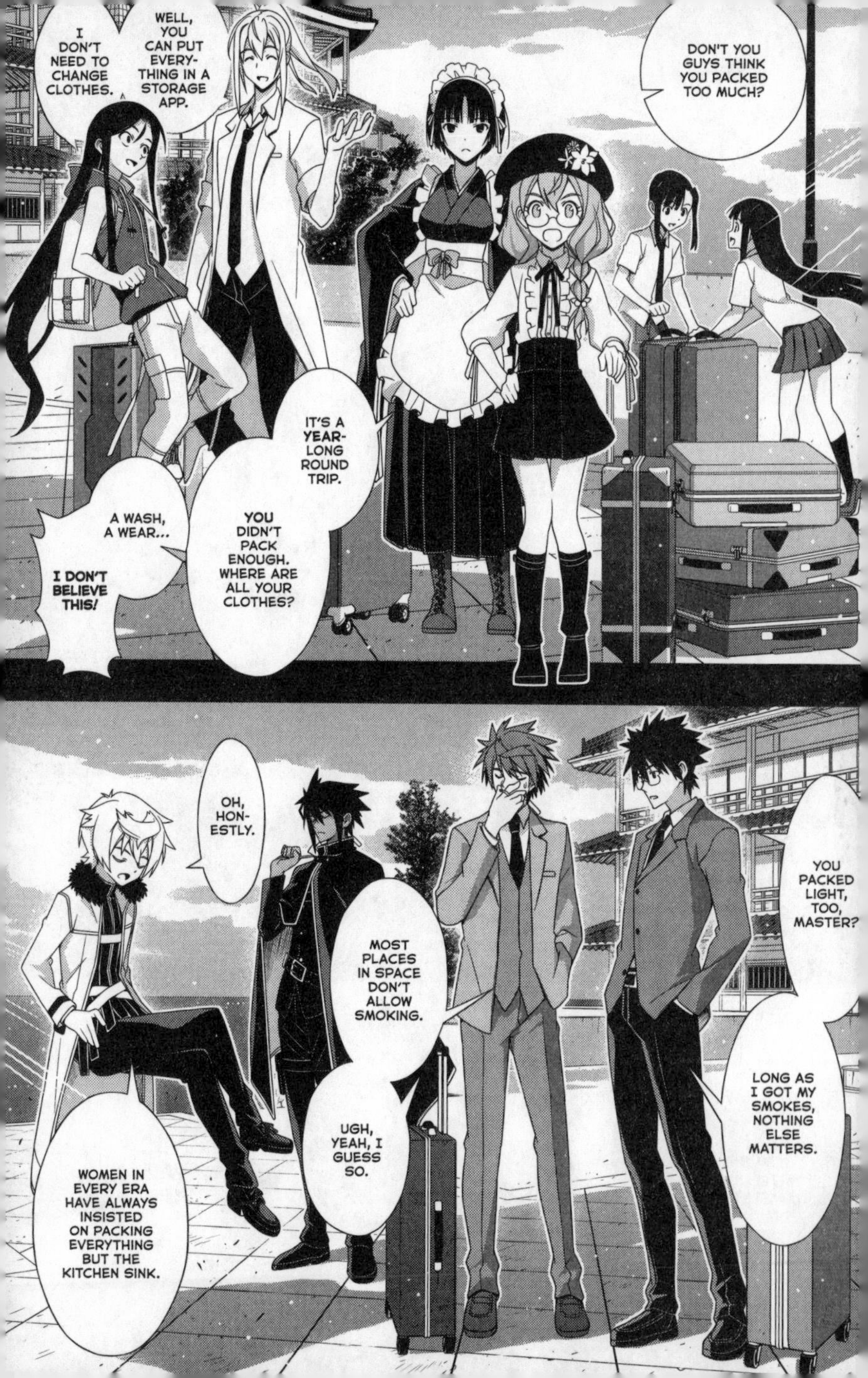
DON'T YOU GUYS THINK YOU PACKED TOO MUCH?
WELL, YOU CAN PUT EVERYTHING IN A STORAGE APP.
I DON'T NEED TO CHANGE CLOTHES.
IT'S A YEAR-LONG ROUND TRIP.
YOU DIDN'T PACK ENOUGH. WHERE ARE ALL YOUR CLOTHES?
A WASH, A WEAR...
I DON'T BELIEVE THIS!
YOU PACKED LIGHT, TOO, MASTER?
LONG AS I GOT MY SMOKES, NOTHING ELSE MATTERS.
OH, HONESTLY.
MOST PLACES IN SPACE DON'T ALLOW SMOKING.
UGH, YEAH, I GUESS SO.
WOMEN IN EVERY ERA HAVE ALWAYS INSISTED ON PACKING EVERYTHING BUT THE KITCHEN SINK.

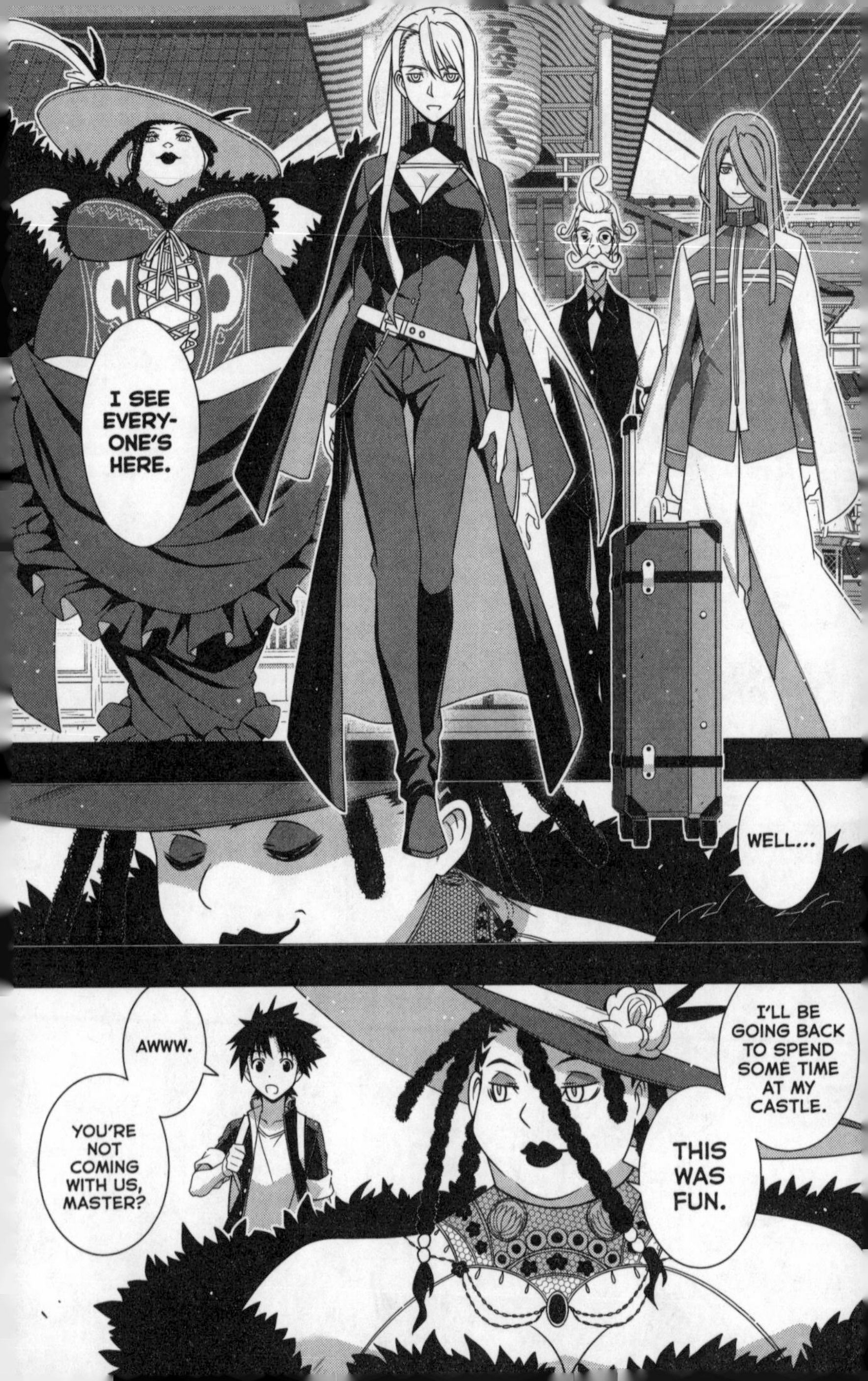
I SEE EVERY-ONE'S HERE.
WELL...
I'LL BE GOING BACK TO SPEND SOME TIME AT MY CASTLE.
THIS WAS FUN.
AWWW.
YOU'RE NOT COMING WITH US, MASTER?

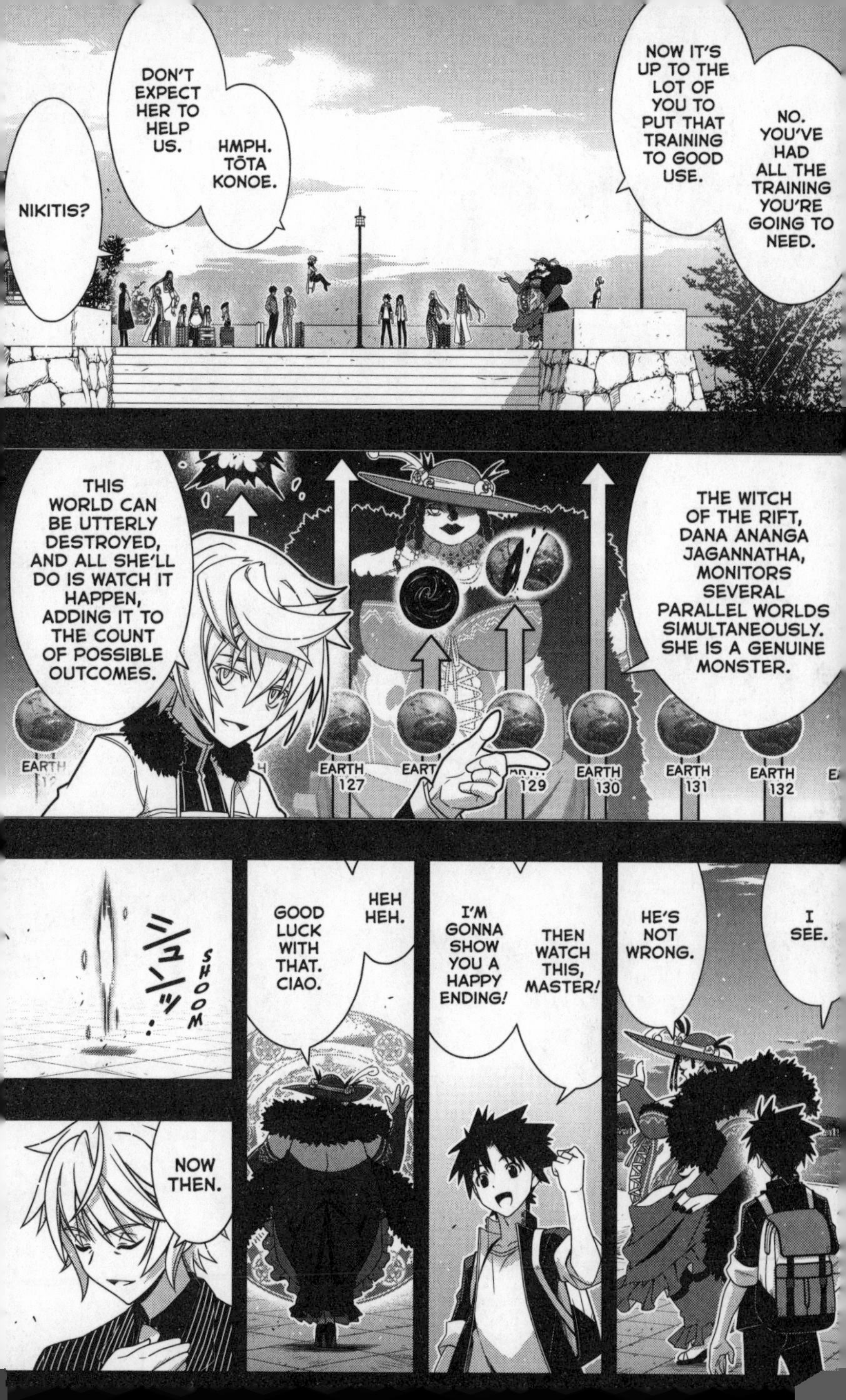
NO. YOU'VE HAD ALL THE TRAINING YOU'RE GOING TO NEED.
NOW IT'S UP TO THE LOT OF YOU TO PUT THAT TRAINING TO GOOD USE.
HMPH. TŌTA KONOE.
DON'T EXPECT HER TO HELP US.
NIKITIS?
THE WITCH OF THE RIFT, DANA ANANGA JAGANNATHA, MONITORS SEVERAL PARALLEL WORLDS SIMULTANEOUSLY. SHE IS A GENUINE MONSTER.
THIS WORLD CAN BE UTTERLY DESTROYED, AND ALL SHE'LL DO IS WATCH IT HAPPEN, ADDING IT TO THE COUNT OF POSSIBLE OUTCOMES.
EARTH 132
EARTH 131
EARTH 130
129
EARTH 127
I SEE.
HE'S NOT WRONG.
THEN WATCH THIS, MASTER!
I'M GONNA SHOW YOU A HAPPY ENDING!
HEH HEH.
GOOD LUCK WITH THAT. CIAO.
SHOOM
NOW THEN.

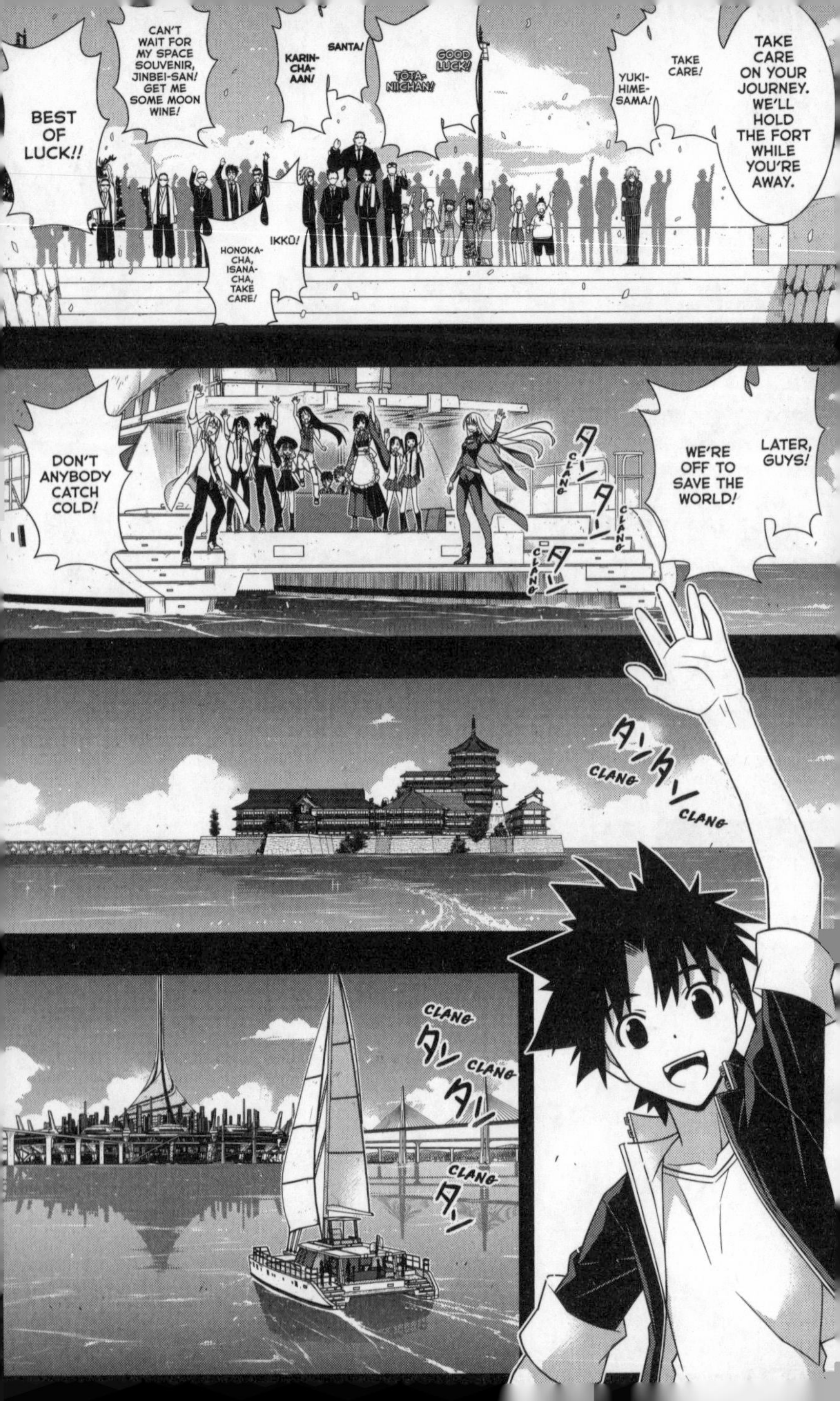
TAKE CARE ON YOUR JOURNEY. WE'LL HOLD THE FORT WHILE YOU'RE AWAY.
TAKE CARE!
YUKI-HIME-SAMA!
GOOD LUCK!!
TŌTA-NIICHAN!
SANTA!
KARIN-CHA-AAN!
CAN'T WAIT FOR MY SPACE SOUVENIR, JINBEI-SAN! GET ME SOME MOON WINE!
BEST OF LUCK!!
IKKŪ!
HONOKA-CHA, ISANA-CHA, TAKE CARE!
LATER, GUYS!
WE'RE OFF TO SAVE THE WORLD!
CLANG
CLANG
CLANG
DON'T ANYBODY CATCH COLD!
CLANG
CLANG
CLANG
CLANG
CLANG

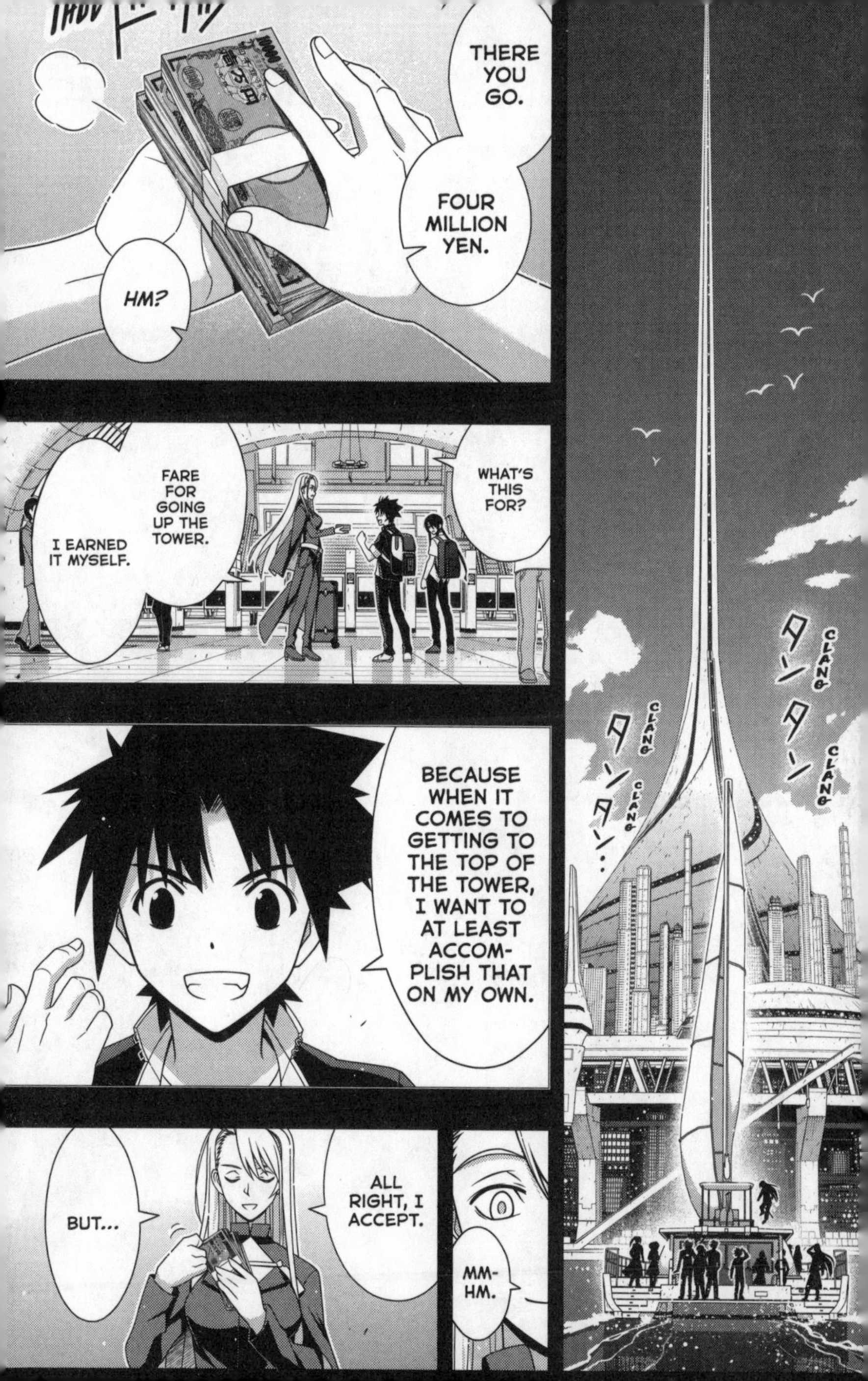
CLANG
CLANG
CLANG
CLANG
THUD
THERE YOU GO.
FOUR MILLION YEN.
HM?
WHAT'S THIS FOR?
FARE FOR GOING UP THE TOWER.
I EARNED IT MYSELF.
BECAUSE WHEN IT COMES TO GETTING TO THE TOP OF THE TOWER, I WANT TO AT LEAST ACCOM-PLISH THAT ON MY OWN.
MM-HM.
ALL RIGHT, I ACCEPT.
BUT...

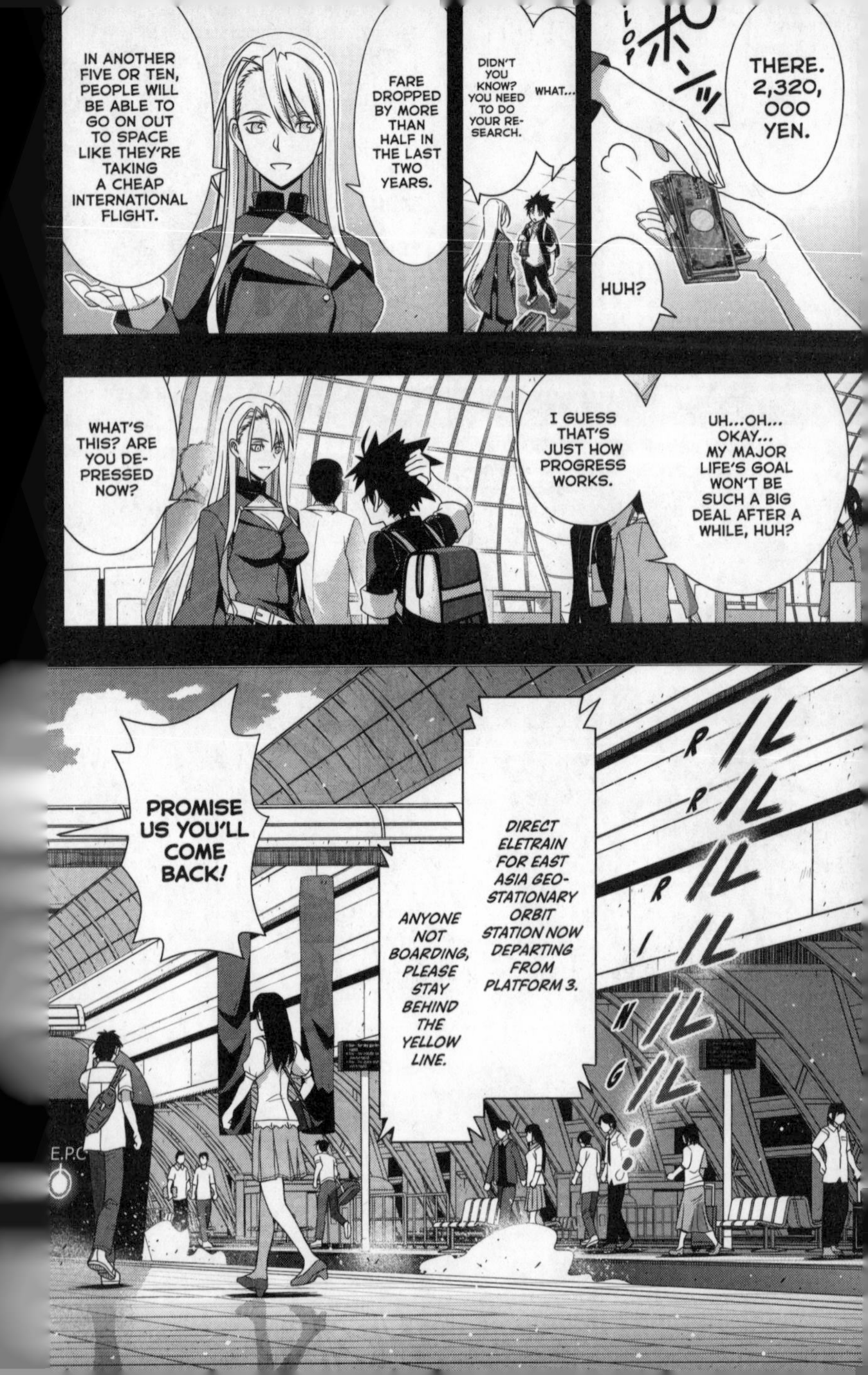
THERE. 2,320,000 YEN.
ポンッ
HUH?
WHAT...
DIDN'T YOU KNOW? YOU NEED TO DO YOUR RESEARCH.
FARE DROPPED BY MORE THAN HALF IN THE LAST TWO YEARS.
IN ANOTHER FIVE OR TEN, PEOPLE WILL BE ABLE TO GO ON OUT TO SPACE LIKE THEY'RE TAKING A CHEAP INTERNATIONAL FLIGHT.
UH...OH... OKAY... MY MAJOR LIFE'S GOAL WON'T BE SUCH A BIG DEAL AFTER A WHILE, HUH?
I GUESS THAT'S JUST HOW PROGRESS WORKS.
WHAT'S THIS? ARE YOU DE-PRESSED NOW?
RRRING
DIRECT ELETRAIN FOR EAST ASIA GEO-STATIONARY ORBIT STATION NOW DEPARTING FROM PLATFORM 3.
ANYONE NOT BOARDING, PLEASE STAY BEHIND THE YELLOW LINE.
PROMISE US YOU'LL COME BACK!
E.P.C

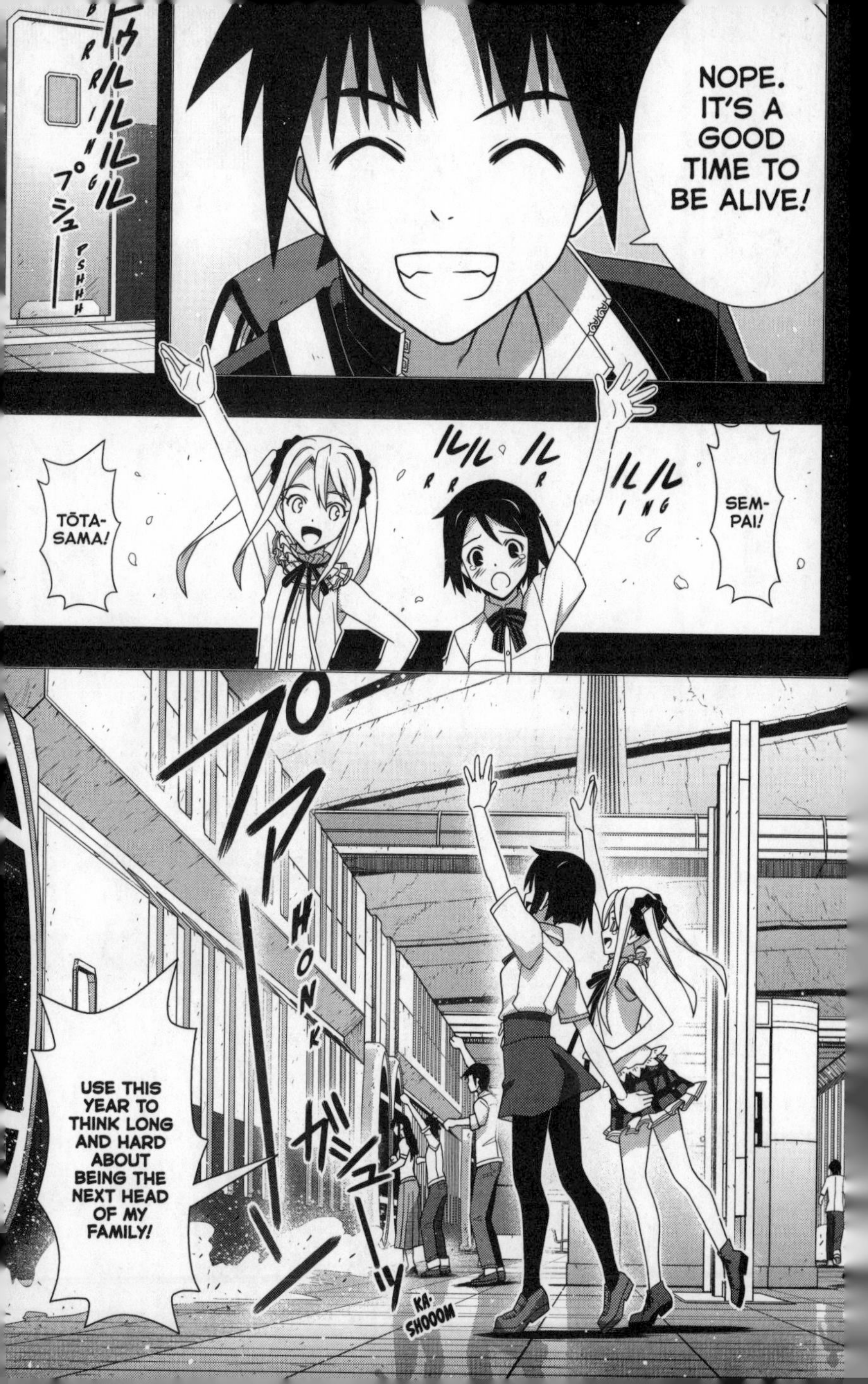

NOPE. IT'S A GOOD TIME TO BE ALIVE!
トゥルルルルル
BRRRRING
プシュー
PSHHH
SEM-PAI!
ルルルルル
RRRING
TŌTA-SAMA!
プァーーーッ
HONK
USE THIS YEAR TO THINK LONG AND HARD ABOUT BEING THE NEXT HEAD OF MY FAMILY!
ガシュ
KA-SHOOOM

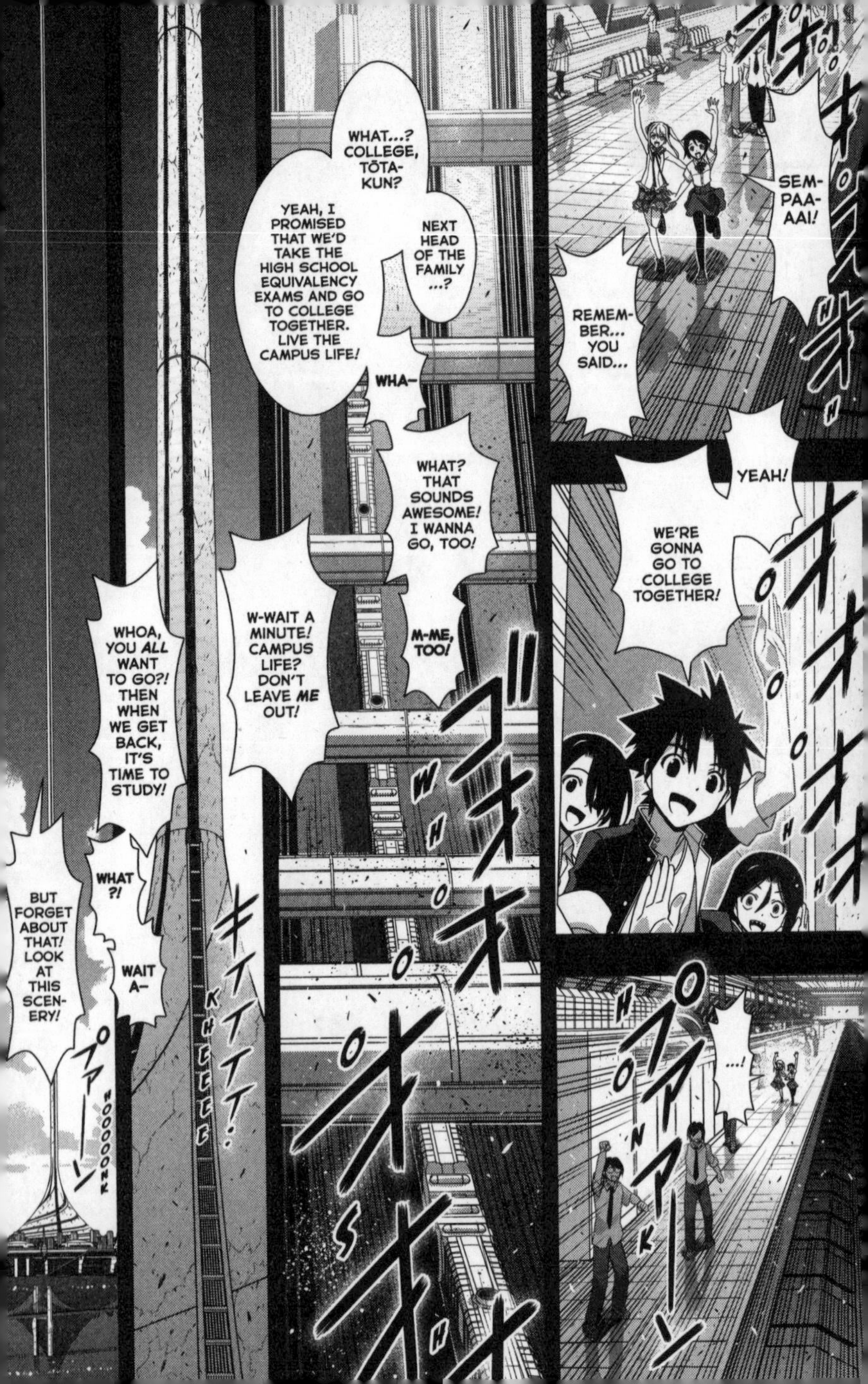
SEM-PAAA-AAI!
HHHH
REMEM-BER... YOU SAID...
YEAH!
WE'RE GONNA GO TO COLLEGE TOGETHER!
HHHH
...!
HONK
WHAT...? COLLEGE, TŌTA-KUN?
NEXT HEAD OF THE FAMILY ...?
YEAH, I PROMISED THAT WE'D TAKE THE HIGH SCHOOL EQUIVALENCY EXAMS AND GO TO COLLEGE TOGETHER. LIVE THE CAMPUS LIFE!
WHA-
WHAT? THAT SOUNDS AWESOME! I WANNA GO, TOO!
M-ME, TOO!
W-WAIT A MINUTE! CAMPUS LIFE? DON'T LEAVE *ME* OUT!
WHOOSH
WHOA, YOU *ALL* WANT TO GO?! THEN WHEN WE GET BACK, IT'S TIME TO STUDY!
WHAT ?!
WAIT A-
BUT FORGET ABOUT THAT! LOOK AT THIS SCEN-ERY!
KHEEEE
HOOOOONK

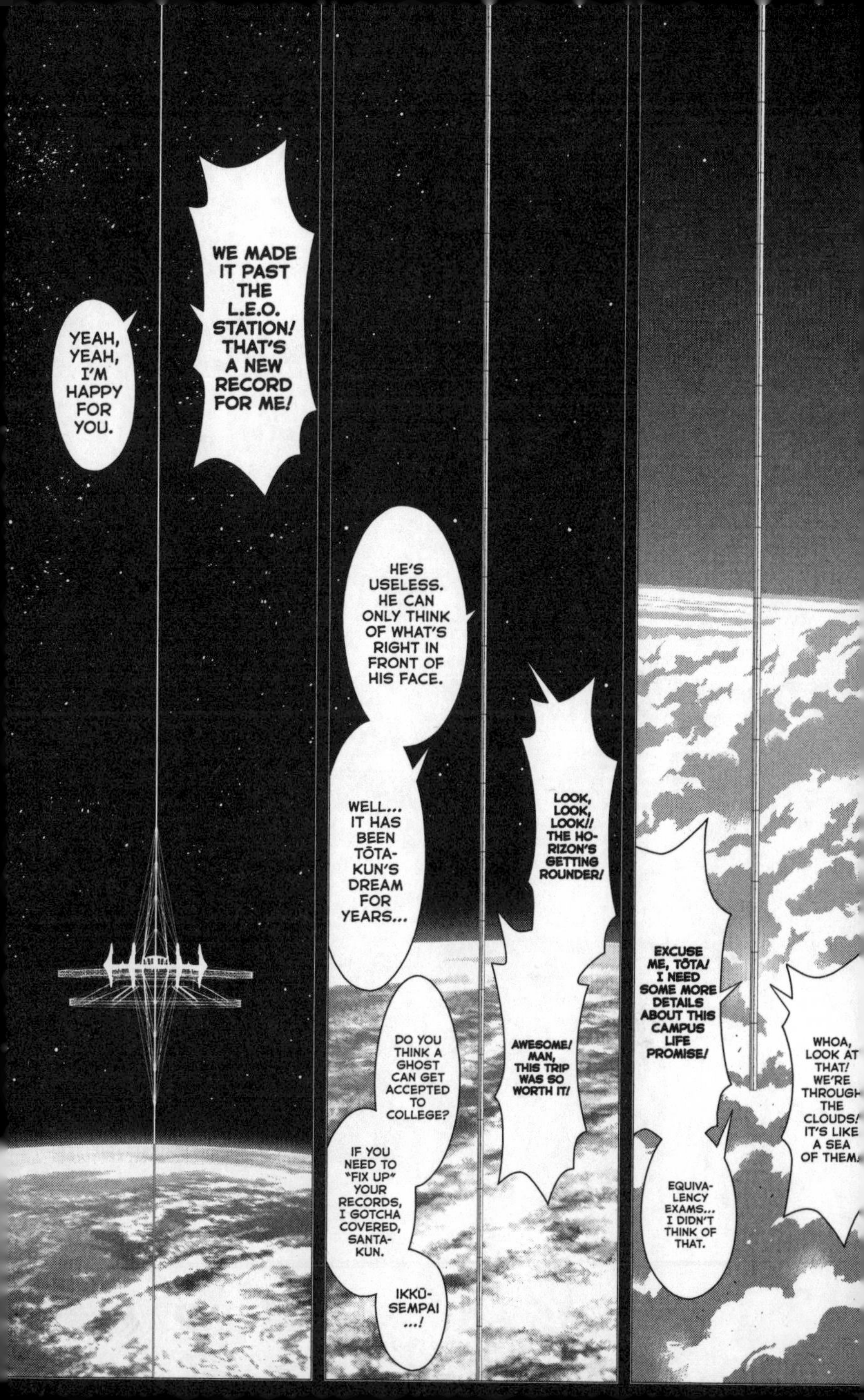
WHOA, LOOK AT THAT! WE'RE THROUGH THE CLOUDS! IT'S LIKE A SEA OF THEM.
EXCUSE ME, TŌTA! I NEED SOME MORE DETAILS ABOUT THIS CAMPUS LIFE PROMISE!
EQUIVALENCY EXAMS... I DIDN'T THINK OF THAT.
LOOK, LOOK, LOOK!! THE HORIZON'S GETTING ROUNDER!
AWESOME! MAN, THIS TRIP WAS SO WORTH IT!
HE'S USELESS. HE CAN ONLY THINK OF WHAT'S RIGHT IN FRONT OF HIS FACE.
WELL... IT HAS BEEN TŌTA-KUN'S DREAM FOR YEARS...
DO YOU THINK A GHOST CAN GET ACCEPTED TO COLLEGE?
IF YOU NEED TO "FIX UP" YOUR RECORDS, I GOTCHA COVERED, SANTA-KUN.
IKKŪ-SEMPAI ...!
WE MADE IT PAST THE L.E.O. STATION! THAT'S A NEW RECORD FOR ME!
YEAH, YEAH, I'M HAPPY FOR YOU.

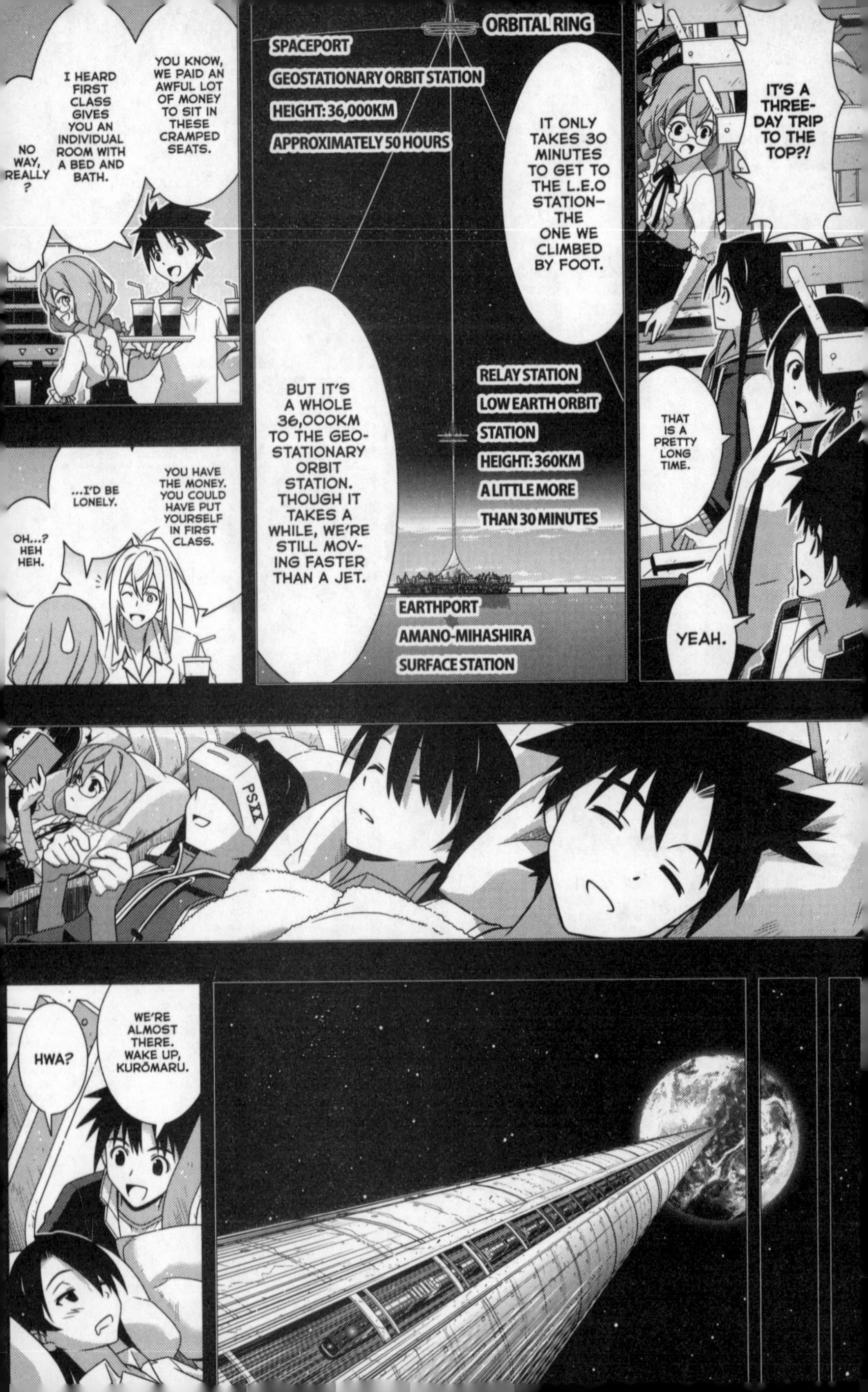
IT'S A THREE-DAY TRIP TO THE TOP?!
THAT IS A PRETTY LONG TIME.
YEAH.
ORBITAL RING
SPACEPORT
GEOSTATIONARY ORBIT STATION
HEIGHT: 36,000KM
APPROXIMATELY 50 HOURS
IT ONLY TAKES 30 MINUTES TO GET TO THE L.E.O STATION— THE ONE WE CLIMBED BY FOOT.
BUT IT'S A WHOLE 36,000KM TO THE GEO-STATIONARY ORBIT STATION. THOUGH IT TAKES A WHILE, WE'RE STILL MOVING FASTER THAN A JET.
RELAY STATION
LOW EARTH ORBIT STATION
HEIGHT: 360KM
A LITTLE MORE THAN 30 MINUTES
EARTHPORT
AMANO-MIHASHIRA SURFACE STATION
YOU KNOW, WE PAID AN AWFUL LOT OF MONEY TO SIT IN THESE CRAMPED SEATS.
I HEARD FIRST CLASS GIVES YOU AN INDIVIDUAL ROOM WITH A BED AND BATH.
NO WAY, REALLY?
YOU HAVE THE MONEY. YOU COULD HAVE PUT YOURSELF IN FIRST CLASS.
...I'D BE LONELY.
OH...? HEH HEH.
WE'RE ALMOST THERE. WAKE UP, KURŌMARU.
HWA?

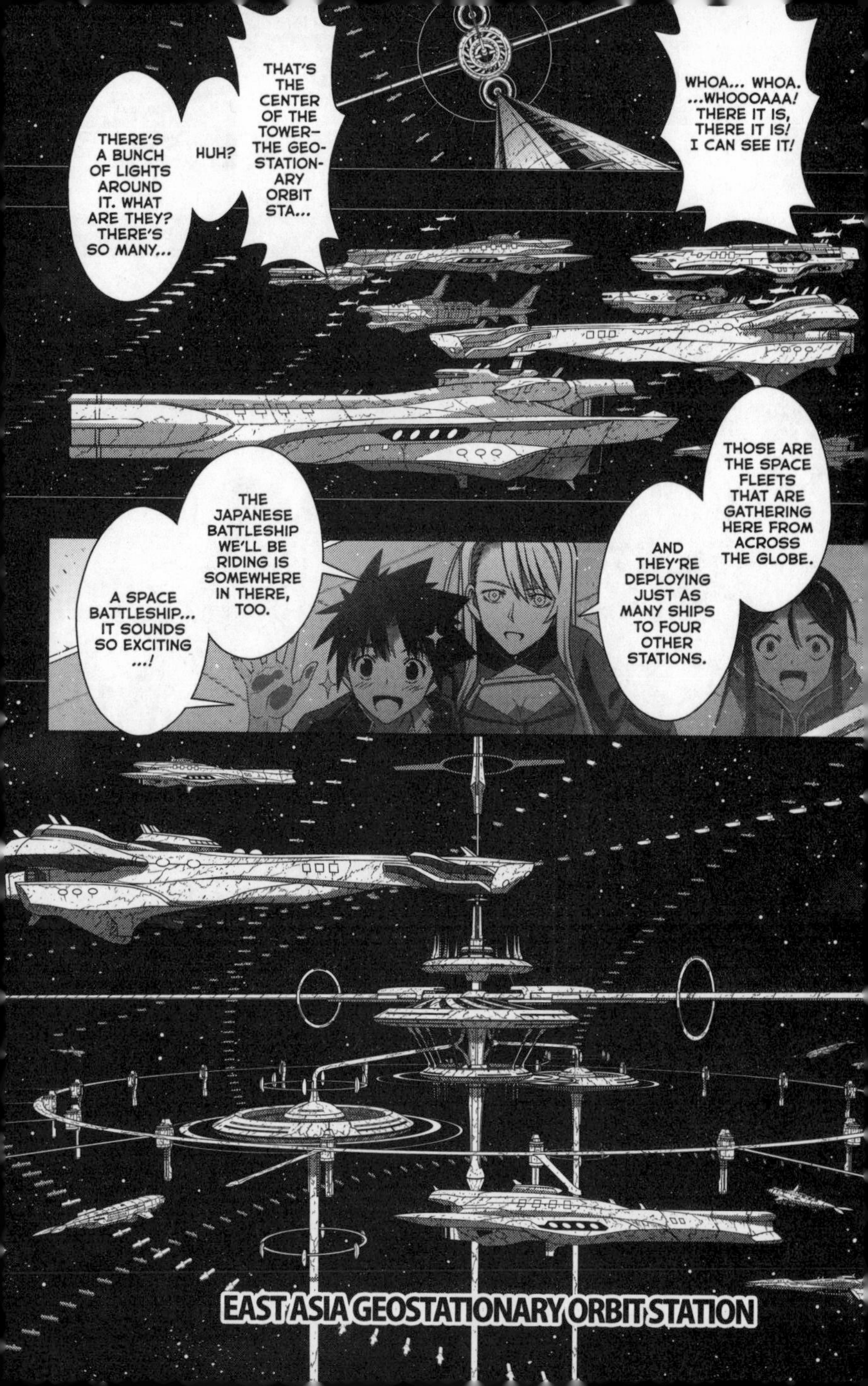

WHOA... WHOA. ...WHOOOAAA! THERE IT IS, THERE IT IS! I CAN SEE IT!
THAT'S THE CENTER OF THE TOWER—THE GEO-STATION-ARY ORBIT STA...
HUH?
THERE'S A BUNCH OF LIGHTS AROUND IT. WHAT ARE THEY? THERE'S SO MANY...
THOSE ARE THE SPACE FLEETS THAT ARE GATHERING HERE FROM ACROSS THE GLOBE.
AND THEY'RE DEPLOYING JUST AS MANY SHIPS TO FOUR OTHER STATIONS.
THE JAPANESE BATTLESHIP WE'LL BE RIDING IS SOMEWHERE IN THERE, TOO.
A SPACE BATTLESHIP... IT SOUNDS SO EXCITING ...!
EAST ASIA GEOSTATIONARY ORBIT STATION

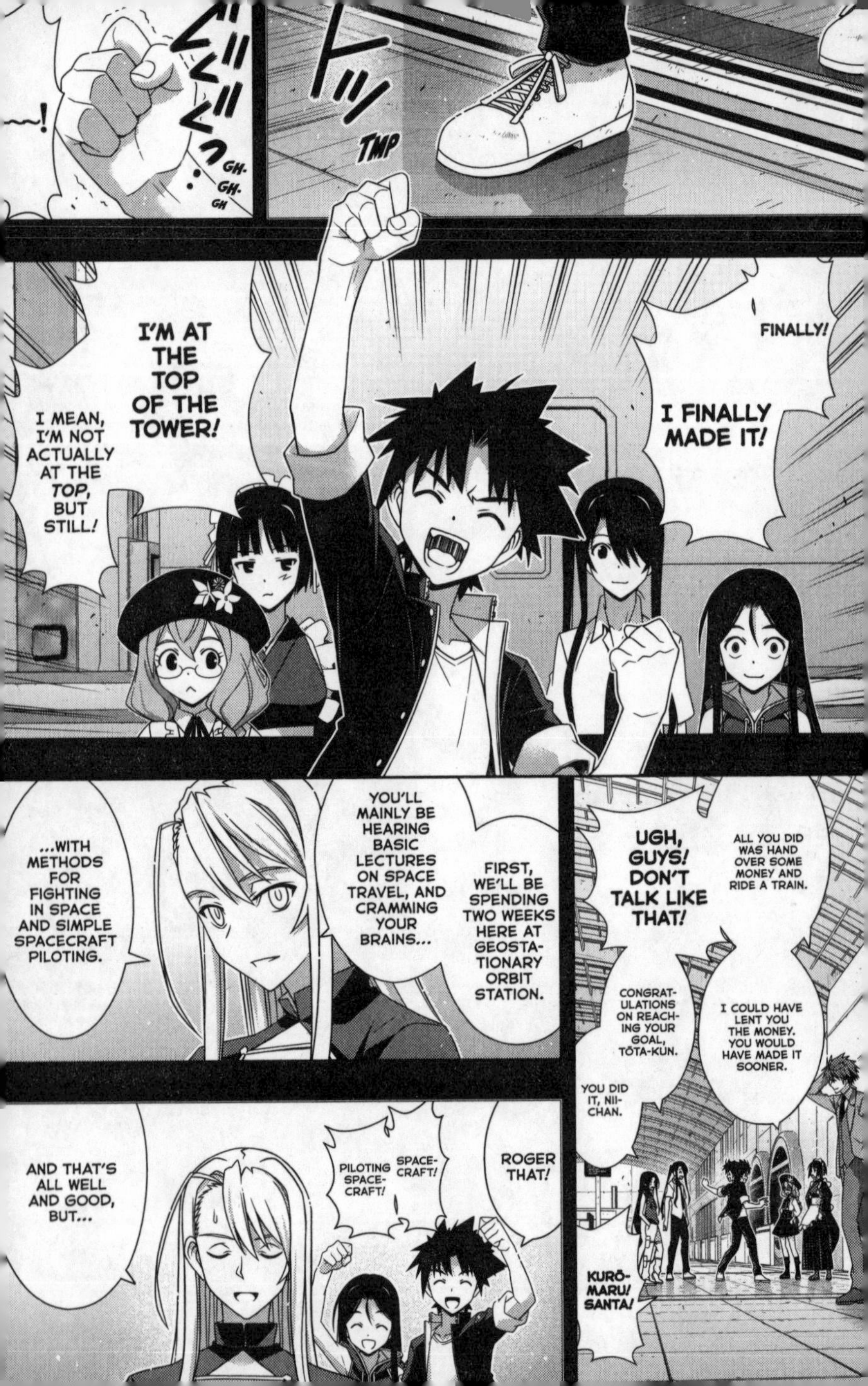
TMP
GH-GH-GH
~~!
FINALLY!
I FINALLY MADE IT!
I'M AT THE TOP OF THE TOWER!
I MEAN, I'M NOT ACTUALLY AT THE *TOP*, BUT STILL!
ALL YOU DID WAS HAND OVER SOME MONEY AND RIDE A TRAIN.
UGH, GUYS! DON'T TALK LIKE THAT!
I COULD HAVE LENT YOU THE MONEY. YOU WOULD HAVE MADE IT SOONER.
CONGRATULATIONS ON REACHING YOUR GOAL, TŌTA-KUN.
YOU DID IT, NII-CHAN.
KURŌMARU! SANTA!
FIRST, WE'LL BE SPENDING TWO WEEKS HERE AT GEOSTATIONARY ORBIT STATION.
YOU'LL MAINLY BE HEARING BASIC LECTURES ON SPACE TRAVEL, AND CRAMMING YOUR BRAINS...
...WITH METHODS FOR FIGHTING IN SPACE AND SIMPLE SPACECRAFT PILOTING.
ROGER THAT!
SPACECRAFT!
PILOTING SPACECRAFT!
AND THAT'S ALL WELL AND GOOD, BUT...

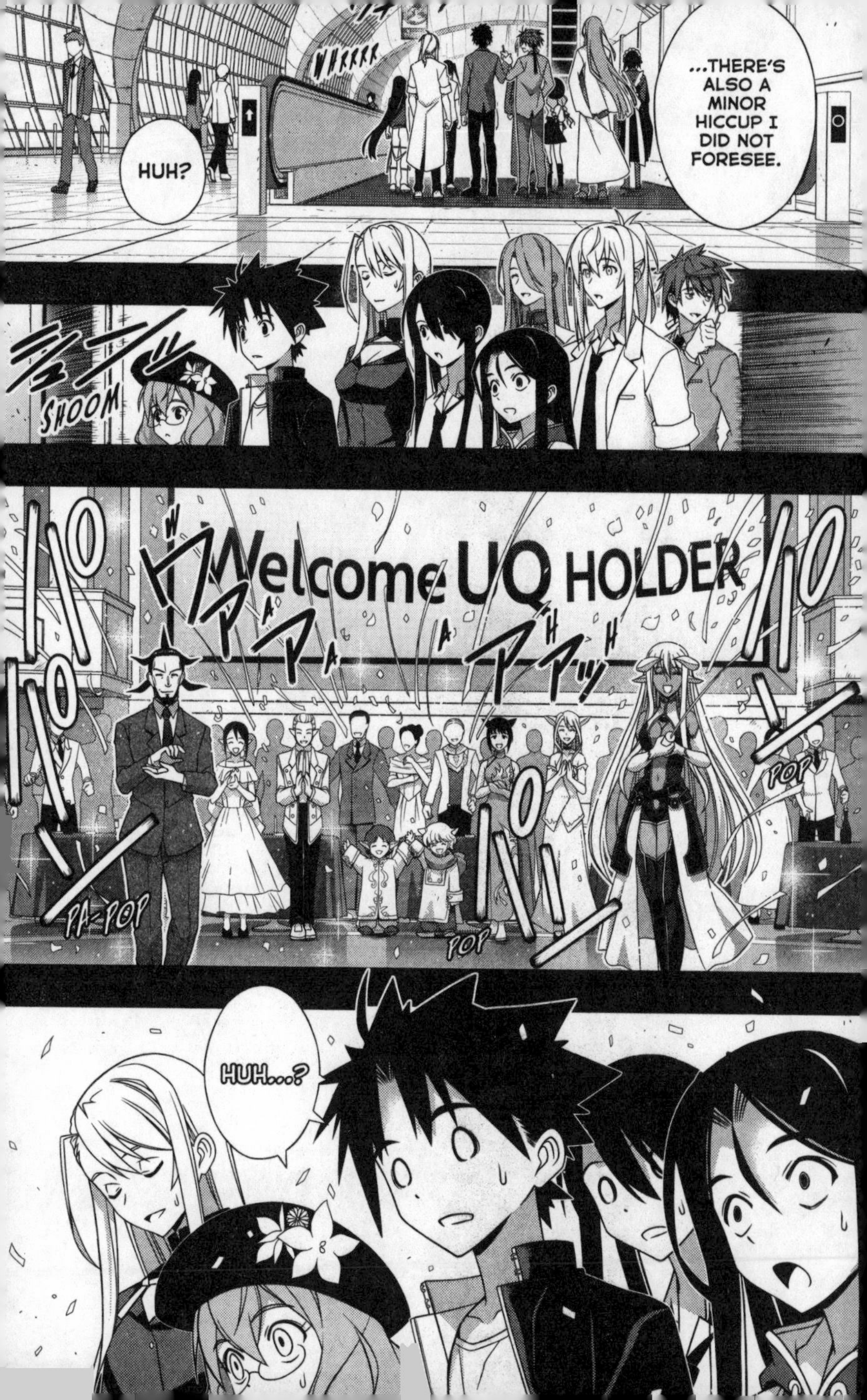
...THERE'S ALSO A MINOR HICCUP I DID NOT FORESEE.
HUH?
SHOOM
Welcome UQ HOLDER
POP
POP
PA-POP
HUH...?

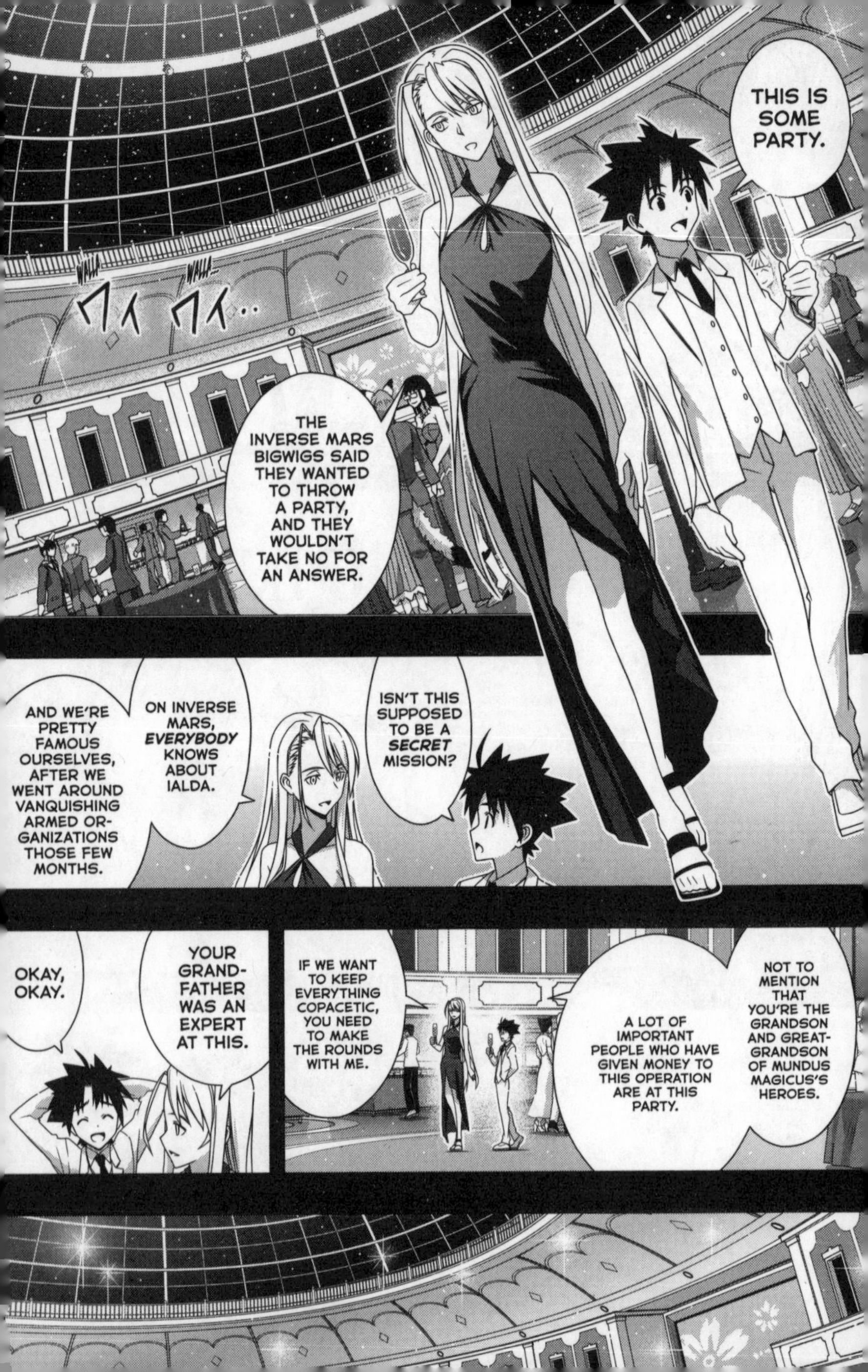
THIS IS SOME PARTY.
WALLA WALLA...
ワイワイ..
THE INVERSE MARS BIGWIGS SAID THEY WANTED TO THROW A PARTY, AND THEY WOULDN'T TAKE NO FOR AN ANSWER.
ISN'T THIS SUPPOSED TO BE A *SECRET* MISSION?
ON INVERSE MARS, *EVERYBODY* KNOWS ABOUT IALDA.
AND WE'RE PRETTY FAMOUS OURSELVES, AFTER WE WENT AROUND VANQUISHING ARMED ORGANIZATIONS THOSE FEW MONTHS.
NOT TO MENTION THAT YOU'RE THE GRANDSON AND GREAT-GRANDSON OF MUNDUS MAGICUS'S HEROES.
A LOT OF IMPORTANT PEOPLE WHO HAVE GIVEN MONEY TO THIS OPERATION ARE AT THIS PARTY.
IF WE WANT TO KEEP EVERYTHING COPACETIC, YOU NEED TO MAKE THE ROUNDS WITH ME.
YOUR GRANDFATHER WAS AN EXPERT AT THIS.
OKAY, OKAY.

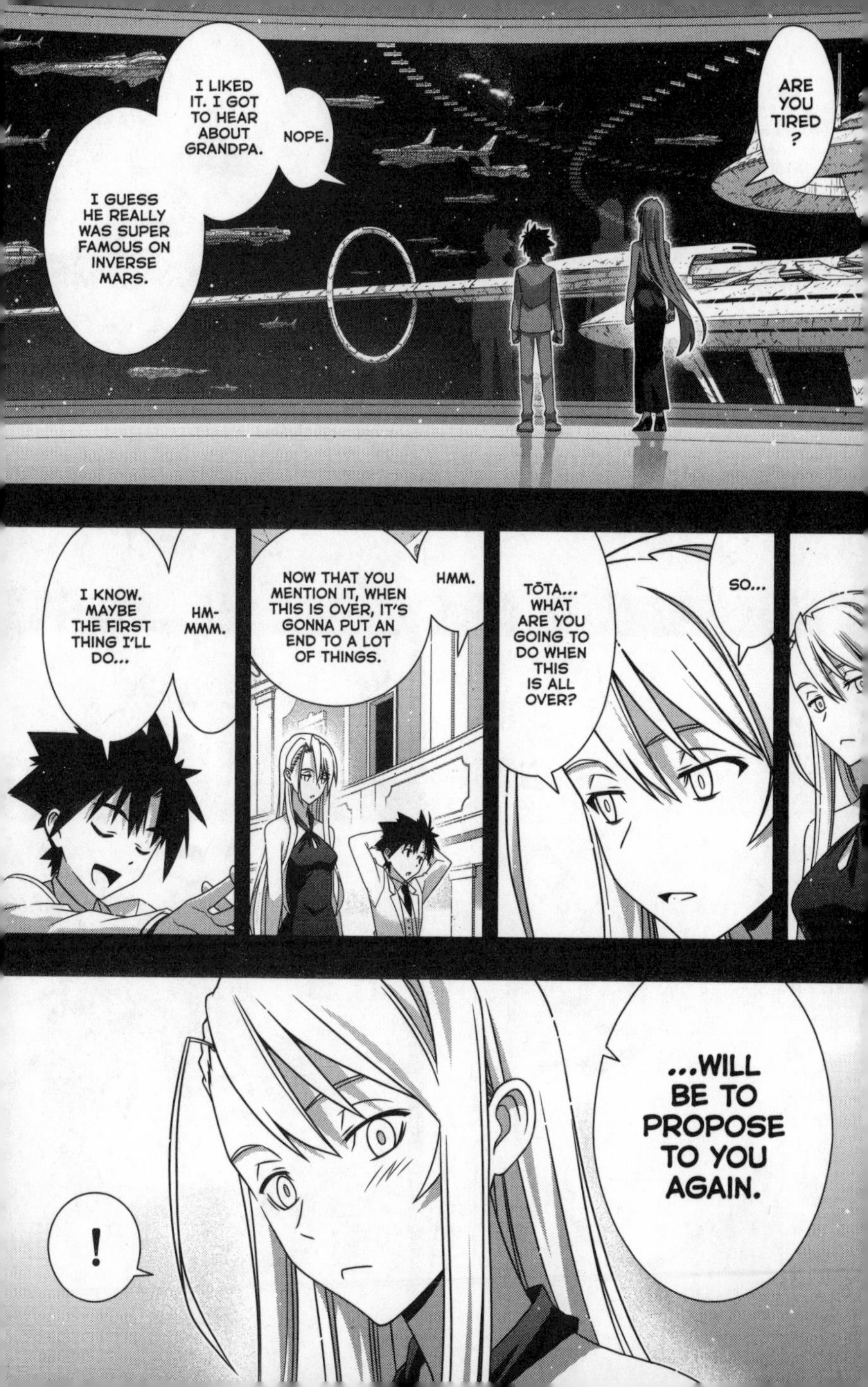
ARE YOU TIRED?
NOPE.
I LIKED IT. I GOT TO HEAR ABOUT GRANDPA.
I GUESS HE REALLY WAS SUPER FAMOUS ON INVERSE MARS.
SO...
TŌTA... WHAT ARE YOU GOING TO DO WHEN THIS IS ALL OVER?
HMM.
NOW THAT YOU MENTION IT, WHEN THIS IS OVER, IT'S GONNA PUT AN END TO A LOT OF THINGS.
HM-MMM.
I KNOW. MAYBE THE FIRST THING I'LL DO...
...WILL BE TO PROPOSE TO YOU AGAIN.
!

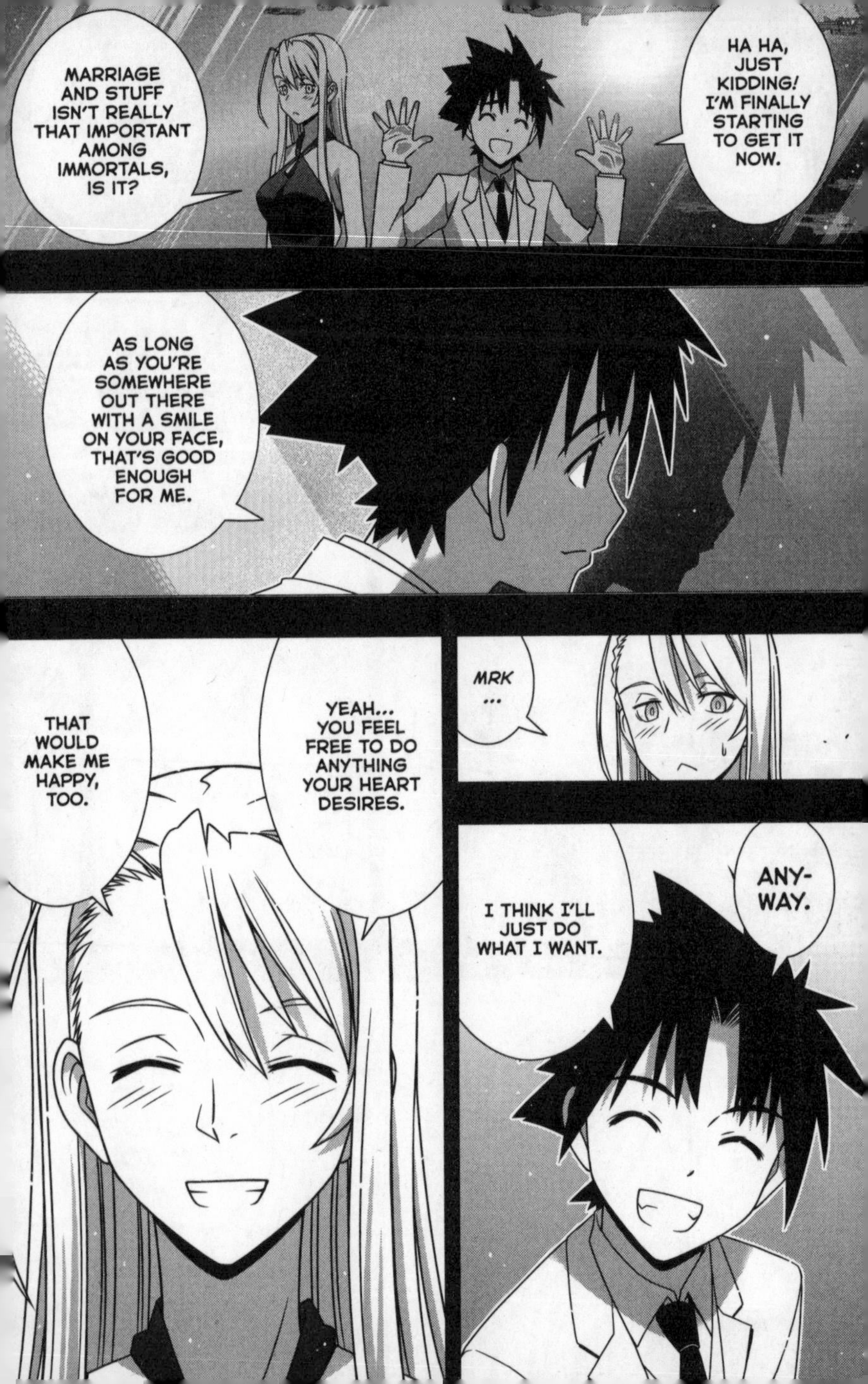
HA HA, JUST KIDDING! I'M FINALLY STARTING TO GET IT NOW.
MARRIAGE AND STUFF ISN'T REALLY THAT IMPORTANT AMONG IMMORTALS, IS IT?
AS LONG AS YOU'RE SOMEWHERE OUT THERE WITH A SMILE ON YOUR FACE, THAT'S GOOD ENOUGH FOR ME.
MRK ...
ANY-WAY.
I THINK I'LL JUST DO WHAT I WANT.
YEAH... YOU FEEL FREE TO DO ANYTHING YOUR HEART DESIRES.
THAT WOULD MAKE ME HAPPY, TOO.

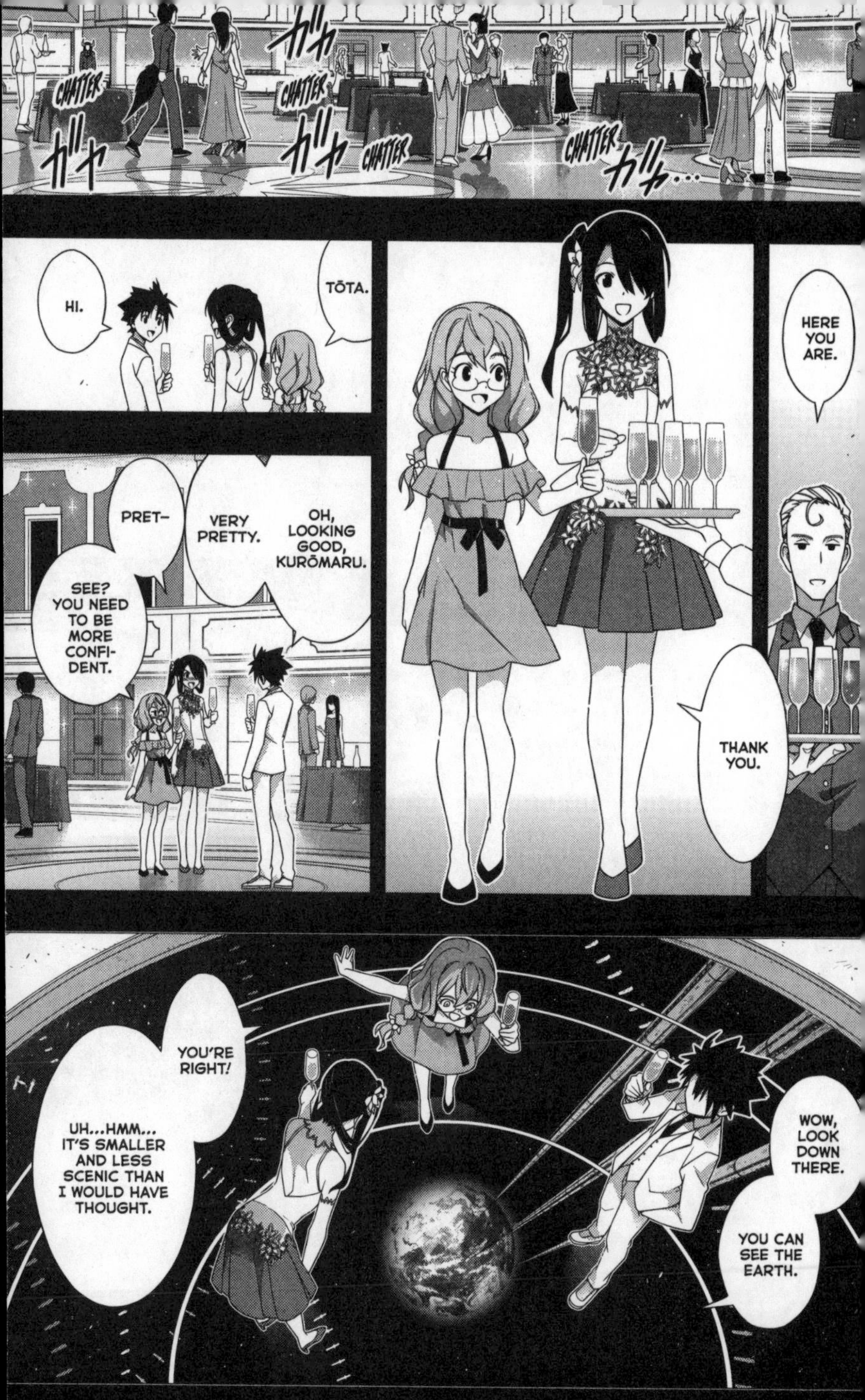
CHATTER
ガヤ…
CHATTER
ガヤ
CHATTER
ガヤ
CHATTER
ガヤ
HERE YOU ARE.
THANK YOU.
TŌTA.
HI.
OH, LOOKING GOOD, KURŌMARU.
VERY PRETTY.
PRET—
SEE? YOU NEED TO BE MORE CONFI-DENT.
WOW, LOOK DOWN THERE.
YOU CAN SEE THE EARTH.
YOU'RE RIGHT!
UH...HMM... IT'S SMALLER AND LESS SCENIC THAN I WOULD HAVE THOUGHT.

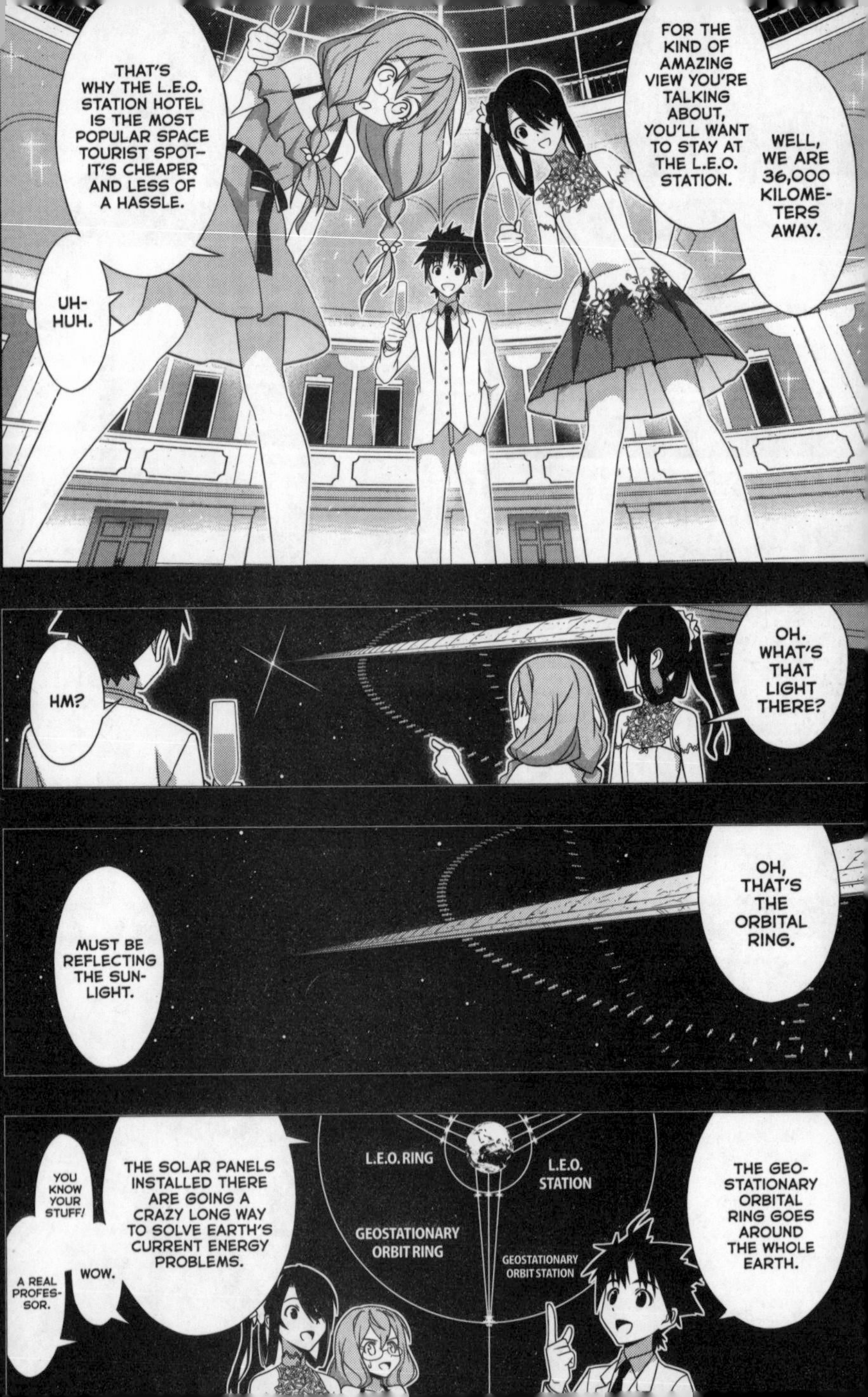
WELL, WE ARE 36,000 KILOMETERS AWAY.
FOR THE KIND OF AMAZING VIEW YOU'RE TALKING ABOUT, YOU'LL WANT TO STAY AT THE L.E.O. STATION.
THAT'S WHY THE L.E.O. STATION HOTEL IS THE MOST POPULAR SPACE TOURIST SPOT—IT'S CHEAPER AND LESS OF A HASSLE.
UH-HUH.
OH. WHAT'S THAT LIGHT THERE?
HM?
OH, THAT'S THE ORBITAL RING.
MUST BE REFLECTING THE SUNLIGHT.
THE GEO-STATIONARY ORBITAL RING GOES AROUND THE WHOLE EARTH.
L.E.O. RING
L.E.O. STATION
GEOSTATIONARY ORBIT RING
GEOSTATIONARY ORBIT STATION
THE SOLAR PANELS INSTALLED THERE ARE GOING A CRAZY LONG WAY TO SOLVE EARTH'S CURRENT ENERGY PROBLEMS.
YOU KNOW YOUR STUFF!
WOW.
A REAL PROFESSOR.

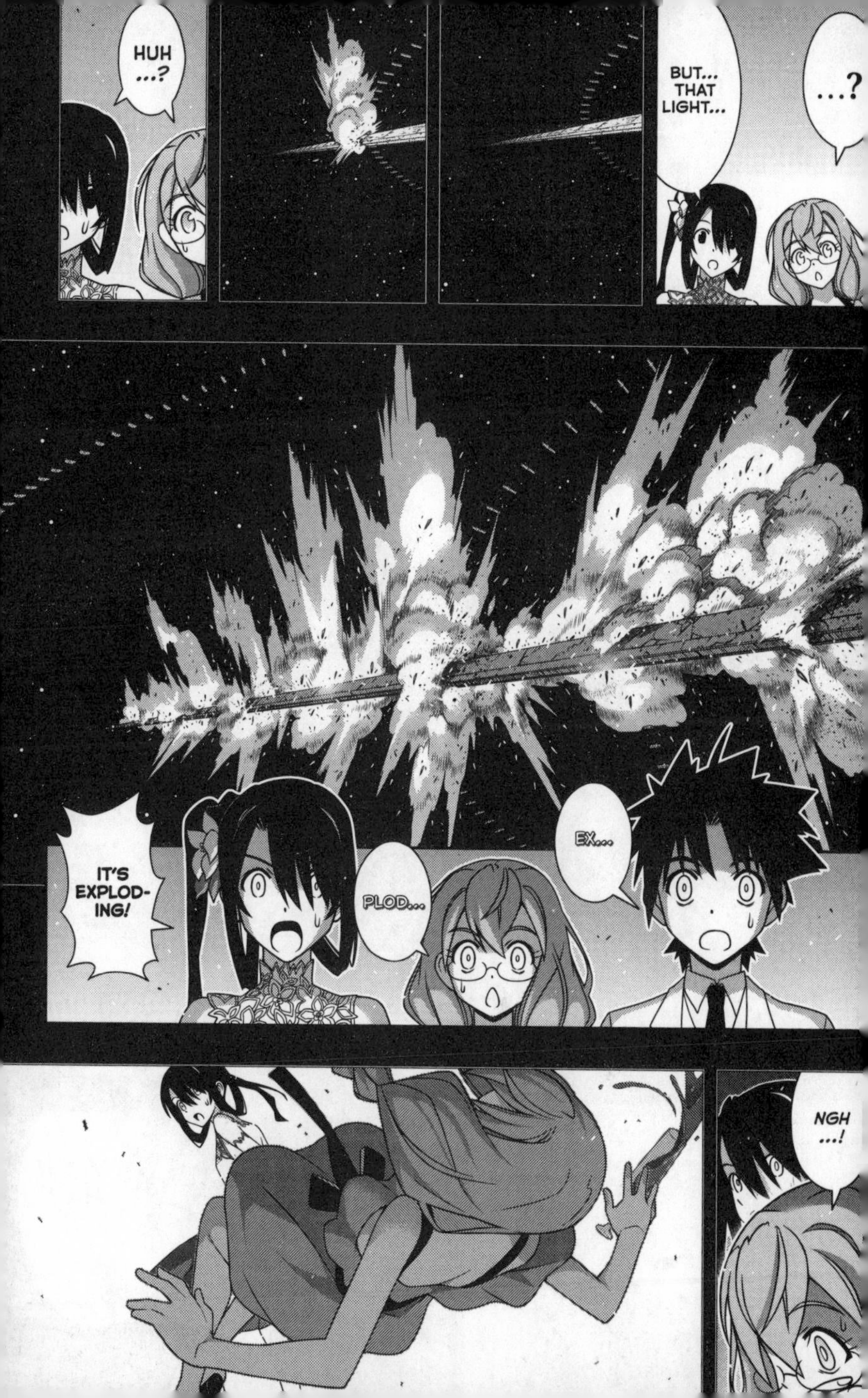
...?
BUT... THAT LIGHT...
HUH ...?
EX...
PLOD...
IT'S EXPLOD-ING!
NGH ...!

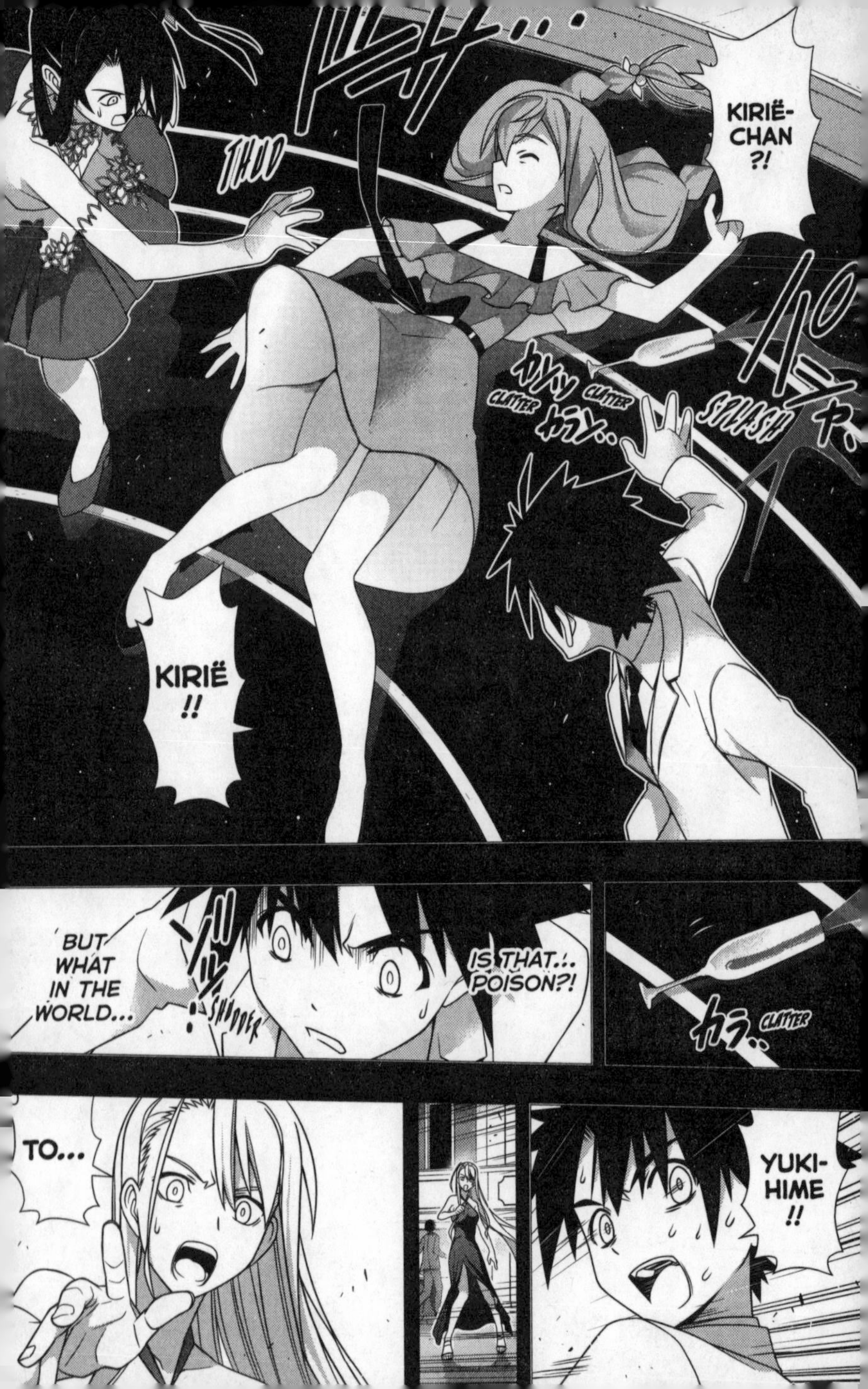
KIRIË-CHAN ?!
THUD
SPLASH
CLATTER
CLATTER
KIRIË !!
CLATTER
IS THAT... POISON?!
SHUDDER
BUT WHAT IN THE WORLD...
YUKI-HIME !!
TO...

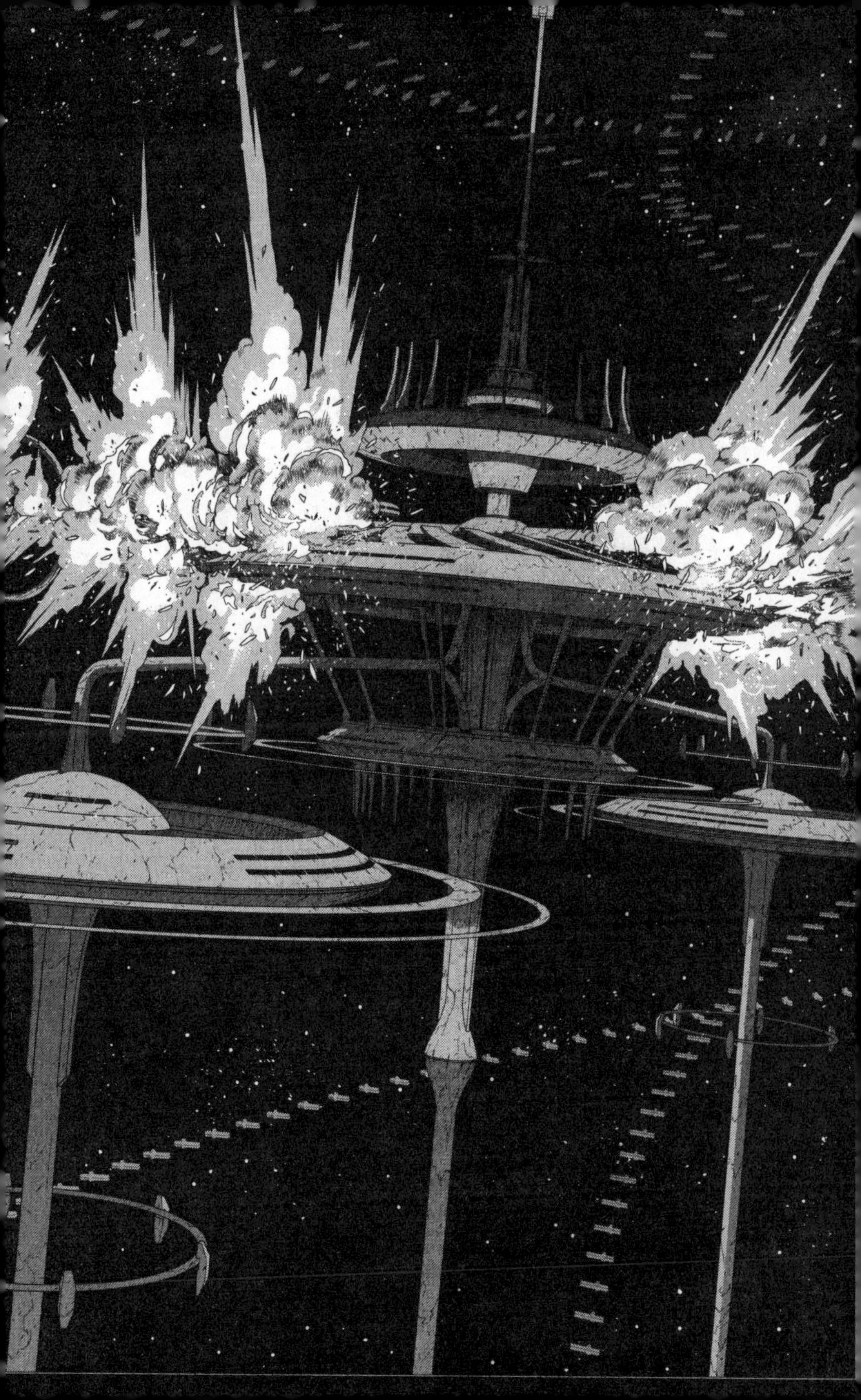

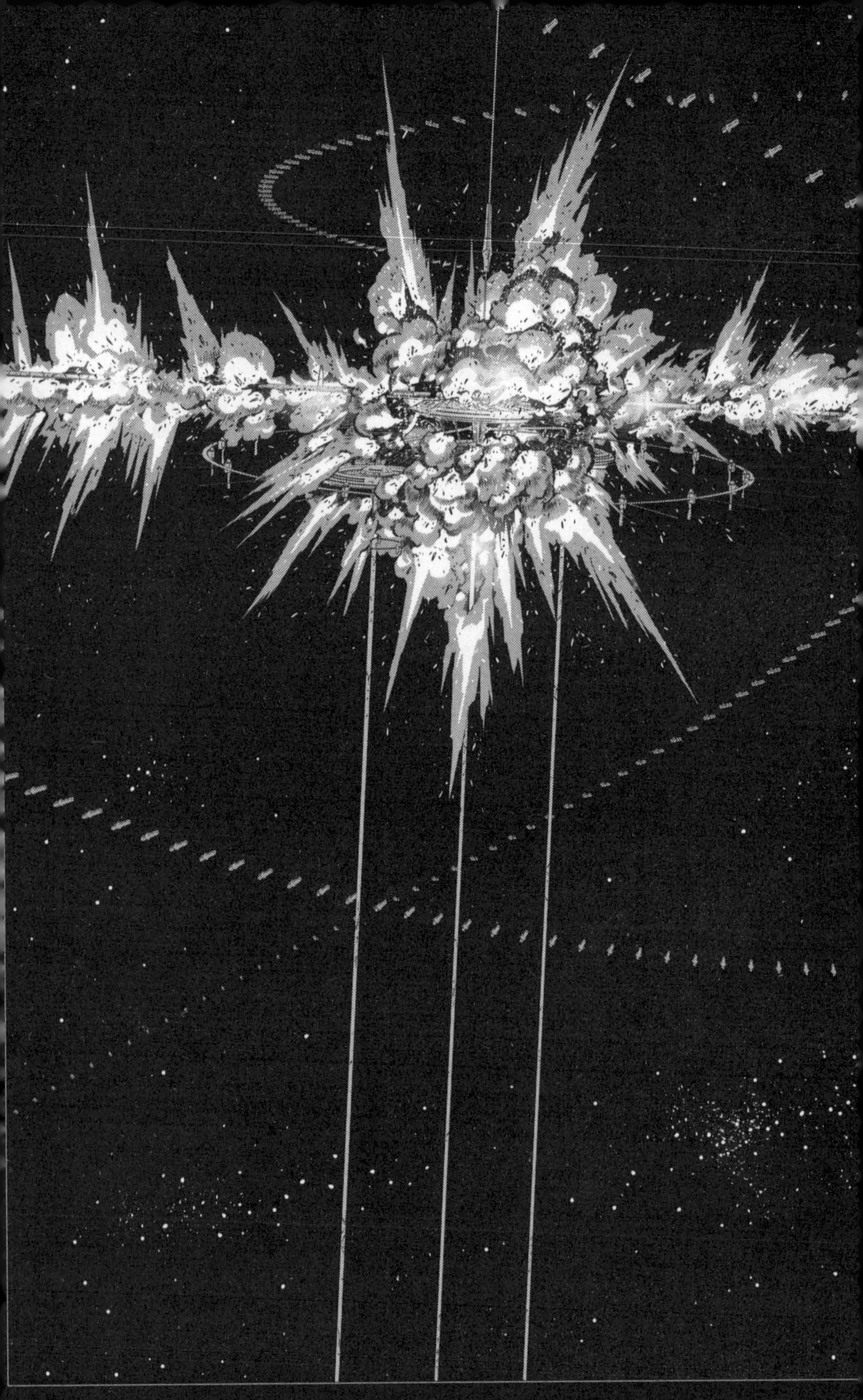

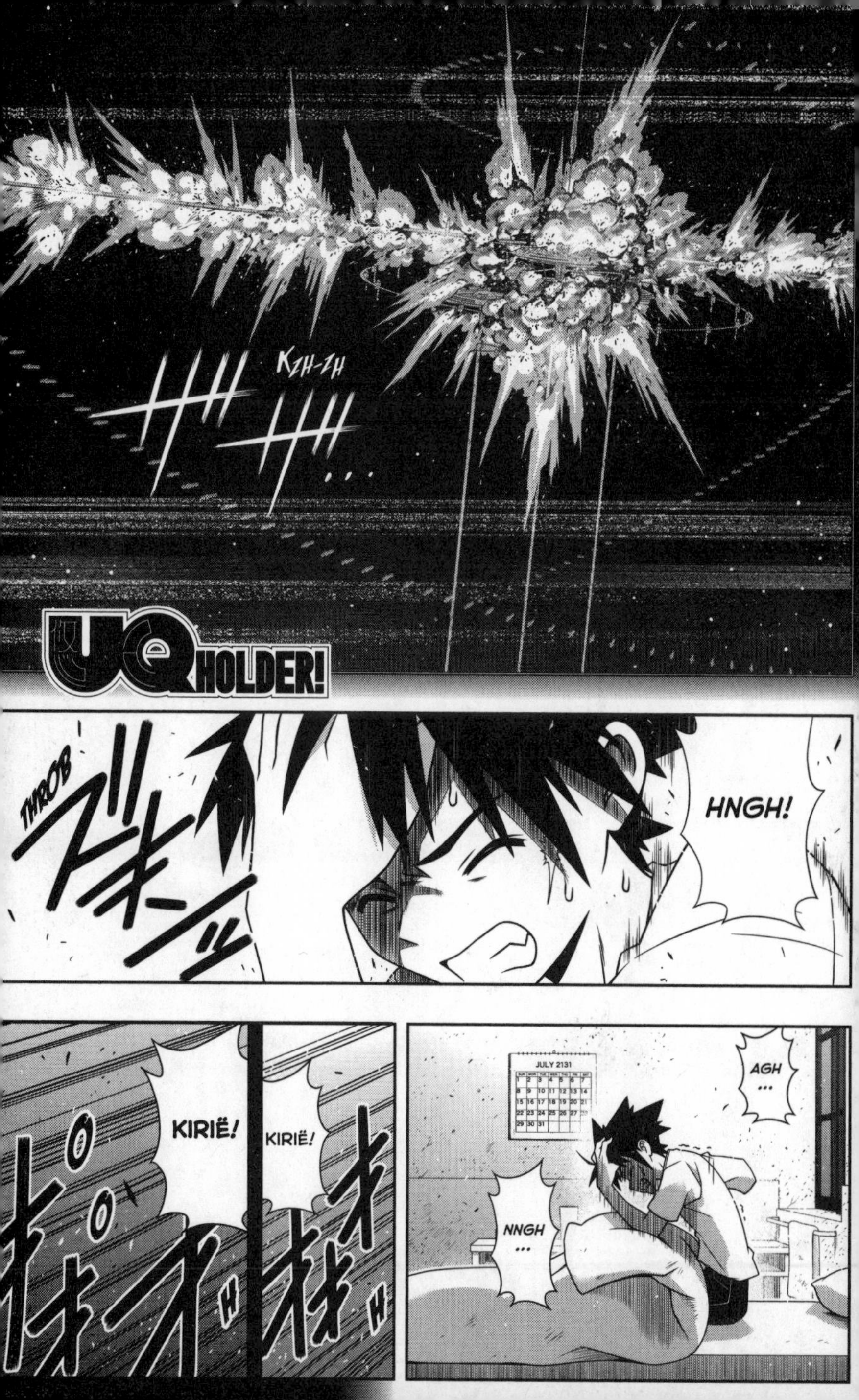
KZH-ZH
...
UQ HOLDER!
THROB
HNGH!
AGH...
JULY 2131
NNGH...
KIRIË!
KIRIË!

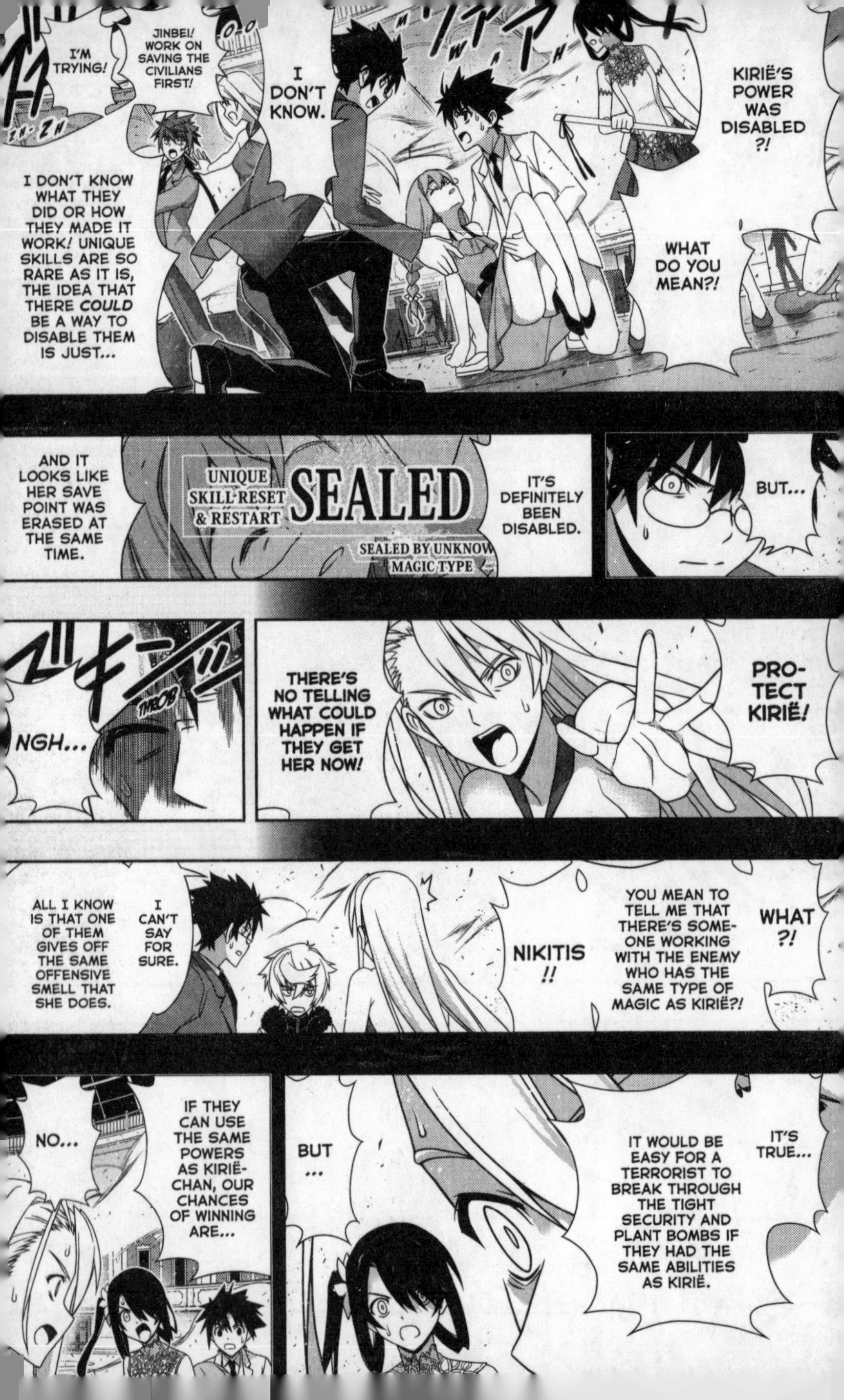

KIRIË'S POWER WAS DISABLED?!
WHAT DO YOU MEAN?!
I DON'T KNOW.
JINBEI! WORK ON SAVING THE CIVILIANS FIRST!
I'M TRYING!
I DON'T KNOW WHAT THEY DID OR HOW THEY MADE IT WORK! UNIQUE SKILLS ARE SO RARE AS IT IS, THE IDEA THAT THERE *COULD* BE A WAY TO DISABLE THEM IS JUST...
BUT...
IT'S DEFINITELY BEEN DISABLED.
UNIQUE SKILL RESET & RESTART
SEALED
SEALED BY UNKNOW MAGIC TYPE
AND IT LOOKS LIKE HER SAVE POINT WAS ERASED AT THE SAME TIME.
PROTECT KIRIË!
THERE'S NO TELLING WHAT COULD HAPPEN IF THEY GET HER NOW!
THROB
NGH...
WHAT?!
YOU MEAN TO TELL ME THAT THERE'S SOMEONE WORKING WITH THE ENEMY WHO HAS THE SAME TYPE OF MAGIC AS KIRIË?!
NIKITIS!!
I CAN'T SAY FOR SURE.
ALL I KNOW IS THAT ONE OF THEM GIVES OFF THE SAME OFFENSIVE SMELL THAT SHE DOES.
IT'S TRUE...
IT WOULD BE EASY FOR A TERRORIST TO BREAK THROUGH THE TIGHT SECURITY AND PLANT BOMBS IF THEY HAD THE SAME ABILITIES AS KIRIË.
BUT...
IF THEY CAN USE THE SAME POWERS AS KIRIË-CHAN, OUR CHANCES OF WINNING ARE...
NO...

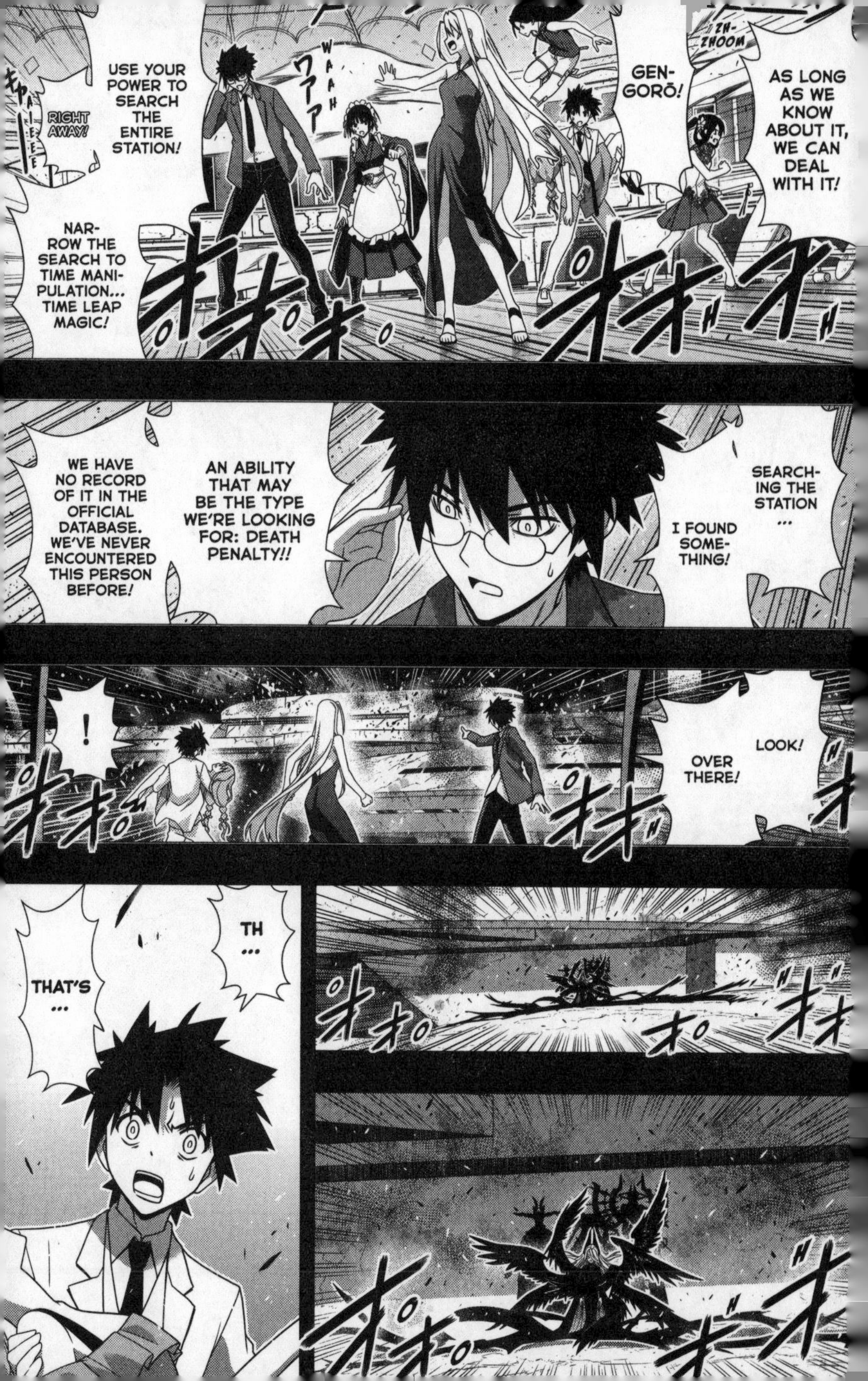
ZH-ZHOOM
AS LONG AS WE KNOW ABOUT IT, WE CAN DEAL WITH IT!
GEN-GORŌ!
ワアア
WAAH
USE YOUR POWER TO SEARCH THE ENTIRE STATION!
RIGHT AWAY!
AIEEE
NARROW THE SEARCH TO TIME MANIPULATION... TIME LEAP MAGIC!
SEARCHING THE STATION...
I FOUND SOMETHING!
AN ABILITY THAT MAY BE THE TYPE WE'RE LOOKING FOR: DEATH PENALTY!!
WE HAVE NO RECORD OF IT IN THE OFFICIAL DATABASE. WE'VE NEVER ENCOUNTERED THIS PERSON BEFORE!
LOOK!
OVER THERE!
!
TH...
THAT'S...

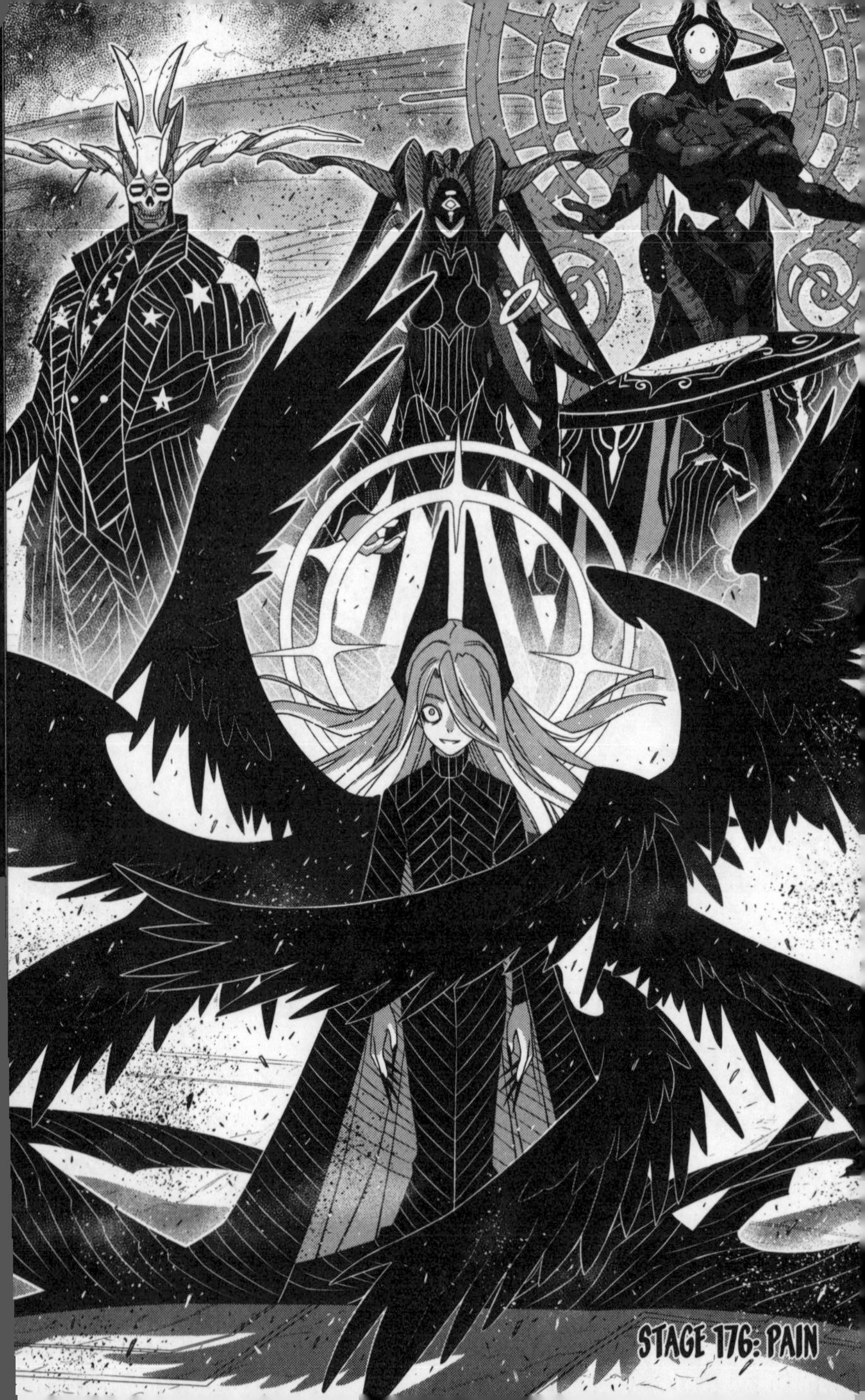
STAGE 176: PAIN

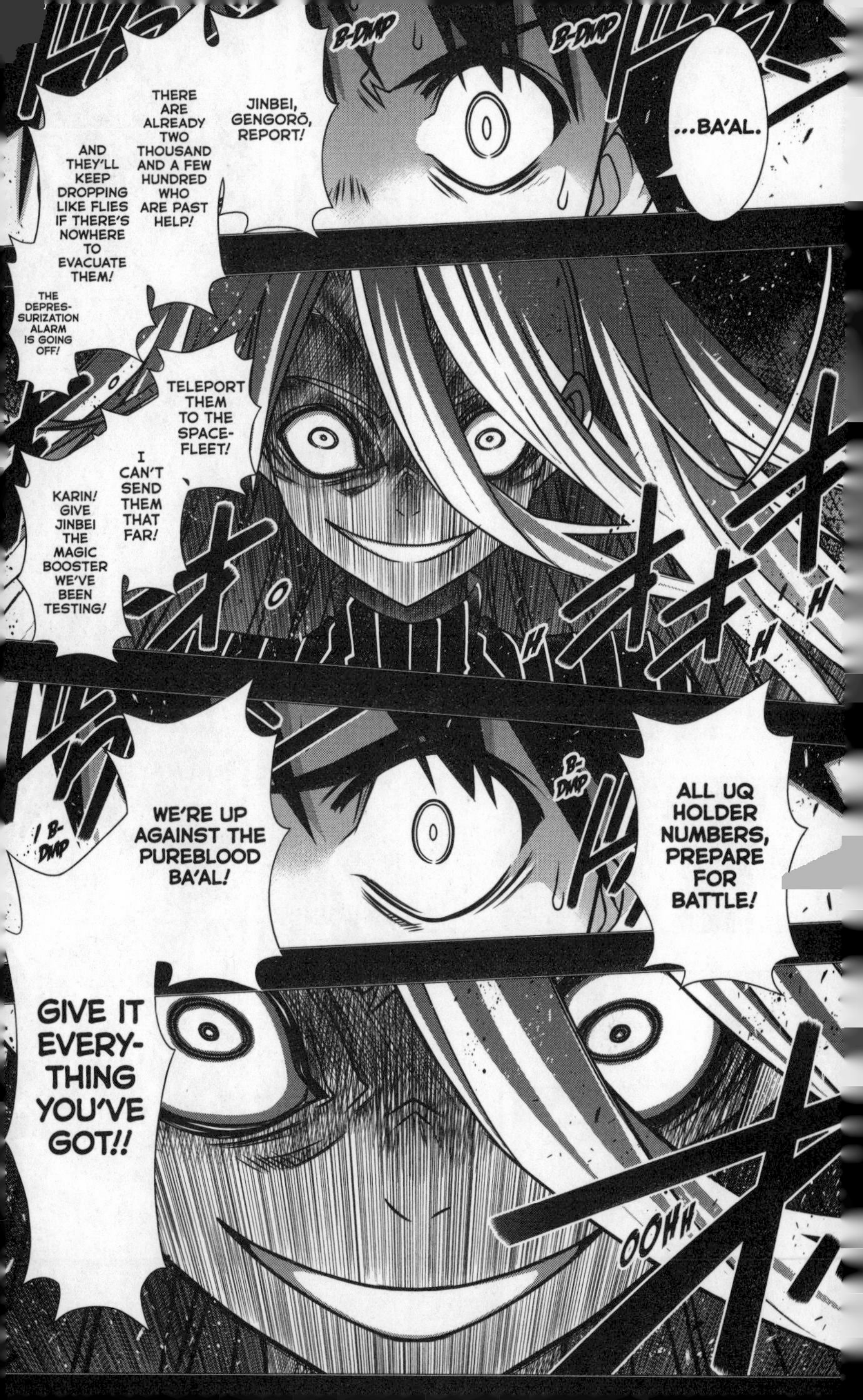
B-DMP
B-DMP
...BA'AL.
JINBEI, GENGORŌ, REPORT!
THERE ARE ALREADY TWO THOUSAND AND A FEW HUNDRED WHO ARE PAST HELP!
AND THEY'LL KEEP DROPPING LIKE FLIES IF THERE'S NOWHERE TO EVACUATE THEM!
THE DEPRES-SURIZATION ALARM IS GOING OFF!
TELEPORT THEM TO THE SPACE-FLEET!
I CAN'T SEND THEM THAT FAR!
KARIN! GIVE JINBEI THE MAGIC BOOSTER WE'VE BEEN TESTING!
H H H H
ALL UQ HOLDER NUMBERS, PREPARE FOR BATTLE!
B-DMP
WE'RE UP AGAINST THE PUREBLOOD BA'AL!
B-DMP
GIVE IT EVERY-THING YOU'VE GOT!!
OOHH

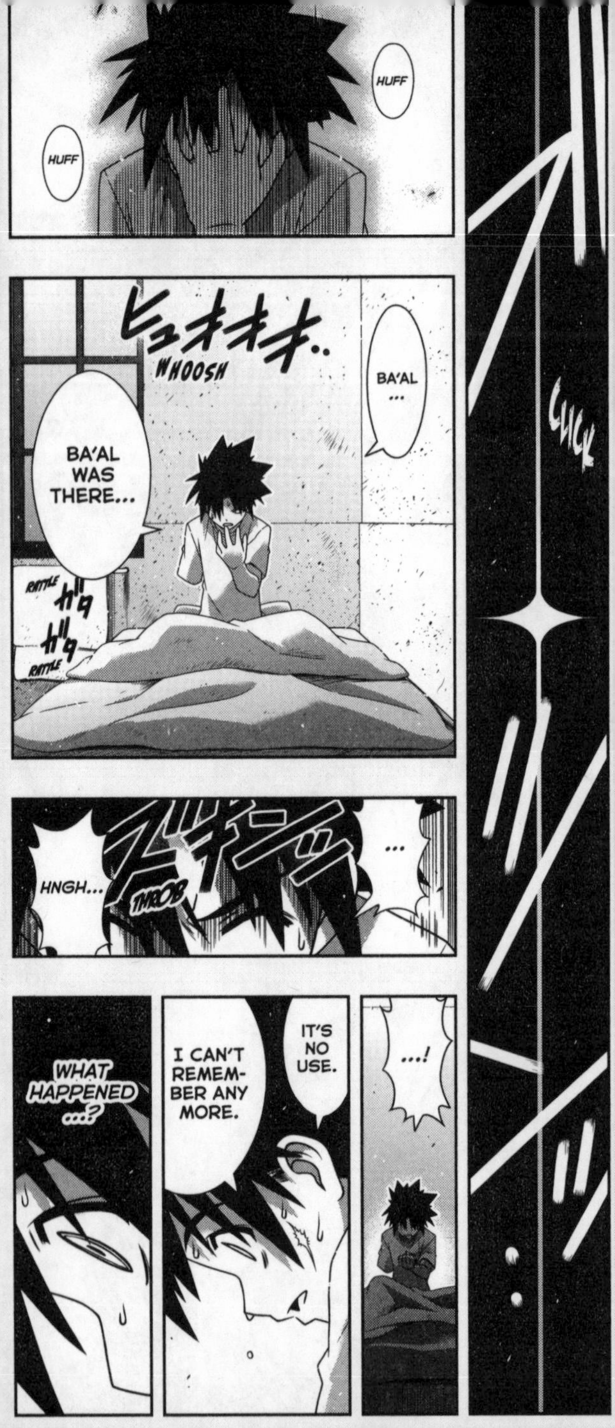
CLICK
HUFF
HUFF
BA'AL...
ヒュオオオ..
WHOOSH
BA'AL WAS THERE...
RATTLE ガタ
ガタ RATTLE
...
THROB
HNGH...
...!
IT'S NO USE.
I CAN'T REMEMBER ANY MORE.
WHAT HAPPENED...?

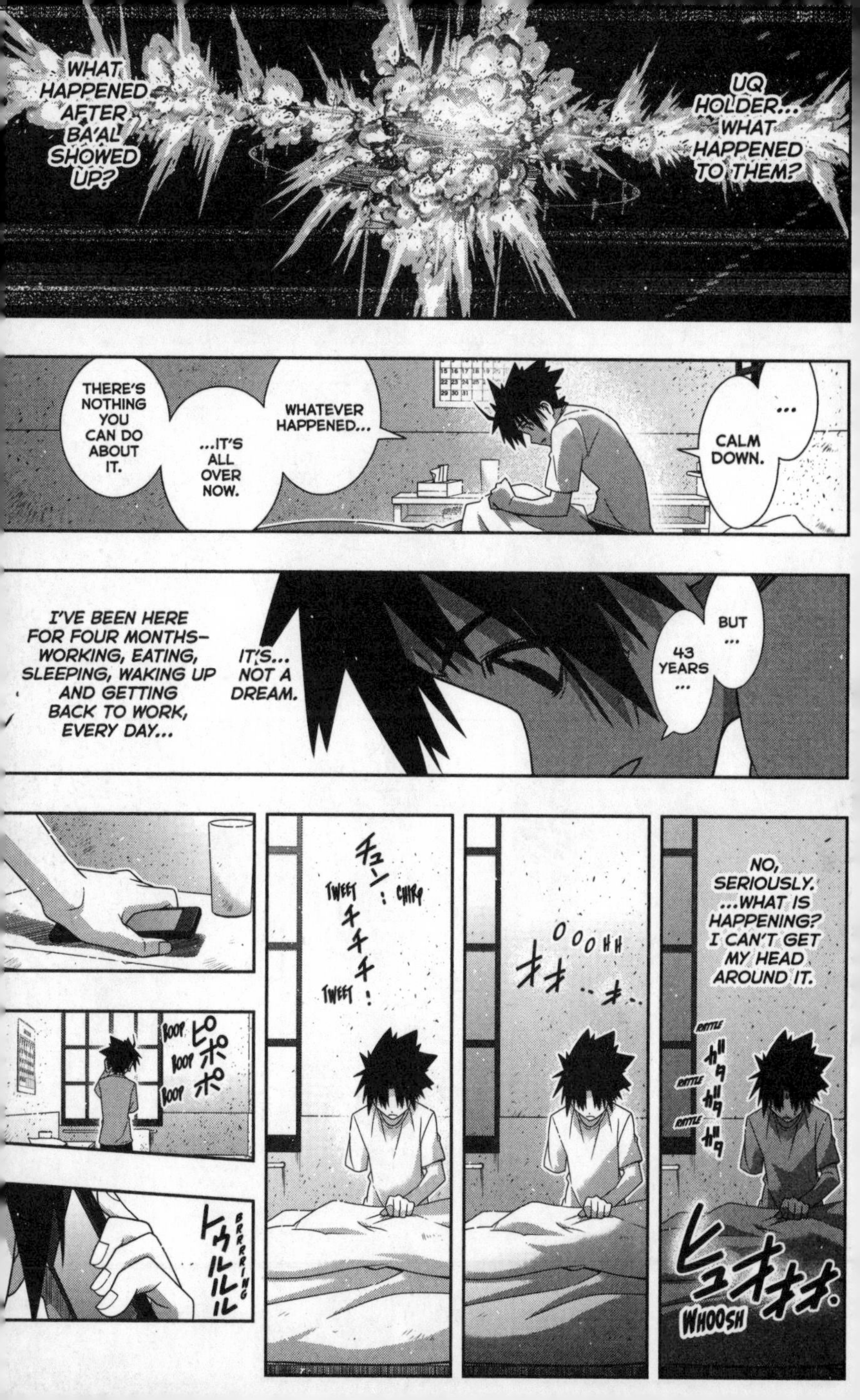
UQ HOLDER... WHAT HAPPENED TO THEM?
WHAT HAPPENED AFTER BA'AL SHOWED UP?
...
CALM DOWN.
WHATEVER HAPPENED...
...IT'S ALL OVER NOW.
THERE'S NOTHING YOU CAN DO ABOUT IT.
BUT... 43 YEARS...
IT'S... NOT A DREAM.
I'VE BEEN HERE FOR FOUR MONTHS— WORKING, EATING, SLEEPING, WAKING UP AND GETTING BACK TO WORK, EVERY DAY...
NO, SERIOUSLY. ...WHAT IS HAPPENING? I CAN'T GET MY HEAD AROUND IT.
ガタ RATTLE
ガタ RATTLE
ガタ RATTLE
ヒュオオオ WHOOSH
オオ…オ… OOOHH
チュン TWEET
チチチ! CHIRP TWEET
ピポポ BOOP BOOP BOOP
トゥルルル BRRRING

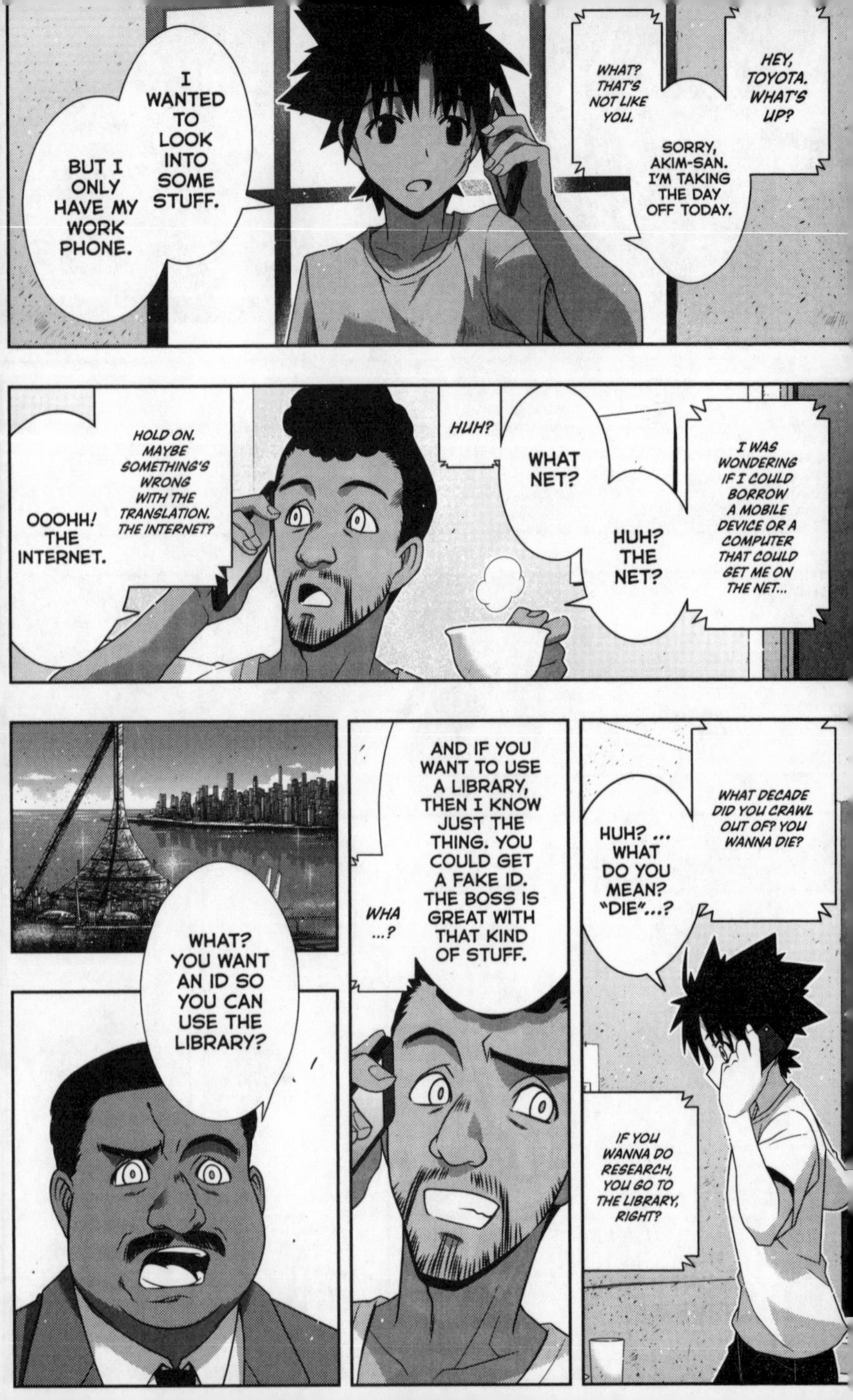
HEY, TOYOTA. WHAT'S UP?
SORRY, AKIM-SAN. I'M TAKING THE DAY OFF TODAY.
WHAT? THAT'S NOT LIKE YOU.
I WANTED TO LOOK INTO SOME STUFF.
BUT I ONLY HAVE MY WORK PHONE.
I WAS WONDERING IF I COULD BORROW A MOBILE DEVICE OR A COMPUTER THAT COULD GET ME ON THE NET...
HUH? THE NET?
WHAT NET?
HUH?
HOLD ON. MAYBE SOMETHING'S WRONG WITH THE TRANSLATION. THE INTERNET?
OOOHH! THE INTERNET.
WHAT DECADE DID YOU CRAWL OUT OF? YOU WANNA DIE?
HUH? ... WHAT DO YOU MEAN? "DIE"...?
IF YOU WANNA DO RESEARCH, YOU GO TO THE LIBRARY, RIGHT?
AND IF YOU WANT TO USE A LIBRARY, THEN I KNOW JUST THE THING. YOU COULD GET A FAKE ID. THE BOSS IS GREAT WITH THAT KIND OF STUFF.
WHA ...?
WHAT? YOU WANT AN ID SO YOU CAN USE THE LIBRARY?

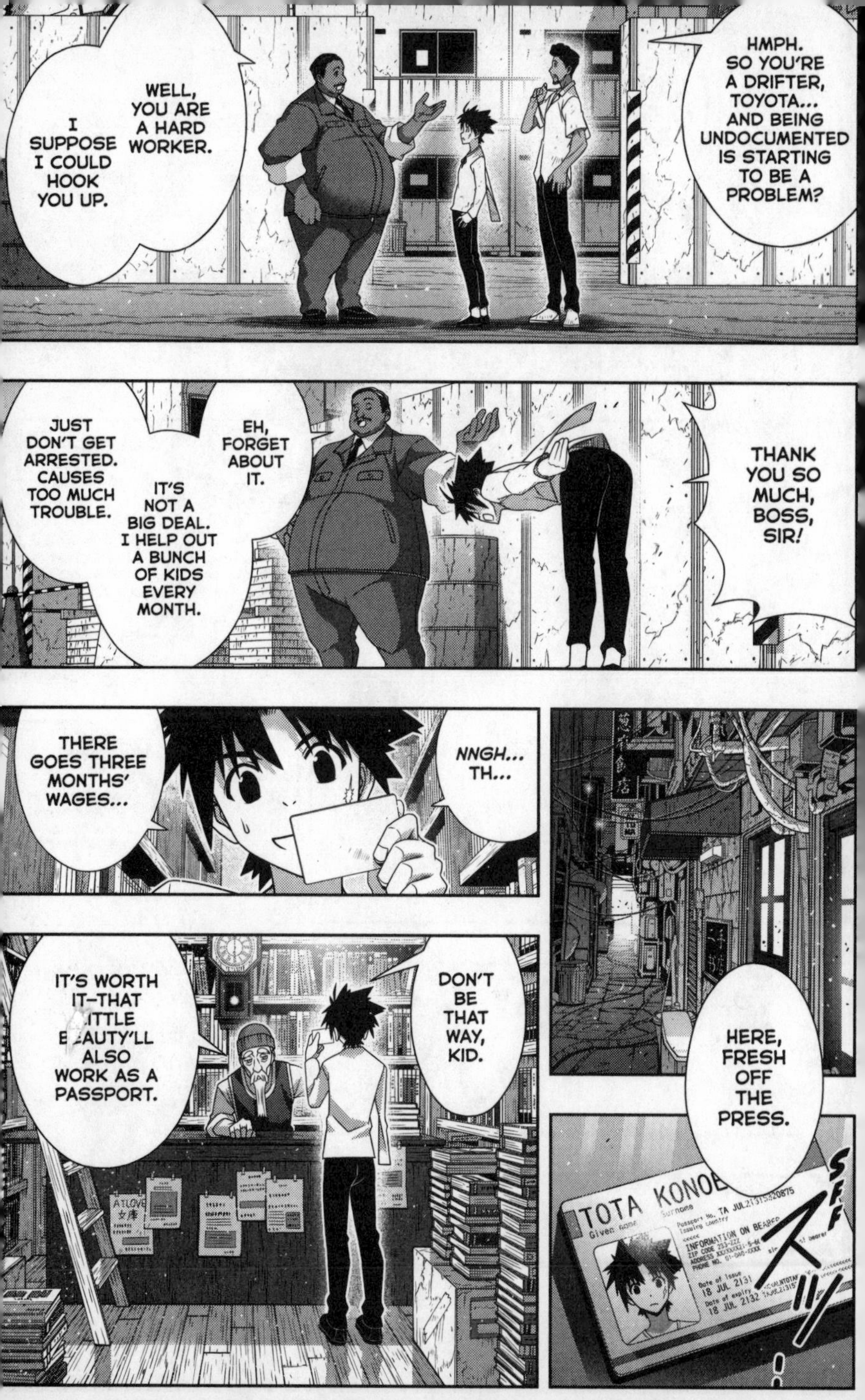
HMPH. SO YOU'RE A DRIFTER, TOYOTA... AND BEING UNDOCUMENTED IS STARTING TO BE A PROBLEM?
WELL, YOU ARE A HARD WORKER.
I SUPPOSE I COULD HOOK YOU UP.
THANK YOU SO MUCH, BOSS, SIR!
EH, FORGET ABOUT IT.
IT'S NOT A BIG DEAL. I HELP OUT A BUNCH OF KIDS EVERY MONTH.
JUST DON'T GET ARRESTED. CAUSES TOO MUCH TROUBLE.
HERE, FRESH OFF THE PRESS.
TOTA KONOE
SFF
NNGH... TH...
THERE GOES THREE MONTHS' WAGES...
DON'T BE THAT WAY, KID.
IT'S WORTH IT—THAT LITTLE BEAUTY'LL ALSO WORK AS A PASSPORT.

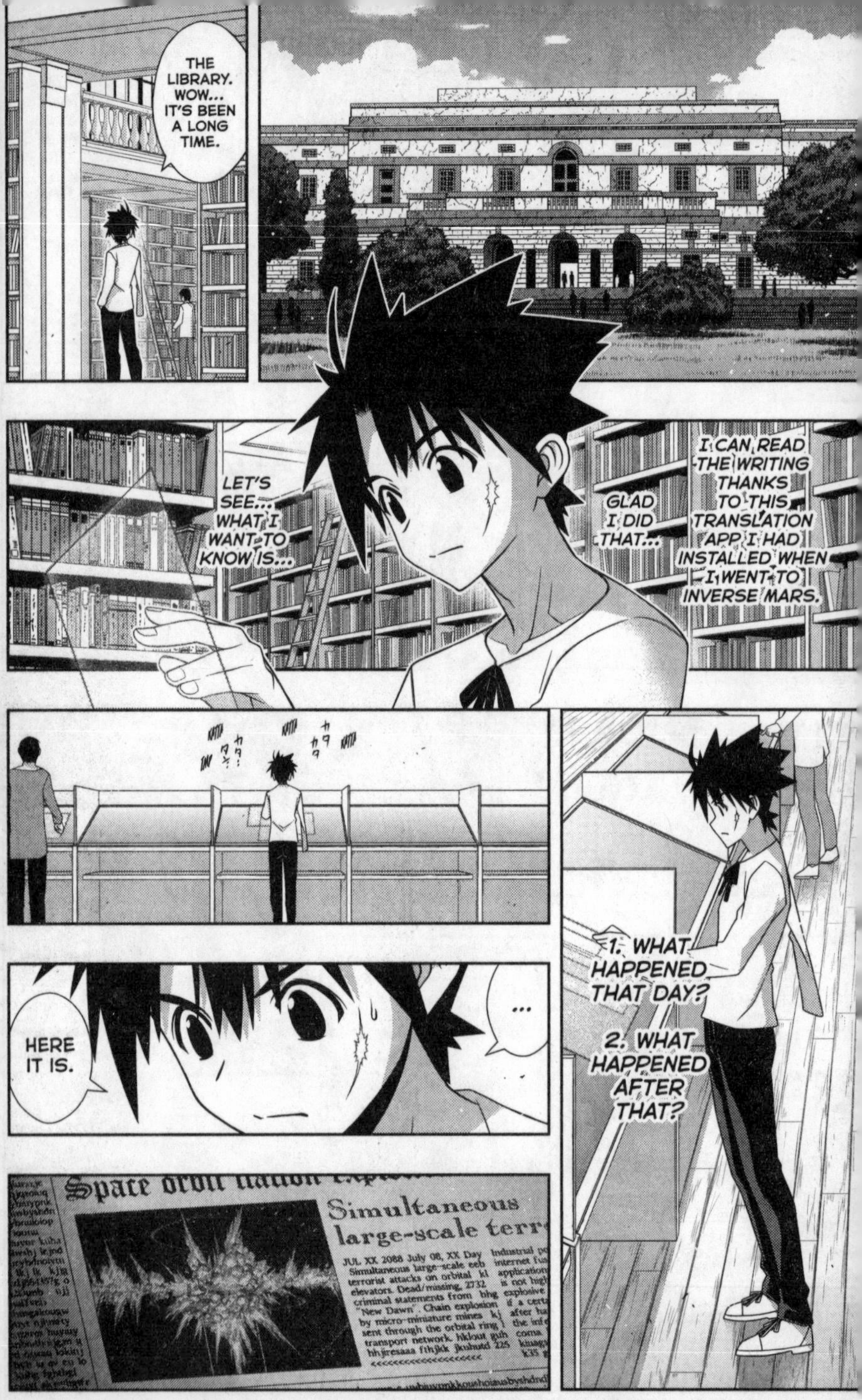
THE LIBRARY. WOW... IT'S BEEN A LONG TIME.
I CAN READ THE WRITING THANKS TO THIS TRANSLATION APP I HAD INSTALLED WHEN I WENT TO INVERSE MARS.
GLAD I DID THAT...
LET'S SEE... WHAT I WANT TO KNOW IS...
1. WHAT HAPPENED THAT DAY?
2. WHAT HAPPENED AFTER THAT?
カタ
カタ
...
HERE IT IS.
Simultaneous
large-scale terr
JUL XX 2088 July 08, XX Day
Simultaneous large-scale eeb
terrorist attacks on orbital kl
elevators. Dead/missing, 2732
criminal statements from bhg
"New Dawn". Chain explosion
by micro-miniature mines kj
sent through the orbital ring
transport network. hkloui guh
hhjiresaaa fthjkk jkuhutd 225

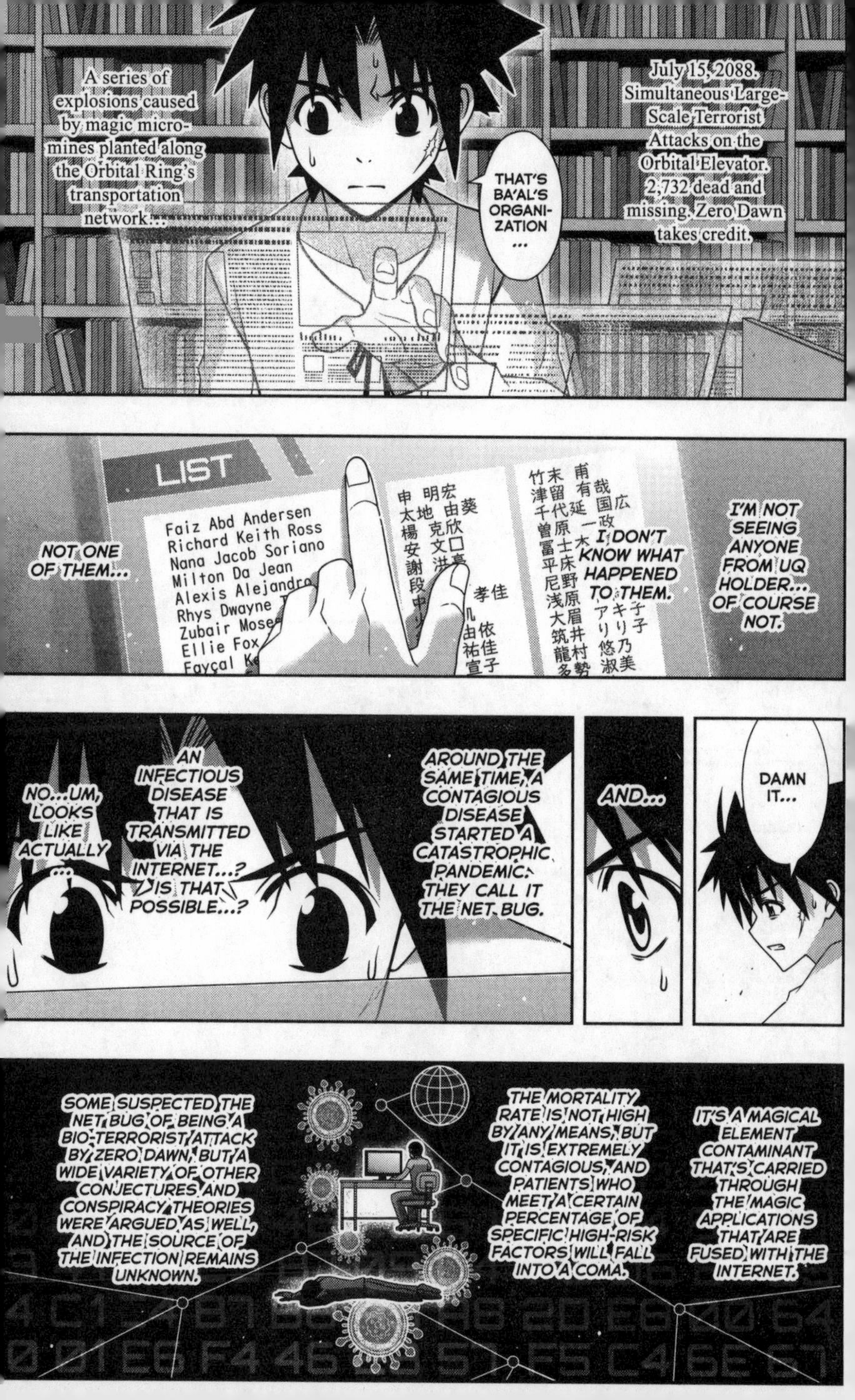
July 15, 2088. Simultaneous Large-Scale Terrorist Attacks on the Orbital Elevator. 2,732 dead and missing. Zero Dawn takes credit.
THAT'S BA'AL'S ORGANIZATION...
A series of explosions caused by magic micro-mines planted along the Orbital Ring's transportation network...
I'M NOT SEEING ANYONE FROM UQ HOLDER... OF COURSE NOT.
I DON'T KNOW WHAT HAPPENED TO THEM.
NOT ONE OF THEM...
LIST
Faiz Abd Andersen
Richard Keith Ross
Nana Jacob Soriano
Milton Da Jean
DAMN IT...
AND...
AROUND THE SAME TIME, A CONTAGIOUS DISEASE STARTED A CATASTROPHIC PANDEMIC. THEY CALL IT THE NET BUG.
AN INFECTIOUS DISEASE THAT IS TRANSMITTED VIA THE INTERNET...? IS THAT POSSIBLE...?
NO...UM, LOOKS LIKE ACTUALLY...
IT'S A MAGICAL ELEMENT CONTAMINANT THAT'S CARRIED THROUGH THE MAGIC APPLICATIONS THAT ARE FUSED WITH THE INTERNET.
THE MORTALITY RATE IS NOT HIGH BY ANY MEANS, BUT IT IS EXTREMELY CONTAGIOUS, AND PATIENTS WHO MEET A CERTAIN PERCENTAGE OF SPECIFIC HIGH-RISK FACTORS WILL FALL INTO A COMA.
SOME SUSPECTED THE NET BUG OF BEING A BIO-TERRORIST ATTACK BY ZERO DAWN, BUT A WIDE VARIETY OF OTHER CONJECTURES AND CONSPIRACY THEORIES WERE ARGUED AS WELL, AND THE SOURCE OF THE INFECTION REMAINS UNKNOWN.

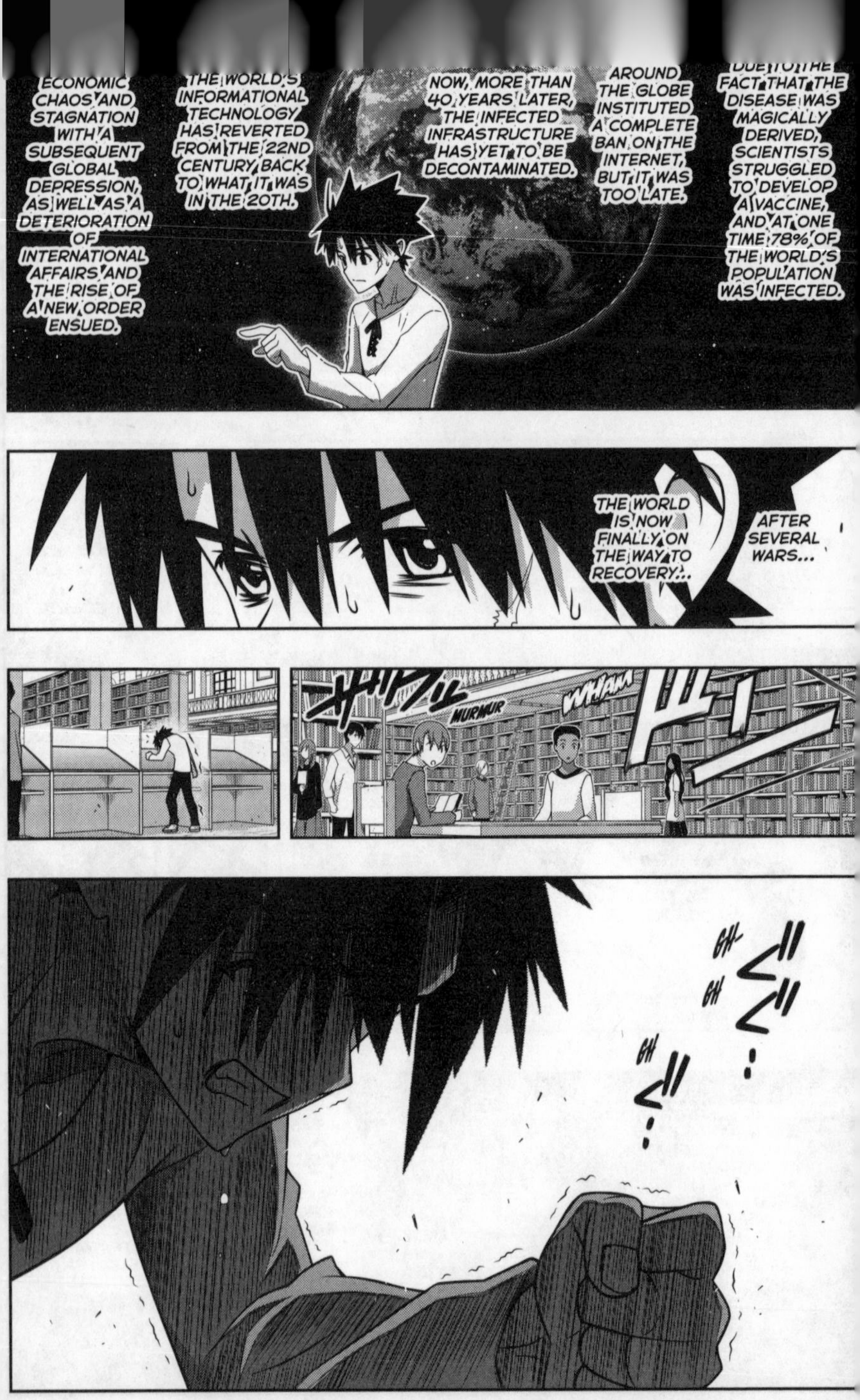
DUE TO THE FACT THAT THE DISEASE WAS MAGICALLY DERIVED, SCIENTISTS STRUGGLED TO DEVELOP A VACCINE, AND AT ONE TIME 78% OF THE WORLD'S POPULATION WAS INFECTED.
AROUND THE GLOBE INSTITUTED A COMPLETE BAN ON THE INTERNET, BUT IT WAS TOO LATE.
NOW, MORE THAN 40 YEARS LATER, THE INFECTED INFRASTRUCTURE HAS YET TO BE DECONTAMINATED.
THE WORLD'S INFORMATIONAL TECHNOLOGY HAS REVERTED FROM THE 22ND CENTURY BACK TO WHAT IT WAS IN THE 20TH.
ECONOMIC CHAOS AND STAGNATION WITH A SUBSEQUENT GLOBAL DEPRESSION, AS WELL AS A DETERIORATION OF INTERNATIONAL AFFAIRS AND THE RISE OF A NEW ORDER ENSUED.
AFTER SEVERAL WARS...
THE WORLD IS NOW FINALLY ON THE WAY TO RECOVERY...
WHAM
MURMUR
GH
GH
GH

I'M JUST GONNA GO SAVE THE WORLD REAL QUICK.

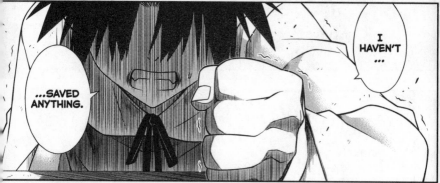

I HAVEN'T...

...SAVED ANYTHING.

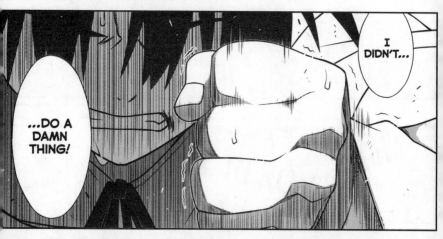

I DIDN'T...

...DO A DAMN THING!

GRNK

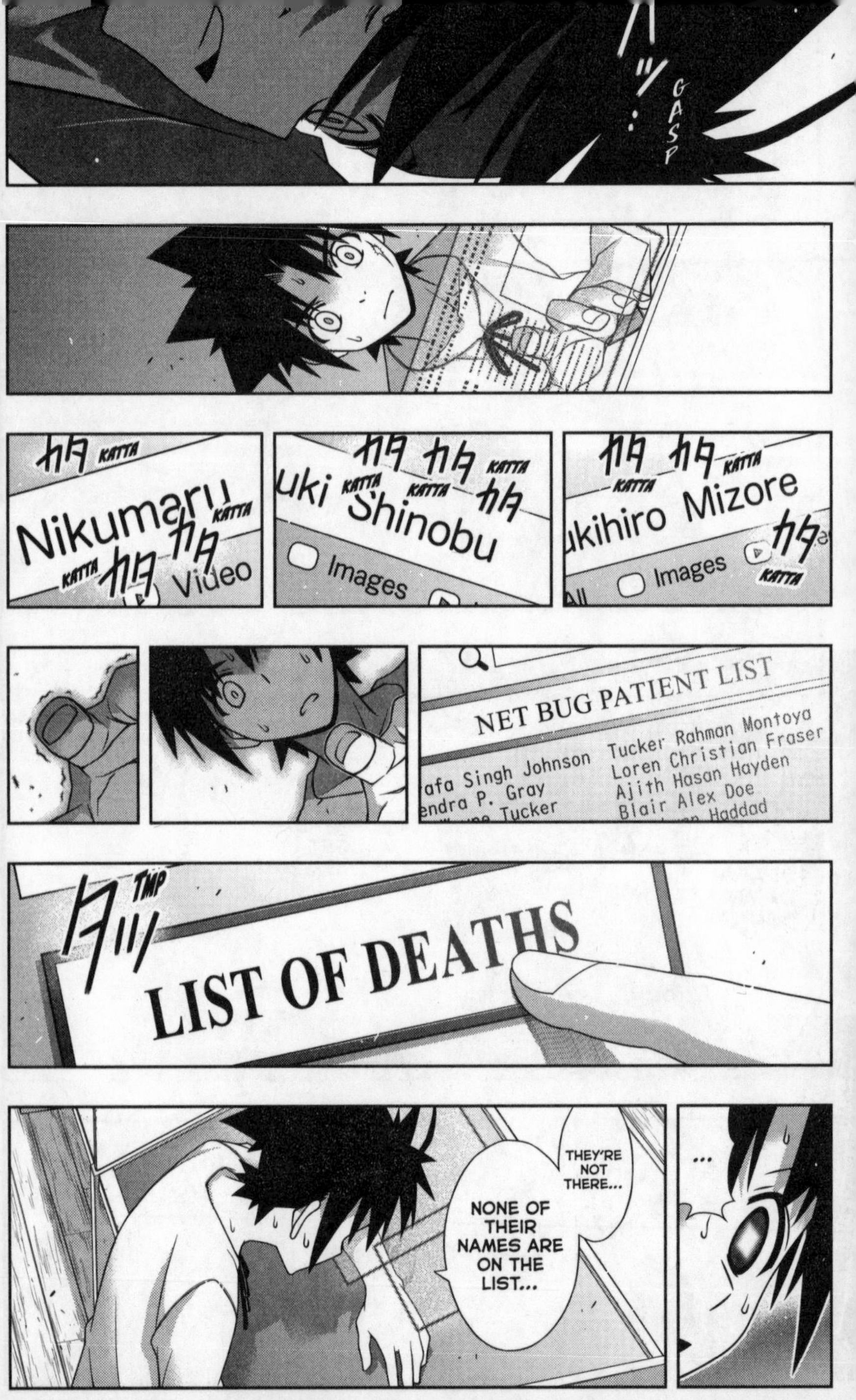
GASP
カタ
KATTA
カタ
KATTA
ukihiro Mizore
Images
カタ
KATTA
カタ
KATTA
カタ
KATTA
カタ
KATTA
uki Shinobu
Images
カタ
KATTA
Nikumaru
カタ
KATTA
カタ
KATTA
Video
NET BUG PATIENT LIST
afa Singh Johnson
endra P. Gray
Tucker Rahman Montoya
Loren Christian Fraser
Ajith Hasan Hayden
Blair Alex Doe
タッ
TMP
LIST OF DEATHS
...
THEY'RE NOT THERE...
NONE OF THEIR NAMES ARE ON THE LIST...

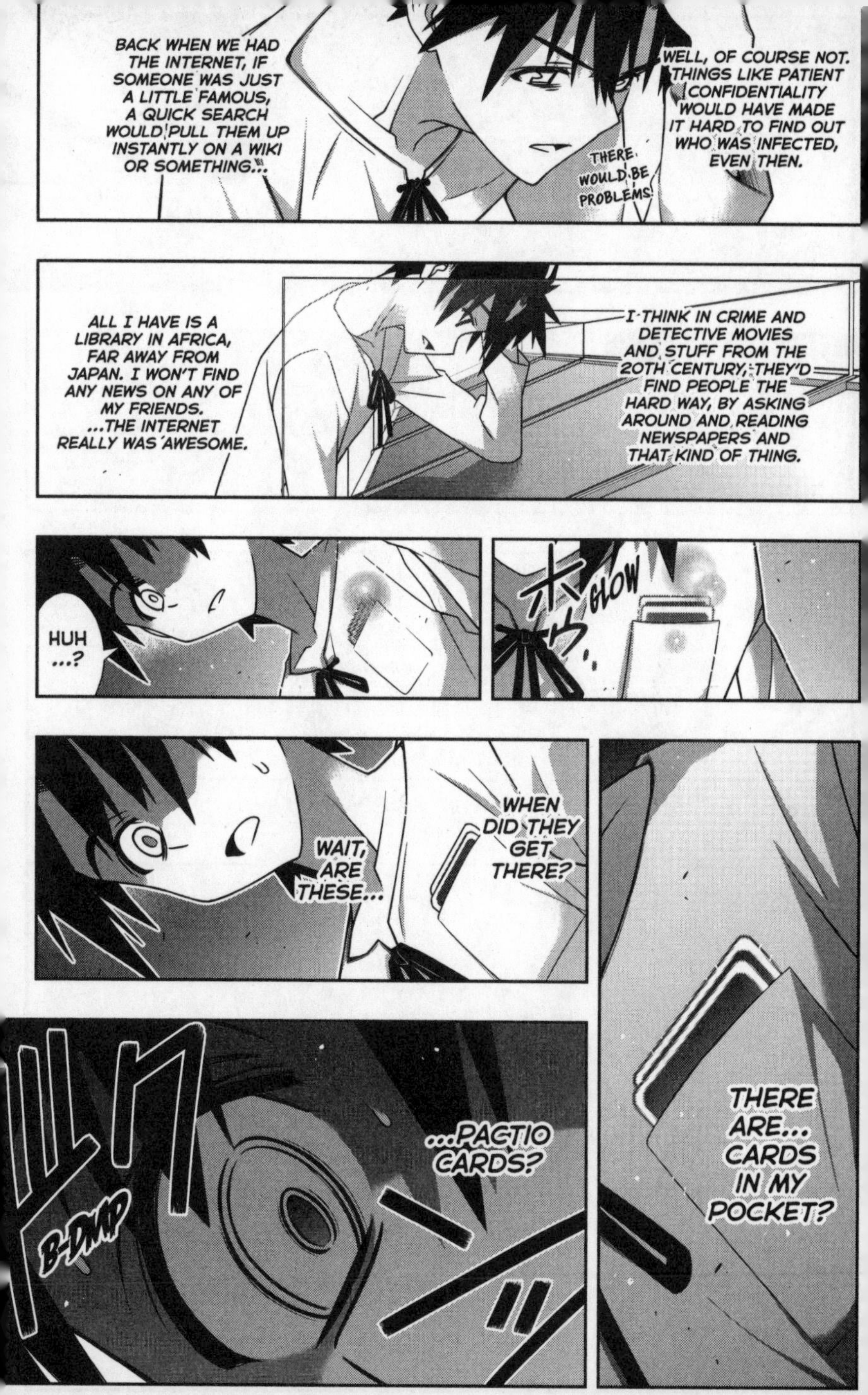
WELL, OF COURSE NOT. THINGS LIKE PATIENT CONFIDENTIALITY WOULD HAVE MADE IT HARD TO FIND OUT WHO WAS INFECTED, EVEN THEN.
THERE WOULD BE PROBLEMS!
BACK WHEN WE HAD THE INTERNET, IF SOMEONE WAS JUST A LITTLE FAMOUS, A QUICK SEARCH WOULD PULL THEM UP INSTANTLY ON A WIKI OR SOMETHING...
I THINK IN CRIME AND DETECTIVE MOVIES AND STUFF FROM THE 20TH CENTURY, THEY'D FIND PEOPLE THE HARD WAY, BY ASKING AROUND AND READING NEWSPAPERS AND THAT KIND OF THING.
ALL I HAVE IS A LIBRARY IN AFRICA, FAR AWAY FROM JAPAN. I WON'T FIND ANY NEWS ON ANY OF MY FRIENDS. ...THE INTERNET REALLY WAS AWESOME.
GLOW
HUH ...?
THERE ARE... CARDS IN MY POCKET?
WHEN DID THEY GET THERE?
WAIT, ARE THESE...
...PACTIO CARDS?
B-DMP

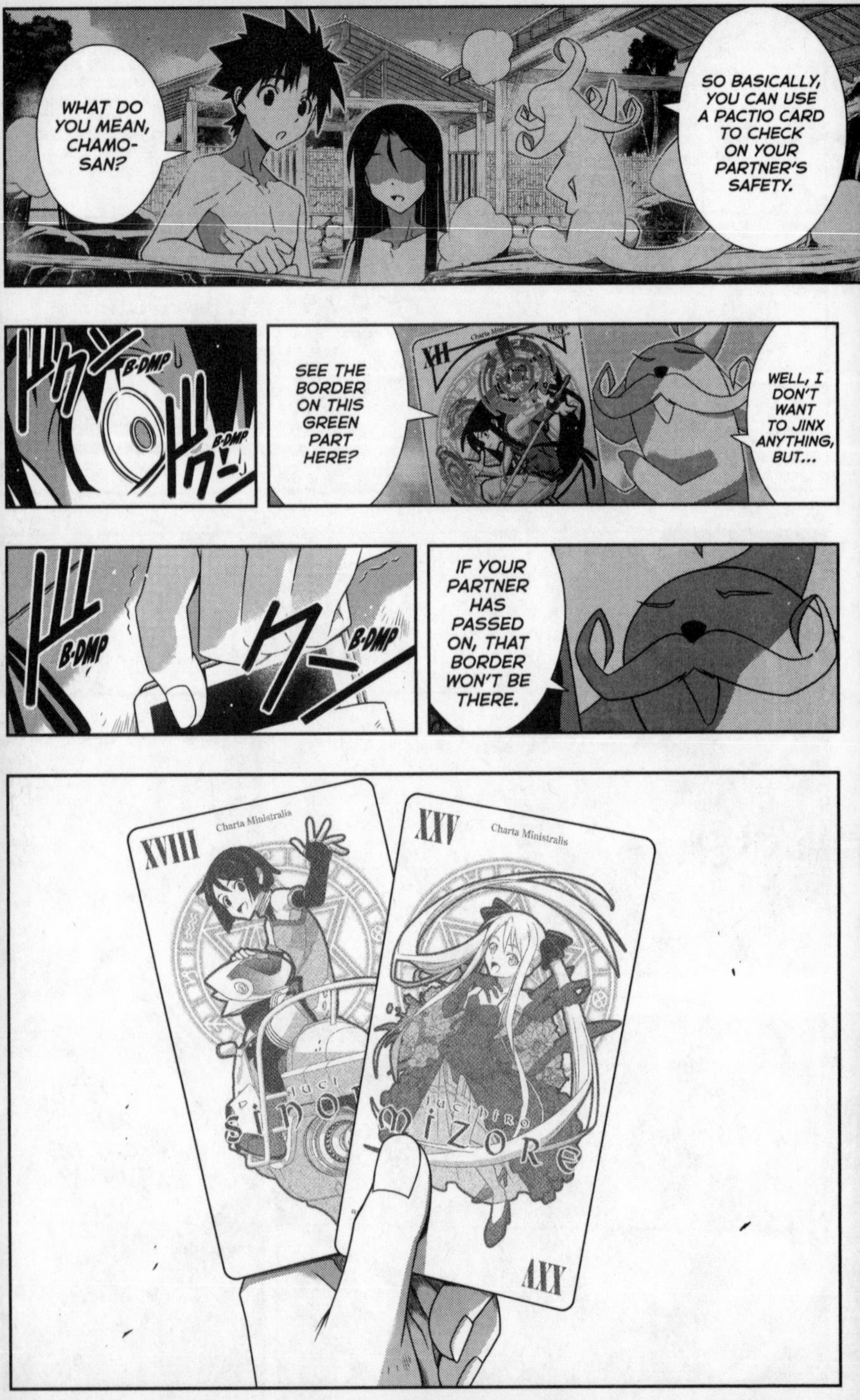
SO BASICALLY, YOU CAN USE A PACTIO CARD TO CHECK ON YOUR PARTNER'S SAFETY.
WHAT DO YOU MEAN, CHAMO-SAN?
WELL, I DON'T WANT TO JINX ANYTHING, BUT...
SEE THE BORDER ON THIS GREEN PART HERE?
B-DMP
B-DMP
IF YOUR PARTNER HAS PASSED ON, THAT BORDER WON'T BE THERE.
B-DMP
B-DMP
XXV
Charta Ministralis
XVIII
Charta Ministralis

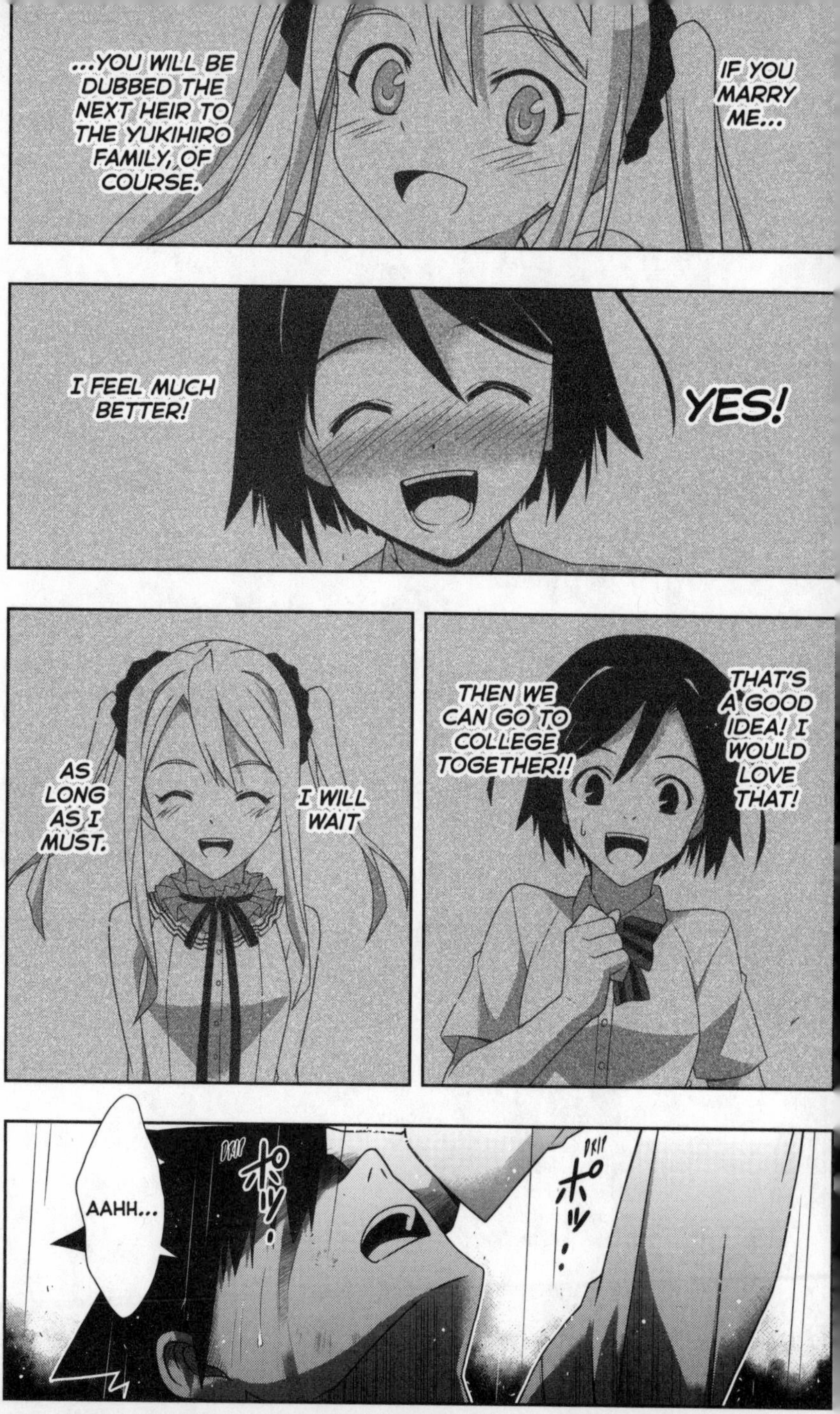
IF YOU MARRY ME...
...YOU WILL BE DUBBED THE NEXT HEIR TO THE YUKIHIRO FAMILY, OF COURSE.
YES!
I FEEL MUCH BETTER!
THAT'S A GOOD IDEA! I WOULD LOVE THAT!
THEN WE CAN GO TO COLLEGE TOGETHER!!
I WILL WAIT
AS LONG AS I MUST.
DRIP
ポッ・・
DRIP
ポッ。
AAHH...

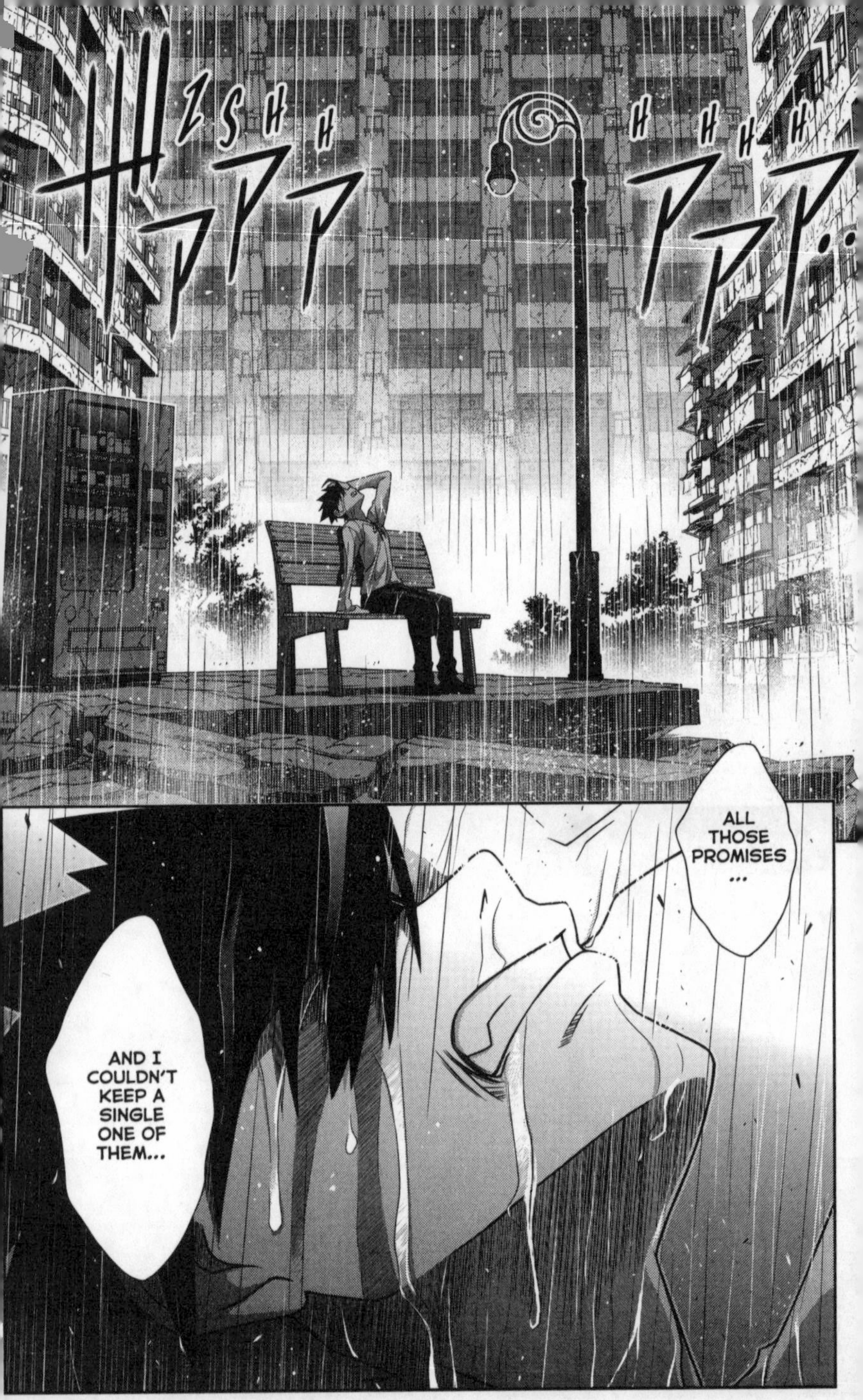
ZSHHHHHH...
ALL THOSE PROMISES...
AND I COULDN'T KEEP A SINGLE ONE OF THEM...

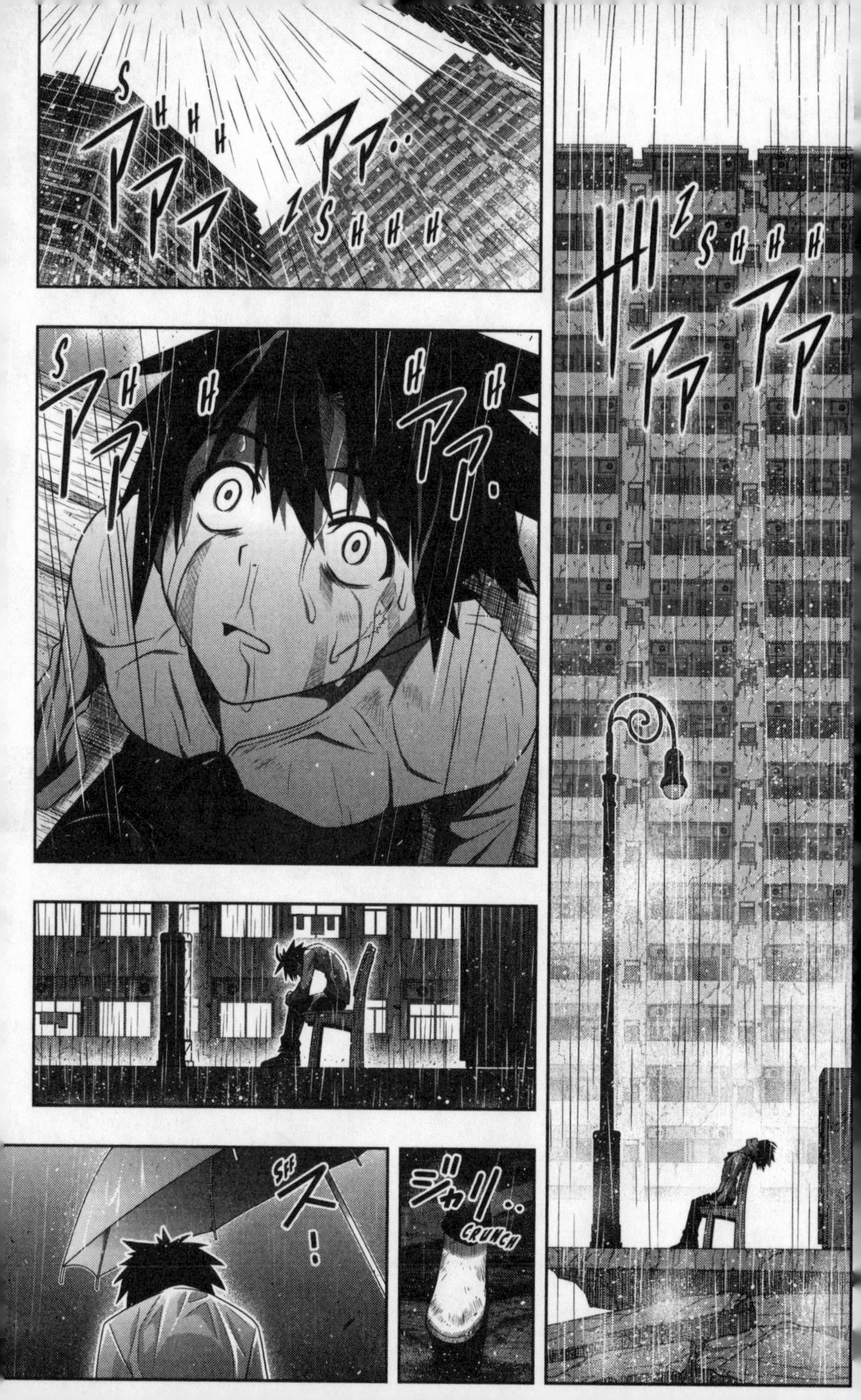
ZSHHHH
SHHHH
ZSHHHH
SHHHHH
CRUNCH
SFF
!

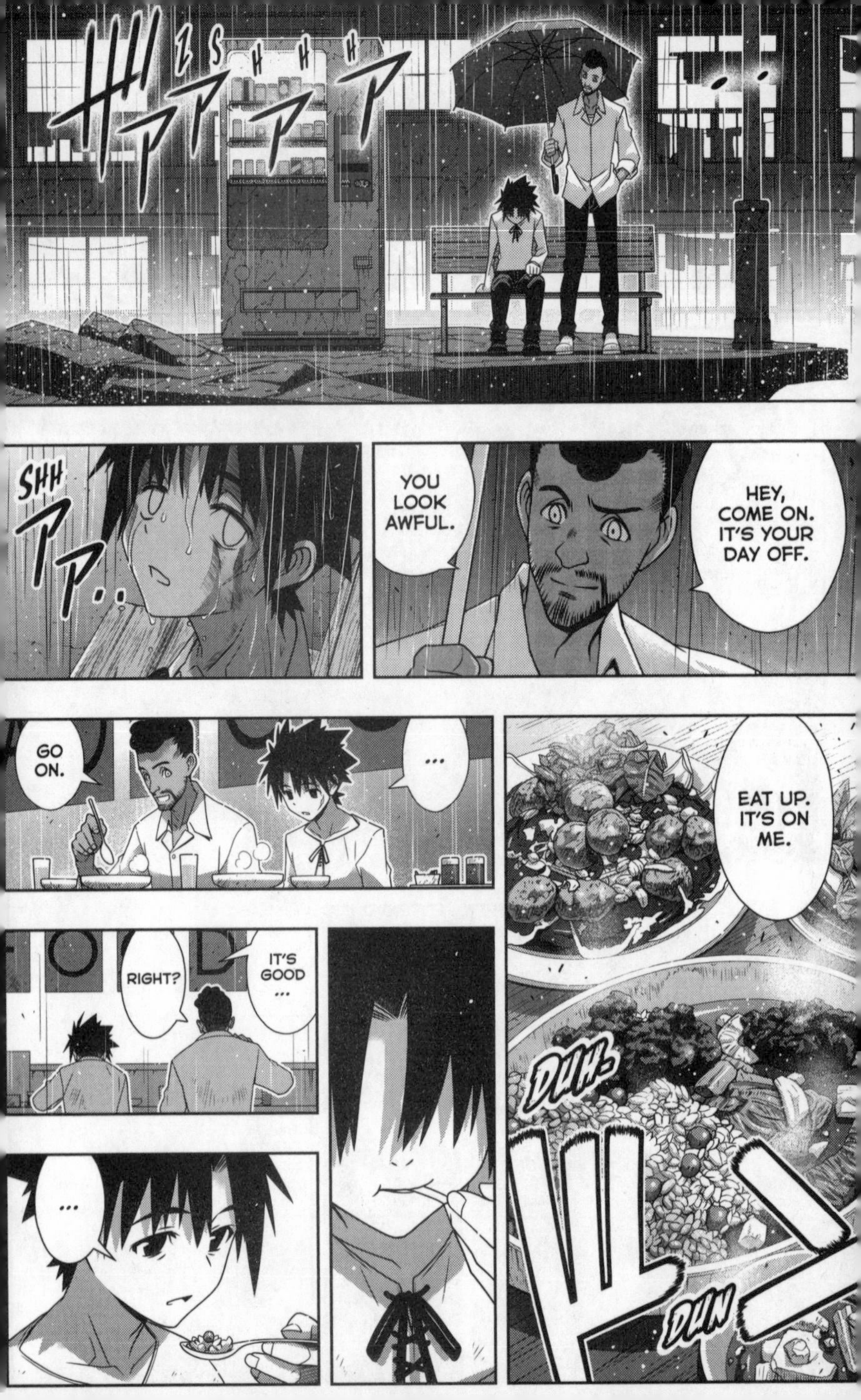
ZSHHH
HEY, COME ON. IT'S YOUR DAY OFF.
YOU LOOK AWFUL.
SHH
EAT UP. IT'S ON ME.
DUH-
DUN
...
GO ON.
IT'S GOOD...
RIGHT?
...

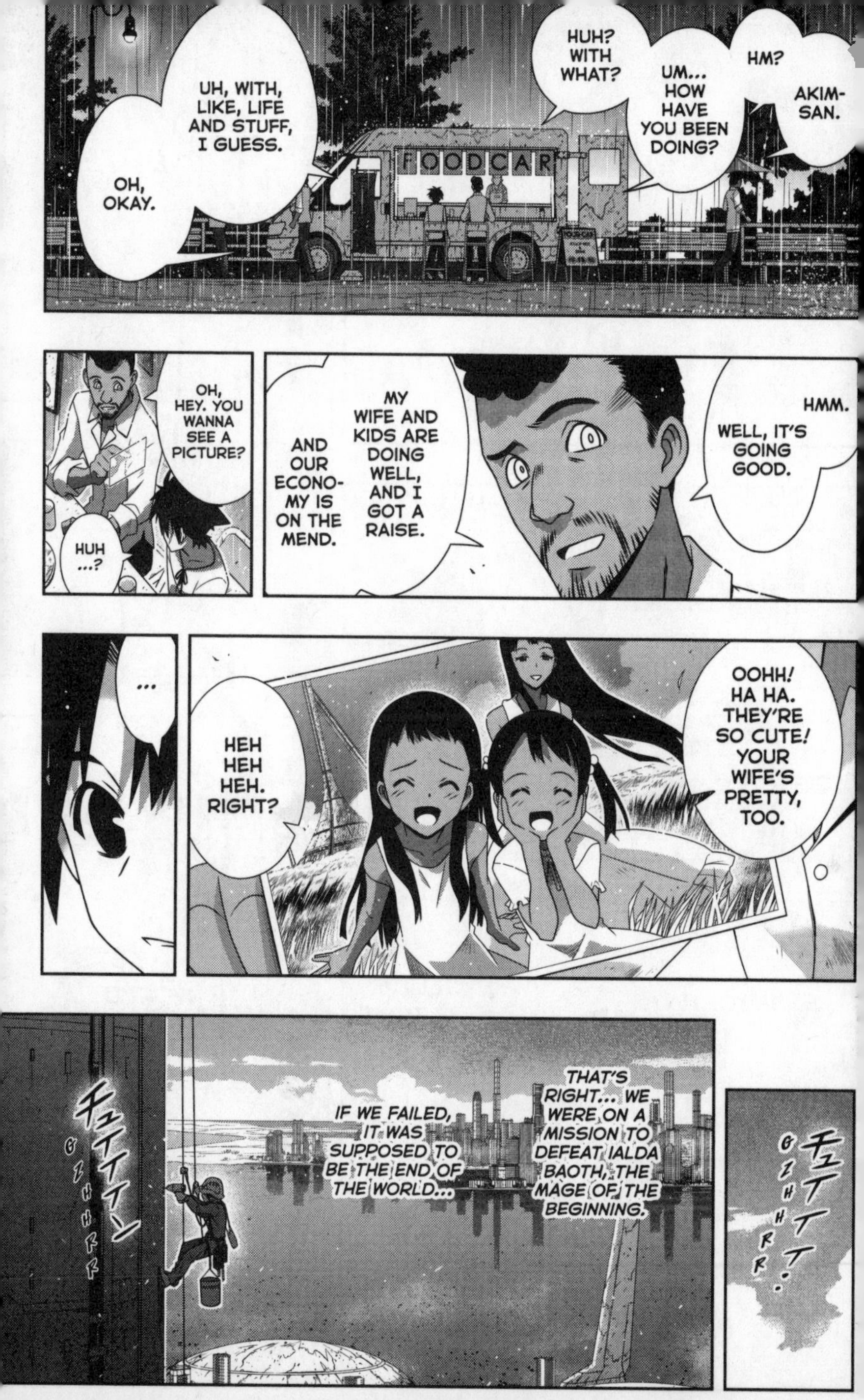
AKIM-SAN.
HM?
UM... HOW HAVE YOU BEEN DOING?
HUH? WITH WHAT?
UH, WITH, LIKE, LIFE AND STUFF, I GUESS.
OH, OKAY.
FOODCAR
HMM.
WELL, IT'S GOING GOOD.
MY WIFE AND KIDS ARE DOING WELL, AND I GOT A RAISE.
AND OUR ECONO-MY IS ON THE MEND.
OH, HEY. YOU WANNA SEE A PICTURE?
HUH ...?
OOHH! HA HA. THEY'RE SO CUTE! YOUR WIFE'S PRETTY, TOO.
HEH HEH HEH. RIGHT?
...
GZHHRR...
THAT'S RIGHT... WE WERE ON A MISSION TO DEFEAT IALDA BAOTH, THE MAGE OF THE BEGINNING.
IF WE FAILED, IT WAS SUPPOSED TO BE THE END OF THE WORLD...
GZHHRR

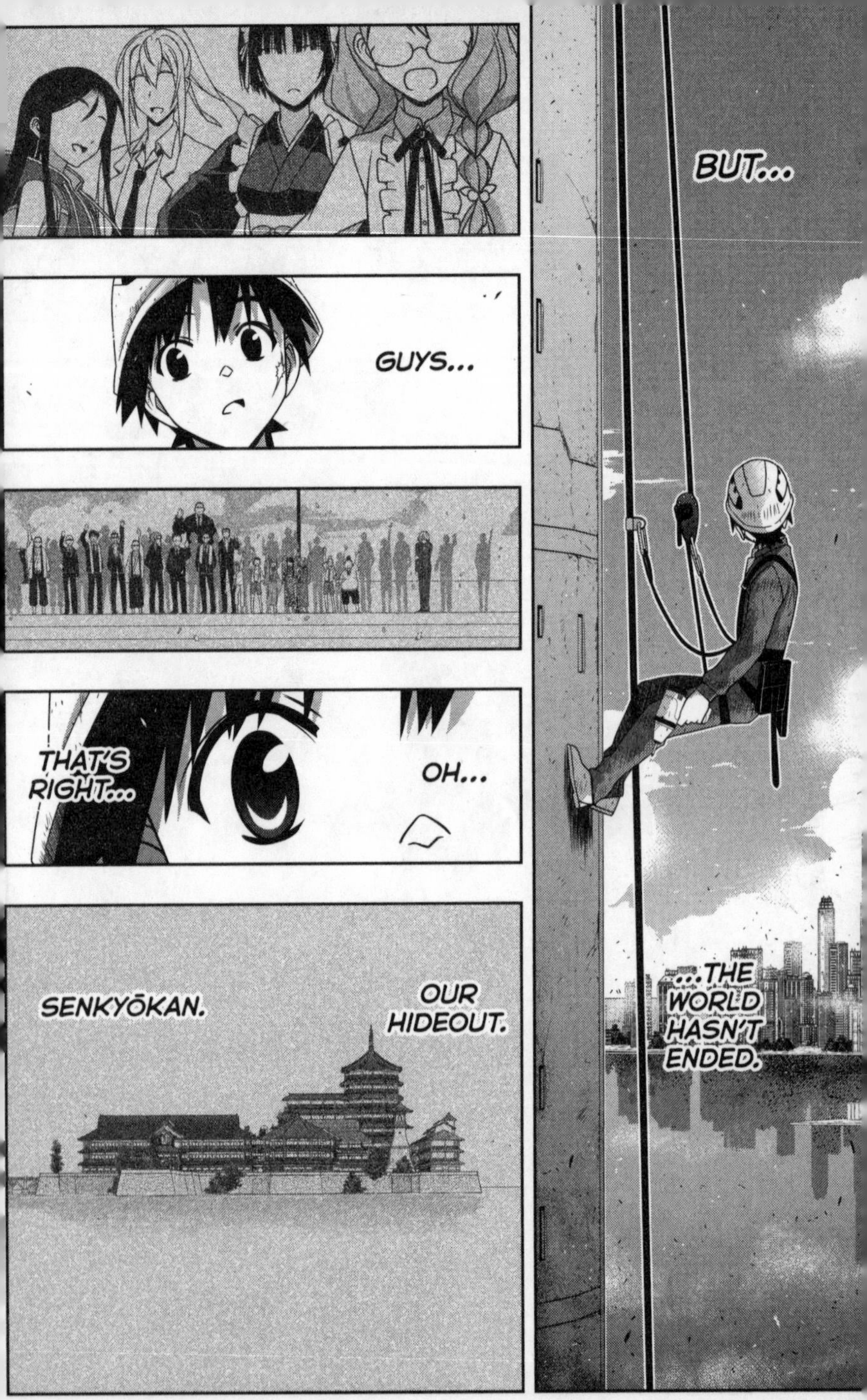
BUT...
...THE WORLD HASN'T ENDED.
GUYS...
OH...
THAT'S RIGHT...
OUR HIDEOUT.
SENKYŌKAN.

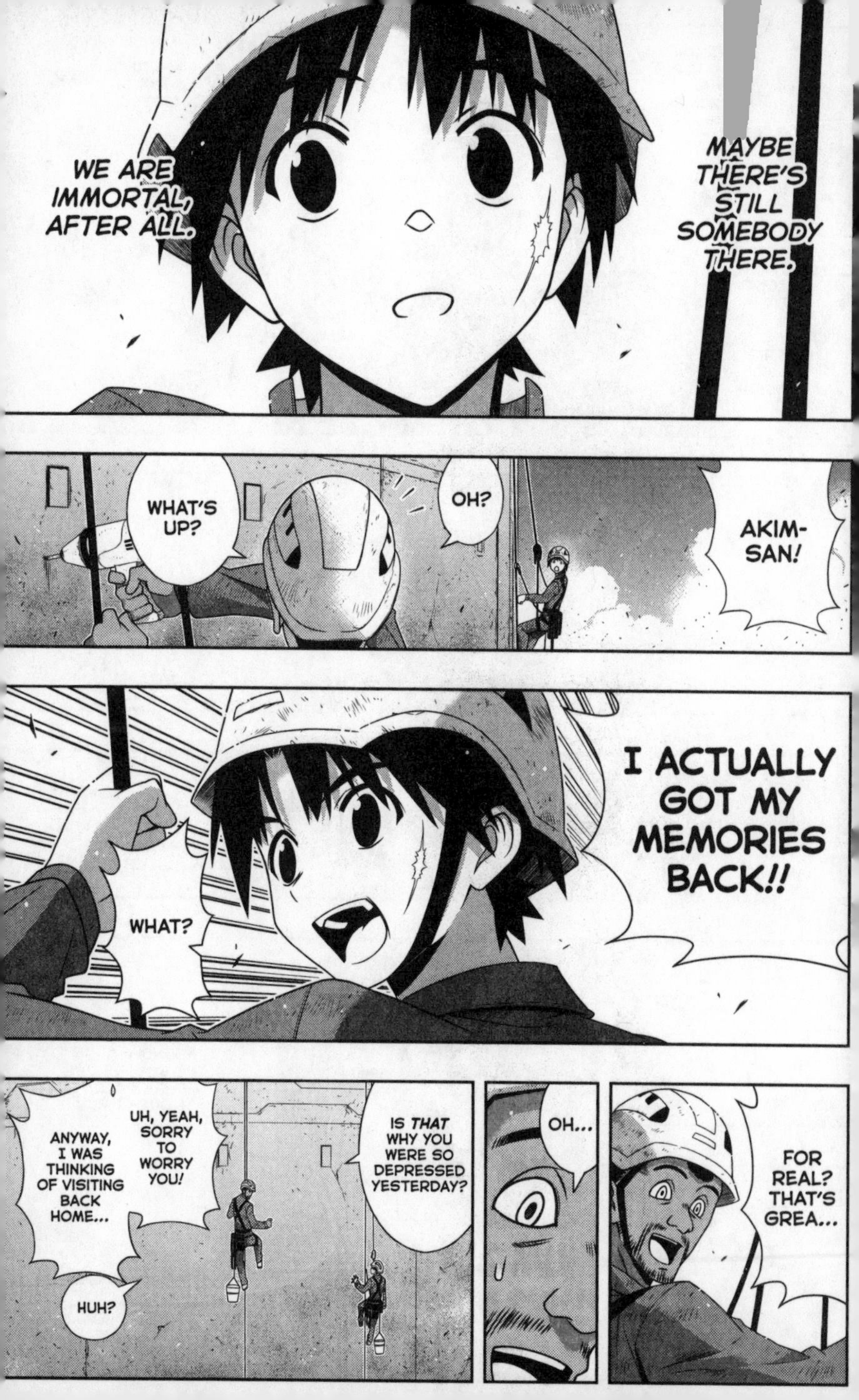
MAYBE THERE'S STILL SOMEBODY THERE.
WE ARE IMMORTAL, AFTER ALL.
AKIM-SAN!
OH?
WHAT'S UP?
I ACTUALLY GOT MY MEMORIES BACK!!
WHAT?
FOR REAL? THAT'S GREA...
OH...
IS *THAT* WHY YOU WERE SO DEPRESSED YESTERDAY?
UH, YEAH, SORRY TO WORRY YOU!
ANYWAY, I WAS THINKING OF VISITING BACK HOME...
HUH?

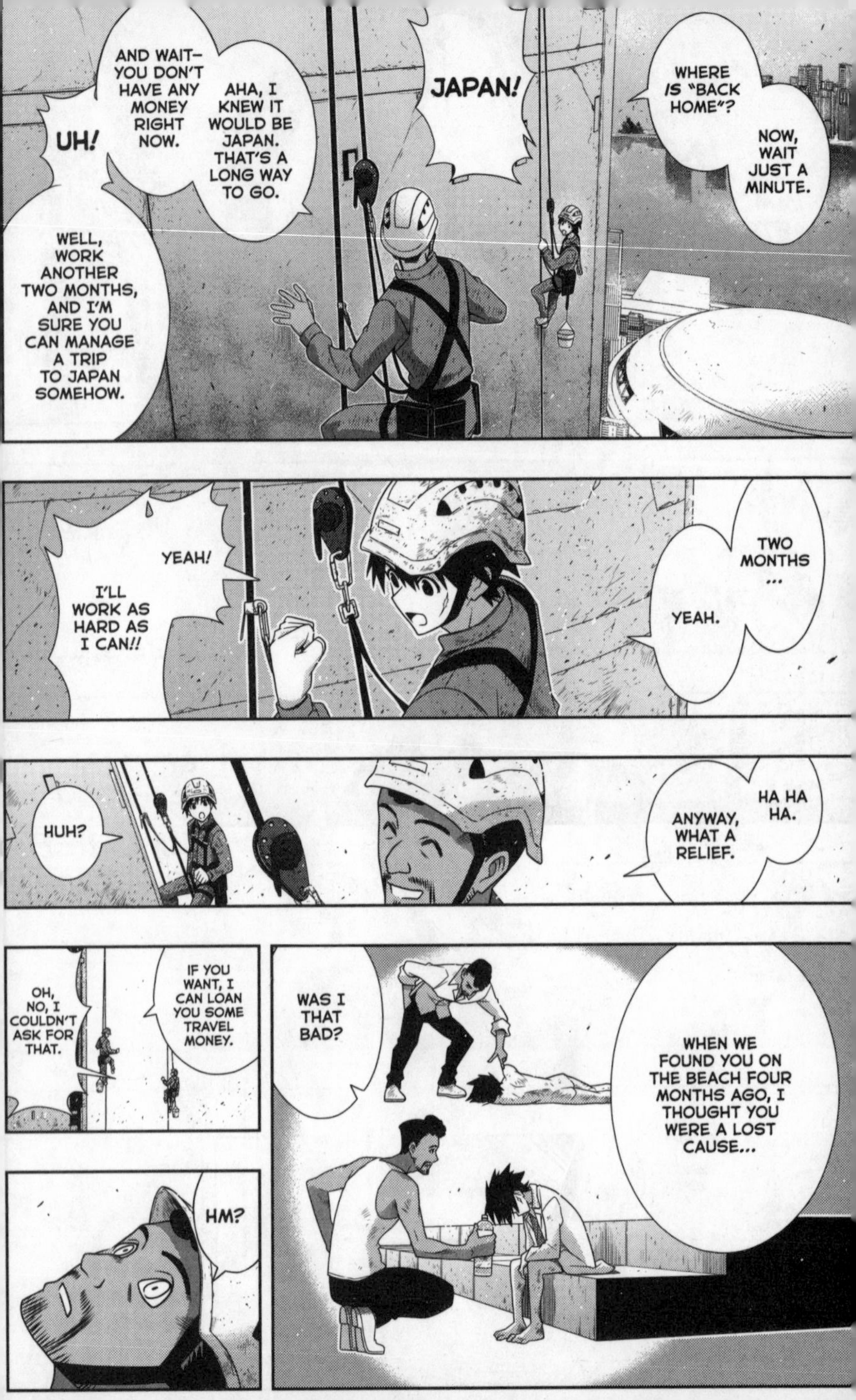
WHERE IS "BACK HOME"?
NOW, WAIT JUST A MINUTE.
JAPAN!
AHA, I KNEW IT WOULD BE JAPAN. THAT'S A LONG WAY TO GO.
AND WAIT— YOU DON'T HAVE ANY MONEY RIGHT NOW.
UH!
WELL, WORK ANOTHER TWO MONTHS, AND I'M SURE YOU CAN MANAGE A TRIP TO JAPAN SOMEHOW.
TWO MONTHS ...
YEAH.
YEAH!
I'LL WORK AS HARD AS I CAN!!
HA HA HA.
ANYWAY, WHAT A RELIEF.
HUH?
WHEN WE FOUND YOU ON THE BEACH FOUR MONTHS AGO, I THOUGHT YOU WERE A LOST CAUSE...
WAS I THAT BAD?
IF YOU WANT, I CAN LOAN YOU SOME TRAVEL MONEY.
OH, NO, I COULDN'T ASK FOR THAT.
HM?

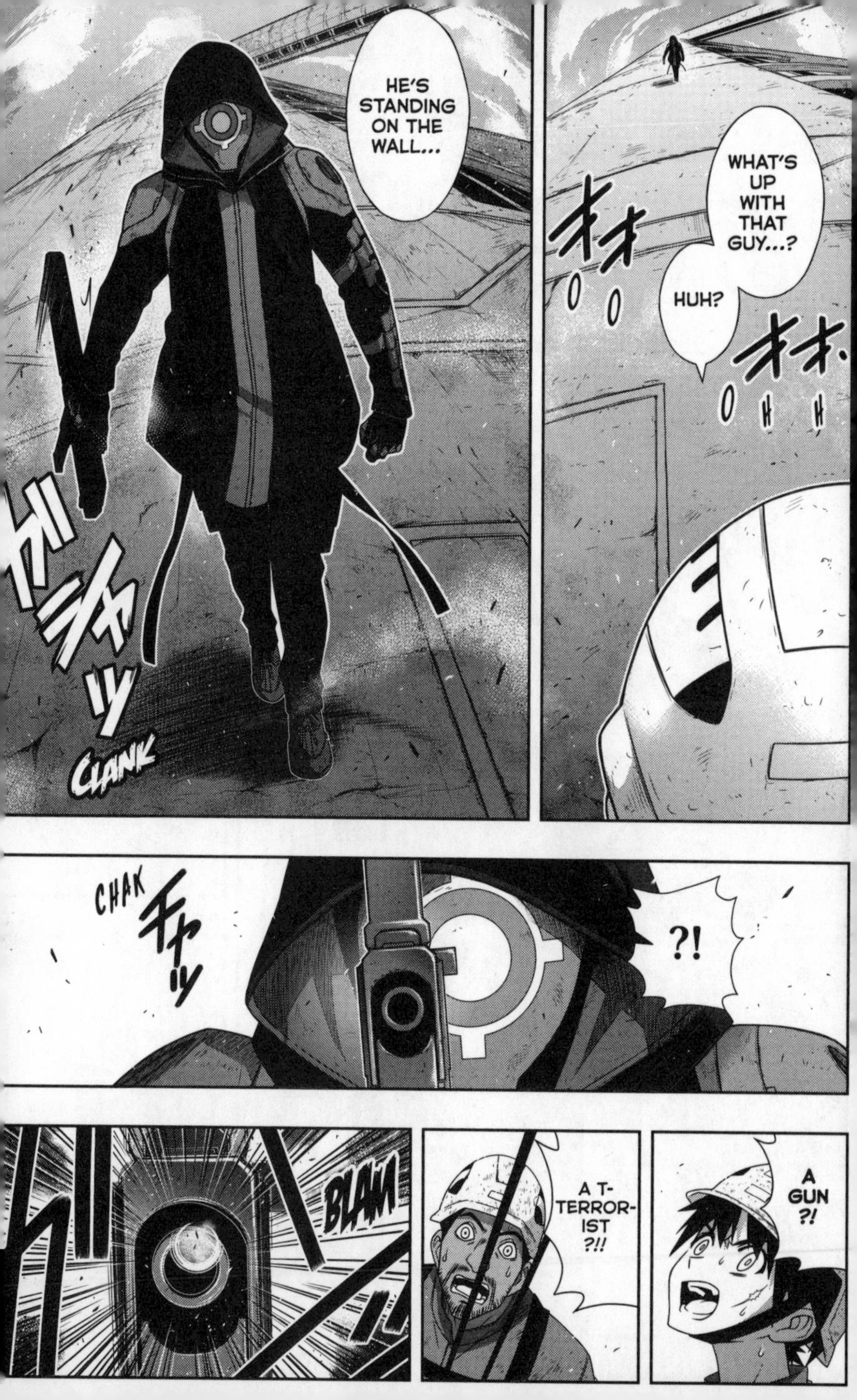

WHAT'S UP WITH THAT GUY...?
HUH?
HE'S STANDING ON THE WALL...
CLANK
?!
CHAK
A GUN ?!
A T-TERRORIST ?!!
BLAM

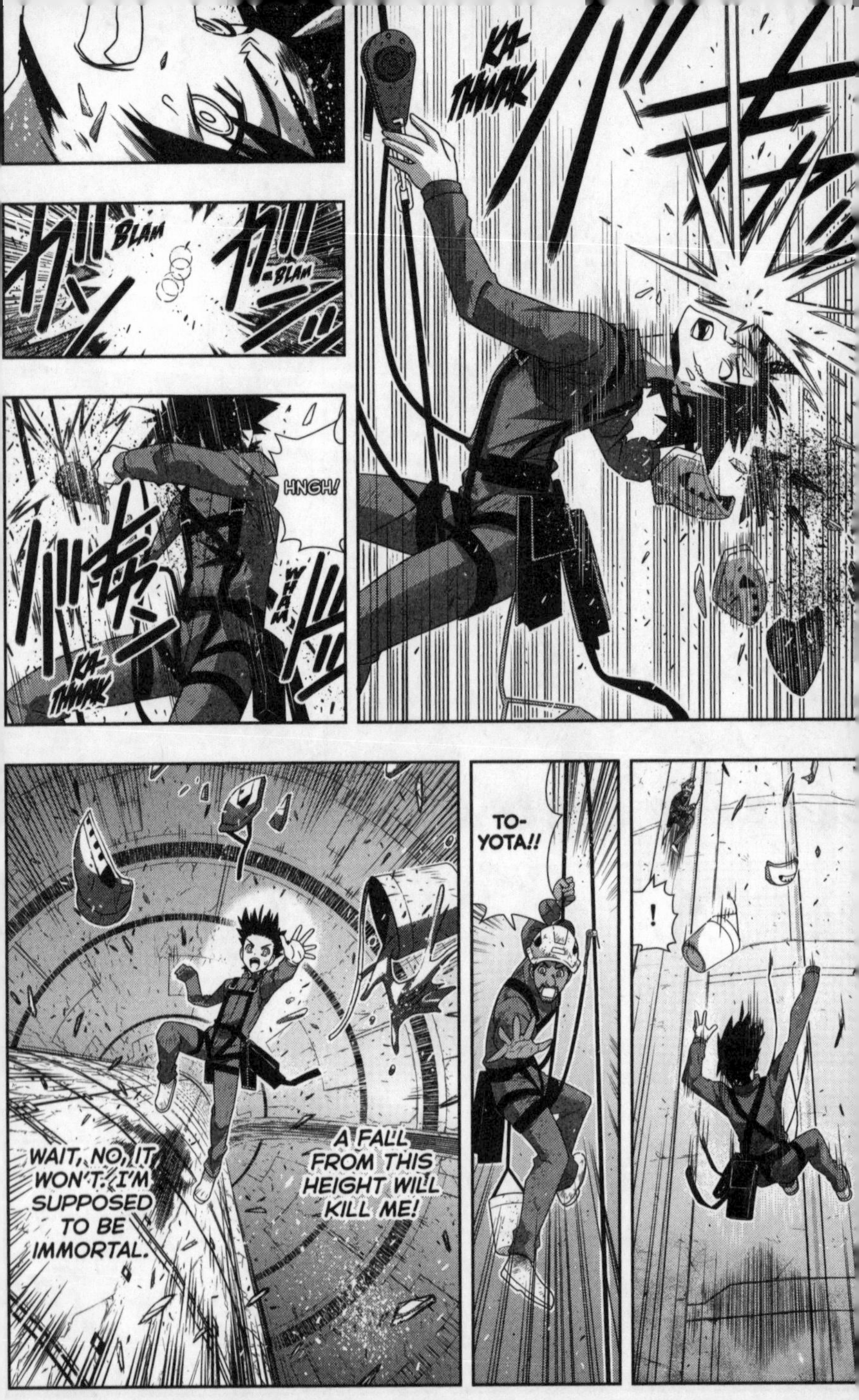
KA-THWAK
BLAM
BLAM
HNGH!
WHAM
KA-THWAK
!
TO-YOTA!!
A FALL FROM THIS HEIGHT WILL KILL ME!
WAIT, NO, IT WON'T. I'M SUPPOSED TO BE IMMORTAL.

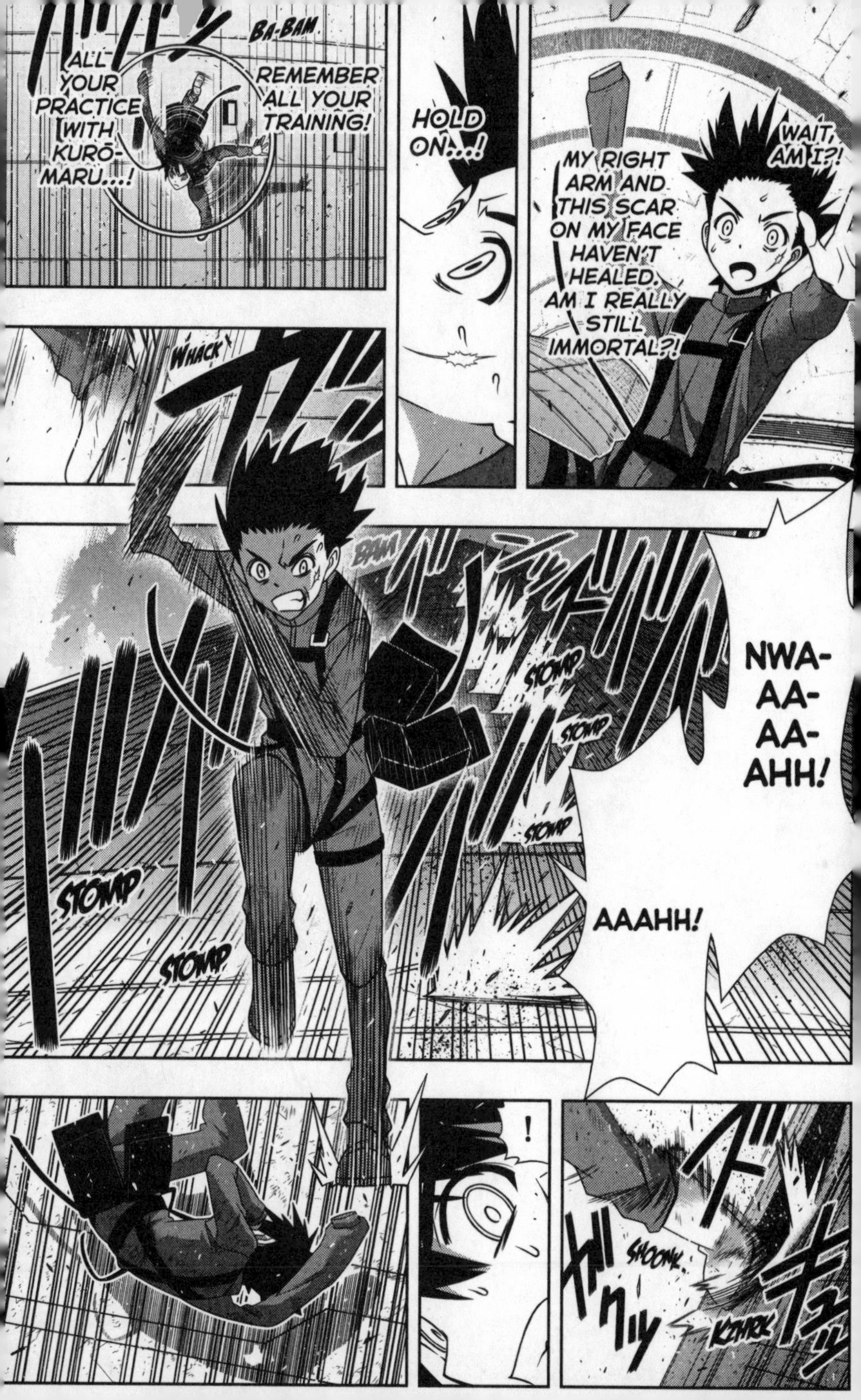
WAIT, AM I?!
MY RIGHT ARM AND THIS SCAR ON MY FACE HAVEN'T HEALED. AM I REALLY STILL IMMORTAL?!
HOLD ON...!
BA-BAM
REMEMBER ALL YOUR TRAINING!
ALL YOUR PRACTICE WITH KURŌ-MARU...!
NWA-AA-AA-AHH!
BAM
WHACK
STOMP
STOMP
STOMP
AAAHH!
STOMP
STOMP
SHOONK
KZHRK
!

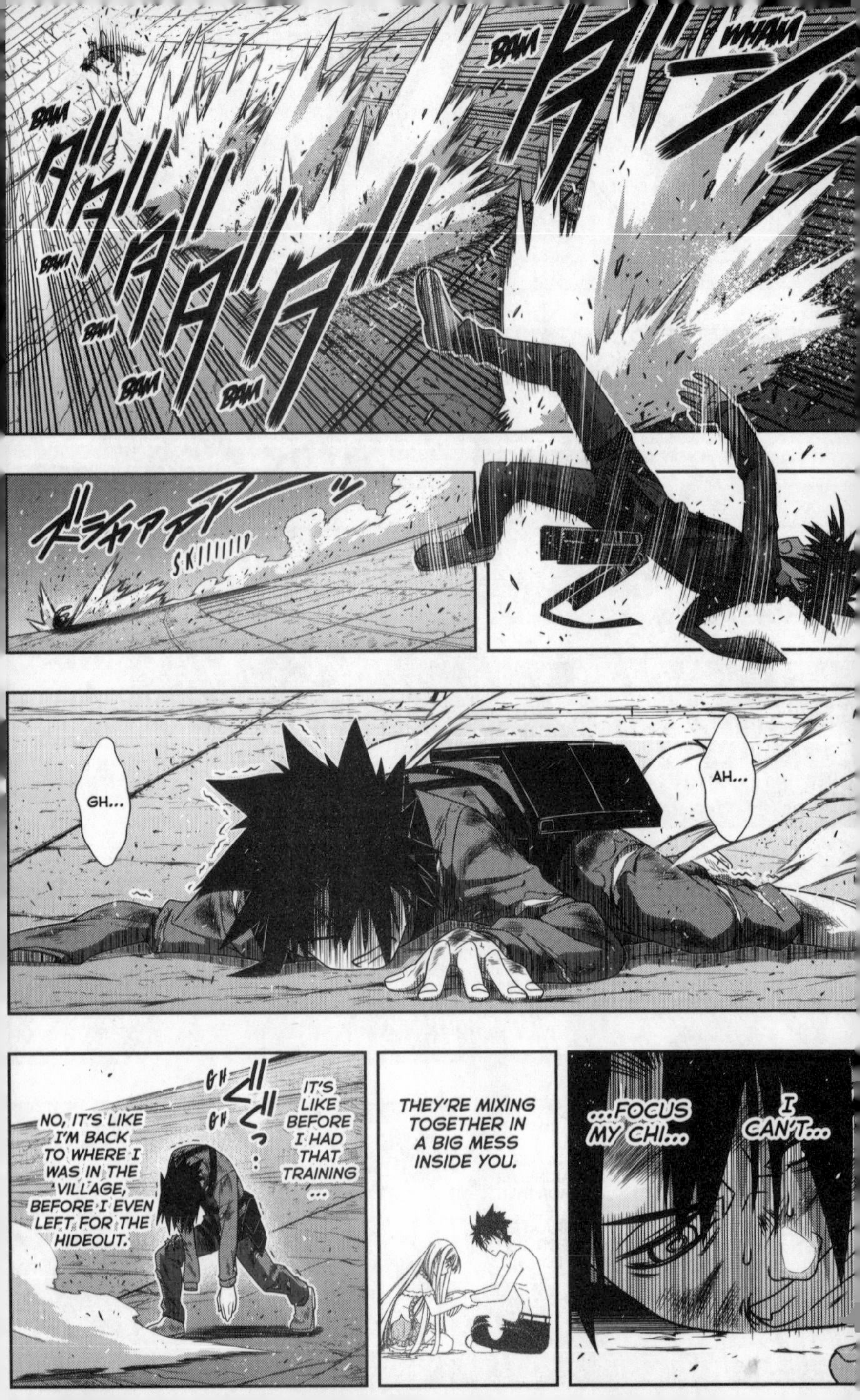
WHAM
BAM
BAM
BAM
BAM
BAM
BAM
SKIIIIIID
AH...
GH...
I CAN'T...
...FOCUS MY CHI...
THEY'RE MIXING TOGETHER IN A BIG MESS INSIDE YOU.
GH
GH
IT'S LIKE BEFORE I HAD THAT TRAINING...
NO, IT'S LIKE I'M BACK TO WHERE I WAS IN THE VILLAGE, BEFORE I EVEN LEFT FOR THE HIDEOUT.

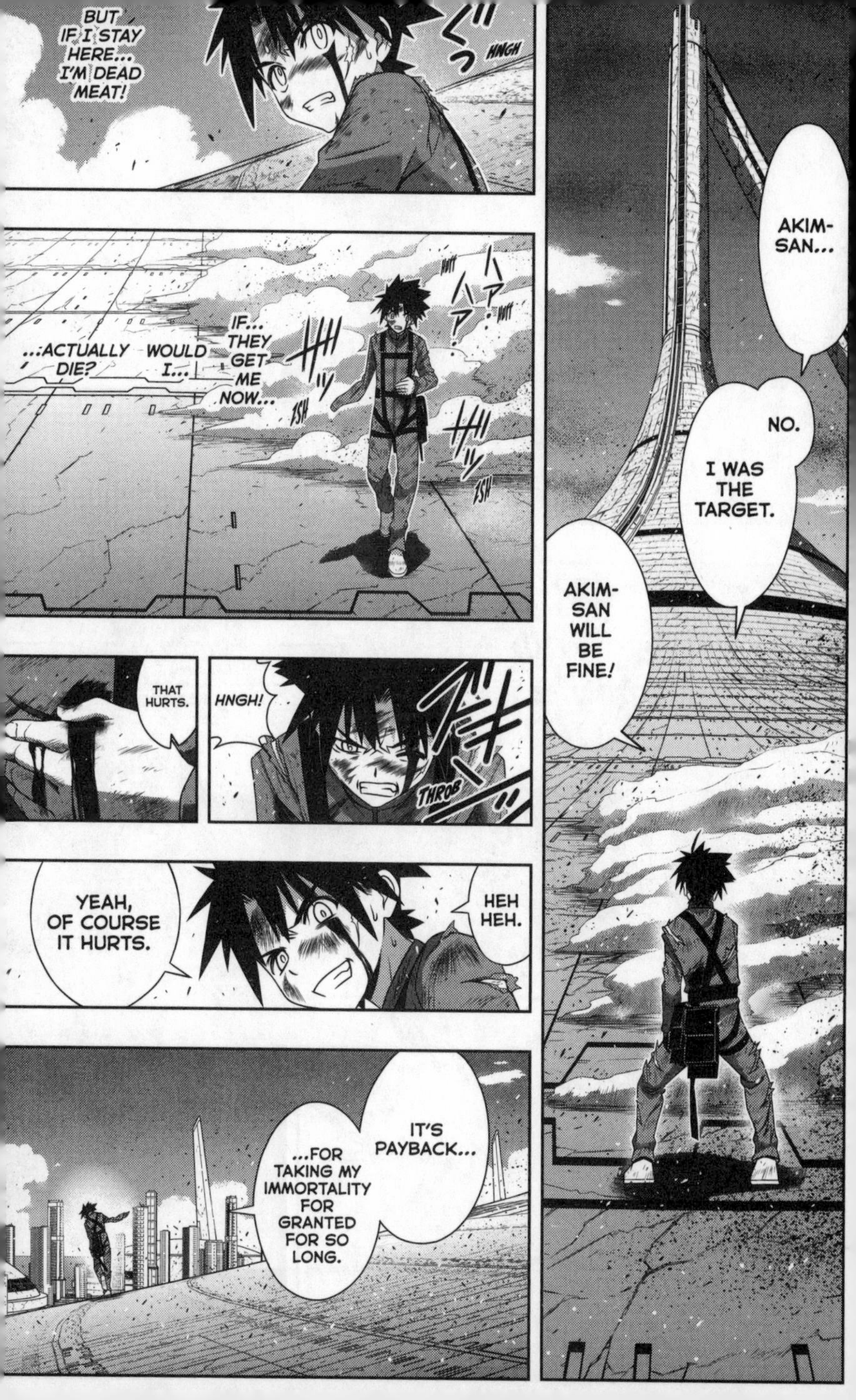
AKIM-SAN...
NO.
I WAS THE TARGET.
AKIM-SAN WILL BE FINE!
HNGH
BUT IF I STAY HERE... I'M DEAD MEAT!
HUFF
HUFF
TSH
TSH
IF... THEY GET ME NOW...
WOULD I...
...ACTUALLY DIE?
THROB
HNGH!
THAT HURTS.
HEH HEH.
YEAH, OF COURSE IT HURTS.
IT'S PAYBACK...
...FOR TAKING MY IMMORTALITY FOR GRANTED FOR SO LONG.

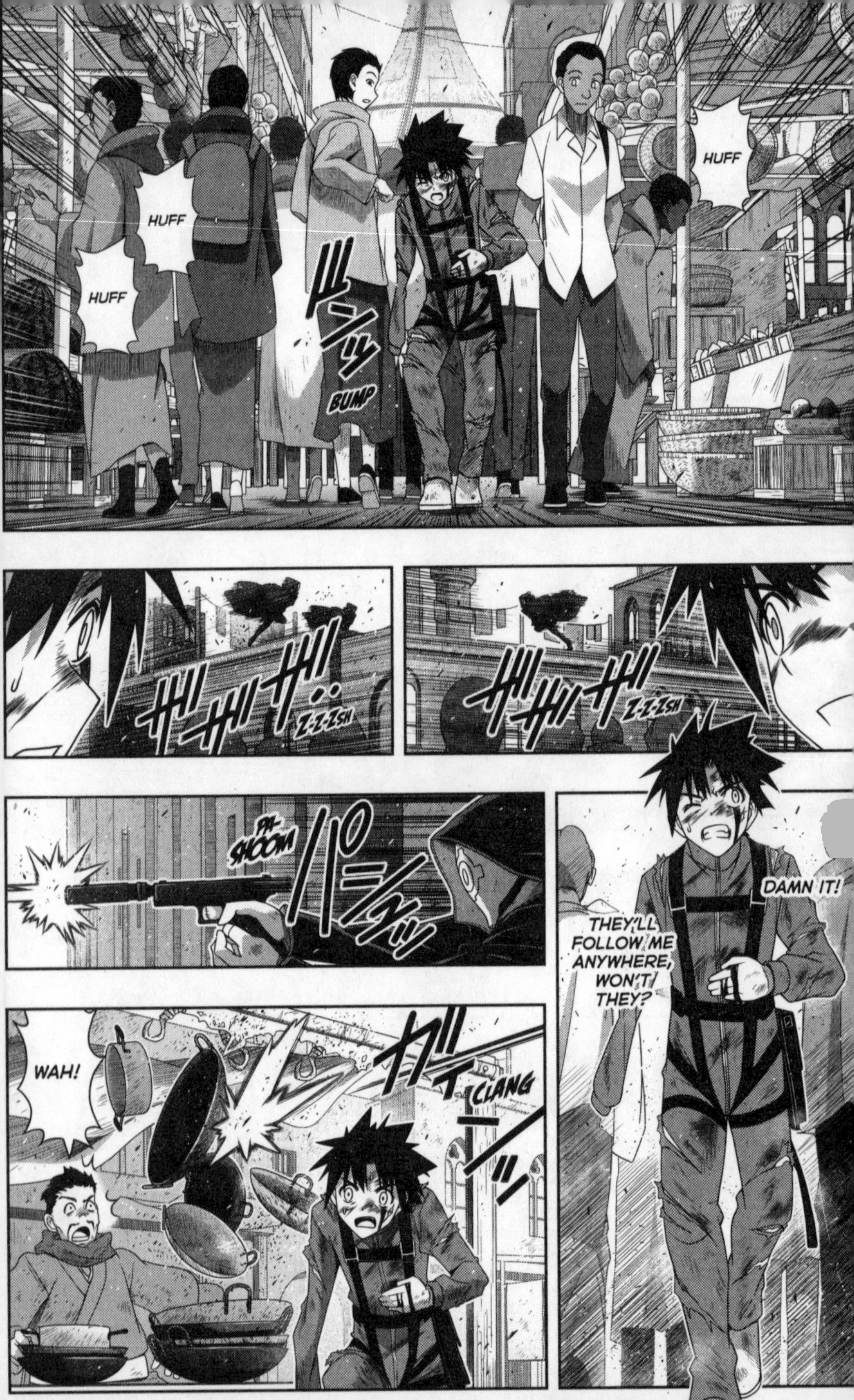
HUFF
HUFF
HUFF
BUMP
Z-Z-ZSH
Z-Z-ZSH
DAMN IT!
THEY'LL FOLLOW ME ANYWHERE, WON'T THEY?
PA-SHOOM
CLANG
WAH!

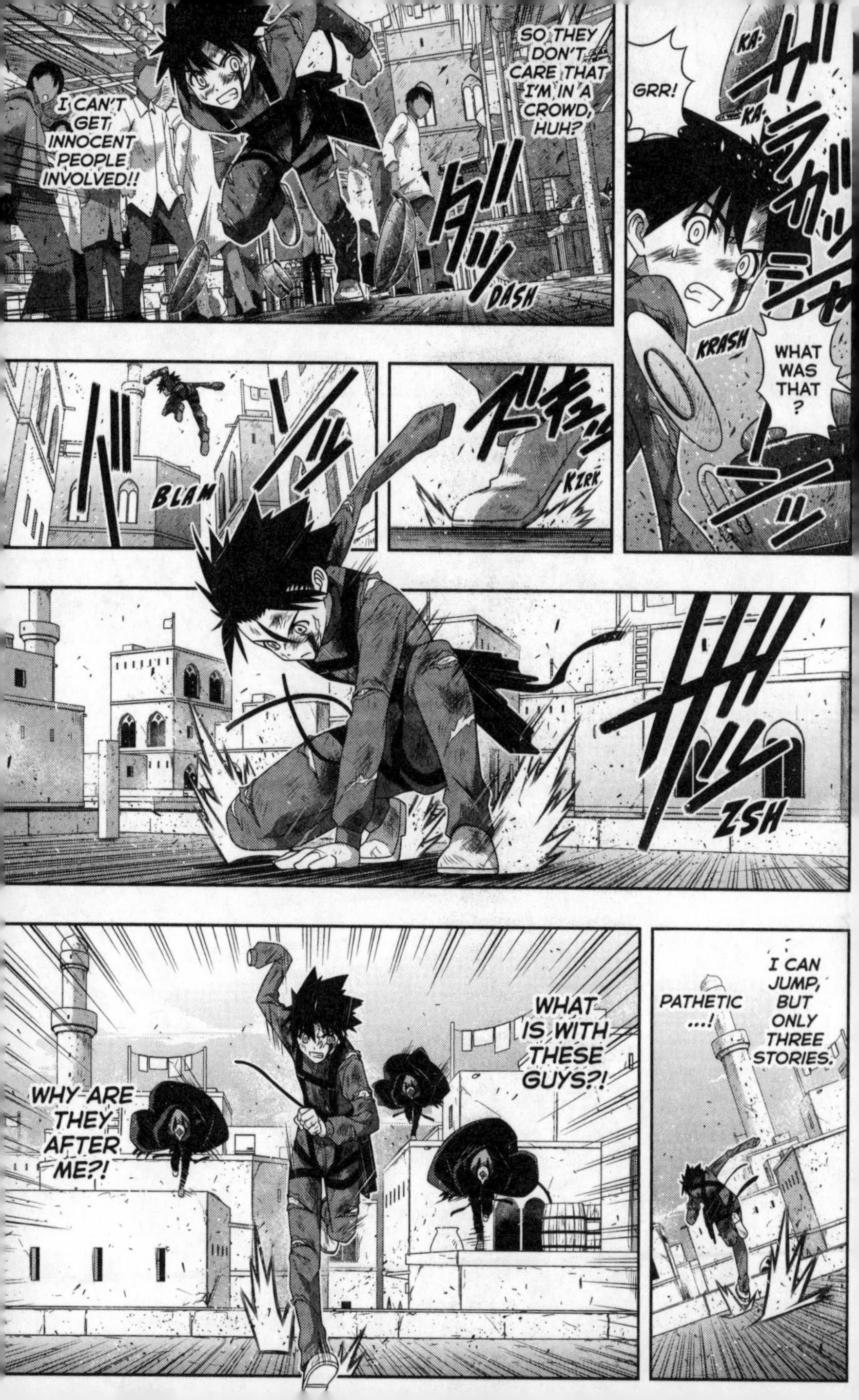
KA-
KA-
GRR!
KRASH
WHAT WAS THAT ?
SO THEY DON'T CARE THAT I'M IN A CROWD, HUH?
I CAN'T GET INNOCENT PEOPLE INVOLVED!!
DASH
KIRK
BLAM
ZSH
I CAN JUMP, BUT ONLY THREE STORIES.
PATHETIC ...!
WHAT IS WITH THESE GUYS?!
WHY ARE THEY AFTER ME?!

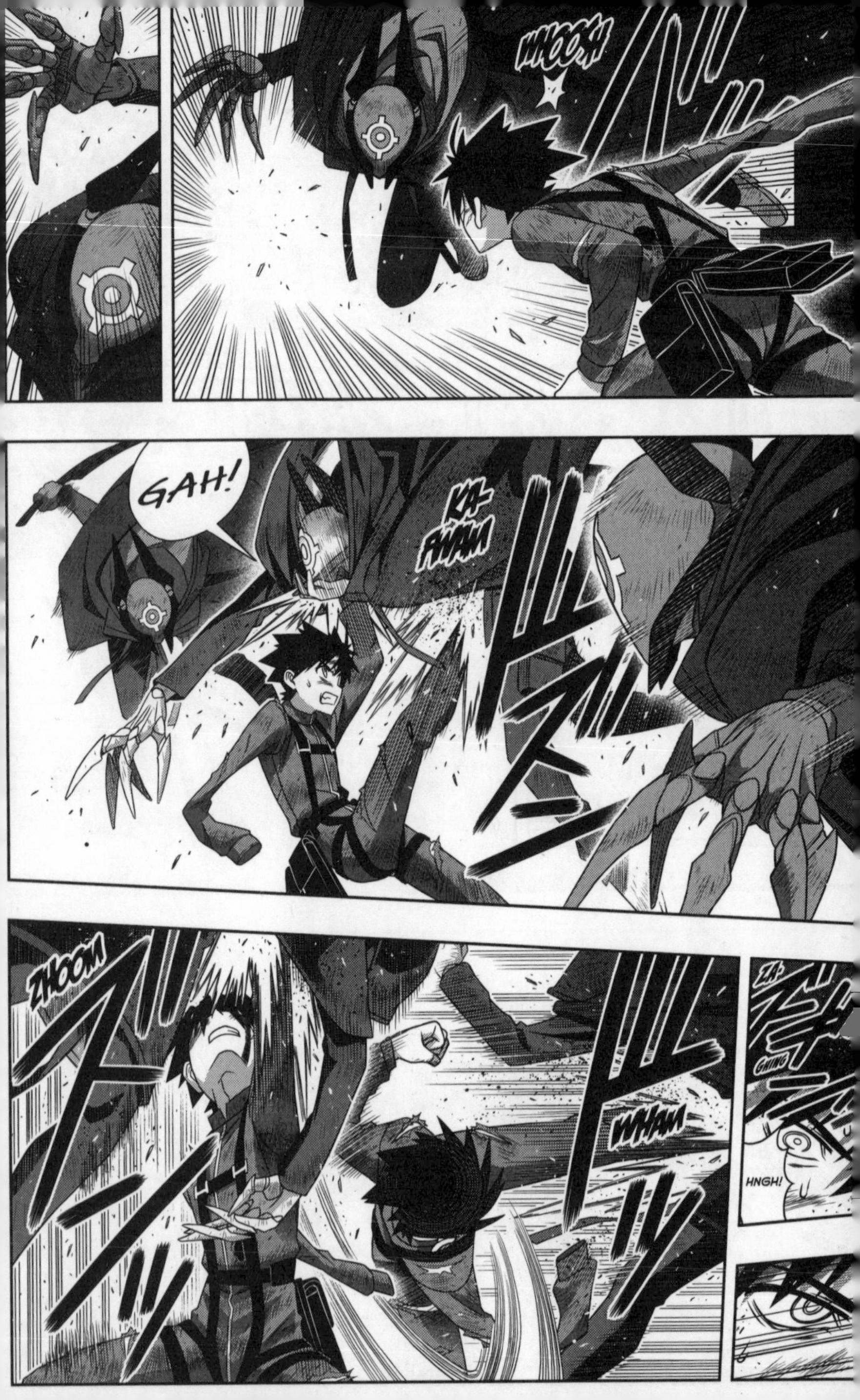
WHOOSH
KA-FWAM
GAH!
ZA-GHING
HNGH!
WHAM
ZHOOM

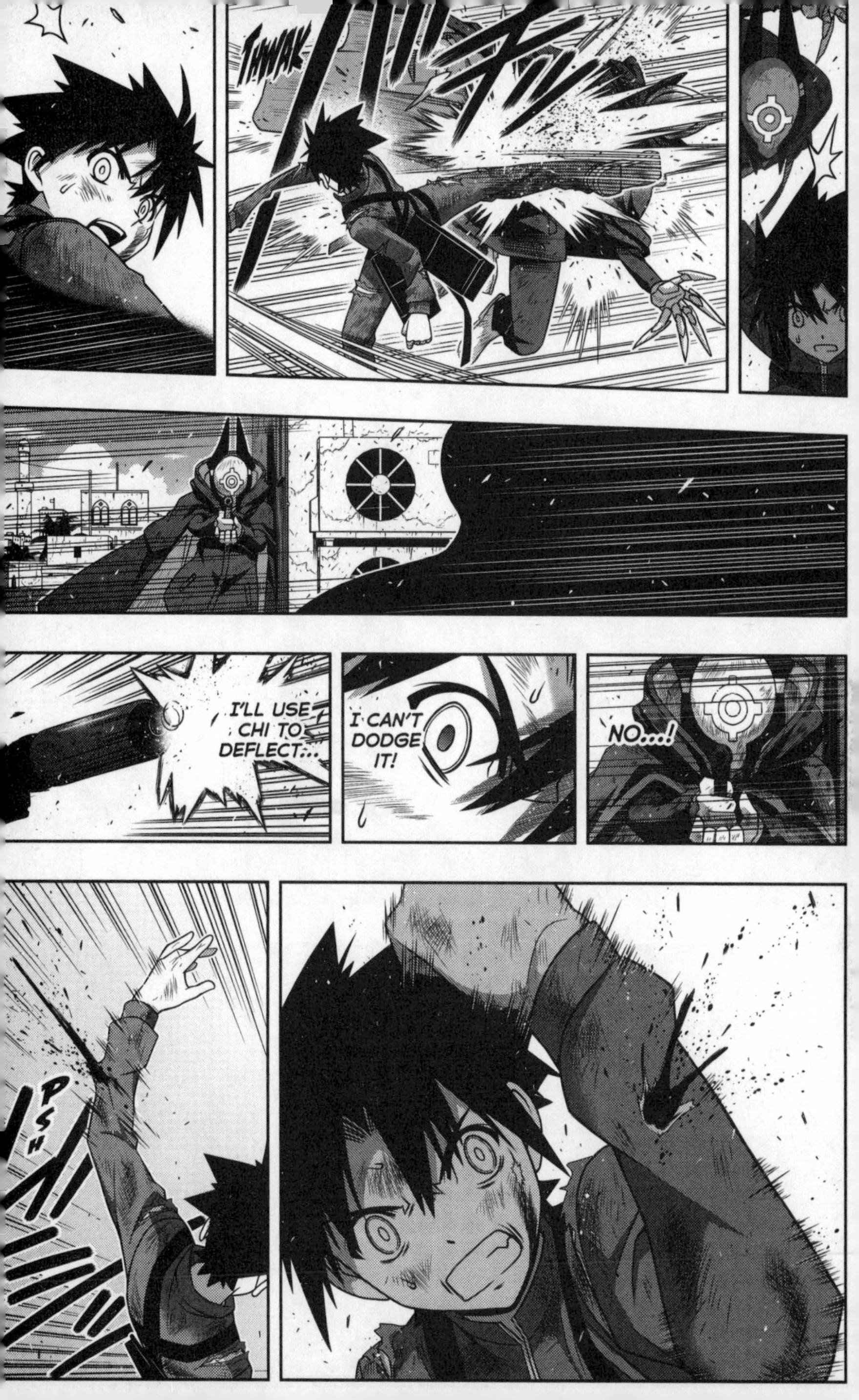
THWAK
NO...!
I CAN'T DODGE IT!
I'LL USE CHI TO DEFLECT...
PSH

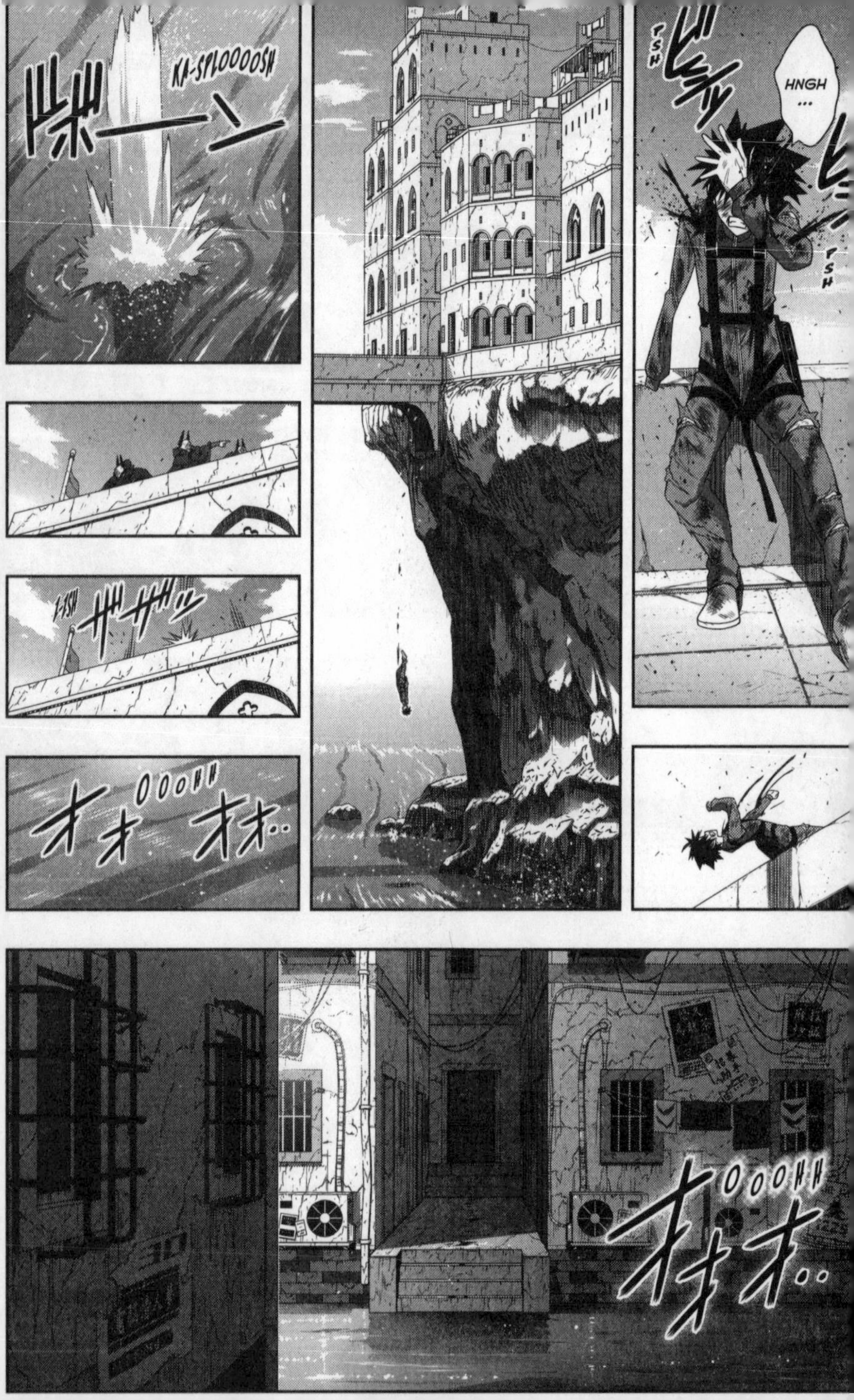

TSH
HNGH ...
TSH
KA-SPLOOOOSH
T-TSH
OOOOHH
OOOOHH

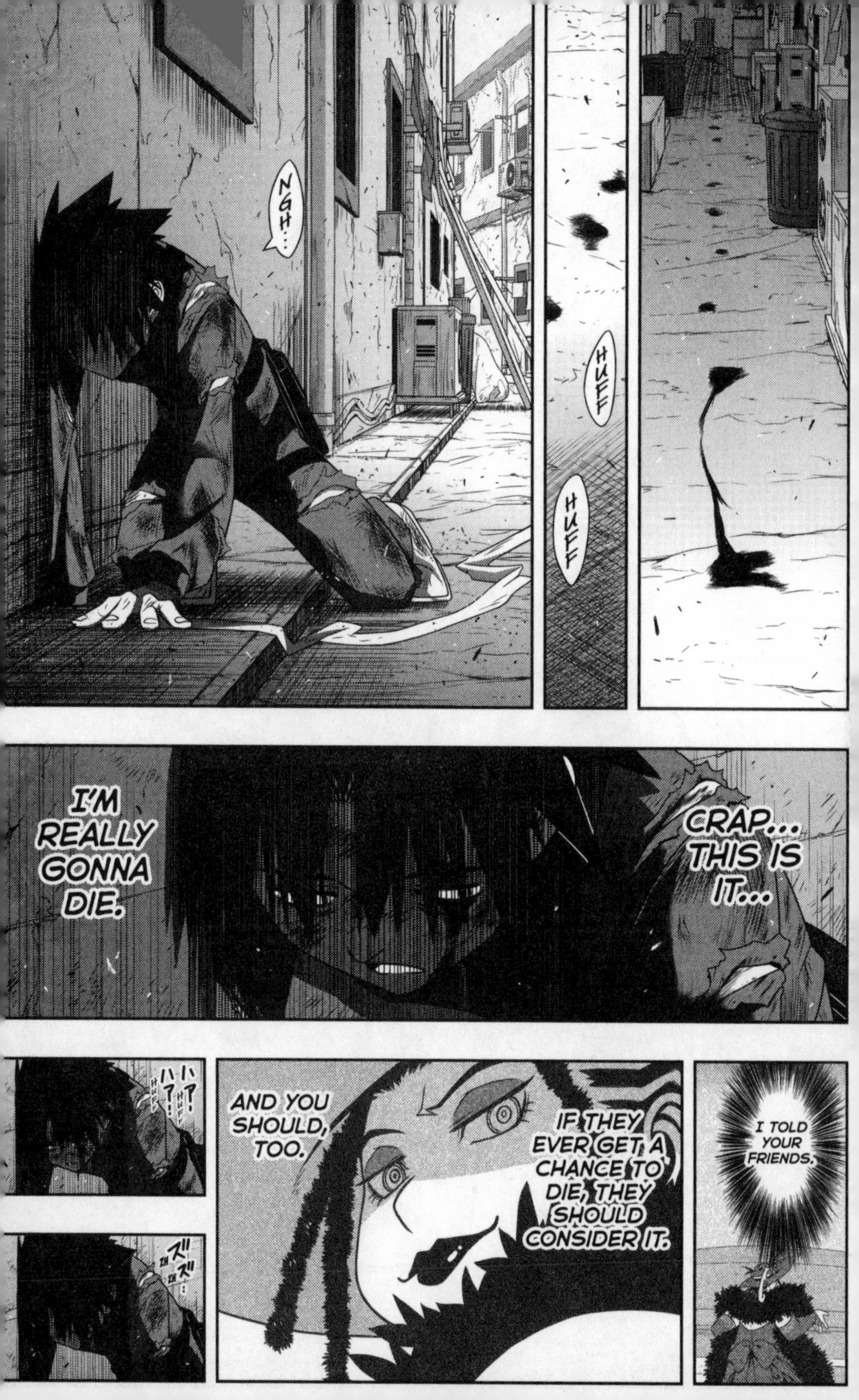
HUFF
HUFF
NGH...
CRAP... THIS IS IT...
I'M REALLY GONNA DIE.
I TOLD YOUR FRIENDS.
IF THEY EVER GET A CHANCE TO DIE, THEY SHOULD CONSIDER IT.
AND YOU SHOULD, TOO.
HUFF HUFF
ZN ZN

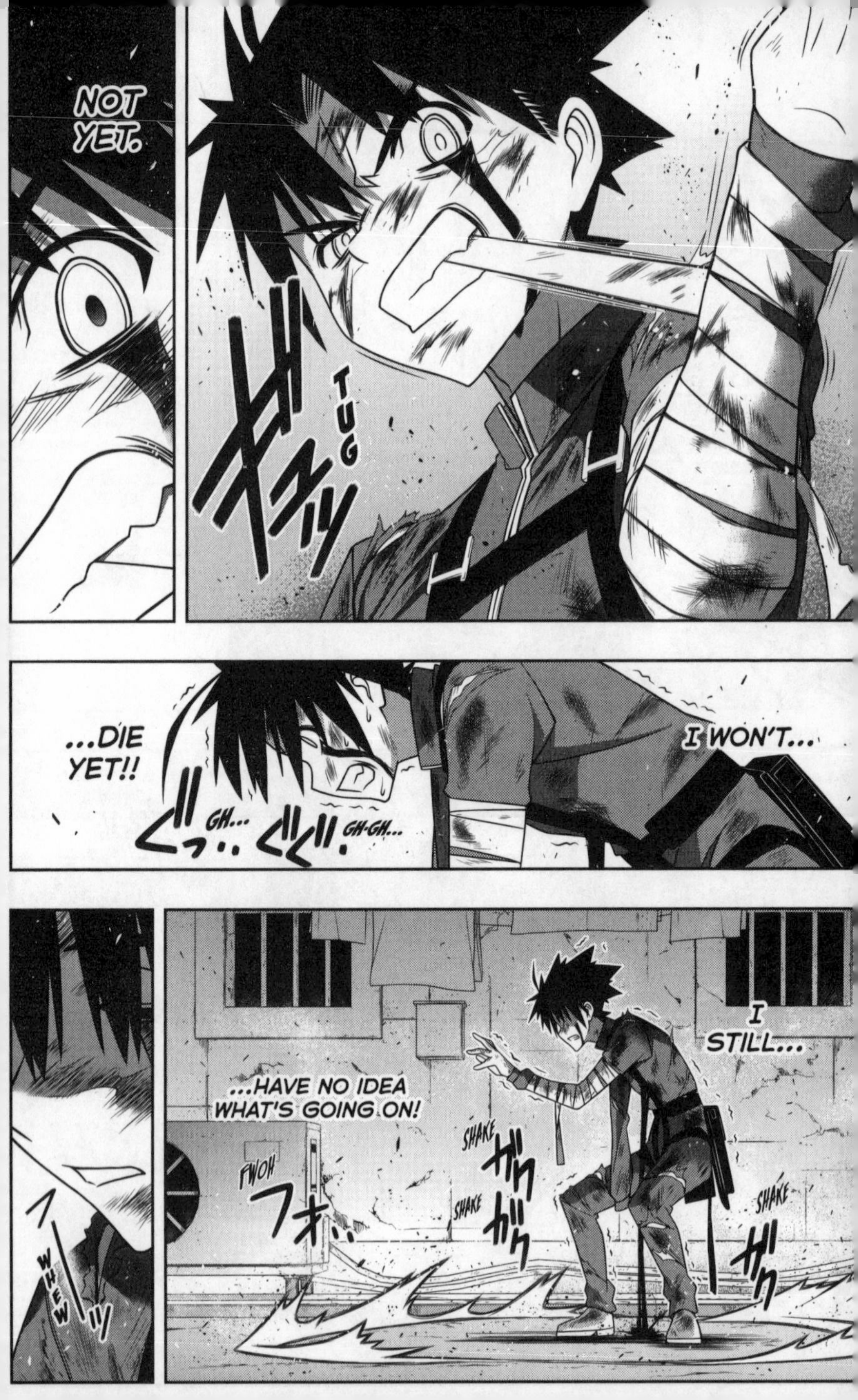
TUG
NOT YET.
I WON'T...
...DIE YET!!
GH...
GH-GH...
I STILL...
...HAVE NO IDEA WHAT'S GOING ON!
SHAKE
SHAKE
SHAKE
FWOH
WHEW

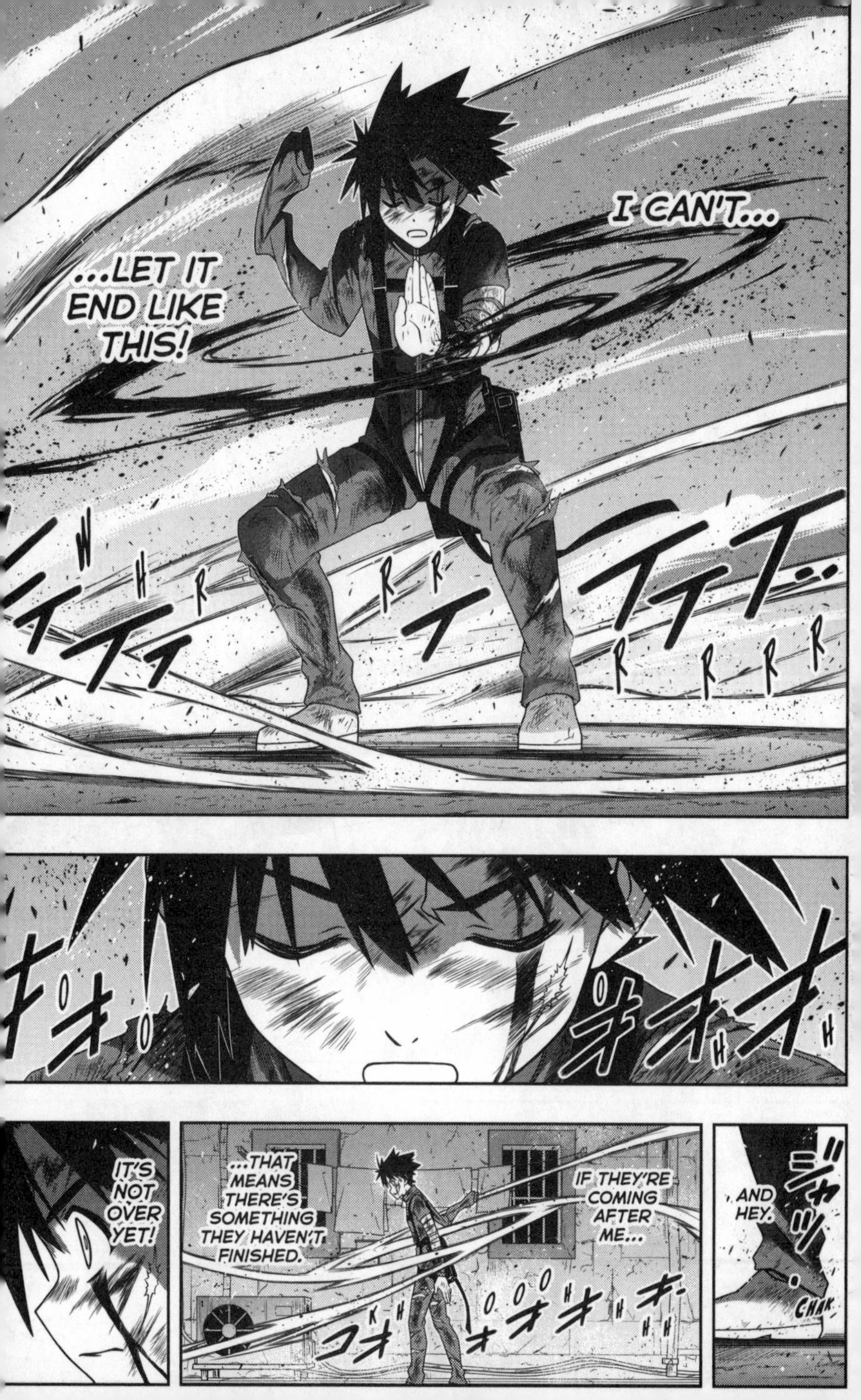
I CAN'T...
...LET IT END LIKE THIS!
AND HEY.
CHAK
IF THEY'RE COMING AFTER ME...
...THAT MEANS THERE'S SOMETHING THEY HAVEN'T FINISHED.
IT'S NOT OVER YET!

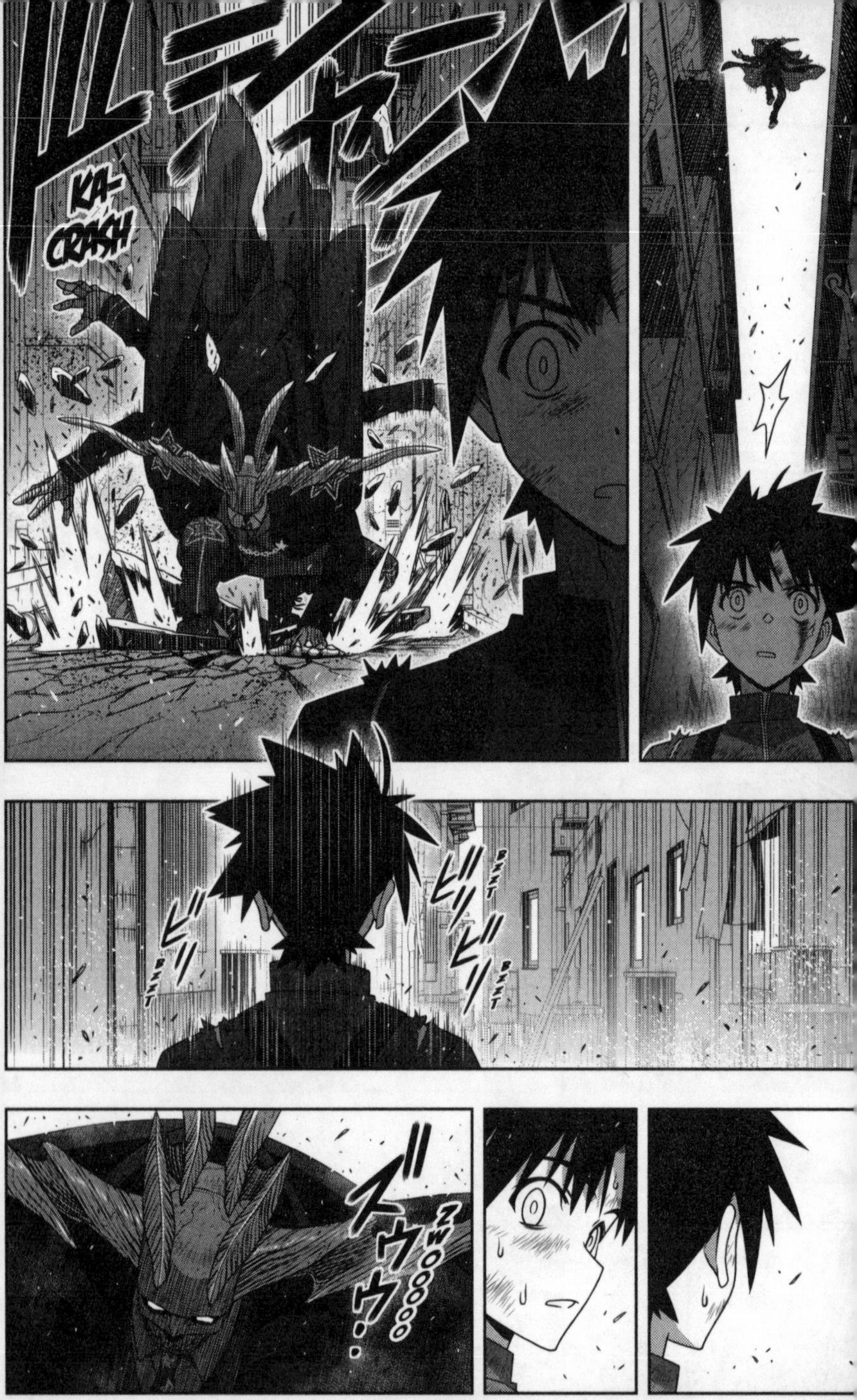
KA-CRASH
BZZT
BZZT
BZZT
ZWOOOOOO

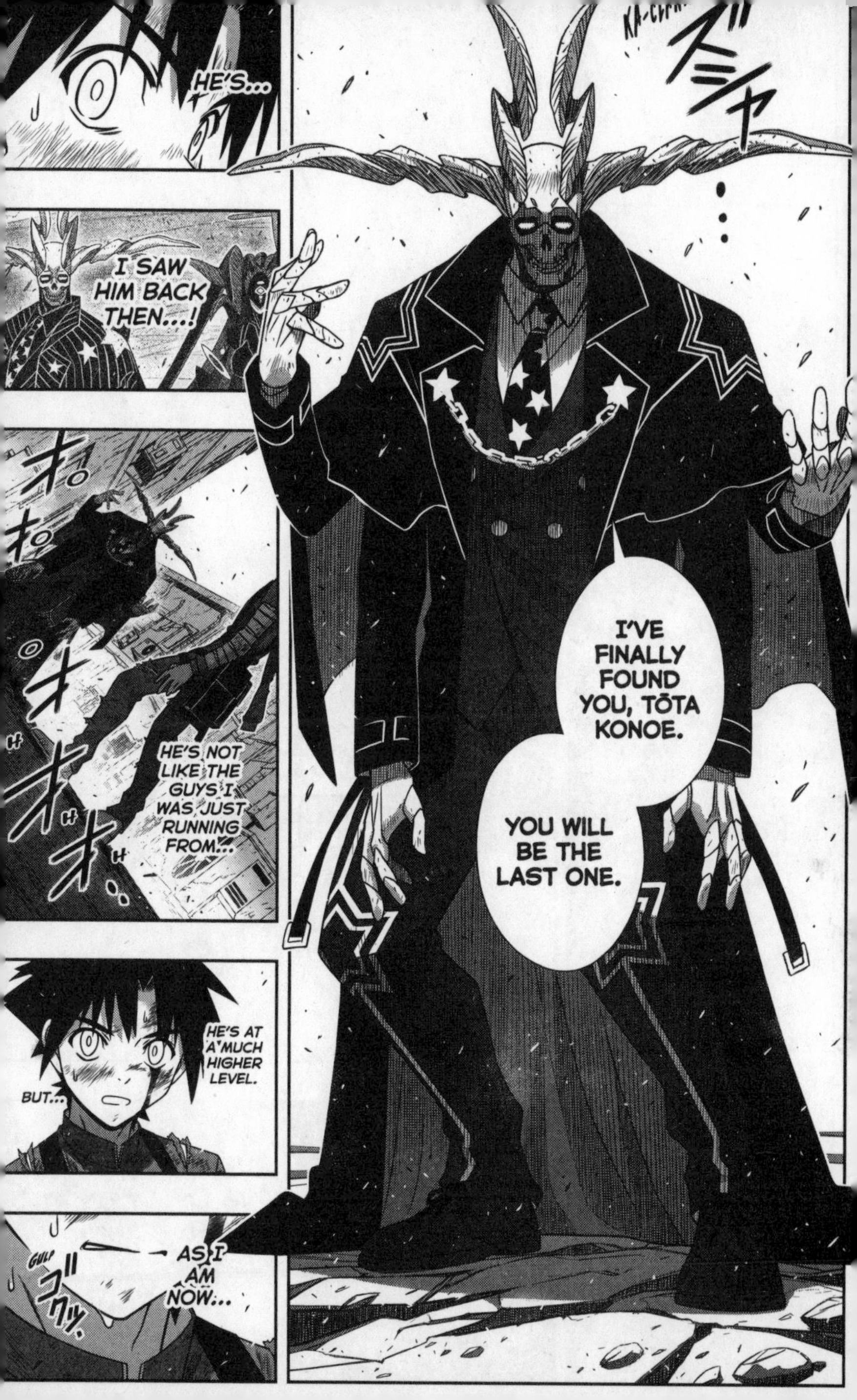
ズシャ
I'VE FINALLY FOUND YOU, TŌTA KONOE.
YOU WILL BE THE LAST ONE.
HE'S...
I SAW HIM BACK THEN...!
HE'S NOT LIKE THE GUYS I WAS JUST RUNNING FROM...
HE'S AT A MUCH HIGHER LEVEL.
BUT...
GULP
ゴクッ
AS I AM NOW...

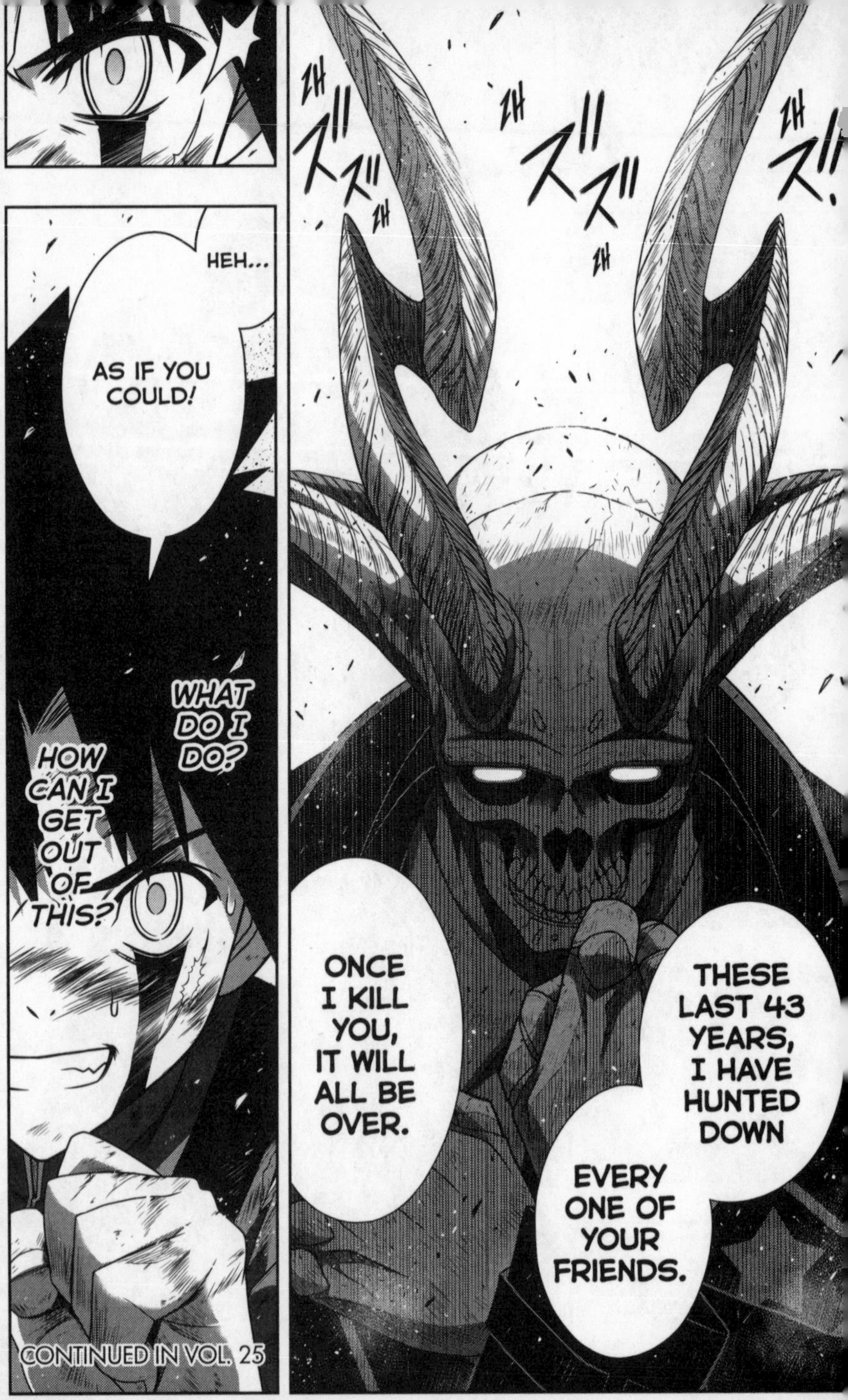
ZH
ZH
ZH
ZH
ZH
THESE LAST 43 YEARS, I HAVE HUNTED DOWN
EVERY ONE OF YOUR FRIENDS.
ONCE I KILL YOU, IT WILL ALL BE OVER.
HEH...
AS IF YOU COULD!
WHAT DO I DO?
HOW CAN I GET OUT OF THIS?
CONTINUED IN VOL. 25

ユーキューホルダー!
悠UQ HOLDER!

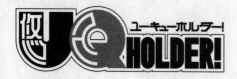

UQ HOLDER!

STAFF

Ken Akamatsu

Takashi Takemoto

Kenichi Nakamura

Keiichi Yamashita

Yuri Sasaki

Madoka Akanuma

Thanks to Ran Ayanaga

Young characters and steampunk setting, like *Howl's Moving Castle* and *Battle Angel Alita*

Beyond the Clouds © 2018 Nicke / Ki-oon

A boy with a talent for machines and a mysterious girl whose wings he's fixed will take you beyond the clouds! In the tradition of the high-flying, resonant adventure stories of Studio Ghibli comes a gorgeous tale about the longing of young hearts for adventure and friendship!

The boys are back, in 400-page hardcovers that are as pretty and badass as they are!

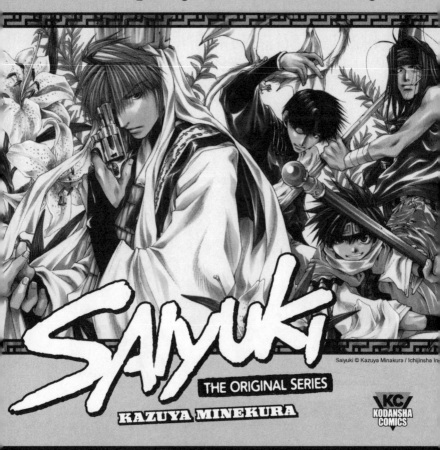

Saiyuki © Kazuya Minakura / Ichijinsha Inc.

SAIYUKI
THE ORIGINAL SERIES
KAZUYA MINEKURA

KC/ KODANSHA COMICS

"AN EDGY COMIC LOOK AT AN ANCIENT CHINESE TALE." —YALSA

Genjo Sanzo is a Buddhist priest in the city of Togenkyo, which is being ravaged by yokai spirits that have fallen out of balance with the natural order. His superiors send him on a journey far to the west to discover why this is happening and how to stop it. His companions are three yokai with human souls. But this is no day trip — the four will encounter many discoveries and horrors on the way.

FEATURES NEW TRANSLATION, COLOR PAGES, AND BEAUTIFUL WRAPAROUND COVER ART!

THE SWEET SCENT OF LOVE IS IN THE AIR! FOR FANS OF OFFBEAT ROMANCES LIKE *WOTAKOI*

Sweat and Soap © Kintetsu Yamada / Kodansha Ltd.

In an office romance, there's a fine line between sexy and awkward... and that line is where Asako — a woman who sweats copiously — meets Koutarou — a perfume developer who can't get enough of Asako's, er, scent. Don't miss a romcom manga like no other!

The adorable new odd-couple cat comedy manga from the creator of the beloved *Chi's Sweet Home*, in full color!

Sue & Tai-chan

Konami Kanata

Sue is an aging housecat who's looking forward to living out her life in peace... but her plans change when the mischievous black tomcat Tai-chan enters the picture! Hey! Sue never signed up to be a catsitter! *Sue & Tai-chan* is the latest from the reigning meow-narch of cute kitty comics, Konami Kanata.

Knight of the ICE

Yayoi Ogawa

Knight of the Ice ©Yayoi Ogawa/Kodansha Ltd.

SKATING THRILLS AND ICY CHILLS WITH THIS NEW TINGLY ROMANCE SERIES!

A rom-com on ice, perfect for fans of *Princess Jellyfish* and *Wotakoi*. Kokoro is the talk of the figure-skating world, winning trophies and hearts. But little do they know... he's actually a huge nerd! From the beloved creator of *You're My Pet* (*Tramps Like Us*).

Chitose is a serious young woman, working for the health magazine *SASSO*. Or at least, she would be, if she wasn't constantly getting distracted by her childhood friend, international figure skating star Kokoro Kijinami! In the public eye and on the ice, Kokoro is a gallant, flawless knight, but behind his glittery costumes and breathtaking spins lies a secret: He's actually a hopelessly romantic otaku, who can only land his quad jumps when Chitose is on hand to recite a spell from his favorite magical girl anime!

UQ HOLDER! 24 is a work of fiction. Names, characters, places, and incidents are the products of the author's imagination or are used fictitiously. Any resemblance to actual events, locales, or persons, living or dead, is entirely coincidental.

A Kodansha Comics Trade Paperback Original

Published in the United States by Kodansha Comics, an imprint of Kodansha USA Publishing, LLC, New York.

Publication rights for this English edition arranged through Kodansha Ltd., Tokyo.

First published in Japan in 2020 by Kodansha Ltd., Tokyo.

ISBN 978-1-64651-309-3

Printed in the United States of America.

www.kodansha.us

1st Printing
Translation: Alethea Nibley & Athena Nibley
Lettering: James Dashiell
Editing: David Yoo
Kodansha Comics edition cover design by Phil Balsman

Publisher: Kiichiro Sugawara

Director of publishing services: Ben Applegate
Associate director of operations: Stephen Pakula
Publishing services managing editors: Madison Salters, Alanna Ruse
Production managers: Emi Lotto, Angela Zurlo